D1454003

AMERICAN INDIANS AND NATIONAL FORESTS

THEODORE CATTON

FOREWORD BY JOEL D. HOLTROP

AMERICAN INDIANS AND

NATIONAL FORESTS

THE UNIVERSITY OF
ARIZONA PRESS

TUCSON

The University of Arizona Press
www.uapress.arizona.edu

© 2016 The Arizona Board of Regents
All rights reserved. Published 2016

Printed in the United States of America
21 20 19 18 17 16   6 5 4 3 2 1

ISBN-13: 978-0-8165-3199-8 (cloth)

Cover designed by Lori Lieber
Cover photo: Ojibwe man and Norway pine, Minnesota, 1902; Minnesota Historical Society.

Publication of this book is made possible in part by the proceeds of a permanent endowment created with the assistance of a Challenge Grant from the National Endowment for the Humanities, a federal agency.

Library of Congress Cataloging-in-Publication Data
Catton, Theodore.
   American Indians and national forests / Theodore Catton ; foreword by Joel D. Holtrop.
      pages cm
   Includes bibliographical references and index.
   ISBN 978-0-8165-3199-8 (cloth : alk. paper)
      1. Forest management—United States—History. 2. United States. Forest Service. Office of Tribal Relations—History. 3. Indians of North America—Government relations—History. 4. Forest policy—United States—History. I. Title.
   SD565.C38 2016
   634.9'208997—dc23

                                   2015022495

⊖ This paper meets the requirements of ANSI/NISO Z39.48–1992 (Permanence of Paper).

CONTENTS

ILLUSTRATIONS

FOREWORD

THE UNITED STATES Forest Service has a rich and complex history reflective of its rich and complex mission. Among U.S. government institutions, it has played a central role in the nation's conservation and land-use policy journey. It has responsibility for managing 193 million acres of National Forest System land. It is home to the leading natural resource research organization. It provides assistance and advice in the management of many more hundreds of millions of acres of state, tribal, and private forests in partnership with state governments, tribal governments, and other partners. The Forest Service is one of the many reasons the U.S. government is a global leader, with ideas and ideals worth being proud of and worth fighting to retain. I am proud to have been a part of that Forest Service history and proud to have taken the high calling of public service. And I'm grateful for the opportunity to have served with passionate and skilled Forest Service colleagues.

As rich and important as the role of the Forest Service is, it pales in significance to the role of Native American indigenous people in shaping the natural resource landscape of America. I have had the privilege of learning from them, of being humbled by their knowledge, of being awed by their love of the same places I love. The depth of Native American connections to their places is beyond my ability to comprehend. It is not beyond my ability to admire.

A characteristic of Forest Service history is that it reflects America's values and needs at each point in time. Another is the agency's ability to reflect and learn from its mistakes. This book on the history of the relationship between Native Americans and the Forest Service is replete with examples of the agency reflecting society norms, and in hindsight some of that is less than admirable. The book also shows how the agency has grown and adjusted as society has changed and as the Forest Service has reflected and learned. This book should assist a dynamic society and agency.

Moving forward, Native Americans must continue to stand up for their rights as they also continue to redeem their responsibilities to their cultures and to the larger society. The Forest Service must continue to adjust and learn to truly embrace the important role of sharing landscapes and resources and passions for the natural and cultural wealth of this great nation. If it were easy, a book like this would not be necessary. If the path forward were obvious, there would be no need to learn from our shared history. If it were not important, the time and resources put into this endeavor would be ill placed.

This is indeed vitally important work for the Forest Service, for Native Americans, and for American society as a whole. It is my hope and expectation that this book will help us on our journey. To fall short would diminish us all.

Joel D. Holtrop
Retired Deputy Chief,
U.S. Forest Service

AMERICAN INDIANS AND NATIONAL FORESTS

INTRODUCTION

A T SUNRISE ON June 16, 2011, six protesters climbed into a pipeline
ditch near the Arizona Snowbowl ski area on the Coconino National
Forest, unfurled a banner with the words Defend the Sacred, and
locked themselves to heavy machinery. Huddling in down parkas in the chill
mountain air, they bravely awaited arrest. They were trying to stop installation
of a pipeline that would bring treated wastewater from Flagstaff to the ski area.
The treated wastewater would be turned into snow and sprayed on the mountainside to enable the ski area's expansion. The lofty San Francisco Peaks in
which the ski area is located are held sacred by thirteen tribes in the Southwest.
To many people, the idea of taking what was once sewage and spraying it on
the mountainside in the form of snow for recreational use is a desecration of
Native religion. As one of the protesters said later after his arrest, "Our actions
were taken to safeguard Indigenous Peoples' cultural survival, our community's
health, and this sensitive mountain ecosystem."[1]

The U.S. Forest Service has been embroiled in litigation with the Navajo,
Hopi, and other Southwest tribes over the Snowbowl permit for many years,
and the contest is likely to go on. While the Forest Service has changed the
terms of the permit to meet the tribes' concerns partway, it has stuck with the
snow making on the grounds that the artificial snow is essential if the ski area
is to remain viable. Although the Forest Service keeps winning in court, no one
in the agency who has been involved in this bitter, long-running controversy
finds any reason to rejoice over the judges' rulings. The tribes and the winter

recreationists are polarized, and the Forest Service finds itself caught in the middle. Indian activists acknowledge that the Forest Service is not unsympathetic to their point of view. Nonetheless, they hold the Forest Service accountable because it has the power, as the decision maker on the Coconino National Forest, to halt the ski-area expansion and protect the San Francisco Peaks from further desecration.

Tribes across the country have followed the developments in Arizona. When the Forest Service recently undertook a series of national listening sessions on the protection of Indian sacred sites nationwide, the Snowbowl case kept getting raised. How could the agency profess a desire to work with tribes to reform its policy when it refused to alter its position in the Snowbowl case, tribes demanded to know.[2]

The Forest Service feels the sting of the San Francisco Peaks controversy precisely because the agency considers it to be an outlier in an overall record of progress in its relations with tribes. There are some 566 federally recognized tribes in the United States with diverse cultures, natural resources, and off-reservation treaty rights and tribal interests. Perhaps half of all tribes assert an interest in public lands under Forest Service jurisdiction based on the tribe's aboriginal occupancy of the area. About 40 percent of tribes have their own forest resources in trust. Forest Service government-to-government relations with these many diverse peoples have by and large undergone a positive transformation over the past twenty-five years or so.

When Congress enacted the American Indian Religious Freedom Act (AIRFA) in 1978, the Forest Service was seen as the most hard nosed of all the federal agencies in its resistance to Native perspectives that would tend to restrict public-land use. At that time, the agency was still strongly oriented to timber production and was protective of its prerogatives to build more logging roads and carry on intensive forestry. A high-elevation logging road on the Six Rivers National Forest in Northern California (from the towns of Gasquet to Orleans, thus called the G-O Road) became the test case for whether AIRFA gave protection to Indian sacred sites on public lands. The U.S. Supreme Court found in *Lyng v. Northwest Indian Cemetery Protective Association* that AIRFA did not have that kind of reach.

The decade in which AIRFA was enacted and the G-O Road controversy began to wend its way to the Supreme Court was also the decade when the nation turned a corner on both Indian policy and environmental policy. For tribes, the most important harbinger of change was the Indian

Self-Determination and Education Act of 1975. For the Forest Service, it was chiefly the National Forest Management Act of 1976, together with other environmental laws. The decade was the beginning of a new era for tribes and the Forest Service alike.

In 1988, Chief of the Forest Service F. Dale Robertson appointed a tribal relations coordinator and committed the agency to improving its relations with Native groups. There were then upward of three hundred federally recognized tribes with incipient government-to-government relations with the federal government. Every tribe was in the process of rebuilding its capacity for self-governance in the aftermath of several generations of administration by the Bureau of Indian Affairs (BIA). All across Indian Country, it was a time of remarkable political and cultural revitalization following more than a century of oppression. And it happened to coincide with a time of significant change for the Forest Service as well, when the agency pivoted away from a primary focus on timber production and began to reinvent itself around a new set of core values grounded in ecology.

By 1990, the Forest Service's new paradigm was "ecosystem management," or EM. Many Indians supported EM in principle, though they preferred to call it "ecological restoration." In the agency's first statement of Indian policy, Chief Robertson expressed his ardent desire that the Forest Service and tribes make a fresh start in working with one another constructively as partners. "The opportunities are at hand," he wrote. "It is time to visit, meet, and walk the land together."[3] Over the next twenty-five years, tribal representatives and Forest Service officials responded to that summons. More and more Indians took employment in the Forest Service, a few coming to occupy key posts in the agency's emerging tribal relations program. In 1999, a task force was appointed to bring more focus to the program. In 2004, another milestone was reached with the establishment of the Office of Tribal Relations (OTR) in the Forest Service's Washington headquarters. In 2009, another Office of Tribal Relations was established in the Forest Service's parent organization, the U.S. Department of Agriculture (USDA). In 2012, Secretary of Agriculture Tom Vilsack joined with three other secretaries in signing an interdepartmental memorandum of understanding to collaborate on better protection of Indian sacred sites. A detailed report by the Forest Service and the USDA was released on the same day, providing a strong foundation for the interdepartmental initiative.

The contentiousness surrounding the San Francisco Peaks notwithstanding, the Forest Service and tribes do share basic values in caring for the land. Gifford

Pinchot, the first chief forester, pointed out those commonalities, and other leaders who came after him did as well. Tribes and the Forest Service both treat the land as a form of heritage to be carefully protected and nurtured for the collective good of the people. The Forest Service is charged with conserving public lands and resources for future generations. Tribal cultures take that same long view in thinking about the welfare of the tribe. Tribes and the Forest Service share an ethic in which tribal or public ownership of land is viewed as inherently more farsighted and enlightened than private ownership of the same.

For both the Forest Service and tribes, using resources is an integral part of maintaining them for the future. The Forest Service manages the national forests for sustained-yield timber production and livestock grazing, for fish and wildlife habitat, and for recreational use as well as for the protection of watersheds and biodiversity. The Forest Service looks at using resources—harvesting trees, for example—as a good thing, provided it is done in the right way. Many tribal communities have that same outlook: if tribal members are not using the resource, then they are not respecting it, or fulfilling their part of the sacred bargain. Tribes have been on the land for millennia, and they view themselves as the land's caretakers, always taking what they need in a way that encourages the land to replenish itself. Many Indians find it easier to accept the Forest Service approach to environmental stewardship than the National Park Service philosophy, with its preservationist ideal of keeping people and nature apart, or, as the saying goes, allowing national park visitors to "take only photographs, leave only footprints."

The Forest Service and tribes also share a sense of stewardship or guardianship over the very same places. All national forestlands were Indian lands at an earlier point in time. Tribes have a cultural memory that extends back to the period when they occupied and claimed the national forestlands as their own. Many Indian reservations border on national forests, and often the national forests take in lands that the tribes once used in their seasonal rounds of hunting and gathering. Although the Forest Service must weigh the interests of many stakeholders in managing the public lands under its charge, it gives special consideration to whatever tribe is the aboriginal people of a given area. Tribes' modern-day interests in their ancestral lands run the gamut from assertion of reserved hunting and gathering rights to protection of burial grounds and other sacred places to having a say in ecological restoration. National forest managers, meanwhile, have their own reasons to seek cooperation from tribes. They want to reach out to tribal forestry programs on adjoining or nearby

Indian reservations for help in fire management, control of forest diseases, and other cross boundary issues. Under the Forest Service's new planning rule, national forest managers are pledged to improve their stewardship through incorporation of tribes' traditional ecological knowledge.

For purposes of understanding how the Forest Service tribal relations program developed after 1988, it is important to recognize that the Forest Service is tasked with more than administering the National Forest System; it also has a separate division that is devoted to research and development, and another division, known as State and Private Forestry, that delivers technical and financial assistance to other forestry programs in the United States outside of the National Forest System. Historically, the Division of State and Private Forestry mostly omitted Indian forests from its cooperative forestry purview, because the Indian forests were under the jurisdiction of the BIA, which had its own forestry division. In the last twenty-five years, as tribes have assumed responsibility over their own forest resources, the situation has completely changed. The division has sought to broaden its reach so that tribes have equal access to its cooperative forestry offerings alongside state governments and private foresters. Tribes have suggested that the Forest Service change the name to State, Private *and Tribal* Forestry to reflect the new scope. While the State and Private Forestry moniker has not changed, it is this division in the Forest Service organization that has mostly overseen development of the Forest Service tribal relations program since 1988. Today, the director of the Office of Tribal Relations reports to the deputy chief of State and Private Forestry, who reports to the chief of the Forest Service. This is so, even though a significant proportion of tribes' issues pertains to national forestlands and falls into the Forest Service's other mission area of National Forest System administration.

A second point that must be emphasized is that Forest Service tribal relations span two distinct land ownerships, public and tribal. Major events and developments in the history of Forest Service tribal relations have occurred in two settings: on national forests and on Indian reservations. Tribes assert a variety of interests on national forestlands by virtue of the fact that those public lands fall within their ancestral homelands; reciprocally, the Forest Service is involved with tribal forests through cooperative forestry. A few tribes have been profoundly affected by transfers of lands back and forth between tribal and public ownership. In the early 1900s, and again in the 1950s, some tribes lost their lands to the National Forest System. Since the 1960s, some public lands have been taken out of the National Forest System and returned to tribes.

The national forests and the Indian forests are comparable systems, though the National Forest System is considerably larger. The National Forest System is composed of 155 national forests and 20 national grasslands, which cover a combined total of 193 million acres. Indian forests and woodlands are located on 240 Indian reservations and cover an area of 25 million acres. Both systems reach across most of the contiguous United States and Alaska, with the lands being concentrated in the West. The commercial timber is somewhat more concentrated in the Pacific Northwest.

Basic forest management guidelines, such as an annual allowable cut (AAC), are common to both systems, yet there are significant differences. Each national forest is managed according to a forest plan that is vetted through a public planning process. Each Indian forest on a reservation is managed according to a tribal or BIA forest plan that is approved by the tribal government and the secretary of the interior. For national forests, the forest plan is mandated by the National Forest Management Act. For Indian forests, the forest plan is mandated by the National Indian Forest Resources Management Act. Indian lands are not part of the public domain and are not subject to federal public-land laws. As Gary Morishima, technical adviser to the Quinault Nation, has said, "Indian lands were set aside for the exclusive use and occupancy of Indians, not to be managed for general public benefit."[4]

The National Forest System was established in the 1890s and was originally administered by the General Land Office in the Department of the Interior. In 1905, the forests were transferred to the Forest Service in the Department of Agriculture. Gifford Pinchot, the chief of the Forest Service from 1905 to 1910, established the basic policy of conservation for use, which became codified in the Multiple-Use Sustained-Yield Act of 1960.

The system of Indian forest management has a more complicated history because it is enfolded in federal Indian policy. Beginning in the 1870s, Congress and the courts defined Indian forests as tribally owned resources held in trust by the federal government. Then, toward the end of the nineteenth century, Congress established the allotment policy to break up Indian reservations into individual allotments of 40, 80, or 160 acres apiece. Although foresters in the Indian Service warned of the difficulties of managing forests that were allotted into many individual land ownerships, the process of allotment went forward to serve the larger goal of Indian assimilation. By the time Congress repealed the allotment policy in 1934, some Indian forests were completely allotted, others remained in tribal ownership, and many were composed of a mix of tribal and allotted lands. According to law, the forests were deemed to be trust assets that went with the land, so the forests themselves were awkwardly checkerboarded with different ownerships.

As long as U.S. Indian policy aimed at breaking up reservations into allotments, tribally owned forests appeared to have little future. Even after allotment ended, the Indian estate continued to shrink as many allotments were sold to non-Indians. Not until the last quarter of the twentieth century were tribes able to stop the land loss. They did so mainly by a combination of converting allotted lands that were held in trust into tribal trust lands and acquiring alienated lands through repurchase.

While tribes' land loss and the allotment policy were both of critical importance to Indian forests, there was also an important evolution in who managed the forest resources. There was an early attempt to place them under Forest Service management. Although the arrangement was short lived, it kept coming up for reconsideration. For most of the twentieth century, Indian forests were under BIA management. Starting in the 1980s, tribal governments began to take over BIA forestry operations. The growth of tribal forestry programs in the late 1980s, 1990s, and early twenty-first century forms the major context for the transformation of Forest Service tribal relations that has occurred over the past twenty-five years.

―――――――――――――

This study was conceived by the Forest Service's Office of Tribal Relations in 2010 as an administrative history of the Forest Service tribal relations program. The purpose of the study was to record the experiences and recollections of the program's early leaders while those people were still available for interviews and to place the development of the program in broad historical context. As OTR director Fred Clark wrote, "Tribal relations in the Forest Service is tied inextricably to the history of Federal/Tribal relations, to the changing political structures in the three branches of the Federal government, to the waves of new initiatives and funding streams in the Agency, to the growing self-governance and self-determination of Tribal governments, and to a variety of international trends."[5] When I discussed the scope of the project with Clark and Chief Historian Lincoln Bramwell, we agreed that the history needed to begin not with the start of the tribal relations program in 1988, nor even with the start of the Forest Service in 1905, but much earlier, so as to explain how the present relationship rests on top of the past five hundred years of joint Indian and European American occupation of the continent.

The importance of that long time frame became more and more apparent during the course of conducting interviews and doing research. Whenever tribes and the Forest Service get together, they bring to the relationship two different views of their shared past. The tribal perspective is based on cultural memory; the Forest Service perspective is based on institutional memory. Institutional memory is notoriously short; that is one reason why we have administrative history. By contrast, the tribes remember things that occurred fifty, one hundred, or two hundred years ago. Those things have a vitality and resonance for tribes in their present relations with the Forest Service that is often lost on their federal partners. Past events that one party in the relationship might regard as "recent" the other party might regard as "remote." Tribes' and Forest Service officials' different perspectives on the past is one of the themes of this study. It is hoped that one benefit of this study will be that it brings about more mutual understanding of that important difference as Forest Service tribal relations continue into the future.

1

INDIANS, NON-INDIANS, AND THE AMERICAN FORESTS TO 1900

INDIAN AND EUROPEAN FOREST ADAPTATIONS

IN EIGHTEENTH-CENTURY backwoods Pennsylvania, Scotch Irish immigrants and Delaware Indians walked the land together. The European newcomers observed that the Natives cultivated garden patches deep within the forest, and they asked them how it was done. First, the Delawares showed the immigrants how they used fire to remove the underbrush. Next, they killed all the trees in the area around where they intended to cultivate. To kill the trees they girdled each one, notching the bark in a circle around its base to cut off the flow of water and nutrients to its limbs and foliage. Where the trees died and stopped producing foliage, sunlight was able to penetrate to the forest floor. Then, when the Delawares had their sunlit patch, they planted corn, beans, squash, and pumpkin seeds in mounds among the trunks and roots of the skeleton trees. They tended this ground for a few years, and when the fertility of the soil declined, they cleared a new patch and allowed the forest to reclaim the abandoned ground. Scholars today refer to the Delawares' traditional form of agriculture as *forest fallowing*. The term is applied to any situation where a given plot of forest ground is cultivated for a few years and then fallowed for a period of twenty years or more while the forest regenerates.

The Scotch Irish quickly adopted the Delawares' method of forest fallowing in preference to the more labor-intensive option of clearing the forest by chopping down trees and grubbing up stumps. Unlike the Delawares, however, the Scotch Irish did not confine their farm patches to creek and river bottoms but cultivated upland slopes as well. And to supplement their small, subsistence yields of grain and vegetables, they practiced open-range herding of cattle and hogs. Besides borrowing techniques from the Delawares, the Scotch Irish in America imported land-use practices from the system of outfield cultivation and livestock raising that they had left behind in Scotland and Ulster, where forests had long since been removed.

The forest-fallowing method of farming in the Pennsylvania backwoods turned out to be well suited for the broken terrain and poor soil conditions found throughout the Appalachian region. After taking hold among the Scotch Irish in western Pennsylvania, this distinctive land-use pattern spread throughout the Mountain South. By the early nineteenth century it extended down the length of the Appalachian highlands and westward to the Ozark plateau in Arkansas and Missouri. It flourished for as long as land was free for the taking and the farming population remained sparse and well dispersed.[1]

The Delawares' use of fire to aid in clearing small patches in the forest for cultivation was but one instance of how Indians practiced light burning to manipulate their environment. Most Indian burning involved low-intensity fires that removed forest underbrush without killing mature trees. Such light burning released nutrients into the ground, stimulating the production of tubers, berry bushes, mushrooms, medicinal herbs, seed grasses, and other plants that Indians ate or utilized in some other way. It also led to a more luxuriant growth of grasses in the following season, which in turn produced a greater abundance of deer and other wildlife. Fire had other beneficial effects as well. It was a control on insect and forest disease infestations. It created a mosaic pattern of forest and meadow. Meadows or clearings in the forest meant more edge effect, the basis for niche habitats where two ecological communities adjoin. The edge of a clearing was not only rich in plant and wildlife diversity and abundance, but it also formed a natural blind for the hunter.

Indians sometimes set fires to aid in the hunt itself. Hunters set fire to the prairie to stampede herds of bison in a certain direction (such as over a cliff). They used fire to flush their quarry out of a sheltered area or force animals into a corral. Indians ignited fires to help them in warfare, too, either to drive the enemy somewhere against their will, or to make smoke for covering their own movements. They used fire to make smoke signals and communicate over long distances. In some parts of North America, Indians regularly burned the woods to make the landscape easier to travel through.[2]

Indians used fire more than any other tool to alter the landscape to suit their needs. Before the coming of Europeans, light burning was so widespread and frequent that most forest and grassland ecosystems across North America fluctuated back and forth between early and middle stages of ecological succession. That is, they were fire-succession ecosystems. Plants and animals in those communities evolved with the presence of fire. While some of that fire was natural, or caused by lightning, much of it was anthropogenic, or produced by humans. As Sheperd Krech III has written, "Through their fires, North American Indians probably played some role in the creation of, and more certainly maintained, a number of fire-succession ecosystems."[3]

Their manipulation of the forest notwithstanding, Indians did not use great amounts of wood in their subsistence economy. They felled trees to make dugout canoes; they used pole-size timbers and bark to construct their homes; they gathered downed limbs for firewood. But Indians had neither the technological means nor the economic incentives to turn trees into milled lumber or clear forests to make farmland.[4]

In contrast with Indian use of the forest, the European colonizers of North America made prodigal use of timber for construction material, heating fuel, and products for export to the mother country. To them, the forest in the New World seemed boundless and inexhaustible. The vast woodlands that English colonists encountered in New England and Virginia stood in sharp contrast to the landed heritage of Great Britain, where centuries of deforestation had turned what little forests remained into guarded commodity resources.

In the new land, the colonists' first order of business was to clear areas for settlement. The forest, therefore, literally stood in the way of progress. As the forest came to define the edge of settlement, colonists saw it as practically synonymous with wilderness, or the antithesis of civilization as they knew it. Indeed, the colonists arrived in the New World with Old World notions that prescribed wilderness as a sinister, forbidding place, the haunt of the devil. The forest was home to the Indians, whom they perceived as heathen and savage. In keeping with those needs and attitudes, they cut down forests and consumed wood without any thought of conservation.[5]

Historians have described the American colonies as having a "timber intensive economy." Colonists used wood to manufacture everything from barrels and boxes to eating utensils. Whole villages were made of wood, including stockades, log cabins, wooden boardwalks, and corduroy roads. The Virginia rail fence was a characteristic feature of their lavish use of wood for construction. Rails were stacked so that the ends crisscrossed, making a sturdy, zigzagging fence. The design required some 3,600 rails for every mile of fence. The fences were easy to erect and repair, and the fact that their zigzagging course made extravagant use of land as well as wood was of no consequence where land was cheap and abundant.[6]

New England colonists burned fantastic amounts of wood to heat their homes in winter. Houses were typically constructed with large open fireplaces, often one per room. Historian William Cronon has estimated that a New England household commonly burned as much as thirty or forty cords of firewood per year and that stocking a woodpile of that size meant clearing an acre of forest per year. By the year 1800, New Englanders burned perhaps eighteen times more wood for fuel than they cut for lumber.[7]

Perhaps the biggest difference between Indian and European use of the forest lay in the fact that European colonists were able to export wood products to foreign markets. With the British Navy requiring tall trees for ship masts, white pine bolls became one of the first exports of the Massachusetts Bay Colony. British naval and mercantile shipping also required large quantities of pitch and tar, which were produced by burning tree trunks and branches at high temperatures. This was achieved by heaping the wood in a huge conical pile and covering the pile with dirt to form a crude kiln. The liquefied tar trickled into a container sunk in the ground next to the pile.[8]

There was also a demand for turpentine, which was made by extracting turpentine gum from pine trees. The colonists' production of turpentine from pines paralleled Indians' extraction of sugar from maples and box elders, but the method used in obtaining the turpentine was so invasive that it generally killed the tree. Often the same tree would be mined for turpentine in one season and then cut down and burned to make tar in the next.

The deforestation wrought by colonists produced a different set of ecological effects compared with the forest burning practiced by Indians. It had diverse ramifications for wildlife habitat and wildlife populations; watersheds, streams, rivers, and lakes; aquatic habitat and fisheries; and even climate. Equally important, the economic values that European colonists brought to the New World tended to redefine forest and land as commodity resources. Colonists sought to exploit and manipulate those resources to serve market demand.

Those differing economic values drew Indians and colonists into conflict over who got to occupy and control the land.

THE LEGACY OF INDIAN DISPOSSESSION

Europeans sought to appropriate Indian lands according to the Doctrine of Discovery. The Doctrine of Discovery has been traced back to a series of papal bulls issued by Pope Alexander VI in 1493 pursuant to Columbus's "discovery" of America. The papal bulls built on earlier papal legal discourse concerning the rights of Christendom in Africa and the Holy Land that dated all the way back to the Crusades. The Doctrine of Discovery held that the discovery of territory by one Christian state before any other state had knowledge of it gave that state a sovereign claim to the territory. In the first instance, the papal bulls of 1493 gave all of the Americas to Spain rather than Portugal because Columbus had sailed for the Spanish sovereign. According to the papal bulls' logic, a sovereign claim by a European state embraced all the indigenous, non-Christian, non-European inhabitants within the territory being claimed by the sovereign. The Doctrine of Discovery was another aspect of that Eurocentric worldview that divided all of humanity into Christians and heathens, or civilized and savage peoples, and it posited that indigenous peoples, being in a "savage state," had no comparable sovereign interests of their own. It provided a rationale for European colonization of the rest of the world and a system for managing imperial rivalries.[9]

When the United States gained independence, it recognized the Doctrine of Discovery as a practical basis for its own claims of territorial expansion. Starting with the Lewis and Clark expedition of 1804 to 1806, the United States government sponsored a series of army explorations of the West that focused on geographic and scientific discovery. Those expeditions were aimed in no small part toward advancing the United States' claims to territory based on the Doctrine of Discovery.[10]

The United States also devised its own approach for conducting relations with Indian peoples. Under the U.S. Constitution, Indian affairs were vested in the federal government. Articles I and II granted authority to the president and Congress to declare war and make treaties. Article III gave Congress exclusive authority to regulate commerce with foreign nations, Indian tribes, and between states. With passage of the Indian Trade and Intercourse Acts, all

Indian trade came under the purview of federally appointed Indian agents, who were responsible for licensing traders in Indian Country and enforcing regulations. All land dealings between Indians and private citizens of the United States were prohibited; the U.S. government had a preemptive or exclusive right to acquire Indian lands either by purchase or conquest. Indian nations were vested with "aboriginal title" over the lands they controlled, meaning they had the right to occupy and use those lands according to their accustomed way of life. Indian nations residing within the territorial limits of the United States could cede aboriginal title to the U.S. government and no other sovereign power. Indian land cessions had to be stipulated by treaty. Indian treaties were subject to ratification by the U.S. Senate.[11]

Treaties were the cornerstone of the young American republic's engagement with Indian peoples. During the presidency of George Washington, the United States concluded a number of treaties aimed at establishing peaceful relations with tribes that had fought on the side of Britain in the Revolutionary War. Historian Francis Paul Prucha, in his seminal work on U.S. Indian policy, *The Great Father*, has observed that the treaties followed legal procedures "similar to those used with foreign nations" and thereby "acknowledged some kind of autonomous nationhood of the Indian tribes" even as the treaty provisions placed the tribes under the protection and control of the United States. "Although the treaties did not touch the autonomy of the tribes in internal affairs, they made it clear that in relations with whites, the Indian nations accepted significant restrictions," Prucha wrote. "The tribes were not free to deal directly with European nations, with individual states, or with private individuals."[12] If the treaties were in some sense contradictory, asserting both tribal sovereignty and U.S. hegemony, they reflected the twin realities that tribes possessed a degree of independent military power and that the United States claimed exclusive control over U.S. territory according to the European Doctrine of Discovery. Indian treaties stayed within that framework through most of the nineteenth century even as Indian military power diminished relative to the power of the United States and even as the primary purpose of Indian treaties shifted from peacemaking to the extraction of Indian land cessions.

In making Indian treaties, the U.S. government sought to engage in government-to-government relations with the Indian nation or nations (or tribes or bands—the various terms carried no legal distinction). On the U.S. side, treaty negotiators were commissioned by the U.S. Congress. On the Indian side, chiefs were sought out who could speak on behalf of their people. Chiefs there were aplenty, for Indian cultures placed a high value on oratorical skill, and good orators often became chiefs for their ability to persuade and forge consensus among the group. But chiefs did not have executive authority in any Western sense of the term. Indian groups did not have constitutional governments with prescribed powers and responsibilities. Even the notion of a tribe, though it might be convenient for making a treaty, tended to imply more political structure and coherence than truly existed in most Indian cultures. Often, the negotiators on the U.S. side, in their zeal to conclude a treaty, made "chiefs" of men on the Indian side who were not recognized as such by their own people. It was not uncommon for chiefs to be compensated with land or something else of value within the terms of the treaty in order to get them to sign. These actions tended to undermine tribal leadership at the very time when the United States wanted to strengthen tribal governments (albeit to serve U.S. aims).[13]

Most treaties began with a declaration of peace and amity between the United States and the Indian tribe. The tribe acknowledged that it was under the protection of the U.S. government, and the United States agreed to take certain measures for the maintenance or betterment of the tribe. As time passed, more and more treaties involved Indian land cessions. Usually the land-cession portion of the treaty consisted of three parts: first, a description of the boundaries of the tribe's territory or lands to which it held aboriginal title; second, a description of the boundaries of the land cession; and third, a description of the boundaries of the territory that the tribe reserved for its permanent home (a reservation). In exchange for each land cession, the United States promised various kinds of assistance, such as farm implements, schools, and annuities (yearly deliveries of food, clothing, and other necessities to the Indian agency for distribution to the whole tribe). Sometimes the tribe reserved the right to hunt and gather on ceded lands as long as the lands remained open and unclaimed, or it reserved the right to fish at accustomed places in common with non-Indian settlers. Usually those reserved rights were perpetual.[14]

The legal language surrounding Indian land cessions barely hints at the titanic clash of values and perspectives that underlay the process of Indian dispossession. Indian peoples regarded the earth as sacred, as an integral part of their spiritual world. They had origin stories that connected their nation or tribe to a given place. Often these stories told of their people emerging out of a specific landform such as a lake or mountain. Their worldviews made them the guardians within their homeland. As guardians over the land, they were imbued with unique privileges and responsibilities that no other people shared. They

FIGURE 1. Treaty council, Fort Laramie, Wyoming, 1868. By the Sioux Treaty of 1868, Lakota and Arapaho peoples secured land and hunting rights in Dakota and Montana territories. Subsequently, when South Dakota became a state in 1889, the Great Sioux Reservation was broken into five smaller reservations, and half the area was opened to white settlement. A portion of that area became the Black Hills National Forest.

PHOTO BY ALEXANDER GARDNER. COURTESY OF NATIONAL ARCHIVES AND RECORDS ADMINISTRATION/WIKIMEDIA COMMONS.

eschewed the idea that land could be bought or sold. "Sell a country!" Tecumseh famously declared. "Why not sell the air, the clouds, and the great sea, as well as the earth? Did not the Great Spirit make them all for the use of his children?"[15] The records of treaty councils are replete with such indignant, incredulous, or anguished pronouncements. Indian leaders agreed to land cessions only under great duress or because they did not fully understand the terms.

White Americans justified taking the Indians' land on religious, moral, and political grounds. They believed it was God's plan for humankind to spread and multiply, turning desolate forests and untilled soil into productive farmland. In the Christian view, farming the land was pleasing to God because it made more of God's creation. When people worked the land, God rewarded them by yielding up a bountiful harvest of grain and fruits that sustained them through the whole year. The farming way of life not only provided economic security by producing a plentiful food supply, it also fostered social stability by giving each family a fixed abode. For nineteenth-century white Americans, farming constituted a leap forward in humankind's march toward higher civilization. As these people found the overwhelming majority of Indians to be unwilling to adopt their own "civilized" ways, they condemned them for being "indolent" (unwilling to take up the hard work of farming) and "improvident" (unwilling to anticipate and prepare for times of scarcity). Nineteenth-century white Americans placed a moral judgment on Indians' subsistence lifeways. By extension, they disapproved of the Indians' relationship to the land.

Early in the nineteenth century, the U.S. government moved toward a policy of "civilizing" Indians or assimilating them into the American way of life. The civilization policy focused on remaking Indians into yeoman farmers. According to the civilization policy, each Indian would be allotted an individual parcel of land and taught how to farm it. Once the Indian became a land owner and a tiller of the soil, it was assumed that the Indian would acquire a respect for laws and be on the path to full American citizenship. The civilization policy dovetailed with Jeffersonian political theory, which identified the yeoman farmer as the ideal republican citizen and the core of the American body politic. Jefferson wanted the nation to expand its territory westward so as to preserve the economic opportunity to take up farms for future generations of Americans. Indians must be taught the arts of civilization so that they would relinquish their lands willingly.

The civilization policy also drew on Enlightenment thought, which held that all of humankind was on a universal path from "savagery" to "civilization." Enlightenment thinkers sought to find an explanation for the enormous diversity of human cultures found around the globe. They tended to believe it was a product of long geographic separation and environmental influence. According to the Enlightenment theory of universal human progress, as "savage" and "civilized" branches of the human race were once more brought into contact by the process of European exploration and colonization, the superior, more advanced European cultures must ultimately prevail. The civilization policy did not countenance the deliberate destruction of Indian peoples, but it did assume that Native cultures would disintegrate under the influence of European contact, and Indians would thereby cease to be "Indian." Advocates of the civilization policy argued that it was more humane to hurry the Indian along on the path to civilization than to let him struggle with his vanishing way of life.

All of these ideas fed into manifest destiny, a belief that the American republic was ordained by God to expand its territory westward and eventually span the continent. The champions of manifest destiny insisted that neither the European states nor the primitive Indian tribes should stand in the way of American expansion. Manifest destiny gave white Americans a still stronger sense of entitlement to Indian lands.[16]

In the course of U.S. westward expansion, the pattern of Indian dispossession differed markedly from era to era and tribe to tribe. As a result, Indian land holdings and treaty rights are unevenly distributed across Indian Country today. In the East and the South, tribes were caught up in the policy of Indian removal implemented in the 1830s. Most of those tribes were forced to abandon their homelands and relocate to a "permanent" Indian Territory west of the Mississippi River. Tribes in the central plains region suffered dislocation both as a result of other tribes moving west and from expanding white settlement. Not many years after a permanent Indian frontier was proclaimed, the U.S. government abandoned the policy of Indian removal in favor of establishing reservations. About the same time, the California gold rush precipitated such a huge and rapid movement of whites that tribes in that state were decimated and pushed out of their accustomed areas with barely a trace of federal protection. During the 1850s and 1860s, the process of Indian land cession shifted to the upper Great Lakes region, the upper Mississippi Valley, and the Pacific Northwest. Treaties negotiated in this era usually carried reserved rights: tribes ceded most of their aboriginal territory to the United States while reserving a smaller area to themselves together with the right to hunt and gather outside the reservation on open and unclaimed lands and to fish at their usual and accustomed fishing places. As national forests later came to be established in some of those ceded areas, twentieth-century courts would find that tribes held reserved rights on those national forestlands based on their nineteenth-century treaties.

The treaty system formed the basis of federal Indian policy for nearly one hundred years, or from the revolutionary era to 1871. In the annual Indian Appropriations Act passed in March 1871, Congress prohibited further treaty making with Indian tribes while pledging to uphold the validity of treaties concluded to that date. Thereafter, the U.S. government negotiated a number of further land-cession "agreements" with tribal councils and turned those agreements into law in a process that was very similar to treaty making. It also established many more reservations by executive order, particularly in the Southwest. Both those practices represented a carryover from the treaty-making era. Thus, even though Congress ended the treaty system in 1871, the era of negotiated tribal land cessions extended into the early twentieth century.[17]

Finally, Alaska Natives (the indigenous peoples of Alaska embracing Indians, Eskimos, and Aleuts) came together not long after Alaska statehood in 1959 to demand settlement of their land claims. The Alaska Native Claim Settlement Act of 1971 extinguished aboriginal title while granting 44 million acres to a dozen Native regional corporations and some two hundred Native village corporations.

Midway through the treaty-making era, Chief Justice John Marshall provided a legal definition of Indian status within the United States in three Supreme Court cases. Together they are known as the Marshall Trilogy. In the first case, *Johnson and Graham's Lessee v. McIntosh* (1823), the court was asked to rule on the validity of two claims to the same piece of land, one based on direct purchase from Indians, the other on a fee patent issued by the government. Upholding the Doctrine of Discovery, Marshall held that Indian title to the land was limited to a "possessory right" of use and occupancy, while the United States held the right of preemption. Indians could not dispose of their possessory interest to anyone but the United States. The decision established the concept of aboriginal title.

In the second case, *Cherokee Nation v. Georgia* (1831), the Cherokees' chief John Ross appealed to the Supreme Court to prevent the state of Georgia from confiscating Cherokee lands. The tribe contended that it was a foreign nation and therefore was not subject to state laws. Marshall found that the Cherokees and other Indian peoples were not foreign nations but rather "domestic dependent nations." The relationship between the Cherokees and the United States, he wrote, was "perhaps unlike that of any other two people in existence." The nearest equivalent was the relationship of a ward to his guardian. This decision introduced the federal trust doctrine, whereby the federal government was cast in the role of a protector or trustee of Indian interests.

Finally, in *Worcester v. Georgia* (1832), the Marshall court considered the case of a missionary by the name of Samuel Worcester who had been charged with violating Georgia law by failing to obtain a permit to live on Cherokee lands within the state. Marshall found the state law unconstitutional because it infringed on the federal-Indian trust relationship. Furthermore, even though the Cherokee nation was in a subordinate position to the United States, it retained the right to govern its internal affairs. The fact that the tribe's relationship to the United States was in the nature of a protectorate did not diminish its right to political independence or tribal sovereignty.[18] The three basic tenets of law established by the Marshall Trilogy—aboriginal title and U.S. preemption, the federal trust doctrine, and tribal sovereignty—continued to underpin federal Indian policy long after the treaty-making era was over.

A TRANSFORMATION OF FOREST VALUES IN INDUSTRIALIZING AMERICA

In 1850, lumber production ranked first among all U.S. manufactures. By 1860, lumber had dropped to second place behind textiles, but the total output of lumber was still growing and would continue to grow for another fifty years. Two major developments fed the rising demand for wood through the second half of the nineteenth century. One was new building construction to house the nation's growing population. As new farms and towns sprang up across the Great Plains and throughout the West, and as Eastern cities spawned new suburbs, much of the sawn wood used in building construction was supplied by a rising national lumber industry. The other major development was railroad construction. The railroads consumed vast quantities of wood for railroad ties, trestle bridges, rolling stock, and associated buildings. Perhaps one-fourth of all lumber production in the 1870s and 1880s went into railroad construction. So great was the demand for track ties alone that fear of an impending "timber famine" arose in the 1890s.[19]

The development of railroads made possible the shipment of lumber products over long distances, thereby giving further stimulus to a national lumber industry. Indeed, by the end of the period, railroads became vital to the timber operations themselves. Until the advent of railroad logging, timber had to be felled near water so that it could be floated to the sawmill. In the era of railroad logging, temporary logging railroads were built into rugged, forested areas that were too remote from navigable waterways to be exploited by the traditional methods of hauling and skidding logs to water. As railroad logging required heavy capital investment, it reinforced other industry trends. The bigger lumbering companies moved from region to region, buying timberlands and building railroads into the woods wherever the supply of timber was sufficiently abundant and close to markets to make their large-scale operation profitable.

Once they had built a logging railroad, these companies wanted to cut nearly every tree within reach in order to recoup their investment. They did not limit themselves to the most valuable species but took everything at once. This cut-and-run pattern of logging occurred on both a local and regional scale. At the regional level, the center of the logging industry moved from New York and Pennsylvania to the upper Great Lakes region after the Civil War. When the vast white pine resources of Michigan, Wisconsin, and Minnesota were finally exhausted around the turn of the twentieth century, the lumber industry pulled up stakes again and migrated to the Pacific Northwest.

As the lumber industry came to be centered in Wisconsin, tribes located in that state were the first tribes to be affected. Indian reservations in the northern part of Wisconsin contained valuable stands of timber. As early as 1854, Menominee tribal leaders sought to exploit their forest resources to produce a tribal cash income, or to barter wood for food. They argued that the tribe

FIGURE 2. Logging camp in Washington State, 1892. Such isolated camps became a common feature of the lumbering industry in the era of railroad logging.

COURTESY OF FOREST HISTORY SOCIETY

owned the reservation timber and it ought to be able to dispose of it in the commercial timber market. The demand presented a quandary for the Office of Indian Affairs, since government policy aimed at making Indians into yeoman farmers, not foresters. Indian desires to enter into the logging industry, even if the Indians were to cut and sell the timber themselves, had no place in the government's overarching civilization policy. Title to the forest was held by the United States in trust for the Menominee. The only legal basis for logging on Indian lands was to clear the land for farming, in which case the United States, as trustee, had a fiduciary responsibility to get a good price for the timber. Since the Office of Indian Affairs was not set up to conduct lumbering, the Wisconsin tribes had to work with local Indian agents to develop their forest resources on a reservation-by-reservation basis. Their efforts were fraught because neither the agents nor the Indians themselves had the practical logging experience, technical training, or market savvy to deal effectively with the lumbermen.[20]

Logging operations on the Lac Courte Oreilles Reservation illustrate the problems encountered. In 1872, Indian agent Seldon N. Clark entered into a contract with lumberman William A. Rust of Eau Claire, Wisconsin, on behalf of the Lac Courte Oreilles Band of Lake Superior Ojibwe. The contract called for the sale and disposal of all pine trees standing within three miles of navigable streams and lakes. Rust was to pay $50,000 in five annual installments, and he was to complete the logging in ten years. The payments were to go to Clark for distribution to the Indians. The chiefs objected to the latter provision but finally gave their consent. As soon as the contract was made, another lumber company offered $100,000, raising the specter that the government had undersold the Indians' timber. Moreover, as Rust commenced logging operations, it became evident that the government had no way to determine how much timber was actually being removed and therefore could not protect the Indians' interests adequately.[21]

About the same time that the Rust contract came under scrutiny, the government brought suit against another Wisconsin lumberman, George Cook, for purchasing logs from a group of Oneida Indians on the Stockbridge and Munsee Reservation. At issue was whether timber on Indian lands could be sold separately from the land for purposes of commercial logging. The case of *United States v. Cook* went to the Supreme Court, and in 1874 the court rendered a decision. Citing Marshall's ruling in *McIntosh*, the court affirmed that Indians had no more than a possessory right to the land and could not sell timber commercially; they could only cut it for personal use or dispose of it for purposes of preparing to farm the land. When such timber was sold illegally, the proceeds belonged to the United States. In the wake of the *Cook* decision, the government apparently canceled the dubious Rust contract along with numerous other contracts.[22]

The *Cook* decision reflected emerging concerns over the protection of timber not just on Indian reservations but on all federal timberlands. One early clarion call for reform came from the philosopher-diplomat George Perkins Marsh. A native Vermonter, Marsh observed for himself the consequences of lumbering, sheep grazing, and soil runoff in his state's Green Mountains. In the 1850s and early 1860s, Marsh served as U.S. minister to Turkey and Italy, where his studies of geography and history of the eastern Mediterranean led to a refinement of his ideas about conservation. His magnum opus, *Man and Nature*, appeared in 1864. Marsh argued that land constituted a nation's wealth, and it was the proper role of government to protect the land against humanity's unwitting destructive influences. Forests must be protected to prevent soil erosion and the degradation of watersheds. Deforestation in the Mediterranean, Marsh believed, had led to the decline of ancient Greece and Rome. The United States must heed the lessons of the past and take proper care of its public domain.[23]

Marsh's message cut against the grain of U.S. public land policy in the mid-nineteenth century, which aimed to convert the public domain to private ownership as rapidly and completely as possible. While the centerpiece of that land policy was the Homestead Act of 1862, the government also made enormous land grants to railroad companies to spur completion of the transcontinental railroads, and it gave away mineral rights to valuable ore deposits to abet the development of mining districts in the West. By the 1870s, however, a few reformers began to see the wisdom in Marsh's warnings and considered alternative approaches to public land management. Franklin B. Hough, a New York physician, led a movement to create an office of forestry in the federal government. Secretary of the Interior Carl Schurz brought attention to the widespread theft of resources occurring on public lands. Major John Wesley Powell, a scientist with the Department of the Interior, called for planning and surveys to ensure a prudent course of development for the nation's arid lands. Congress heeded these warnings with half measures. For example, it passed two acts for the protection of timber on public lands in 1878, but the laws were so weak that their practical effect was to encourage timber thieves to flout the laws because neither the penalties nor the threat of enforcement were real deterrents.[24]

Congress did appropriate funds in 1876 for the appointment of a specialist in the Department of Agriculture to study the forest problem. Hough was selected for the job and produced a four-volume *Report upon Forestry* that added weight to Marsh's plea for informed, public stewardship of the land. In 1886, Congress made the Division of Forestry a standing institution in the Department of Agriculture. However, when Hough's successor, Chief of Forestry Bernhard E. Fernow, drafted a bill for the protection of forests, Congress proved to be unreceptive. The idea of permanently retaining some of the public domain in government hands had not yet ripened.[25]

Western Indian tribes were able to offer very little on these matters during the 1870s and 1880s despite being the forests' original stewards. Confined to reservations and dependent on government rations to fend off starvation, they were in no position to make themselves heard. When Indian leaders did speak out in public, their views hardly counted, for by this period Indian peoples had become completely marginalized in American society. If they did manage to stir some sympathy in their white audiences, as when Chief Standing Bear of the Ponca tribe went on a lecture tour in the East to protest his people's mistreatment by the army, the general effect was to reinforce Indian reformers' opinion that Indian reservations were hellholes that had to be liquidated for the Indians' own good. Of course, that was not the answer to their problems that tribal leaders were seeking. By the 1880s, the land issue of overwhelming importance to tribes was how to stop the government's initiative to break up reservations through the process of individual land allotment.[26]

Indian allotment created a fresh opportunity for lumbermen to buy Indians' timber. While *United States v. Cook* prohibited commercial logging on tribal lands, it did allow sale of timber when the primary purpose of logging was to clear the land for farming. Since allotment ostensibly aimed at turning Indians into farmers, it opened the way for lumbermen to purchase timber from allottees. Land-cession treaties in Wisconsin and Minnesota provided for allotment even before Congress passed the General Allotment Act of 1887. Consequently, the tribes located in northern Wisconsin and Minnesota were once again on the battle lines where the lumbering industry sought access to Indian-owned timber. Under pressure from the lumber interests, the Office of Indian Affairs ruled that Indian allottees could sell three-quarters of the timber on their allotment, retaining one-quarter as a woodlot for fuel and fencing material. Following this ruling in September 1882, the rush was on.

In the early going, the government required that all wage work connected with the timber sales must be reserved for Indians. However, lumbermen soon insisted that they could operate more efficiently if they were allowed to employ white crews. Supposedly, allottees would stand to get a higher return on their timber if the lumbermen could reduce labor costs. It was a spurious argument. Yet the new administration of President Grover Cleveland went for it, dropping the requirement that all wage jobs be reserved for Indians. Allotment timber sales mushroomed after 1885. As they did, prices paid on the timber actually fell slightly while Indian wage earnings dropped off precipitously. Republican members of Congress denounced the administration's handling of the timber sales and called for an investigation. The Senate committee report in 1889 found that the allottees' timber had been sold at rock-bottom prices. In the course of its investigation, the committee heard testimony from a number of Ojibwe. Speaking through interpreters, those witnesses expressed their bewilderment over the whole allotment process and stated that they had been pressured to take their allotment and sell the timber. One witness said he had refused to sell the timber but that it was logged off anyway. As with the earlier phase of Indian logging that ended with the *Cook* decision, the Office of Indian Affairs was ill prepared to deal with the market pressures that came to bear on allotment logging.[27]

Some claimed that the pressure to allow timber sales was not chiefly coming from white lumbermen but rather from the Indian land owners. Allottees frequently asked to sell the timber from their lands in full knowledge that the timber would be removed in one fell swoop. Looking back on these years, the leading Indian forester in the early twentieth century, J. P. Kinney, said that the allottees' request to sell was not typically a farsighted economic decision (with a view to clearing the land to farm it, as reformers hoped). Rather, it was born of the allottee's dire need for cash to survive in the white man's individualistic money economy.[28]

Some tribes continued to agitate for the right to sell timber from their lands. The Menominee tribe was the most notable example. The tribe's desire to enter into the commercial lumbering market appears to have been calculated to protect tribal sovereignty by creating a new tribal economy rooted in capitalism. Jobs in the woods and even a large sawmill operation would be maintained under tribal auspices.[29]

Pressure from the Menominee tribe and Wisconsin lumbermen led Congress to pass legislation in 1889 known as the Dead and Down Act. The measure aimed to satisfy lumbermen and alleviate Indians' suffering on the one hand and meet the federal government's fiduciary responsibility to protect Indian forests in trust on the other. It settled on a new formula to get around the *Cook* decision. Commercial logging on Indian lands would be limited to the removal of "dead and down" timber only. Green trees would be preserved. Where evidence was presented to government officials that trees had been killed beforehand to make them eligible for cutting, the sale would be disallowed.[30]

One year after passing the Dead and Down Act, Congress responded to further demands of the Menominee Tribe by passing a law that authorized commercial logging of green timber on the Menominee Reservation only. This singular legislation recognized tribal ownership of the forest and launched what was at that time the nation's only tribal forest enterprise. Key provisions included an annual maximum cut of 20 million board feet, a loan fund to provide for capital start-up costs, and a deduction of one-fifth of annual stumpage revenues for a tribal fund for the support of a hospital and relief of the poor.[31] Viewed against the backdrop of Indian land allotment and the government's longstanding effort to make Indians into yeoman farmers, the Menominees' tribal forest enterprise might appear to be a surprising initiative. But viewed in connection with the dawning national conservation movement, it can be seen as a pilot project for public-lands forestry. Indeed, professor of forestry Alan G. McQuillan has termed the act "the first law in the nation that provided for the management of any 'public' forestlands for economic purposes"—since fee title to the Menominee Tribe's forest was held in trust by the United States and could be considered "public" in that narrow sense. It was an important precedent for all of U.S. forestry, McQuillan observes, because the law authorized commercial logging of green timber under government supervision where the land and living forest were to remain in U.S. ownership.[32]

The following year, Congress enacted what is now called the Forest Reserve Act of 1891, the foundation for the future National Forest System. The law authorized the president to establish areas of the public domain that were partially or wholly covered with forest as "public reservations." (The designation was soon changed to "forest reserve" and then "national forest.") The measure was actually inserted at the eleventh hour as a rider in a public-lands bill at the initiative of Secretary of the Interior John W. Noble, and so it became law without congressional debate. President Benjamin Harrison used the new executive authority to establish the nation's first public forests, totaling some 13 million acres. Looking back on it from a later era, Secretary of the Interior Stewart L. Udall described the legislation as a fluke: "One of the most far-reaching conservation decisions ever made was ironically consummated in half-hidden haste."[33] In a similar vein, historian Harold K. Steen wrote that the obscure manner in which this critical piece of legislation became law was "unfortunate."[34] Certainly there would have been substantial public support for such a measure had it been given more daylight. Concerns about timber fraud, despoliation, waste, theft (more often referred to as "trespass"), and an impending nationwide wood shortage (a so-called timber famine) all gained currency as the decade wore on.

As soon as Harrison created the first forest reserves, conservation-minded people in and out of government pressed for further legislation to provide for the reserves' administration. The American Forestry Association urged some kind of federal supervision over lumbering operations. From inside the Department of Agriculture, Bernhard E. Fernow, chief of the Division of Forestry, spoke of the need for regulations to guide timber cutting on the forest reserves as well as data with which to identify more forestlands for protection. When Grover Cleveland returned for a second presidential term in 1893, he made Hoke Smith his secretary of the interior. Smith wanted Congress to appoint a forestry commission to advise the General Land Office on how to administer the reserves. Six months into his second term, President Cleveland designated two more areas totaling 5 million acres; he then resisted adding any more areas until Congress provided a system for administration. But Congress was in no hurry to act.[35]

At the end of his second presidential term, Cleveland finally gave up on securing the desired legislation and went ahead in proclaiming thirteen more forest reserves covering a total of 21 million acres. His bold action carried considerable political risk, because Westerners strongly objected to what they saw as a "lockup" of Western states' resources, and Western senators threatened to take the whole system down. However, out of the resulting political furor emerged a compromise bill that promised to establish the forest reserves on a sounder footing. What became known as the Organic Act had three main provisions. First, the essential purposes of forest reserves were to protect watersheds and provide for timber production, and all future forest reserves had to meet those criteria. Second, the secretary of the interior was directed to make rules and regulations for their protection, which included supervision of timber sales. And third, the thirteen newly proclaimed reserves were suspended for nine months to give land claimants in those areas an opportunity to file for lieu lands elsewhere. (This last item was essential to dispel Westerners' opposition.) President William McKinley signed the measure into law on June 4, 1897.

The Organic Act marks the beginning of a federally managed National Forest System. At the outset, forest administration came under the Department of the Interior. The secretary of the interior assigned responsibility to the General Land Office (GLO), which established a forestry unit that came to be designated Division "R" (Forestry). Despite its name, most GLO forest supervisors and rangers lacked professional training in forestry, and the secretary of the interior looked to the Division of Forestry in the Department of Agriculture for actual forestry expertise. In 1898, Gifford Pinchot succeeded Fernow as chief of the Division of Forestry in the Department of Agriculture. Pinchot believed the forest reserves ought to be under the administration of professional foresters and therefore ought to be transferred from Interior to Agriculture. After an assassin ended the life of President McKinley and elevated Pinchot's friend Vice President Theodore Roosevelt to the presidency, the chief forester soon found his way clear to obtain the land transfer. The Transfer Act of 1905 placed the forest reserves under the Department of Agriculture and turned the research-oriented Division of Forestry into a premier federal land-management agency, the U.S. Forest Service. Two years later, the forest reserves took the more illustrious name of National Forests.[36]

TRIBES AND NATIONAL FORESTS AT THE END OF THE NINETEENTH CENTURY

When the National Forest System came into being at the end of the nineteenth century, relations between the public forests' administrators and Indian tribes were far from most people's minds. Tribes were too preoccupied with problems on the reservation to assert tribal interests on neighboring lands. Federal and state agencies and the courts as well as the surrounding non-Indian communities were not friendly to any type of tribal assertiveness. State and federal courts barely recognized tribes' off-reservation treaty rights. The federal government's overall campaign of Indian assimilation had so reduced the standing of tribal governments within the American political system that virtually all of a tribe's official dealings with the outside world had to be conducted through the local officer of the Bureau of Indian Affairs (BIA), usually a reservation superintendent. The BIA superintendent operated within an organizational culture that had long treated tribes paternalistically, interpreting and screening tribes' communications to the outside.

In 1900, the future of the Indian estate appeared doubtful. Indian land holdings had been reduced to about 78 million acres, and the assimilation policy

FIGURE 3. Ojibwe man and Norway pine, Minnesota, 1902. After creating the
Minnesota (later Chippewa) National Forest from the Winnibigoshish Reservation
and a portion of the Leech Lake Reservation, the U.S. government cut down this
Norway pine forest in spite of objections by the resident Pillager band of Ojibwe.

COURTESY OF MINNESOTA HISTORICAL SOCIETY

aimed at allotting or selling off all that remained. In stark contrast, the amount
of acreage in forest reserves stood at 46 million acres in 1900 on its way to 75 million acres just five years later. The Indian estate and the National Forest System were on opposite trajectories, one dwindling while the other grew. Indian
reservations and the National Forest System already abutted one another in
numerous places in 1900, yet they did not then appear to be permanent or even
long-term neighbors. The adage "good fences make good neighbors" was not
particularly apt under the changing circumstances.

The main principles of public forestry in 1900 were hardly applicable to
the Indian reservations, nor did they resonate with traditional Indian forest
values. Early professional forestry in the United States has been characterized
as "Prussian forestry" because of the strong influence of German concepts of

forestry on the leading American practitioners. Bernhard Fernow came from Germany, as did Carl Schurz, and Gifford Pinchot received part of his higher education there. Prussian forestry was committed to ordering nature, or at least controlling the growth of trees. Its basic aim was to achieve sustained yield of wood production.

As Professor Samuel Trask Dana explained in his classic treatise, *Forest and Range Policy*, Prussian forestry emanated from the basic forest conditions found in nineteenth-century Germany. There, land was scarce; trees were also scarce and yet indispensable to the nation's life, economy, and defense; and the nation had a dense population with abundant labor and a fair degree of social stability. Those conditions led to several assumptions about forest management that could be summed up in three axioms involving scarcity, stability, and certainty. First, *scarcity* of land in Germany ensured scarcity of wood. Second, as wood would always be in demand, and as Germany had a high degree of social *stability*, the demand for wood would remain stable. And third, because wood was scarce and demand was stable, it created *certainty* about the appropriate standards for forest management: the consumption of wood must be limited to the growth potential of the forest—a sustained yield. The assumptions behind Prussian forestry were simply not applicable in the American context. Professor Dana summed up the contradictions this way: "Land was not scarce, timber was not scarce, the social structure was fluid, and new sources of supply were constantly being brought within economic reach. Moreover, consumption patterns, utilization, and technology were constantly changing."[37]

The managerial and scientific basis of Prussian forestry was obviously alien to the traditional Indian perspective of living lightly on the land and being a part of the forest community. (Still today, Indians tend to bridle at the notion that humans *manage* the land, insisting that humans only *care* for the land.) Despite their cultural heritage, however, Indians were not immune to market forces, and when the lumber industry moved into their area and they found that they had a valuable commodity to sell, then they demanded the right to sell it. Prices for timber were anything but stable, and reservation economies were cash poor, so Indians could be expected to want to sell timber when they had the opportunity. Moreover, when Indian reservations were divided into allotments, forestry principles of sustained-yield management became even more inapplicable. How could forestry be practiced on an individual property of 40 to 160 acres? Even when the BIA was able to combine numerous allotments into one timber sale unit to achieve economy of scale, forest managers could not expect allottees to wait twenty or thirty years for a cutting when they needed the income immediately.[38]

Yet the conservation movement did promote values that were, in a very general sense, far more compatible with Indian perspectives than previous U.S. land policy had been. The idea that not all land should be turned into private property, that some land should be held in public trust, came closer to the tribal perspective that the welfare of the group came before that of the individual. Conservation's premise that resource use must take into account the needs not only of the present generation but of future generations as well more closely resembled the indigenous people's view that the tribe is the perpetual guardian of the tribal homeland. Even conservation's notion of wise stewardship of the land was more nearly akin to the Indian's view that all of the Earth is sacred. These basic commonalities between conservation and the indigenous point of view were nothing less than the seeds of a positive, constructive relationship that would finally begin to germinate some sixty to seventy years later.

Just over midway through the twentieth century, Secretary of the Interior Stewart L. Udall saw those tender shoots of mutual understanding and respect at last beginning to appear. He wrote eloquently of the Indians' "land wisdom" in his 1963 classic on the American conservation movement, *The Quiet Crisis*:

> It is ironical that today the conservation movement finds itself turning back to ancient Indian land ideas, to the Indian understanding that we are not outside of nature, but of it. From this wisdom we can learn how to conserve the best parts of our continent.
>
> In recent decades we have slowly come back to some of the truths that the Indians knew from the beginning: that unborn generations have a claim on the land equal to our own; that men need to learn from nature; to keep an ear to the earth, and to replenish their spirits in frequent contacts with animals and wild land. And most important of all, we are recovering a sense of reverence for the land.[39]

CHAPTER SUMMARY

Two centuries of European colonization and another century and more of U.S. national expansion laid the foundation for Forest Service tribal relations commencing around 1900. Four major elements went into that foundation. First, there was a major clash of values in the way Indian peoples and European Americans inhabited and used North American forests. Indians used fire to manipulate forests for a variety of purposes, such as to increase deer populations or to improve berry production. European Americans cut down forests for wood and cleared forests for farmland. The different values that Indians and European Americans placed on forests produced different environmental consequences, which led to conflict over who had the right to occupy and steward the land.

The second major element that went into the foundation of Forest Service tribal relations was the U.S. government's treatment of Indian peoples from the nation's founding to 1900. Federal Indian policy was rooted in the European Doctrine of Discovery and the U.S. Constitution. United States–Indian relations took definite shape under the treaty system and the Marshall court, both of which defined a special trust relationship between the federal government and tribes. An important legacy of the treaty system for Forest Service tribal relations was that Indian reservations and reserved treaty rights came to be distributed unevenly across the nation.

The third and fourth major elements in the foundation were the rise of a national lumber industry and the concomitant growth of a forest conservation movement. At the end of the nineteenth century, the foundation was in place for the U.S. Forest Service to commence management of the National Forest System. But as yet there was only a faint glimmer of an idea that traditional Native land-use practices and the forest conservation movement were in some ways alike, or that the Forest Service and tribes might one day walk the land together and partner as environmental stewards. How that idea began to emerge in the first quarter of the twentieth century is the subject of the next chapter.

2

PUBLIC FORESTS AND FORESTS IN TRUST

The Early Twentieth Century

MAKING NATIONAL FORESTS, DISPOSSESSING THE INDIANS

PRESIDENT THEODORE ROOSEVELT and Chief Forester Gifford Pinchot are firmly linked in the public's mind with the rise of the conservation movement at the start of the twentieth century. Roosevelt believed passionately in the federal government's responsibility to conserve the nation's resources, and he relied on his friend Pinchot to help him marshal the powers of the executive branch to that end. Not the least of Roosevelt's executive powers was the presidential authority to proclaim forest reserves. During his two terms in office, Roosevelt more than quadrupled the size of the National Forest System, expanding it from 43 million acres to about 174 million acres.[1]

As Roosevelt approached the end of his second term as president, he and Pinchot and the other men in the president's inner circle on conservation matters began to form doubts that William H. Taft, the president-elect, whom they regarded as Roosevelt's chosen successor, would remain faithful to the conservation movement. In the administration's final days, Roosevelt directed Pinchot and Secretary of the Interior James Garfield to prepare a final set of presidential proclamations to put more lands into the National Forest System before Taft took over the reins of government. Pinchot and his staff worked feverishly on the proclamations, and on March 2, 1909, the president's second-to-last day in office, the chief forester hand-delivered them all to the White House for the president's signature, each one accompanied by maps and elaborate legal descriptions of the lands involved. In all, the proclamations enlarged thirteen national forests in Arizona, New Mexico, California, Nevada, and Washington, and added approximately 16 million acres to the National Forest System.[2] The eleventh-hour collaboration by Pinchot and Roosevelt is a well-known vignette of Forest Service history. A legendary big win in the annals of conservation, it also illustrates the extraordinarily close relationship the chief forester enjoyed with the chief executive, the likes of which the American conservation movement has not seen since.

In this oft-told tale, the critical piece that invariably gets overlooked is the fact that the proclamations targeted tribal forests for transfer to the U.S. Forest Service. In all, the thirteen proclamations called for the conveyance of seven tribal forests to adjacent national forests. For a period of twenty-five years, each proclamation declared, the secretary of the interior and the commissioner of Indian affairs would retain full authority to make allotments to individual Indians on the lands conveyed and to use timber for the construction of school and agency buildings and for other tribal purposes. Over the same period, the tribes would continue to derive income from the leasing of grazing privileges and the disposal of dead and down timber under rules and regulations prescribed by the secretary of agriculture. At the end of the twenty-five-year period, all those lands not allotted to individual Indians would pass to the complete control of the Forest Service.[3] In short, the proclamations aimed to absorb the better part of seven Indian reservations into the National Forest System. Not one of the tribes was consulted. The proclamations made no provision for compensating the tribes for land or timber once it left federal trusteeship even though the eventual transfer of land title and timber to the National Forest System would clearly be a taking.

To Roosevelt, Pinchot, and other conservation-minded white Americans of their era, it seemed only proper that Indian forests should be brought under public ownership. At the beginning of the twentieth century, U.S. Indian policy aimed at assimilating Indians into American society on the basis of individual U.S. citizenship. To the contemporary way of thinking, that meant breaking down Indians' tribal identity, disposing of tribal assets, and liquidating reservations. Since the goal was to Americanize the Indian and extinguish the tribe, Indian forests could not be maintained in tribal ownership in perpetuity; they must either become private or public. Given the alternative of seeing the forest fall into private hands and get cut down, Roosevelt and Pinchot believed it was in the Indians' best interest to have their forests converted to public ownership.[4]

Pinchot thought a natural affinity existed between Indian peoples and the Forest Service. Referring to Native Americans as the continent's "first conservationists," he noted that Native cultures exhibited patterns of resource use that effectively maintained healthy populations of fish and game on the continent before the arrival of Europeans. Traditional Native religions and social structures kept in check the wanton destruction and overexploitation of resources. Regrettably, European colonists lacked "this Native wisdom," Pinchot wrote, and as they and their descendants spread across the continent during the eighteenth and nineteenth centuries, they dispossessed the Indians and converted their lands into farms and settlements without regard for sustaining animal and plant communities as the Indians had. And yet, Pinchot observed, European traditions eventually gave rise to scientific forestry, providing a new foundation for conservation at the dawn of the twentieth century.[5]

As much as Pinchot admired the Indians' land wisdom, he saw it as a quaint relic of the past, not as something to be seriously studied or consulted by contemporary land managers. It was practically axiomatic in turn-of-the-century America that Indian peoples belonged to a "vanishing race." Traditional tribal cultures, whites assumed, would not be able to persist much longer against the shocks of Western civilization and the pressures of overwhelming numbers of non-Indians invading their space. And so they were destined for oblivion. What many Americans of Pinchot's time predicted was the complete amalgamation of Indian peoples into the white race. "Kill the Indian, save the man," went the reformers' motto. What those chilling words meant was that the sooner individual Indians could be shorn of their tribal allegiances, supposedly the better off they would be.[6]

The Forest Service came into being in 1905 in a time when the Indian estate was being rapidly broken up and sold off to non-Indians. The centerpiece of federal Indian policy during the Theodore Roosevelt administration was still the General Allotment Act of 1887, also known as the Dawes Severalty Act. The intent of this law was to allot parcels of land to individual Indians in order to instill in them the white man's values of private property ownership, thereby preparing them for U.S. citizenship. Since President Jefferson's day, Indian reformers had argued that the key to "civilizing" Indians or absorbing them into the American nation was to give them their own land and the wherewithal to become small farmers. Once Indians became private property owners, the reformers' argument ran, they would acquire the white man's desire to accumulate wealth and learn his respect for civil law. Only then would Indians be prepared to enter American life with all the rights and responsibilities of citizenship. The General Allotment Act took this old idea and declared that the time had come to implement it. In passing the law, Congress envisioned a point in the not-too-distant future when all Indians would be U.S. citizens, Indian reservations would no longer exist, and the Office of Indian Affairs (or Bureau of Indian Affairs, as it came to be known in the twentieth century) would have put itself out of business.

The mechanics of the General Allotment Act were fairly simple. Reservations were to be surveyed into lots and allotted to individual tribal members at the rate of 160 acres to each adult head of family, forty acres to each family dependent, and eighty acres to each single adult without family and to each orphan under the age of eighteen. Each allotment was to be held in trust by the U.S. government for a period of twenty-five years, meaning that it could not be sold. At the expiration of the trust period, the Indian's trust patent would be converted into a fee patent, and he or she would be conferred U.S. citizenship.

The law further provided that when all Indians residing on a reservation had been allotted, the remaining area would be deemed "surplus" and made available for land entry or purchase by non-Indians. Westerners strongly supported that provision of the law since it promised access to Indian resources. The Indian forests that Pinchot eyed for absorption into the National Forest System in 1909 were vulnerable to expropriation by non-Indians precisely because of that provision. What he and Roosevelt feared was that once those reservation lands were declared "surplus," tribes would be powerless to prevent private lumbering companies from buying up the land for the value of a single timber crop. After removing the timber, the private landowner would have no long-term economic incentive to grow another forest on it and would simply abandon the cutover land or sell it for almost nothing in its despoiled condition. To avoid that eventuality, Pinchot wanted those Indian forests converted to public ownership so that they could be properly managed for sustained-yield forestry and watershed protection.

As enacted in 1887, the General Allotment Act included certain safeguards to protect tribes from the rapaciousness of Westerners intent on breaking up reservations as quickly as possible. The responsibility for deciding when to allot a given tribe rested with the president, and the disposal of "surplus" lands following allotment required the concurrence of the tribe. Subsequent legislative amendments and court decisions weakened those protections. The law was amended in 1891 to allow the secretary of the interior to lease Indian allotments to non-Indians, which opened the door for non-Indians to move onto the reservation and earn a livelihood farming the Indians' land. Though they earned a small rental income from their allotments, these displaced Indians became virtual landless paupers on their own turf. Then, in 1903, the Supreme Court ruled in *Lonewolf v. Hitchcock* that Congress had plenary power to abrogate an Indian treaty and dispose of surplus reservation lands over a tribe's objections. The specific case involved the Kiowa in Oklahoma, where tribal leaders protested the sale of surplus lands based on the Treaty of Medicine Lodge Creek of 1867, which required the consent of three-fourths of adult males for any further cession of Kiowa land. In the wake of the high court's decision in *Lonewolf*, tribal governments were practically powerless to stop Congress and the Roosevelt administration from selling off Indian lands.[7]

FIGURE 4. Chief Charlo (1830–1910) of the Bitterroot Salish. Despite pursuing a policy of peace with local white settlers, Chief Charlo and his people had to give up their home in western Montana's Bitterroot Valley and move to the Flathead Reservation in 1891.

Another crucial change in allotment policy came with passage of the Burke Act in 1906. The law did away with the mandatory twenty-five-year period in which each allotment was held in trust by the U.S. government. In its place, it authorized the secretary of the interior to determine when an allottee was "competent" to receive a fee patent. Along with the fee patent came all the rights of citizenship but also the onus of taxation on the land. Ostensibly, the law aimed at emancipating Indians who were held down by their status as wards, but what it did in practical terms was hasten the day when allottees disposed of their allotments for cash. Many Indians who were deemed "competent" and issued their fee patents were soon forced by economic circumstances to sell their land to non-Indians. Others lost their land for failure to pay taxes. The allotment policy went forward in the face of mounting evidence that it had become just another means of taking away the Indians' land.[8]

In fact, the process of allotment reached full tide during the Roosevelt administration. By the time Roosevelt took office as president in 1900, some 56,000 allotments had been made among a total U.S. Indian population of around 237,000. Over the next ten years, the number of allotments rose to more than 190,000. Thereafter, the pace of allotment slowed as officials grew more cautious about the policy's failings and as the most suitable lands for allotment got used up.[9] The irony is inescapable. At the same time that Roosevelt and Pinchot built up the National Forest System, they also played a major role in shrinking the Indian estate. From 1905 to 1909, the National Forest System increased in size by around 97 million acres, while allotment led in fairly short order to Indians' loss of around 86 million acres. The rise of conservation dovetailed with a national closeout sale on the Indians' landed heritage.[10]

FROM INDIAN LAND TO NATIONAL FOREST: THE CASE OF MINNESOTA

The origin of the Chippewa National Forest in northern Minnesota offers a prime example of how Indian lands became national forestlands. The national forest was the first to be created by an act of Congress, and it played an important role in bringing about the establishment of the Forest Service.

In 1855, the Ojibwe (or Chippewa) Indians of Minnesota signed a treaty ceding all of the northern part of the state except for several small reservations. By the 1880s, their reservations contained the last big stands of white pine still remaining in the state. Two years after Congress enacted the General Allotment Act, Representative Knute Nelson of Minnesota, a Republican with close ties to the state's lumber barons, sponsored a bill aimed at getting those reservations allotted and opened for logging. (Pinchot described him most unkindly as a "hardboiled, tobacco-chewing, short and powerful squarehead Norwegian.") Nelson gave his legislation the euphemistic title, "An Act for the relief and civilization of the Chippewa in the State of Minnesota," for the law purported to answer the demands of numerous mixed-blood Ojibwe who wanted to be allotted so that they could sell their timber to market. Under the terms of the so-called Nelson Act, passed in 1889, a government commission negotiated with the several bands of Ojibwe to obtain their consent to allotment. Each band agreed to cede its remaining lands in return for individual allotments plus payment on the value of the surplus land when it sold. As logging operations began, however, allegations arose that the government was selling the land far below value, the actual volume of timber logged being more than double what the Office of Indian Affairs had estimated in some cases. In response, the Office of Indian Affairs curtailed land sales and logging operations, much to the lumbermen's dismay.[11]

In 1897, Congress amended the Nelson Act to correct the problem. Now, only "dead and down" timber could be logged, and only Indians could be licensed to do the logging. But the new law brought a train of other abuses. Green timber was cut fraudulently. Fires were set to kill the timber so it could qualify as "dead." Many Indians who were licensed to do the logging but lacked the means sold their permits to non-Indian operators for as little as one fourth of their actual value.[12]

The controversy over fraudulent "dead and down" logging sparked a movement to protect the core area in either a national park or forest reserve. Soon a coalition of conservationists formed to advance the proposal. Led by the Minnesota Federation of Women's Clubs, it included state foresters, one prominent Chicago sportsman, and a few well-placed spokespersons for the Ojibwe. Representative Page Morris of Minnesota prepared a bill, which the leader of the coalition, Mrs. W. E. Bramhall, found unacceptable because it failed to establish a public reserve of any kind. The bill was circulated among the members of Minnesota's congressional delegation, and finally the whole delegation met in council with Gifford Pinchot, then in charge of the Bureau of Forestry, and H. H. Chapman, superintendent of the North Central Experiment Station in Grand Rapids, Minnesota. The four-hour meeting ended with a decision in favor of establishing a forest reserve, and Pinchot was given the task of drawing up a bill.[13]

The resulting Morris Act of 1902 appeared to contain something for everybody. It got land sales and logging moving again for Indians and lumbermen. It preserved ten sections (6,400 acres) of islands and lakeshore as parkland. Most significantly, it established a forest reserve over about nine-tenths of the Leech Lake Reservation and gave the Bureau of Forestry responsibility for selecting the lands and prescribing rules and regulations for logging. Not all were in accord with the measure, however. Most Indians on the reservation were opposed. One week after the Morris Act was enacted, Chief Flatmouth of the Pillager band of Ojibwe lambasted it in a speech at a Fourth of July celebration at the Leech Lake Agency. "The white men are bound to crowd out the poor Indian," he was quoted by a newspaper reporter. "The people that passed the Morris bill are not honest. The Indian should have more money for his land and pine."[14]

The Indians' objections notwithstanding, the Morris Act stood. Mandating a forest reserve of 225,000 acres, the law marked the first time that a forest reserve was established by Congress. The legislation elevated the Bureau of Forestry from a research and advisory body to a land-managing agency. By placing ceded Indian lands under the care of the Department of Agriculture, the Morris Act anticipated Congress's passage of the Transfer Act of 1905 two and a half years later. As everyone familiar with Forest Service history knows, the Transfer Act moved all forest reserves from the Department of the Interior to the Department of Agriculture and created the Forest Service to administer them. Pinchot, in writing his autobiography many years later, gleefully proclaimed the importance of the Morris Act, devoting an entire chapter to it. By providing that "the said Forester shall have power at all times to patrol and protect said lands and forests, and to enforce all rules and regulations made by him," the law did nothing less than launch government forestry on the ground.[15]

In Pinchot's first report to the secretary of agriculture as chief of the Forest Service, he proudly described how the work was proceeding on the Leech Lake Reservation, the future Chippewa National Forest. Under rules and regulations prepared by his office and approved by the secretary of the interior, 5 percent of trees were marked with a "U.S." stamp for retention as seed trees for reforestation. Then the remaining 95 percent of timber on selected lands was sold at public auction. After the trees were felled and removed, the operators were required to pile and burn brush to reduce fire hazard. "The success of the plan

FIGURE 5. Logging camp on the Chippewa National Forest. The Morris Act of 1902 turned most of the Leech Lake Indian Reservation into national forest land.

COURTESY OF MINNESOTA HISTORICAL SOCIETY

adopted to secure the perpetuation of the forest is entirely assured," Pinchot wrote; "Already young seedlings are springing up in abundance, and there can be no question that an ample supply of young growth will be established over the entire forest area."[16]

To Pinchot, the selective cutting under Forest Service regulations formed a striking contrast to previous logging operations in northern Minnesota, which left nothing but stumps and slash behind. To the resident Ojibwe, however, the advent of Forest Service management made a far different impression. They saw their forest cut down. For them, the making of the Chippewa National Forest created an indelible cultural memory, and the Leech Lake Band of Ojibwe of today has not forgotten it. The band's website includes a time line of major historical events in the life of the people, including the establishment of the Chippewa National Forest. This brief narrative points out that "the establishment of this forest did absolutely nothing to curb the widespread destruction of the majestic pine from the logging industry as intended. Over 95 percent of the white and red pine that was still standing when the Chippewa National Forest was established has been cut."[17]

THE MENOMINEE AND THE COOPERATIVE AGREEMENT OF 1908–1909

In the wake of the Morris Act, the Roosevelt administration soon found opportunities to reappraise more Indian forests in light of conservation policy. In 1903, the secretary of the interior requested the secretary of agriculture to provide a field study of forest conditions on the Menominee, Lac Courte Oreille, and La Pointe Indian reservations, all in Wisconsin. In each case, Pinchot's Bureau of Forestry was to prepare a description of the forest, a plan for fire protection, and recommendations for lumbering, including rules and regulations for timber sale contracts to be overseen by an agent of the Bureau of Forestry.[18]

The Menominee Indians by this time had a history of lumbering on their reservation. As early as 1871, the secretary of the interior authorized limited cutting of reservation timber to clear land for agricultural use. Over the next three decades, the Menominee became increasingly involved in the lumber industry, so that by 1905 a faction of the tribe was eager to expand logging operations on the reservation and participate more fulsomely in the larger market economy. That year, a windstorm knocked down thousands of trees on the reservation, leaving an estimated 25 million to 40 million board feet of downed timber in danger of going to waste. The proindustry faction—generally composed of the more educated, prosperous, and acculturated members of the tribe—formed the Business Committee of the Menominee Tribe and lobbied Congress for legislation to authorize salvage logging. Congress responded by enacting a law that placed the Menominee Business Committee in charge of all logging operations on the reservation even though it was not the tribal government. The law was a recipe for graft, particularly as members of the business committee were known to have ties to the state's lumber barons.[19]

Following passage of the law, the secretary of the interior again turned to the secretary of agriculture and the Bureau of Forestry for assistance. In 1907, James A. Howarth, a forest supervisor in the Forest Service, was dispatched to the Menominee Reservation to review the business committee's work. Howarth reported in December that the logging operations were a disaster. As suspected, members of the business committee had proceeded to award lucrative contracts to themselves and their associates. The holders of the contracts had then subcontracted to unscrupulous lumbermen from outside the reservation community, and those operators had made a mess of the work, high-grading the merchantable timber, discarding tops and branches, and piling the brush haphazardly. According to Howarth, many people believed the Menominee Business Committee had been set up to fail in the expectation that Congress would then have to pass legislation opening up the reservation to non-Indian lumbermen.[20]

A month after Howarth filed his report, the secretary of the interior and the secretary of agriculture entered a cooperative agreement, dated January 22, 1908, that placed the Forest Service in charge of all forestry on Indian reservations. As soon as the Forest Service took charge on the Menominee Reservation under the terms of this agreement, it confirmed Howarth's allegations of massive fraud and halted payments on the fraudulent contracts. Meanwhile, Senator Robert M. LaFollette of Wisconsin, a Progressive Republican and staunch ally of the Roosevelt administration, had been steering a bill through Congress to put the Menominee forest industry on a new footing with the Forest Service firmly in charge. The LaFollette Act of March 28, 1908, repealed the act of 1906 and called on the Forest Service to oversee cutting of green as well as dead and down timber by the Menominee. It also called on the Forest Service to construct a sawmill on the reservation to anchor the new operations. The mill would be tribally owned and operated. The Forest Service immediately set to work building a large sawmill with one hundred thousand board feet daily capacity, and by June 30, 1909, the mill had produced about 10 million board feet of lumber from the salvaged timber.[21]

The Menominee operations were the Forest Service's most important undertaking on Indian lands during the short-lived cooperative agreement between the Department of the Interior and the Department of Agriculture. But the Forest Service's activities were by no means limited to the Menominee Reservation: it took over supervision of timber sales on seven other reservations (three in Wisconsin, three in Minnesota, and one in Montana); it oversaw cutting for personal use by tribal members on the Klamath, Pine Ridge, Rosebud, and San Carlos reservations; it made forest examinations on the Coeur d'Alene, Flathead, Hupa Valley, Klamath, Lac Courte Oreille, Leech Lake, Nez Perce, Northern Cheyenne, Qualla, Red Lake, Siletz, and Spokane reservations; and it prepared planting plans for reforesting five reservations in Oklahoma.[22]

All these far-flung efforts notwithstanding, the cooperation between the Forest Service and the Indian Office did not go smoothly. The two staffs dickered over who was in charge of the work and who was paying for it. According

FIGURE 6. Menominee Indian Reservation Mills, 1911. The facility
was built by the Forest Service and owned and operated by the tribe.

to the cooperative agreement, the Forest Service was to prescribe rules and regulations for all timber sales and lumbering on Indian lands, determine which
Indian lands were best suited for forestry purposes, and prepare plans for their
protection. The Indian Office, for its part, was to pay all salaries and other
expenses connected with the work. But in practice the lines became blurred. In
some cases, work was disrupted when funds fell short; in other cases, officials
disagreed over areas of responsibility.[23]

Pinchot claimed in his autobiography that when Roosevelt left office, all
was well with the arrangement between the Department of Agriculture and the
Department of the Interior. "The agreement was in complete accord with T.R.'s
often expressed desire for the fullest co-operation between the two Departments, and was fully approved by him," Pinchot wrote.[24] When the Taft administration took over in the spring of 1909, the cooperative effort no longer had that
presidential seal of approval, and it soon fell apart. Although Pinchot kept his
position as forester after Taft became president, he soon found himself at logger-
heads with Taft's new secretary of the interior, Richard A. Ballinger. Among the

two men's several points of disagreement was the Forest Service's role in Indian forestry. On July 19, 1909, Ballinger abrogated the cooperative agreement, citing a recent ruling by the comptroller that found it illegal to detail employees from one department to another. While Ballinger based his decision on this narrow legality (a court subsequently ruled that such transfers were permissible after all), he was probably influenced by more substantive concerns about the divergent aims and responsibilities of the Indian Office and the Forest Service.[25]

Pinchot found Ballinger's decision most unfortunate and disappointing. Around this same time, he also quarreled with Ballinger over withdrawals for ranger station and water power sites. While Ballinger based his decisions on these matters on legal interpretations, too, Pinchot saw in them a nefarious intent to roll back the previous administration's conservation policy. His brewing conflict with Ballinger erupted into open warfare when Pinchot raised allegations of misconduct by the secretary of the interior in the fall of 1909. The case involved Ballinger's approval of thirty-three coal claims in Alaska that were of doubtful validity. Pinchot was alerted to the controversy by a junior official in the General Land Office, L. R. Glavis. Ballinger fired Glavis, and when Pinchot raised a furor over the firing, Taft dismissed Pinchot for insubordination.[26]

In December 1909, Congress appointed a joint Senate and House committee to investigate the Department of the Interior and the Forest Service. By then the scandal over the Alaska coal claims overshadowed all else, including the issue of how the Indian forests were being managed. Nonetheless, when the chairman of the joint committee, Senator Knute Nelson of Minnesota, wrote to Pinchot asking him what topics should be investigated, Pinchot responded with three, listing Indian forests third. He framed the issue thus: "Are the laws governing disposal of timber on Indian lands leading to their destruction by fire and unskilled management?"[27]

The joint investigating committee held hearings during the spring of 1910 and finally rendered a partisan, split decision. The Republican majority exonerated Ballinger while the Democratic minority sided with Pinchot. The testimony on Indian forests was inconclusive. Its main result was to embitter relations between the Indian Office and the Forest Service. J. P. Kinney, a forester with the Indian Office who soon rose to head its new Branch of Forestry, would later provide this assessment of the congressional testimony and actual conditions:

> There was plenty of evidence that the forests on Indian lands had never been given the consideration that their importance warranted, but the allegations of

FIGURE 7. Gifford Pinchot (1865–1946)

COURTESY OF NATIONAL PARK SERVICE

mismanagement were greatly exaggerated. On the other hand the claims that were made by the Forest Service as to the improvement effected during the eighteen months that its representatives had charge of Indian forests, from January 22, 1908 to July 17, 1909, were very extravagant and in most instances unsupported by facts.[28]

As for the effect that the Ballinger-Pinchot affair had on Indian forestry going forward, Kinney wrote:

> The net result was that I and others in the Indian Service, who tried to remain neutral in the Ballinger-Pinchot controversy, were distrusted by ardent pro-Pinchot partisans as not being sincere conservationists, and were disliked by the anti-Pinchot partisans as being luke-warm to the defense that the Ballinger forces were making against what they sincerely believed to be an unfair and unjustified attack upon the Interior Department.[29]

By an act of June 25, 1910, Congress authorized the selling of timber on Indian lands under regulations prescribed by the secretary of the interior. Congress initiated an annual appropriation of $100,000 to manage the Indians' forest resources, and the commissioner of Indian affairs established the Branch of Forestry within the Indian Service. Kinney later observed in his book, *A Continent Lost—A Civilization Won*, that the law marked a watershed in the history of Indian forestry. "At last the Congress had reached the conclusion that the forests on Indian reservations could generally be made to contribute to the support and advancement of the Indians through the sale of the products of the forest instead of through the sale of the land with the timber thereon," he wrote. This was the fork in the road where forestry on Indian lands was set up as a distinct entity separate and apart from forestry on the national forests.[30]

President Taft, it must be said, was no friend of Indian forestry. Even though his administration saw to the formation of a forestry unit within the Indian Service, he had little enthusiasm for the idea that Indian forests should be conserved for the long-term benefit of present and future generations of Indians. Such a notion tended to conflict with the federal government's goal of winding down the Office of Indian Affairs and liquidating everything tribal. Rather, he simply recognized the fact that Indians, not the U.S. government, owned those forests. The government held the forests for Indians as trustee; therefore, the government had to maintain the forests for the beneficial interest of the Indians, not the good of the public. As a former jurist, Taft saw the justice in the Indian Office's claim that Indian forests could not be transferred to the National Forest System by executive fiat. Whatever way the government might dispose of the Indian forests, as trustee it had to be sure the Indians were fairly compensated. Consequently, Taft found Roosevelt's presidential proclamations of March 2, 1909, to be improper, for they had incorporated seven Indian forests into adjacent national forests without paying for them. On February 17, 1912, President Taft restored those same Indian lands to their respective reservations through a matching set of executive orders. The seven affected reservations were the White Mountain Apache, Mescalero Apache, Jicarilla Apache, Navajo, Zuni, Hupa Valley, and Tule River reservations in Arizona, New Mexico, and California. Ironically—for it was not what Taft intended—those forests remain in tribal hands to this day.[31]

INDIAN FORESTRY UNDER SIEGE

On September 29, 1919, Republican Representative Homer P. Snyder of New York, chairman of the House Committee on Indian Affairs, gaveled his committee to order in a hearing room in the Capitol building. His committee was charged with investigating the conduct of the BIA. It was the first congressional investigation of the Indian Office since the Ballinger-Pinchot affair. As in the prior investigation, the members of Congress were interested to know what the Forest Service could do for Indian forests. At this hearing, the sixth of the investigation, the committee's lead witness was Chief of the Forest Service Henry S. Graves.[32]

Representative Snyder began his line of questioning by asking Graves about the Forest Service's record of work on the Indian forests in the period from 1908 to 1909. Then he came to the point: was the Forest Service capable of taking over management of the Indian forests from the BIA? Graves indicated that he thought the prior attempt at cooperation had been problematic, and he was not in favor of trying it again. When Snyder pressed him, though, Graves conceded "it could be done." The main issue, he explained, was whether Congress intended to dispose of those forests or not. If they were classified as permanent reservations, "the problem would be very much simpler, because then the administration of the forestlands for the Indian Bureau would be substantially the same problem that we have."[33]

Another member of the committee, Representative Carl Hayden of Arizona, a Democrat, quizzed the chief about a timber sale that the Forest Service had recently administered that combined timber on the Sitgreaves National Forest with timber on the adjacent Fort Apache Reservation. Then Hayden brought up the Indian forests that had once belonged to the Five Civilized Tribes in Oklahoma. The forests had been allotted and mostly cut down, a situation Graves found regrettable. Finally, the Arizona congressman summarized what he thought Graves was driving at through his responses:

> The distinction between your bureau and the Indian Bureau is briefly this: The Forest Service looks forward to the retention under Government supervision of forest lands for practically all time to come, having in mind a plan to increase the stock of timber, to promote its growth, so as to have something for future generations to use for public benefit. The Indian Bureau is supposed to be a bureau that is gradually going out of business trying to individualize the Indian, divide up the tribal property and get rid of communal ownership of the forests. So that the two policies are totally different and look in opposite directions. That, as I gather from your statement, is the distinction between the two bureaus.[34]

Other members of the committee followed Hayden with similar lines of questioning. Their overall point was clear. BIA forestry presented a conundrum. Inasmuch as the forestry program sought to manage Indian forests as permanent tribal resources, it cut against the grain of both allotment policy and the BIA's professed goal to put itself out of business. In the House committee's final report of its investigation of the BIA, it recommended that BIA forestry be transferred to the Forest Service.[35]

In January 1921, Representative Snyder introduced four bills in Congress, each involving a reorganization of the BIA. The first bill provided in part that "Hereafter all Indian timberlands shall be administered by the Forest Service of the Department of Agriculture." Each subsequent bill contained a variant of that provision. A Progressive Republican, Snyder's main objective seems to have been to shrink the BIA and goose the government's effort to "emancipate" Indians from their status as wards. The forests themselves were not his primary concern. Indeed, the bills were odd in that they directed the secretary of the interior to keep on selling the Indians' "surplus" lands, including forested lands, even as the forests were put under Forest Service management. All four bills died in committee.[36]

Meanwhile, another Republican congressman from New York, Bertrand Snell, a former lumberman and paper manufacturer, introduced two more bills concerning Indian forests. In contrast to Snyder's legislation, Snell's bills aimed directly at transferring Indian forests to the national forests. Snell's first bill simply authorized the transfer. His second bill provided for a general survey of all federally owned or controlled forestlands, including Indian forests. All lands classified as chiefly valuable for timber production or watershed protection would be withheld from all forms of entry, appropriation, or allotment (in the case of Indian lands). Further, it authorized the president to incorporate all such lands in the national forests, taking into account existing "rights, equities, or title of any Indian tribes." Snell had no more success with his legislation than Snyder did. However, some of the material that Snell obtained from the Forest Service for his legislation was published in the *Journal of Forestry*. Associate Forester Edward A. Sherman presented the material in the form of a paper to the Society of American Foresters. The society then saw to its publication as an article in its *Journal of Forestry*.[37]

In the article, titled "A Plan for the Disposal of Indian Reservation Timberlands," Sherman made two main points. First, he noted that unallotted timber lands on Indian reservations were already surveyed, classified, and inventoried—at least in a preliminary way. His plan listed the estimated acreage and quantity of timber by reservation, with the total acreage amounting to 5,287,849 acres. Of these lands, the Forest Service recommended 4,533,838 acres for possible additions to national forests. The acreages were only tentative, pending "careful field work" by the Department of Agriculture, but they gave a general picture of the area involved.[38]

Sherman's second point was that the Forest Service stood ready to receive the entire staff of BIA forestry into its organization. According to the second Snell bill, the BIA forestry staff would be transferred as a unit to the Forest Service in the Department of Agriculture, where it would form a new Indian Forest Division within the larger agency. "The amalgamation of the two organizations in a single Bureau," Sherman wrote, "would bring to bear upon the line of work the combined experience, vision, and initiative of both organizations." The Forest Service would bring advantages of size and depth, while the BIA foresters would bring a sensitivity to Indian interests.[39]

The BIA's head forester, J. P. Kinney, answered Sherman in a letter printed in the October 1921 issue of *Journal of Forestry*, followed by an article in the December 1921 issue. He argued that the BIA Branch of Forestry should be left in the BIA where it could remain fully engaged with other aspects of the federal-Indian trust relationship.[40]

Throughout the 1920s, BIA forestry had to fend off other proposals for placing tribal forests under Forest Service administration. In 1923, Secretary of Agriculture Henry C. Wallace advocated that all unallotted Indian timberlands be incorporated into the National Forest System "subject to suitable liquidation of the Indian equities."[41] In 1926, Chief of the Forest Service William B. Greeley wrote to Commissioner of Indian Affairs Charles H. Burke suggesting that the BIA give its support to a plan for the purchase of all those tribal lands. Burke replied that "the time has not yet arrived." At the end of the decade, Assistant Forester E. E. Carter of the Forest Service and Kinney of the BIA prepared a lengthy joint memorandum on the subject. They estimated the cost of purchasing all unallotted Indian timberlands at over $100,000,000, excluding the value of the timber. The price tag seemed prohibitive and reason enough to set aside further discussion of merging the two forestry organizations. Until such time as the forestlands actually changed hands, Carter and Kinney agreed, it was best to keep the forestry organizations separate.[42]

CHAPTER SUMMARY

In the early twentieth century, the conservation estate grew while the Indian estate shrank. Most of the national forests were created from lands in the public domain where tribes had ceded title to the U.S. government a few decades earlier. In the case of the Minnesota National Forest and in other rare instances, the Indian estate was transferred directly over to the conservation estate.[43] Government leaders and the American people accepted Indian land loss as an inevitable by-product of Indian people's assimilation into the dominant society.

As Indian reservations were allotted to tribal members and surplus lands were opened to non-Indian settlement, questions arose over how the U.S. government should administer Indian forests that it held in trust for tribes and individual allottees. One impulse was to place Indian forests under Forest Service management until such time as the lands could be absorbed into the conservation estate. However, differences between the Forest Service and the Department of the Interior prevented that from occurring. Instead, the Indian forests remained in trust under BIA administration. The BIA formed its own Branch of Forestry. Whereas the Forest Service managed public forests for the public good, BIA forestry managed Indian forests in trust for the benefit of the Indian owners.

Despite that clear distinction in purpose, BIA forestry had the paradoxical mission of managing tribal forests according to principles of conservation when the federal government was otherwise intent on liquidating tribal assets and breaking down individual Indians' tribal identification. Cognizant of that paradox, Congress remained interested in transferring tribal forests to the National Forest System. It demurred in part because of the cost involved, for tribes would have to be compensated for the value of their trust assets by the U.S. Treasury.

As long as tribes continued to see their lands taken away, they could not view the Forest Service as their friend. Tribes could only consider partnering with the Forest Service after their land base was secure.

3

THE INDIAN NEW DEAL AND
THE FOREST SERVICE

TRIBAL FORESTS CONFIRMED

A S LONG AS assimilation formed the basis of federal Indian policy, all tribal forests hung like so much ripe fruit waiting to drop into the Forest Service's basket. BIA forestry was at best an uncertain enterprise because the future ownership of the Indian forest remained so much in doubt. Kinney himself considered it likely that "surplus" Indian timberland would eventually be transferred to the national forests. It was paradoxical to invest in those forests for the future of the tribe when the government's aim was to bring an end to tribes as separate political and economic entities. As for allotted timberland, Kinney wrote, the BIA could not require an individual Indian to practice forestry on his or her allotment. BIA foresters did attempt to combine allotments into larger units and manage them on a twenty-five- or fifty-year cutting cycle, but almost invariably they ran into problems when individual allottees called for a quick sale of their timber. "To anyone having the slightest acquaintance with the character and mental make-up of the Indian," Kinney stated, "it should be at once apparent that co-operative management of allotments as forest lands is impracticable. Many of these allotments are held by old men and women who have never adapted themselves to the habits of the white. Hundreds of them live face to face with destitution. The only means that the Indian Service has through which to keep these unfortunate people from starvation is to derive as large a revenue as possible from their timber."[1] Forest conservation formed an ill fit with the government's program to remake Indians into yeoman farmers. Even in those cases where the 40- or 160-acre allotment was best suited for growing timber, good forestry practice aimed at producing a long-term economic benefit, not a year-to-year income.[2]

The 1932 election of Franklin D. Roosevelt for president led to a dramatic reversal in federal Indian policy that in turn put management of the Indian forests on a sounder footing. Roosevelt chose Harold Ickes, a sharp critic of Indian administration, to be his secretary of the interior. Ickes selected John Collier for commissioner of Indian affairs. The choice of Collier to head the BIA signaled a major change of direction. A social reformer who had championed the cause of Pueblo Indians in the early 1920s, Collier had emerged by the end of the decade as the most vociferous and forceful critic of the government's policy of assimilation. Far from desiring to see Indian peoples assimilated in the conventional sense of being Americanized and detribalized, Collier wanted to bring Indians into the life of the nation with their traditional cultures and tribal structures intact. Indeed, in his view Indian tribalism held many advantages over the hyperindividualistic and materialistic tendencies of the dominant society in the modern age.[3]

Collier appointed Robert Marshall, a conservationist and socialist with a PhD in forestry, to head BIA forestry. Collier and Marshall shared similar ideas about Indian land tenure. Both men saw the allotment policy as having been an unmitigated disaster. Both thought the most important step toward improving the lives of Indian peoples was to repeal the General Allotment Act and restore as much of the Indians' land base as possible. Both were enthusiastic about the potentialities of tribal land ownership in the modern context. In his book *The People's Forests* (1933), Marshall expounded on the many advantages of public over private ownership of forestlands. For Marshall, tribal ownership was attractive because of its similarities to public ownership. Collier, for his part, drew inspiration for his program of Indian reform from the deep connections between culture, community, and place that he had discovered at Taos Pueblo.[4]

In an article titled "The Indians and Their Lands" (which Collier and Marshall coauthored that same year with Collier's adviser on soil conservation, Ward Shepard), the authors suggested that tribal land ownership should be understood as being analogous to public ownership on a community level. Just as management of lands in public ownership could be directed toward the welfare of the whole society, so too the management of tribally owned resources could be directed toward the good of the tribal community.[5]

The authors went on to explain that Indian forestry must be understood as part of the larger problem of Indian peoples' land tenure. The allotment policy had attached like a cancer to the Indians' lands. As a result of "the allotment system and its attendant evils," Indians had lost some 63 million acres, or almost two-thirds of all the area remaining in their possession in 1887. Some lands had been lost through disposal of so-called surplus lands by public auction, some through tax delinquency and forfeiture, and some through direct sale by allottees to non-Indians. In addition, many allotted lands still held in trust by the government were falling into a messy divided ownership known as "heirship status." When an allottee died, it was necessary to divide the land title among the heirs. Already some allotments had been handed down two generations, creating complicated fractional interests. For lands in "heirship status," proceeds from timber sales or grazing leases might have to be divided into so many shares that the allotments almost became useless. Certainly they were harder to manage. The first aim of Indian forestry, then, was to address the land tenure problem by stopping further diminishment of the Indian estate, reacquiring lands that had been lost, restoring allotted lands to tribal ownership through purchase, and consolidating tribal lands through exchange.[6]

The next aim of Indian forestry was to reorganize the forest industry so that Indians were employed in logging and milling operations. The BIA would foster tribal enterprises. Reservation timber would be sold to the tribal enterprise so that the forest would generate revenue for the tribe not just as standing timber but as finished lumber. And tribal members would derive income not just from per capita shares in the stumpage value but also from wages. "All of the capital," the authors wrote, "including both the forest and the machinery necessary to develop it, will be communally owned by the entire Indian nation." With smaller capital outlays, the change to tribally owned forest enterprises would entail new methods of cutting and milling. Reservation logging would be done by tractor and truck instead of by railroad. Light selective cutting would replace clear cutting. Most milling would be done by portable and semi-portable sawmills. Collier and his assistants pictured a gratifying end result. "Through these tribal forest industries it should actually be possible to give all able-bodied men on the timbered reservation a permanent chance for work," they wrote. "Thus the Indian will develop a stable life, with a steady income which will give them the material necessities for happiness, instead of the old, sporadic income with its accompanying splurge."[7]

FIGURE 8. Bob Marshall (1901–1939). Chief of forestry in
the Bureau of Indian Affairs from 1933 to 1937 and head
of recreation management in the Forest Service from 1938
to 1939, he cofounded The Wilderness Society in 1935.

COURTESY OF FOREST HISTORY SOCIETY

As chief forester in the BIA from 1933 to 1937, Marshall had much opportunity to ponder Indian peoples' relationship to the environment past and present. It was ironic, in view of aboriginal Indians' record of living "in balance with
nature," that contemporary tribes confronted severe environmental problems
on their reservations. This sad state of affairs, Marshall explained in an article
titled "Ecology and the Indians," had come about as a consequence of their having been pushed westward, forced to cede the most fertile lands to non-Indians,

and ultimately confined to small reservations. Indeed, most Indian reservations occupied arid, semi-arid, or mountainous places. The roughly third of a million Indians living in the United States in the 1930s did not have enough land left to them to be self-supporting. No wonder, then, that Indian reservations had become substantially overgrazed, while logging operations had often taken more timber than a plan of sustained-yield forestry would permit.[8]

In 1934, Congress passed the Indian Reorganization Act (IRA), the centerpiece of a new Indian policy that the Franklin D. Roosevelt administration proclaimed to be the Indian New Deal. The law aimed primarily at stopping further Indian land loss and even turning the tide so that tribes could reacquire a bit of what they had lost. Furthermore, the law called for the conservation of Indians' natural resources, including forest, range, and soil. It specifically mandated that Indian forests would be managed according to principles of sustained yield and that Indian range would be managed according to each range unit's carrying capacity for livestock. It was the first time those key concepts of conservation appeared in a U.S. statute.[9]

Most importantly, the IRA repealed the General Allotment Act. The Indian New Deal could not undo more than fifty years of land loss, but it did put a halt to further allotment, lowered the boom on fee patenting for thousands of allotments that were still held in trust, and provided opportunities for tribes to reacquire a small part of what had been sold off.[10]

Besides revamping the government's approach to Indian land tenure, the law encouraged tribal enterprise and tribal sovereignty. Its opening title promised "to grant certain rights of home rule to Indians." Reservation by reservation, it gave tribes the opportunity to form a government under its own constitution and bylaws. Each tribal government would go into effect following approval of the constitution and charter by the secretary of the interior and ratification by a majority of adult members of the tribe.[11]

Collier has been criticized for implementing his own form of federal paternalism. Although the IRA aimed at tribal revitalization, its provisions for tribal self-determination were restrictive and imposed from outside. Historian George Pierre Castile writes, "Governments were created, but the IRA constitutions were based on models drawn up by BIA lawyers, not locally cobbled together from scratch. All of the tribal governments were more alike than not, and the new governments were scarcely 'Indian' if by that one means some form of traditional precontact organization."[12]

It must be remembered that at the time the IRA was enacted, tribal culture and leadership had been suppressed by the U.S. government for some forty years on most Indian reservations. Collier aimed to reverse course and restore the very same attributes of tribalism that the federal government had previously sought to extinguish. Still, the new IRA governments were allowed relatively little scope to exercise self-governance. "They did not have power over federal funds spent on the reservations, nor over the BIA staff, who continued to run things day to day," Castile writes. "Despite Collier's good intentions, in the end the new IRA tribal governments were still 'feeble organizations' that 'existed by administrative sufferance.'" As in the allotment era, the BIA superintendent on each reservation wielded enormous power. What Collier had created, Castile observes, "were the forms of self-government without the actual authority of government. During Collier's era, tribally elected councils did little actual governing. Most of them were little more than advisory bodies, allowed only to ratify decisions made, as before, by the bureau."[13]

In 1937, John Collier signed and Secretary Ickes approved an order designating 4.8 million acres of Indian lands as "roadless" or "wild" areas. As recommended by Bob Marshall, these areas were to be preserved from all road development and mechanized entry. While many of these designated areas featured desert rather than forestlands, approximately 1 million acres overlapped what the BIA classified as Indian timberlands on seven reservations. These were Makah, Grand Portage, Yakama, Warm Springs, Flathead, Colville, and Wind River. In a number of cases, such as the Warm Springs and Colville reservations in Oregon and Washington, the Interior order took in one fourth or more of the reservation's unallotted timberlands. The remainder of the 4.8 million acres covered desert or canyon lands on the Navajo, Fort Apache, San Carlos, Hualapai, and Consolidated Ute reservations. Following the pattern of Teddy Roosevelt's presidential proclamations in 1909, the federal authorities in Interior acted on their own judgment without consulting the tribes even though tribal assets were at stake.[14]

Marshall was a leading advocate for the preservation of wilderness, and the order looks suspiciously like a land grab for the federal wilderness system he so much desired. Yet Marshall did assert that he had the Indians' interests at heart when he recommended that the areas remain undeveloped. He believed that the Indian forests possessed cultural as well as economic value. To conserve portions of the Indians' forested heritage in a primitive condition was to promote the cultural revitalization of these Indian groups. If tribes possessed their

FIGURE 9. Flathead Indians and Mission Mountains. The area became
part of the 125,000-acre Mission Range Roadless Area in 1937.

COURTESY OF NATIONAL PARK SERVICE

own wilderness areas, the tribal members would always have a place to "escape
from constant contact with white men." This was vital to their cultural autonomy, since "almost everywhere they go the Indians encounter the competition
and disturbances of the white race."[15]

The Indian roadless and wild areas eventually got disestablished. Amid
the debate over national wilderness legislation that began in the mid-1950s,
tribes became leery that those areas might be included in a national wilderness system. At tribes' request, all but one area (Wind River) was disestablished
between 1956 and 1960. Tribes saw the disposition of those lands as a sovereign
issue, and wilderness advocates finally had to concede they were right. Collier
himself admitted that he had made a mistake not to consult the tribes in the
first place.[16] The vital issue of tribal sovereignty aside, Marshall's pronouncement that Indians should have a wilderness refuge for their exclusive use, without the presence of non-Indians, would find an echo forty years later in the
push for protection of Indian sacred sites.

THE FOREST SERVICE, INDIANS, AND THE CIVILIAN CONSERVATION CORPS

During the presidential campaign in 1932, Roosevelt proposed an economic relief program for putting unemployed young men to work on conservation projects. Shortly after taking office, Roosevelt sent a proposal to Congress that led to passage of the Emergency Conservation Work Act on March 31, 1933. The law provided for the enrollment of three hundred thousand men in camps under a temporary organization to be called the Civilian Conservation Corps (CCC). The Labor Department was given responsibility for enrollment, the War Department was to construct and administer the camps, and the Agriculture and Interior departments were to develop work projects primarily on the national forests and in the national parks, respectively. The Department of Agriculture came to administer roughly three quarters of all CCC projects, and of that number the Forest Service was responsible for the majority. Nearly half of all CCC camps were located on national forests. The rapid mobilization of so many untrained young men severely tested the Forest Service, but over time the CCC proved its worth in fire suppression, road and trail construction, blister rust control, and myriad other kinds of manual work.[17]

Kinney and other BIA officials immediately pointed out how the emergency relief program would benefit Indian Country. Besides offering much needed employment to Indians, it would provide reservations with badly needed forest protection, soil erosion control, and range improvements.[18] From the outset they argued for a separate, parallel division of the CCC that would hire Indian men of all ages and deploy exclusively on Indian lands. Their rationale was that without that separation, Indians would suffer discrimination in the camps. And with fewer enrollments, Indian Country would miss out on getting its fair share of conservation work done. Secretary Ickes forwarded this recommendation to the newly appointed head of the CCC, Robert Fechner. Within a month of the congressional authorization, Roosevelt approved a plan to establish an Indian division, the CCC-ID, along the lines that Ickes suggested.[19]

One place where Indians had no separate CCC but instead worked directly under Forest Service supervision was in Alaska. Because of the territory's remoteness and small population, the Forest Service was put in charge of the whole CCC program there, including camp construction, recruitment, and project administration. While the CCC in Alaska initially centered on the immense Tongass National Forest, it eventually came to involve the Forest Service in projects located far outside the National Forest System—from Eskimo villages in the far north, where Forest Service officials oversaw construction of community buildings and aircraft landing strips, to Nunivak Island in the Bering Sea, where CCC enrollees built a musk ox corral.[20] More importantly, the CCC program in Alaska provided the Forest Service with its first opportunity in nearly thirty years to work hand in hand with Native peoples.

At the outset of the Alaskan CCC experience, the BIA's concerns about racial discrimination were borne out. Forest Service officials resisted hiring Alaska Natives in the belief that "mixed camps" of Natives and whites would be "wholly impracticable." At that time, Alaska Natives constituted about half of the territory's total population of around sixty thousand people, but the two races mostly lived apart. Whites inhabited the mining towns and sea ports; Alaska Natives lived in widely scattered villages. Even in southeast Alaska, where many Tlingit and Haida Indians worked in the salmon industry, the population was largely segregated. When the CCC was launched in the summer of 1933, the Forest Service recruited in the white communities only, and when Natives applied, they were told the rolls were filled. In the mostly white town of Sitka, two young Tlingit applicants were rejected on the grounds that Natives and whites could mix on a work site but they could not share living quarters. "Eating from the same dishes would be unworkable," one Forest Service official stated. The district ranger in Craig, when later pressed by his superior to describe whether the enrollment process had been discriminatory, replied, "We did continue to enroll applicants of the breed class, who had adopted the white man's mode of living and could be placed in the regular CCC camp."[21]

In November 1933, a Tlingit-Haida organization called the Alaska Native Brotherhood (ANB) passed two resolutions charging the Forest Service with discrimination against Indians. ANB leaders raised the matter with the Forest Service, the BIA, the governor of Alaska, the secretaries of Agriculture and Interior, and members of Congress. The next month, Regional Forester Charles H. Flory replied to Judson Brown, grand secretary of the ANB, that the federal government would provide relief to Alaska Natives through other emergency relief programs. Over the next three years, that did in fact become the arrangement: CCC camps were reserved for employment of young men of the white race, while smaller amounts of federal relief trickled out to the Native villages to afford employment opportunities there, too, but usually on a short-term, day-labor basis. Most of the federal relief to Native villages came from other programs by way of the BIA, though some of it came out of CCC funds through the Forest Service. The ANB remained unsatisfied and continued to press the issue of racial discrimination by the Forest Service. Finally, in 1937, it got what it was after. The cap on CCC enrollment in Alaska was raised from 325 to 600 man-years, with 50 percent reserved for Alaska Natives. Chief Forester William A. Silcox allocated $1 million to the expanded program in its first year. This sum included a contribution of $150,000 by the BIA for new camp construction. Alaska newspapers presented the expanded program as a Forest Service initiative. But behind the facade of federal largesse, the ANB had achieved a hard-won victory to force the government's hand.[22]

It is important to note that the influential ANB was a fraternal organization, not a tribal government. As such, it was practically unique. Founded in 1912 by a group of highly acculturated Tlingit men, it reflected the effect of the Presbyterian Board of Home Missions on Alaska Native affairs in the late nineteenth century. ANB membership was open to all Alaska Natives who professed the Christian faith; it cost each member ten dollars to join and six dollars per year thereafter. In its early years, the ANB fought for the advancement of Alaska Natives on the basis of political equality and separate but equal public education. Besides lobbying for Native political interests, the ANB offered sick benefits and assistance for funeral expenses. By the 1930s, it had a wide membership among the Tlingit and Haida tribes, with chapters or "local camps" located in most towns and villages throughout southeast Alaska. When the American Federation of Labor (AFL) and the Congress of Industrial Organizations (CIO) came to southeast Alaska in the mid-1930s, the ANB found that labor organizers were chiefly concerned with protecting the interests of white resident and nonresident fishermen. So in 1937 the ANB began its own collective bargaining work on behalf of its member fishermen and cannery workers. Each local camp of the ANB became a plant unit for negotiating fish prices, cannery wages, and closed-shop hiring practices with local cannery operators. For several years the ANB acted in the capacity of bargaining agent for Native workers. Then, at its grand camp meeting in 1947, it voted to shed that function and allow its members to join the CIO-affiliated Alaska Fisherman's Union.[23]

The ANB approached the issue of discrimination in the CCC in the same way that it approached collective bargaining in the 1930s: it wanted separate but equal treatment, not integration of Natives and whites in the same camps. Separation was not simply to shield enrollees from race prejudice; the CCC's six-month enrollment period was an awkward fit with the seasonal rhythm of traditional Native life. Forest officials agreed. In 1936 (when the Forest Service was still trying to defend its discriminatory enrollment policy) District Ranger W. A. Chipperfield explained the difficulty with Native enrollees this way:

> The rules and regulations of the CCC [do] not appeal to the natives. In the summer they are all following the fishing industry; the fall is their hunting season; in the spring they go after the hair and fur seal and in the winter they cut fuel wood and trap. All of these are their native customs and it is hard for them to change. It follows that they would not care to enroll for a period of six months in the CCC. They might feel they should be given relief for a shorter period, but when the work interfered with their long established customs, they would stick to the customs and not to the enrollment.[24]

Under the new program that began in 1937, the Forest Service basically formed its own miniature CCC-ID in Alaska. Much in the same way that the BIA ran the CCC-ID, the Forest Service modified the CCC structure as it approached working with Alaska Natives. When it came to enrollment, it waived the age limitation, accepted married as well as unmarried men, and dropped the six-month requirement. When the Forest Service considered how best to use Native labor, it looked for projects where camps could be situated right in the Native community, allowing enrollees to continue to live with their families.[25]

One very successful CCC project to emerge from these circumstances involved the preservation of totem poles. As many as five hundred totem poles stood in numerous locations throughout southeast Alaska. Many were found clustered in old village sites that the Tlingit and Haida had abandoned during the last decades of the nineteenth century. Impressively tall, handsomely carved and painted, they were found in various stages of disrepair, some toppled over and vandalized, and all slowly decaying under the influence of the region's extraordinarily wet climate. As few Indian carvers still practiced their craft in the 1930s, the totem poles appeared to be vestiges of an indigenous art form on the brink of extinction.[26]

Forest Service officials had long debated what to do with the relics. In 1916, President Woodrow Wilson signed a proclamation creating Old Kasaan National Monument around a large grouping of totem poles located at a former village site near Ketchikan. The Forest Service had nominal responsibility for the national monument, but there was no money for protecting it. In 1921, Regional Forester Flory recommended that those totem poles be moved to Sitka National Monument, the site of a battle between Tlingits and Russians, and consolidated with the totem pole collection there. Nothing came of the plan until 1934, when the Forest Service joined the National Park Service (NPS) in developing a similar proposal—with the added condition that Native carvers would be employed in restoring them. As the idea was to transfer the salvageable totem poles and then abandon the Old Kasaan site, the Forest Service conveyed all photographs and papers relating to Old Kasaan to the NPS. However, no further action was taken on this plan, either, until the new infusion of money into the CCC program in 1937 presented an opportunity.[27]

Over the next three years, the CCC worked on totem pole restoration at several locations, including Old Kasaan and Sitka. One of the first projects involved preserving the totem poles at Sitka. The crew consisted of John Maurstad, foreman, George Benson, chief carver, and nine Indian workmen. As each totem pole was restored, it was treated with a chemical preservative, Permatox D, similar to spar varnish. Totem poles brought from Old Kasaan were used in building a community house.[28]

The Forest Service replicated this success at numerous other sites around southeast Alaska. At each location, a master carver emerged from among the older men in the local Native population, and other, mostly younger, men went to work under his tutelage. The Native carvers used handmade tools modeled on traditional ones and produced paints according to traditional methods. The work was conducted year-round in sheds erected for the purpose. Old poles were carried into the sheds and placed on skids. If they were not too badly deteriorated, the carvers worked on restoring the originals. If they were beyond salvage, then careful measurements were taken, a new cedar log was laid beside the original, and the old pole was copied.[29]

Totem pole restoration fostered a cultural revival in the Native villages. It revitalized the art of carving and brought out clan stories as told in the totem poles. Chief Forester B. Frank Heintzleman used CCC funds to employ an ethnographer, Dr. Viola Garfield, who traveled from village to village to research the stories and photograph the carvings. Her notes and pictures eventually filled twenty-seven volumes. Meanwhile, Forest Service officials approached the Native village councils about ways to display the poles once they were restored. Village after village set aside town lots for totem parks. Some totem parks featured a new community house; others were located where they would attract touring steamships. Natives in the mostly white town of Wrangell planned a traditional potlatch ceremony on the occasion of their totem park's

FIGURE 10. Totem pole being transported by Forest Service boat to undergo restoration. The CCC totem pole project fostered a revival of Native traditional carving in southeast Alaska.

COURTESY OF ALASKA HISTORICAL SOCIETY

grand opening. When the Wrangell Chamber of Commerce pitched in several thousand dollars, the Natives showed their gratitude by adopting the whole chamber of commerce into their clan. Heintzleman, together with the BIA's senior official in Alaska, Claude Hirst, attended Wrangell's big event.[30]

Forest Service historian Lawrence Rakestraw called the totem pole project a "marvelous achievement," especially considering that it happened years before the agency had developed any semblance of a formal cultural resources management program. Forest Service officials who managed the project relied on their own intuition and judgment rather than professional training in archeology, anthropology, or history. "The quality of work varied, as would be expected in a project of this type," Rakestraw stated. "Some was outstanding; in general it was good. Both as a relief project and as an artistic project, the CCC totem pole work was a great success."[31]

John Autrey, an archeologist and tribal relations specialist on the Tongass National Forest since 1978, pointed out that the totem pole project deserves notice as a signal achievement in Forest Service–tribal relations. The Forest Service demonstrated that it could work constructively with Native communities. Forest officials recognized that the totem poles were the cultural property of Native villages in some instances and the individual property of chiefs in others. Every totem pole was covered by a legal document before its removal and restoration. The protocol went hand in glove with efforts to develop ethnographic information about each pole and to bring forth a decision on how it would be exhibited. The totem pole project, Autrey suggested, was tantamount to an early experiment in tribal consultation.[32]

THE FOREST SERVICE AND INDIAN RANGE

The Indian New Deal mostly quieted talk of transferring tribal lands to the National Forest System. But it did not completely silence the issue. In 1936, the Forest Service produced a detailed study of the western range in which it suggested that Indian rangelands be brought under Forest Service management. In a throwback to the bygone allotment era, the report stated,

> Any sound program for the administration of Indian range lands must comprehend the ultimate integration of the Indian into the social and economic life of the Nation. When this has been accomplished there will be no further need for special guardianship of Indian rights nor for special care of Indian property as a separate ownership class. Meanwhile the administration of an Indian-owned natural resource should aim first toward the maximum sustained contribution to the progress of the Indian people, and, secondly, the conservation of a resource which is of magnitude to be of national importance.[33]

Although the Forest Service stopped short of calling for outright transfer, it remained alert to the prospect of acquiring more Indian lands and kept that notion alive.

The Forest Service's examination of Indian rangelands in the mid-1930s must be put in context. It came toward the end of the Dust Bowl years, when the lands at issue were in a deplorable condition: drought stricken, badly eroded, and overgrazed. In 1934, Congress passed the Taylor Grazing Act, which ended open-range grazing on the public domain and created the U.S. Grazing Service, the future Bureau of Land Management. The new agency was to administer livestock use of grazing districts under a new grazing permit system. Although the Forest Service favored the measure in principle, it opposed the legislation on the grounds that it was too lax and would create a weak federal agency under the control of livestock interests. After the Taylor Grazing Act was enacted, the U.S. Senate passed a resolution calling on Secretary of Agriculture Henry A. Wallace to provide a report that would fully explain the Forest Service's concerns. Wallace gave the Forest Service wide scope in preparing its response. Associate Chief Forester Earle H. Clapp headed a team of thirty-five experts who examined range management and the condition of the natural resource across all types of land ownership, including Indian lands. The result, a 620-page tome entitled *The Western Range*, made the case for all federal grazing administration to be consolidated under the Department of Agriculture. Forest Service historian Harold K. Steen found that *The Western Range* was "unusually blunt for an official document." It predicted that the Taylor Grazing Act would fail in its intended purpose, and it advocated "in no uncertain terms" that the Forest Service take responsibility over all federal ranges.[34]

The authors of *The Western Range* were a little more circumspect when they approached the subject of Indian range. First, they put Indian range management in historical perspective. Federal oversight of the resource had commenced only after the creation of the BIA Branch of Forestry in 1910. Shortly thereafter, range management had been turned over to the reservation superintendents. For the better part of two decades, the BIA had emphasized collection of grazing fees rather than range control. BIA foresters had only taken charge of the resource again in 1930; consequently, measures to curtail overgrazing had been in effect for just a few years. By the mid-1930s, they were only beginning to make a difference. On three-quarters of Indian rangelands conditions were still in a downward trend.[35]

The authors of *The Western Range* further noted that the BIA's efforts to institute grazing controls were resisted by non-Indian livestock operators. But the sharpest opposition to grazing controls came from Indians who were themselves owners of livestock. On the Navajo Reservation, Collier's BIA was embroiled in a controversial program of livestock reduction. In spite of accompanying extension work aimed at improving the Navajos' knowledge and understanding of range management, the BIA's progress toward sustained-yield management was making slow headway.

The Forest Service's report also pointed to the difficulties of managing Indian range where ownership was broken up by allotments. The report recognized three main categories of land ownership within reservation boundaries: tribal, allotted, and ceded (or so-called surplus land surrendered under allotment acts—most of which had passed into non-Indian ownership). Allotted lands were further divided into trust allotments and alienated allotments. Although the BIA was attempting to consolidate Indian allotments into range units for purposes of managing the range resource, the presence of alienated allotments and trust allotments in heirship status tended to complicate that effort considerably.

The authors tried to be sensitive to Indian rights and privileges stemming from the Indians' tribal heritage. For example, they noted that Indians were not "prevented from grazing semi-wild and almost worthless ponies yearlong on seriously depleted spring ranges." To the contrary, BIA administrators sought to give their wards wide latitude in handling their own property so as to allow them opportunities to develop their own "habits of industry"—even when that meant turning a blind eye to bad range practices. Furthermore, BIA administrators could not deny individual Indians the right to seek immediate cash income over long-term benefits from their allotments even when it involved knowingly overstocking the range.

Summing up the conditions on Indian reservations, the authors of *The Western Range* pointed to the need for further reduction in numbers of livestock, especially in the Southwest; the preparation of range-management plans; the improvement of the range by reseeding, fencing, and soil conservation; the continued manipulation of divided land ownerships into range units; and the furtherance of extension work among Indian livestock owners.[36] These needs were distinct from range problems elsewhere.

In the end, the authors of *The Western Range* lumped Indian lands with everything else, arguing broadly that all forest and range work by the federal government ought to be consolidated in the Department of Agriculture. "The best division of functions between the two departments is on the basis of organic and inorganic resources," the report stated. "The organic or 'renewable' resources are those which have to do with growth from the soil, with plant and animal life, and the interrelationships of soil, plants, and water. These are the resources of the national forests and the grazing districts, and logically their administration should be in the Department of Agriculture." The inorganic or nonrenewable resources—mining, coal, oil, and gas—logically belonged in Interior. The authors did not specifically address whether Indian-owned natural resources ought to be bifurcated along these same lines. However, they did suggest that the Forest Service's mission to protect watersheds was closely aligned with the federal government's trust responsibility to protect reserved Indian water rights. Watershed protection was essential for maintaining stream flow for Indian irrigation projects and for protecting healthy fish populations on Indian reservations. Ultimately, protecting watersheds on Indian lands was of national interest, they said, because many reservations were located at or below the headwaters of rivers that were of vital interest to the West.[37]

The Forest Service's work on *The Western Range* demonstrated that many people within the agency still conceived of Indian lands according to the old paradigm of Indian assimilation. They assumed that tribes would eventually fade away as distinct political entities, leaving the tribes' land holdings up for grabs.

CHAPTER SUMMARY

The Indian New Deal secured the tribal forests in trust and confirmed that they would not be transferred to the National Forest System. Tribes recovered a measure of self-determination, but tribal forests were still largely managed by the BIA.

The Forest Service had a singular opportunity to work with Indians when it was given responsibility to administer the entire CCC in Alaska. The totem pole project was a success story, demonstrating that the Forest Service could partner with tribal communities in support of their cultural revitalization.

At the same time, in authoring *The Western Range*, the Forest Service revealed that it still harbored thoughts of taking over management of Indian lands after their transfer to the conservation estate.

4

INDIAN USE OF THE
NATIONAL FORESTS TO 1950

SYMBOLS OF OPPRESSION

I N 1931, THE OGLALA SIOUX spiritual leader Black Elk remarked that his people lived like "prisoners of war" on their Pine Ridge Reservation in western South Dakota, cut off from their former hunting grounds.[1] "Once we were happy in our own country and we were seldom hungry, for then the two-leggeds and the four-leggeds lived together like relatives, and there was plenty for them and for us," Black Elk stated. "But the Wasichus came, and they have made little islands for us and other little islands for the four-leggeds, and always these islands are becoming smaller."[2] Black Elk expressed sentiments that were widely shared among Indians in the early decades of the twentieth century. From their perspective, national forests and national parks were not places for them to use and enjoy, but rather they formed part of a political landscape of oppression.

There were myriad reasons why Indians did not feel welcome to use the national forests during the early decades of the twentieth century. Perhaps the most elemental reason was that Forest Service rangers in uniform reminded many Indians of their people's bitter experiences with the U.S. military. Their aversion to the official uniform constituted in many cases a cultural memory that had been passed down generation to generation.

Pauline Esteves, a Timbisha Shoshone who was born in Death Valley, California, in 1924, still remembered the day the National Park Service arrived after her homeland was made into a national monument in 1933. She was then nine years old. "My people thought that the army had pulled in, because they were all in uniform," she recounted many years later. "We were told to be wary of them, not to speak back to them or anything like that."[3] Even as Esteves and the other children became somewhat emboldened by curiosity and began talking to the park rangers, the adults remained suspicious. The rangers probably had no idea of the effect their Park Service uniforms had on the Indians. Yet the effect was intimidating and unsettling, and with good reason, for the uniform of the Park Service ranger in those days was modeled on the uniform of the nineteenth-century U.S. cavalryman.

The Forest Service ranger uniform in that period was only quasi-military in style; nevertheless, it used the army's olive drab color scheme and often included cavalry-style riding breeches.[4] And Indians' memories of the U.S. cavalry uniform were not always a generation or two removed. Black Elk, for one, had firsthand memories of fighting the U.S. cavalry. He had participated in the Battle of the Little Big Horn when he was nine years old and had suffered wounds in the Wounded Knee massacre when he was a young man. How might he have responded, then, to the sight of forest rangers in uniform patrolling the Black Hills National Forest in 1931?

Another reason why Indians saw the national forests and national parks as symbols of oppression was that they found themselves restricted from hunting on those lands. Early wildlife conservation efforts focused on protecting game in the national parks and national forests as well as a handful of national wildlife refuges. In national parks, all hunting was prohibited by federal law. On the national forests, hunting was regulated by state law, and forest rangers helped state wardens to enforce the state game laws. When Indians went on the national forests to hunt, they generally did so without obtaining state hunting licenses. Western states contested Indians' rights to hunt off reservation on all types of public lands: national parks, national forests, federally owned public domain lands, and state lands. Legal outcomes varied depending on the land ownership as well as each Indian's tribal affiliation and treaty rights. Western states' efforts to suppress Indian off-reservation hunting were undergirded by the U.S. Supreme Court's decision in *Ward v. Race Horse* (1896). In that landmark decision, the high court found that the federal act granting statehood to

Wyoming terminated the treaty right of the Bannock Indians of the Fort Hall Reservation in Idaho to hunt off reservation in Wyoming.[5]

When Indians went on the national forests they faced other forms of oppression, too. Their traditional practice of setting low-intensity fires to manipulate ground cover and wildlife habitat was anathema to forest rangers, for whom fire prevention and total fire suppression were the primary tasks of forest protection. Consequently, forest rangers often looked with suspicion on Indian use of the national forests. If Indians traveled to the national forests by horse, they were apt to get crosswise with stockmen who held grazing leases. The stockmen did not want the Indian ponies competing with their own livestock for graze.

Finally, it must be pointed out that most Indians in the first half of the twentieth century were still too marginalized or discriminated against by the dominant society to partake in many of the national forests' recognized public uses. Most Indians had no interest in obtaining grazing leases on the national forests, no means to avail themselves of summer home lots, no desire to share campground and picnicking facilities with non-Indians, and usually no vehicle

FIGURE 11. Campers on the Cleveland National Forest, California, 1923. Burgeoning recreational use of national forests came in conflict with Indians' traditional hunting and gathering practices.

COURTESY OF FOREST HISTORY SOCIETY

for driving on national forest roads. While the Forest Service dedicated itself to managing the national forests for the public good, it nevertheless operated within a political system and capitalist economy that relegated Indian tribes to the very margins of the public good.

THE YAKAMA AND THE HANDSHAKE AGREEMENT OF 1932

While we may assume that a good deal of Indian use of the national forests went on without ever being recognized or remarked on by forest rangers, sometimes Indians and forest officials did talk to each other and arrange some kind of formal relationship. One early instance of Forest Service–tribal relations involved the Yakama tribe and the use of huckleberry fields located on the former Columbia National Forest (today's Gifford Pinchot National Forest) in Washington State. In this case, the dialogue between tribal leaders and forest officials culminated in a historic agreement that gave tribal members exclusive use of a prescribed area of about 2,800 acres during the huckleberry season. Historian Andrew H. Fisher has pieced together the correspondence and council minutes behind the agreement from administrative records held at the Mount Adams Ranger Station and the national forest headquarters. He concludes in his article that "the 1932 Handshake Agreement stands out as a striking case of accommodation in an often bleak record of bureaucratic indifference or even antagonism toward Native American cultural and religious concerns."[6]

The Handshake Agreement was a reflection of the Yakamas' desire to maintain cultural traditions, preserve their ancestral ties to the land, and exercise rights that their forefathers had reserved in the Yakama Treaty of 1855. Traditionally, the Yakama occupied a variety of environments throughout the seasons of the year. In the winter, they congregated in permanent villages along the Columbia River, where they subsisted on stored foods and occasional game and applied themselves to making fishing nets and other material items for the coming year. In the spring, they dispersed in extended family groups to their various fishing stations on the river, where they caught and dried salmon. When summer arrived, they moved to the foothills and then farther into the mountains, gathering edible plants as the plants ripened at progressively higher elevations as well as hunting large and small game. Late summer brought them to the mountain meadows on the east slope of the Cascade Range, where huckleberries grew in profusion. At each stage of their seasonal rounds, the Yakamas came together to hold a thanksgiving feast in honor of the Creator and in celebration of the bounty of the new season's harvest. Each feast featured one of their four sacred staples of salmon, deer, roots, and berries.[7]

The huckleberry season, or *wiwnumi*, was known as a particularly social time of the year. Yakamas camped in the same vicinity with Umatillas, Wyams, and Klickitats. All spoke mutually intelligible Sahaptin dialects, and the different peoples renewed their bonds of friendship through marriage and trade. Yakamas also met in the mountains with more distant tribes coming from the Pacific coast and the northern plains, trading with them to enrich their variety of foods and material culture. By around 1730, they acquired the horse; a couple generations later, they were trading for items of European manufacture including metal cookware and tools, guns, mirrors, and glass beads.[8]

In 1855, the U.S. government appointed Isaac Stevens governor of Washington Territory and commissioned him to negotiate treaties of land cession and amity with the many tribes. At the Walla Walla Council in June of that year, the Yakamas signed a treaty by which they ceded much of their territory to the United States while reserving a core area for their exclusive use and occupation—the present-day Yakama Reservation. In article 2 of the treaty, the Yakamas allowed that the ceded area would be open to settlement by citizens of the United States, and in article 3 they reserved the right of "taking fish at all usual and accustomed places, in common with the citizens of the Territory . . . together with the privilege of hunting, gathering roots and berries, and pasturing their horses and cattle upon open and unclaimed land."[9] The Yakama chiefs understood these terms according to what they heard stated and translated for them in council. "We do not want you to agree not to get roots and berries and not to go off to the buffalo," the governor declared. "We want you to have your roots and to get your berries, and to kill your game."[10] Hence, the treaty established the tribe on a reservation while also reserving to the tribe certain off-reservation rights in perpetuity. In time, those off-reservation rights came to exist on national forestlands when large swaths of the Cascade Range were set aside as forest reserve or national forest in the 1890s and 1900s.

With changing times, the courts interpreted the exact meaning of the Indians' off-reservation rights in various ways. The pressure of increasing non-Indian settlement and land use, together with the subsequent establishment of national parks and forest reserves within the Yakama's ceded area, led to different interpretations over the meaning of continued access to "open and unclaimed lands."

New forms of commercial fishing as well as growing competition over the fishery resource led to disputes over what it meant to fish "in common . . . at usual and accustomed places." When Washington was granted statehood in 1889, it acquired the authority to regulate the taking of fish and game within its territory under the equal footing doctrine. All new states admitted to the Union came in on an "equal footing," endowed with the same powers and reserved rights as the original thirteen states. Those powers included the authority to regulate the taking of fish and game within their territory. As Washington state enacted fish and game laws, state wardens and even federal rangers sometimes arrested Yakamas for hunting out of season off-reservation. Yakamas objected, claiming they had the right to hunt on open and unclaimed lands without interference. The U.S. Supreme Court upheld the Yakamas' off-reservation treaty right in *United States v. Winans* (1905). But the Washington State Supreme Court in *State v. Towessnute* (1916) ruled that Yakamas hunting outside the reservation had to abide by state law.[11] More recently, the courts have found that state law can only be applied to Indians outside their reservation where it would not "impair a right granted or reserved by federal law." Thus, off-reservation fishing and hunting rights are now seen to override the state power to regulate the taking of fish and game.[12] But for much of the twentieth century, the courts' interpretation of off-reservation rights remained unsettled, and Forest Service policy tended to back the state's view.[13]

The Forest Service had several reasons for discouraging Yakamas from continuing to use mountain areas that had come under the agency's control. For one thing, the Forest Service sought to suppress all forest fire. Forest officials were well aware of the Yakamas' traditional use of light burning to encourage growth of huckleberry bushes and improve graze for their horses in the following year. Forest rangers took every opportunity to admonish them for what they considered a reckless and misguided use of fire.[14]

The Forest Service also tended to side with non-Indian stockmen who complained that Indians trespassed with their horses on the stockmen's grazing leases. The Forest Service divided the national forest into grazing units, advertised them for competitive bidding, and leased each one to the highest bidder. The purpose was to regulate grazing use and demonstrate that national forests were for use. The stockmen were the Forest Service's first significant client, for it would be many years before timber sales occurred on the western national forests. The stockmen paid a fee for their grazing leases and entered into cooperative associations for managing the grazing resource. Under those circumstances, forest officials tended to support the stockmen's claims that the Yakamas' horses intruded on summer range that rightfully belonged to them, the leaseholders. On the other hand, when Yakamas pointed out to the Forest Service that domestic sheep made a mess of the huckleberry fields, their complaints initially fell on deaf ears.[15]

Yakamas began to clash with recreational users on the national forest, too. As Americans adopted the automobile, they took to car camping, hiking, picnicking, and recreational fishing as popular pastimes. In the 1920s, the Forest Service started touting recreation as another important public use of the national forests. Yakamas resented the fact that the Forest Service encouraged more recreational use by constructing roads and campgrounds in areas where the Yakamas made their seasonal camps for picking huckleberries. Cultural differences arose where Indians and non-Indians camped in close proximity. Non-Indians swam and bathed in lakes and streams that Yakamas regarded as sacred. The non-Indian presence inhibited Yakamas from engaging in religious practices such as sweats and vision quests that had long been part of their experience in going to the huckleberry fields year after year. For their part, non-Indians complained at finding refuse such as animal bones scattered about after the Yakamas broke camp and returned to the reservation.[16]

The clash of cultures intensified when the Great Depression brought thousands of unemployed migrant workers into the area. These destitute non-Indians, besides finding comfort in numbers where they overflowed the free campgrounds, occupied a good part of their time picking huckleberries, which they sold to canneries in nearby cities for fifty cents a gallon. Yakamas did not like the outsiders encroaching on what they had long regarded as their own huckleberry patches, nor did they appreciate the commercialization of their sacred food.[17]

Negotiations between the Yakamas and the Forest Service began on August 25, 1929, with a council held at the Meadow Creek campground. Forest Supervisor F. V. Horton and District Ranger Harvey Welty represented the agency, while an estimated 150 tribal members attended on behalf of the tribe. The Yakamas voiced their many grievances over the state's hunting and fishing law enforcement, sheep grazing, and recreational use, while the forest officials expressed their concern about forest fires. No specific proposals came from the meeting, but a Nez Perce delegate praised the two officers for giving them a respectful hearing.[18]

In 1931, when the conflict intensified after migrant workers swarmed into the area, the consultation between the Forest Service and Yakama leaders resumed.

FIGURE 12. Yakama woman and children gathering huckleberries, 1933. Forest Service photographer K. D. Swan took this photo on the Columbia National Forest (now the Gifford Pinchot National Forest), Washington. The Handshake Agreement provided for the tribe's exclusive use of the area for berry picking.

The Yakamas stated that they would accept the presence of the non-Indians in the Twin Buttes area of the national forest if they could be assured privacy in one small tract containing a few berry patches. In other words, the Yakamas would drop their claim to exclusive use over most of the berry fields if the Forest Service would guarantee their people exclusive use of that small area. At the same time, they would reserve the right to pick berries in common with non-Indians outside of that area. (Interestingly, the proposal mirrored the 1855 treaty in miniature, for it would secure a small reservation within a larger ceded area while reserving the Yakamas' right to share in the resource in the ceded area.) Forest officials balked at these terms at first, but the new forest supervisor, J. R. Bruckart, argued to his superiors that it presented a fair and workable arrangement. He agreed to another council, which was held on August 23, 1932, at Surprise Lakes Indian camp.[19]

It was at this third council that the Handshake Agreement was forged. Chief William Yallup spoke for the Yakamas. Much of his people's angst centered on the state's attempts to abrogate their off-reservation hunting rights on the national forest. After going over that matter, Yallup turned to the huckleberry picking. Bruckart listened sympathetically, but with regard to the hunting issue he said there was little he could offer. As for protecting their use of the huckleberry fields, he was constrained on that issue, too. "I myself was placed here by the Great White Father to see that all people enjoyed the forest equally," he stated. "I cannot exclude the White Man from the berry fields or I would also have to exclude the Indians." However, that said, he agreed to set aside the Meadow Creek, Surprise Lakes, and Cold Springs campgrounds for the Yakamas' exclusive use during the huckleberry season. The area encompassed about 2,800 acres. Yallup then stood and thanked Bruckart. "I have spoken to the end. Nothing is hidden in my heart. Your words give me happiness. You are my friend. Now all is well between my people and your people." And the two shook hands on the agreement.[20]

In the following months, federal officials pondered how the agreement might be implemented. The BIA superintendent of the Yakama Agency, C. R. Whitlock, proposed that the BIA and the Forest Service seek an act of Congress to secure it. The Forest Service did not want to elevate it to that level, believing that to exclude the general public from an area by legislation would be so contrary to the multiple-use principle of the National Forest System that the area would have to be transferred out of its control. Rather, Bruckart wanted to appeal to non-Indians to respect the agreement on a voluntary basis. Believing that the Handshake Agreement should be kept on a strictly personal level, he met with Yallup and recommitted to it year after year, and he persuaded his successor, K. P. Cecil, to do the same. The Forest Service publicized the agreement to non-Indians by putting up signs and handing out brochures. A 1936 pamphlet for the Twin Buttes Recreation Area depicted the Yakamas' exclusive-use area on a map and explained its connection to the 1855 treaty.[21]

The Handshake Agreement endured. While the annual council and handshake ritual ended after a few years, the Forest Service continued to publicize the agreement in brochures decade after decade. It was written into the forest plan in 1990. Public respect for the agreement stood the test of time. Social conflicts were not unknown: a few non-Indians encroached on the exclusive-use area or helped themselves to the Yakamas' tipi poles and turned them into firewood. Boundary signs were vandalized. But voluntary compliance with the exclusion was generally high. Nowadays the most serious threat to the Yakamas' traditional gathering of huckleberries comes from another quarter. After a century of forest fire suppression, the huckleberry fields are being engulfed by forest growth. One study by the Forest Service found that the huckleberry fields have diminished by about two-thirds since the 1930s and could disappear altogether in a few more decades.[22]

The Handshake Agreement has been characterized as a "historical quirk" with few contemporary analogues on other national forests.[23] Yet the circumstances surrounding the agreement were emblematic of conditions shaping Forest Service–tribal relations generally. Indians continued to make traditional use of national forestlands in virtually every part of the country. Often the same issues arose on other forests—over Indians' off-reservation hunting rights, their supposed carelessness with fire, their competition with stockmen over grazing privileges, and their general incompatibility with non-Indian campers and other types of recreationists. What made the Handshake Agreement unusual in its day was the Yakamas' success in opening a fruitful dialogue with forest officials and the forest supervisor's willingness to take a stand in demanding public respect for the tribe's rights and cultural autonomy.

THE TLINGIT AND HAIDA AND THE TONGASS TIMBER ACT OF 1947

One region where Indian rights on the national forest made the Forest Service nervous was in southeast Alaska. The Forest Service proposed to establish a pulpwood industry on the enormous 16-million-acre Tongass National Forest. Many Alaskans, including the Alaska Territory's appointed governor, Ernest Gruening, saw the development as a key stepping stone on the path to statehood. The chief obstacle to attracting industry, however, was the uncertainty surrounding Indian rights in the land. When the Department of the Interior took action in the mid-1940s toward the establishment of reservations around the fourteen Tlingit and Haida villages located on the Tongass, it caused several interested pulpwood companies to pull back and cancel their field investigations. An editorial in the *Journal of Forestry* in June 1945 stated that the Indians' land claims were "viewed with real alarm." It called for Congress to resolve the situation by imposing a legislative settlement that would "safeguard such rights as the Indians may actually possess, without jeopardizing the economic and social development of the territory as a whole."[24]

The Tlingit and Haida land claims stemmed from a complicated history. In precontact times, the land tenure of the Tlingit and Haida tribes was based on clan territories. Clans were divided into two moieties, Eagle and Raven, and as the culture dictated that marriage partners could not be from the same moiety, clans of different moieties came together in winter villages. In the late nineteenth century there were some three times as many Native villages as now exist in southeast Alaska. From the 1880s to the early 1900s, when the Tlingit and Haida came under the combined influence of missionaries, miners, the commercial fishing industry, government agents, and an incipient tourism industry, many abandoned their winter villages and moved to larger population centers to work in canneries, enroll their children in schools, and seek other opportunities. Perhaps as many as two dozen villages were deserted, and subsistence patterns shifted accordingly.[25]

For a long time, the U.S. government did not recognize tribes or tribal governments in Alaska. After the United States purchased Alaska from Russia in 1867, the federal government made no effort to extinguish aboriginal title there as it did in the American West during the nineteenth century. The Organic Act of 1884 promised that Indians would "not be disturbed in the possession of any lands actually in their use or occupation," but enforcement was practically nil.[26] The Tongass National Forest was established by three presidential proclamations in 1902, 1907, and 1909 without tribal consultation or any acknowledgment of Native rights of use and occupancy. Taking in practically the whole Alaskan panhandle, the proclamations offhandedly treated the Tlingits and Haidas as though they were landless villagers. Subsequent exclusions from the national forest gave each of the fourteen surviving Tlingit and Haida villages a small land base, but each village community in fact relied on a much wider area to sustain its mixed economy of commercial and subsistence fishing, hunting, and gathering. The Forest Service failed to acknowledge the extent to which those Native villages used the surrounding lands for their subsistence and assumed they were tied to the cash economy more firmly than they actually were.[27]

In 1929, the Alaska Native Brotherhood (ANB) passed a resolution to bring suit in the U.S. Court of Claims for a settlement of Tlingit and Haida land claims arising from the establishment of the Tongass National Forest and Glacier Bay National Monument. In 1935, Congress passed a law allowing the Tlingit and Haida to file their claim as one tribe, and subsequently *The Tlingit and Haida Tribe of Alaska v. the United States* was entered on the court's docket. The following year, Congress passed the Alaska Reorganization Act, which adapted the provisions of the Indian Reorganization Act (the Indian New Deal) for conditions in Alaska. Under one of the law's provisions, Secretary of the Interior Ickes and Commissioner of Indian Affairs Collier proposed to establish small Indian reservations in southeast Alaska for the Tlingit and Haida tribe's protection. However, there were legal questions about whether lands that were not actually occupied by the Natives could be so designated. Pushing the issue would raise the question of whether Natives had abandoned certain places, which would likely exacerbate race relations and injure the Tlingit and Haida claim.[28]

There the matter rested until 1942, when a ruling by the U.S. Supreme Court in *United States v. Santa Fe Pacific Railroad Company* conveniently provided the Department of the Interior's solicitors with a new legal interpretation of aboriginal rights. The justices found that (1) aboriginal occupancy established rights of possession, (2) possessory rights need not be based on treaty or statute, and (3) extinguishment of possessory rights might not be inferred from general legislation or administrative action. Based on that ruling, Interior solicitors Felix Cohen and Nathan R. Margold thought the department could challenge the Forest Service's position that the United States held clear title to the Tongass National Forest by right of abandonment. In a solicitor's opinion issued on February 13, 1942, Margold held that Alaska Native possessory rights had never been extinguished by the United States and that, moreover, their possessory rights extended to the submerged lands or waters traditionally used for fishing. Regulations permitting control of such areas by non-Natives were unauthorized and illegal.[29] The implications of the solicitor's opinion were

FIGURE 13. Native village on the Tongass National Forest, 1941. Such communities used surrounding lands for subsistence hunting and gathering.

COURTESY OF FOREST HISTORY SOCIETY

momentous, posing a challenge to the salmon fishing industry as well as the pulpwood industry.

Ickes moved quickly to take advantage of the new finding in law. On March 13, 1942, he announced new Alaskan fisheries regulations that prohibited the use of fish traps on Indians' property without their consent. Then he invited the Native village councils to request hearings by the department to delineate the extent of their possessory interests. His intent was clear: once those possessory interests were substantiated, he would have authority under the Alaska Reorganization Act to establish Indian reservations, thereby securing those fishing grounds for Indian use only. Further action on this initiative had to be suspended during the middle years of World War II as Alaska became an important staging area in the war with Japan. Finally, in September 1944, a first round of hearings was held in the villages of Klawock, Kake, and Hydaburg, Judge Richard H. Hanna presiding.[30] By then, the Interior secretary's move to establish Indian reservations in Alaska incited a strong negative reaction among the non-Native population of Alaska as well as commercial interests based outside the territory. "The fate of Alaska hangs in the balance," an editorial in *The Alaska Fishing News* shouted. "It must now be apparent to everyone that Secretary Ickes is planning one of the biggest land grabs ever attempted by a bureau chief."[31]

Judge Hanna, a former justice on the New Mexico Supreme Court who was remembered for his staunch support of Pueblo land claims in the 1920s, found that the villages of Klawock, Kake, and Hydaburg had a valid claim to some 275,000 acres. However, that was less than a tenth of the area that the three Native villages petitioned for. In fact, Hanna's report leaned toward the Forest Service's position that the Tlingits and Haidas had abandoned many of their aboriginal rights to fishing places and hunting territories. Despite the disappointing findings in Hanna's report, Ickes recommended the establishment of Indian reservations around Klawock, Kake, and Hydaburg based on the smaller acreages and submitted his recommendations for a vote by the residents in each village. Reluctant to accept the smaller territories, the three villages did not bring the proposals to a vote.[32]

Ickes resigned in February 1946. His replacement, Julius A. Krug, initially followed the same tack on Alaska Native land claims. On June 10, 1946, the Department of the Interior invited more petitions from Native villages by promulgating "Rules of Procedure for Hearings for Possessory Claims to Lands and Waters Used and Occupied by Natives of Alaska." That month, Krug appointed Theodore Haas, the BIA's chief counsel, and Dr. Walter Goldschmidt, an anthropologist in the Department of Agriculture, to conduct hearings. Haas and Goldschmidt traveled to the several Tlingit villages not previously visited by Judge Hanna and obtained extensive testimony on past and present subsistence patterns. Sympathetic listeners, they also heard numerous accounts of how government agents or the government's surrogates among the non-Native population had driven the Tlingits out of their traditional use areas. At the end of the year, Haas and Goldschmidt filed their report, "Possessory Rights of the Natives of Southeast Alaska." Applying the standards set by the department, they found Native possessory rights on nearly 2 million acres in southeast Alaska, which included about 10 percent of the Tongass National

Forest. Krug endorsed their finding and tasked his new assistant secretary, Warner W. Gardner, to work with the BIA and the Forest Service in developing a legislative solution to the Alaska Native land claims.[33]

While Interior was moving ahead with its determination of Alaska Native possessory rights, the Senate formed a special subcommittee to investigate the nation's newsprint shortage and sent the chairman of the subcommittee, Republican Homer E. Capehart of Indiana, to investigate the Forest Service's plan to develop a pulpwood industry on the Tongass. Capehart consulted with Regional Forester B. Frank Heintzleman. At that time, in 1946, the Tongass plan called for construction of five mills under fifty-year contracts, with each separate lumbering and milling operation to employ approximately 1,250 people. Counting the new service people who would be required in each of the mill towns, the industry would bring an estimated 6,500 jobs to southeast Alaska. Capehart was favorably impressed with the plan and advised investors to go ahead in their negotiations with the Forest Service, notwithstanding the unresolved claims of Alaska Natives.[34]

Governor Gruening and Alaska's single delegate in Congress, E. L. "Bob" Bartlett, also urged the pulpwood industry to go forward. As both politicians championed the cause of Alaska statehood, they noted that the industry would boost Alaska's population and raise the tax base needed to support state government. In October 1946, the territory held a referendum on whether to pursue statehood, and Alaskans voted in favor of the measure by a two-to-one margin, setting in motion the final campaign for legislation by Congress. The timing of the referendum effectively tied the Forest Service's Tongass initiative to the popular statehood movement.[35]

Buoyed by all the political interest in its plan for the Tongass, the Forest Service refused to accept the Haas and Goldschmidt report as a basis for addressing Indian rights in southeast Alaska. Indeed, the agency held to its position that the Tlingits and Haidas had abandoned many of their traditional use areas on the Tongass through their process of relocation and acculturation early in the century. It did not agree with the Department of the Interior's theory about what constituted Native possessory interests. If the land was unoccupied, then it was under the Forest Service's administration and control.[36]

In 1947, the clash over Indian rights on the Tongass National Forest came rapidly to a head. At the start of the year, Interior officials offered a compromise by which 10 percent of the land area in southeast Alaska would be withheld from timber operations until such time as the Native land claims could be resolved. But in February, Agriculture Undersecretary W. E. Dodd informed Interior Assistant Secretary Gardner that the 10 percent offer could not be accepted; the Forest Service could not support such a bill because it would create a muddle of "competing jurisdictions," hampering pulpwood operations. Then in March, a solicitor in the Department of Agriculture, Edward Mynatt, came forward with another formula: maybe the Forest Service would provisionally recognize a Native claim of 1 million acres, or 6.5 percent of the forestland, based on an allotment of 160 acres for each Native. Interior Solicitor Felix Cohen responded to this offer by adding a second proviso: 10 percent of all timber sale receipts would be paid to the Tlingit and Haida Tribes to fund their legal expenses in the U.S. Court of Claims. In May, the Agriculture and Interior secretaries agreed to those terms and arranged with the executive secretary of the National Congress of American Indians (NCAI), Ruth Muskrat Bronson, to go to Alaska and obtain the tribes' support for the compromise proposal.[37]

However, when the impending deal was leaked to the salmon canning industry's lobbyists, they raised a hue and cry. The 10 percent payment to the Indians of timber sale receipts, they said, was tantamount to an admission of the validity of the Indians' land claim. And if the Indians won their claim, it would cause irreparable damage to Alaska's prospects for industrial development. Getting an earful from the industry's lobbyists, Alaska's two leading politicians, Gruening and Bartlett, withdrew their support for the idea to pay out a percentage of timber sale receipts.[38]

Interior officials now feared they would get nothing in the bill to protect the Native land claim. Regional Forester Heintzleman and others in the Agriculture Department were on record favoring legislation that would simply extinguish aboriginal title and invite the Tlingit and Haida to sue for damages. To salvage some semblance of a compromise, Gardner suggested that all receipts from timber sales would be put in an escrow account until such time as the Alaska Native claims could be settled. In the meantime, nothing in the act would be construed to affect the standing of the claims one way or the other. The Forest Service agreed to Gardner's proposal, confident that it would not slow the pulpwood development one iota.[39]

The bill was introduced in Congress on May 16. The House Committee on Agriculture held hearings on it over a two-week span in May and June, receiving testimony from Gruening, attorneys for the government and the tribe, and a delegation of tribal members who arrived from Alaska on the second to last day of the schedule. Despite the Indians' strong objections to it, the bill passed both houses of Congress with little debate at the end of July, and President Harry S. Truman signed the Tongass Timber Act into law on August 8.[40]

In the final analysis, Congress enacted legislation that brushed aside the Native land claims issue in the interest of promoting industrial development in the northern territory. Pulpwood production commenced with the opening of the first mill in Ketchikan in 1953 and expanded with the opening of a second one in Sitka in 1959, the year Alaska achieved statehood. That was also the year that the U.S. Court of Claims at last rendered a preliminary decision in *Tlingit and Haida Indians of Alaska v. United States*, recognizing the loss of the tribe's lands. Tribal attorneys then sought a judgment of $80 million for damages, but the judges finally recommended an award of just $7.5 million, which Congress authorized in 1968. Three years later, the Alaska Native Claims Settlement Act (ANCSA) provided for a renewal of Tlingit and Haida land holdings through an elaborate process of land selection. The total amount of land that eventually transferred from the Tongass National Forest to the Native villages under ANCSA remained far less than either the 10 percent recommended by Gardner or the 6.5 percent recommended by Mynatt in 1947.[41]

Alaska historian Stephen W. Haycox has rendered the following historical judgment on the legislative settlement in 1947:

> The story of the Tongass Timber Act is one of a conflict of values and the policies which embodied them. For the Forest Service and advocates of Alaska statehood, the primacy of modern capitalist development in the Tongass National Forest was more important than the protection and safeguard of potential Indian land rights and resources, which they interpreted as a threat to that development. . . . On the other hand, supporters of the Indians argued for the primacy of aboriginal title and protection of Indian rights. To secure Indian lands, and Indian culture and identity, they placed the sanctity of Indian land title above the value of economic development.[42]

CHAPTER SUMMARY

Indians continued to use national forestlands for hunting and gathering, vision quests, and other traditional purposes through the first half of the twentieth century in spite of the dominant society's discouragement of virtually all such uses. The Forest Service discouraged Indian use mainly in the interest of forest fire protection, in support of state game law enforcement, and in solidarity with non-Indian stock growers who held grazing leases.

In the Handshake Agreement of 1932, the Yakama tribe obtained assurances of continued access to and exclusive use of certain huckleberry grounds on the Columbia National Forest. It was an exceptional case in which local Forest Service officials partnered with a tribe to accommodate the tribe's traditional use of the national forest. While the Handshake Agreement was an enduring achievement that foreshadowed how other types of Indian traditional use would be accommodated on other national forests many years hence, it was a singular event in its day.

Federal and state courts interpreted tribes' possessory interests and treaty-reserved rights on national forests more narrowly in the first half of the twentieth century than in subsequent decades. When Indian and non-Indian interests clashed on the Tongass National Forest in the 1930s and 40s, the Forest Service took a hard line against accommodating Indian traditional use. It rejected claims by the Tlingit and Haida tribes that they had possessory interests in traditional use areas because the tribes' claims would impede plans to develop a pulpwood industry. The Forest Service got its way when Congress passed the Tongass Timber Act of 1947. The story of Tlingit and Haida land claims is not only vital historical background for an understanding of contemporary Forest Service tribal relations in southeast Alaska, but it also reflects how tribes everywhere at midcentury still faced long odds when they took their grievances to the courts or Congress.

5

THE TERMINATION ERA

The 1950s and 1960s

THE TERMINATION POLICY

FEDERAL INDIAN POLICY in the twentieth century has swung like a pendulum between two opposing and indomitable ideas. The first, assimilation, presumes that Indians will inevitably merge into the general American population; therefore, the government's trust responsibility is to smooth that road for them. The second, self-determination, holds that Indians have the ability and right to live as tribal peoples in our modern pluralistic society. It upholds the doctrine of tribal sovereignty, which recognizes Indian tribes as domestic, dependent nations existing within the larger nation. The ideas of assimilation and self-determination have taken turns dominating policy, neither one ever fully vanquishing the other. The Indian New Deal saw the pendulum swing to self-determination; the termination era saw it swing back to assimilation.

The termination era began after World War II when the Republican Party took control of Congress. The movement's name, "termination," referred to breaking or terminating the federal trust relationship in Indian affairs. The program was based on winding down the BIA and eventually terminating all BIA services to Indians. Taking a phased approach, the government would begin handing off those BIA services one by one to state and local governments. Some services would be terminated outright. The withdrawal of federal responsibility for Indians would proceed tribe by tribe, with the most assimilated tribes going first. This overall scheme of a phased withdrawal first took shape in February 1947 when the Senate Committee on the Civil Service held a hearing. Acting Commissioner of Indian Affairs William Zimmerman was called to testify before the committee on the relative importance of BIA services for all federally recognized tribes. Zimmerman gave the committee three lists. The first list included those tribes that could supposedly do without BIA services immediately. The second list comprised those that could be essentially cut loose after ten years. All the remaining federally recognized tribes, which made up the last list, would need more time. The information provided by Zimmerman became known as the Zimmerman Plan and served as a road map for subsequent congressional bills that targeted specific tribes for termination.[1]

FIGURE 14. Tribal representatives at the founding meeting of the National Congress of American Indians (NCAI) in Denver, 1944. The NCAI was formed to resist the federal government's assimilation and termination policies and protect American Indian and Alaska Native sovereign rights.

Political momentum for termination built over the next six years and climaxed in the first term of President Eisenhower. In 1954, Congress enacted a handful of termination acts featuring the Klamath Tribe in Oregon, the Menominee Tribe in Wisconsin, and several smaller tribes in Oklahoma, California, Utah, and elsewhere. When Democrats took back control of the Senate in 1956, the drive for termination slowed. There was bitter opposition to the policy across Indian Country, and problems soon surfaced where termination acts were put into effect. As a result, the Menominee and Klamath remained the two prominent examples of terminated tribes in the nation.

In its decisive phase, the termination policy was short lived. When the burst of termination acts ended, terminated tribes numbered 13,263 individuals, or only about 3 percent of federally recognized Indians. Likewise, the Indian lands divested of federal trust status amounted to about 3 percent of all Indian trust lands. Nonetheless, the termination policy had wider repercussions. Virtually all Indians experienced cutbacks in BIA services, and perhaps more importantly over the long run, the termination policy sent a shockwave of dismay through Indian Country. Indian resistance to termination finally caught the ear of Congress, which caused the political pendulum to swing once more toward Indian self-determination in the 1960s.

THE KLAMATH TRIBE AND ITS FOREST

The Forest Service was drawn into the termination process for the Klamath Tribe because the Klamath Reservation contained a large tribal forest. It was the last time in the twentieth century that a tribal forest was converted into a national forest.

Historian Donald L. Parman has suggested that intense factionalism within the Klamath Tribe made it vulnerable to the termination impulse in Congress whereas other tribes put up a stronger resistance to it. A sizable minority among the Klamath people had achieved a level of formal education equal to the surrounding non-Indian population, and many of them lived off reservation in mostly non-Indian communities. The leader of the protermination faction, Wade Crawford, advocated selling off the tribal forest for a onetime per capita payment to all tribal members. He was able to put together a winning coalition that combined the most assimilated tribal members with the most desperate ones who were attracted by the short-term promise of a per capita payment.

The self-destructive factionalism in the Klamath Tribe contrasted with the united front that the Confederated Salish and Kootenai tribes presented when Congress considered a termination bill for them. Like the Klamath Reservation, their Flathead Reservation in western Montana contained a valuable tribal forest. When the Senate held a hearing on the Flathead termination bill, tribal chairman Walter McDonald brought a delegation of tribal leaders and traditionalists to Capitol Hill to show the tribe's solidarity against it.[2]

The termination act for the Klamath Tribe declared that at midnight on the date of the act, the tribal roll would be closed and no child born thereafter would be eligible for enrollment. The tribe was to prepare a final roll of its members. Once the roll became finalized, all tribal property would be deemed personal property divided equally among the persons on the roll. The secretary of the interior was to have an appraisal made of the tribal forest based on its "fair market value by practicable logging or other appropriate economic units"— the appraisal to be accomplished within four years. Upon completion of the appraisal, each tribal member would vote on whether to withdraw from the tribe and receive a per capita share in the tribe's assets or stay in the tribe. For those choosing to keep their tribal affiliation, whatever was left after the per capita distribution would be turned over to a "trustee, corporation, or other legal entity" yet to be named. The end result, as defined in section 1 of the act, would be the "termination of Federal supervision over the trust and restricted property of the Klamath Tribe of Indians . . . and of the individual members thereof."[3]

The Klamath Reservation included 693,997 acres of commercial and non-commercial forest containing an estimated 4.5 billion board feet of ponderosa and sugar pine and 1.8 million cords of pulpwood. BIA foresters had opened the reservation to commercial logging in 1913, inaugurating a timber cutting program that brought millions of dollars to the tribe over the next four decades. As the BIA managed the forest according to sustained-yield principles, cutting reached an all-time high of 240 million feet in 1926 and averaged 109 million feet per year over the longer term. At the start of World War II, BIA foresters administered ten timber sales with a required minimum cut for that year of 127 million feet. With its system of competitive bidding on timber sales, its marking rules, and its program of fire protection, BIA administration of the Klamath tribal forest was not dissimilar to Forest Service management of national forests.[4]

With the passage of the termination act, the possibility loomed that the Klamath Tribe's forest would be sold off and logged at a much faster rate than previously. The law mandated sale of the forest at market value so that all those who elected to withdraw from the tribe might receive their share of the tribal wealth in a lump-sum payment. Preliminary indications revealed that as much as 70 percent of the tribe might withdraw, necessitating sale of 70 percent of the commercial forest to private lumbering companies to pay them off. That would amount to a whopping 2.7 billion board feet being dumped on the local lumber market in a few years. In addition, individual owners of allotments would be free to sell their timber, which amounted to another 225 million board feet. The prospect of sudden forest liquidation raised a variety of concerns. Local lumbermen feared that a flood of Klamath timber would depress lumber prices. Area ranchers and farmers worried about the effects of clear-cutting on watersheds and their water supply. Conservationists bemoaned the loss of forest and the effects on wildlife. Of particular concern was what might happen to the twenty-three-thousand-acre wetland on the reservation, which was important both as a water source for agricultural lands and as a waterfowl breeding area.[5]

Under the leadership of Senator Richard L. Neuberger of Oregon, a Democrat, Congress began to consider ways to amend the Klamath termination act to avoid those pitfalls. The Forest Service was called to testify before Neuberger's committee. The Forest Service representatives warned that the sudden liquidation of the Klamath Indian forest would depress timber sale business for at least four neighboring national forests: the Rogue River, Deschutes, and Fremont in Oregon and the Modoc in California. "Such an impact would, in turn, result in a reduction in the amount of funds returned to local levels out of national forest receipts," those officials explained. "There would be a reduction in the payments where under 25 percent of the receipts of each national forest are paid to the States for the benefit of public schools." No fewer than ten counties in Oregon and California would feel the bite.[6]

Through 1957, pressure grew to amend or repeal the Klamath termination act and forestall those negative effects. The Forest Service suggested that a requirement of sustained-yield management could be attached to the sale of Klamath forestlands, ensuring that the timber would enter the market in an orderly fashion as before. Western lumbermen by and large opposed that idea because they resisted government regulation of logging on private lands on principle. However, lumber magnate George Weyerhaeuser supported the Forest Service proposal, seeing it as a practical alternative to the free-for-all by timber buyers that would cause market instability. Senator Neuberger went one step farther, suggesting that if private companies declined to purchase the Klamath forestland under those restrictive terms, then the United States would buy it and make it part of the National Forest System.[7]

Congress amended the Klamath termination act by a law enacted August 23, 1958. The Forest Service clearly influenced the legislation. Under the amended law, the secretaries of agriculture and the interior would jointly determine lands on the Klamath Reservation with commercial timber, and they would group those lands into units for sale on the basis of competitive bids. The units would be sold to private purchasers who agreed to manage them according to sustained-yield procedures. Plans for sustained-yield management were to be submitted with each bid and enforced by the secretary of agriculture. Forest units which did not sell by April 1, 1961, would be bought by the United States and put into the National Forest System.[8]

As termination went into effect, 77 percent of Klamath tribal members voted to withdraw from the tribe and receive a per capita payment of $43,700. To raise the money for this payout, 617,000 acres of the Klamath Reservation were divided into eleven sale units plus several small tracts. The Crown Zellerbach Corporation purchased 92,000 acres, while the U.S. government eventually purchased the remaining 525,000 acres after the clock ran out in 1961. Another 16,400 acres went into the Klamath Marsh National Wildlife Refuge. Those tribal members who voted to stay in the tribe retained a rump reservation of 145,000 acres, which was conveyed to the National Bank of Portland as their trustee.[9]

On July 26, 1961, President Kennedy proclaimed the Winema National Forest. It comprised 419,000 acres of former Klamath Indian land plus small areas transferred from the Rogue River, Deschutes, and Fremont national forests. By the same proclamation, the president added 106,000 acres of former Klamath land to the Fremont National Forest.[10]

TAOS PUEBLO AND THE RETURN OF BLUE LAKE

In 1946, Congress established the Indian Claims Commission. Its mission was to take all Indian land claim cases that had gotten stalled in the U.S. Court of Claims or had not yet been brought to court, expedite those cases, and help prepare the way for the government to "get out of the Indian business."[11] Congress intended for the Indian Claims Commission to complete its work in five years; however, because of the volume of tribal claims against the United States, the life of the commission had to be repeatedly extended until it finally closed shop in 1978.[12]

While the Indian Claims Commission brought attention to the history of U.S. land takings in violation of Indian treaties, Congress made it clear that restitution would be made through monetary settlements only. Congress would not return confiscated lands back to the Indians. In northern New Mexico, the Taos Pueblo Indians challenged that framework, insisting that the tribe could not be made whole without the return of its sacred lake and some fifty thousand acres of mountainous terrain surrounding it. The Taos Indians finally succeeded in their quest when President Richard Nixon came to the tribe's support and pushed a bill through Congress in 1970. The restoration of Blue Lake to the Taos Indians marked the first time in the history of federal-Indian relations that land was returned to a tribe to settle a claim.[13] Since the area at issue was on the Carson National Forest, the Forest Service was directly involved in the tribe's long struggle.

Blue Lake is sacred to the Taos Indians because they consider its waters to be the lifeblood of their people. For centuries they have irrigated their crops from the river that emanates from the sublimely beautiful lake, which lies cradled in a cirque at an altitude of eleven thousand feet in the Sangre de Cristo Mountains. For generations, all able-bodied persons in the tribe have gone on an annual pilgrimage to the lake to perform religious rites. The Taos Indians are extremely secretive about their native religion—a cultural conditioning that stems in no small part from the frightful religious persecution they suffered after the Spanish conquest. But in spite of their secretiveness they have made one thing clear to the outside world: Blue Lake lies at the center of their cosmology and symbolizes their sacred connection with nature.[14]

Pueblo land title has a distinct history. Because the various Pueblo groups dwelt in permanent villages, practiced subsistence agriculture, and were inclined toward peaceful relations, the Spanish gave each group a land grant of one square league surrounding the pueblo. After Mexico gained independence in 1821, the Mexican government made the Pueblo Indians citizens of the state and tried to prevent non-Indians from encroaching on their Spanish land grants. The Treaty of Guadalupe Hidalgo, which concluded the Mexican-American War of 1846–1848, made the Pueblos, together with the Hispanic inhabitants of what became New Mexico, all citizens of the United States. Sixteen years later, President Abraham Lincoln issued patents to seventeen Pueblos covering their Spanish land grants, and through the superintendent of Indian affairs in New

FIGURE 15. Blue Lake, Carson National Forest, New Mexico

COURTESY OF THE PALACE OF THE GOVERNORS

Mexico he presented each Pueblo governor with a cane. The so-called "Lincoln canes," picking up an earlier tradition followed by Spanish and Mexican officialdom, were meant to symbolize federal recognition of the Pueblos' right to self-governance. But the Pueblos' independence came at a price. In *United States v. Joseph* (1876) the Supreme Court confirmed that Pueblos were not Indians in a legal sense, meaning they did not come under federal guardianship. Lacking federal protection, the Pueblos were unable to hold back the rising tide of non-Indian settlement on their lands.[15]

In 1906, the first President Roosevelt made the lands surrounding Blue Lake part of the Carson National Forest, ignoring the fact that the Taos Indians considered that area to be their spiritual homeland since time immemorial. (The area did not come within their Spanish land grant.) Given the Pueblos' peculiar legal status, U.S. officials gave no thought to the Pueblos' aboriginal title. In *United States v. Sandoval* (1913) the Supreme Court reversed its earlier decision in *Joseph* and found that the Pueblos, like other Indians, were wards of the government after all. However, the ruling came too late to rectify the situation surrounding Blue Lake and the Taos Indians. Twice following the *Sandoval* decision, the Taos Indians petitioned the federal government for an executive order Indian reservation to protect their interest in the Blue Lake area, but both requests were denied.[16]

Eleven years after *Sandoval*, Congress passed the Pueblo Lands Act of 1924, which set up a Pueblo Lands Board to settle disputes between Pueblos and non-Indian squatters. When the lands board initiated its work at Taos in 1926, the tribal leaders presented an offer that they had made to the commissioner of Indian affairs five years earlier: the Taos Pueblo would drop its challenge to the non-Indians who had taken up residence on their Spanish land grant in return for a reservation covering the Blue Lake area. As the presidential authority to establish Indian reservations by executive order no longer existed, it would require an act of Congress.[17]

The head of the lands board, H. J. Hagerman, consulted the BIA about the Taos Indians' offer, but he declined to recommend the deal to Congress. Hagerman was unsympathetic to the Indians' desire to protect their sacred area because the government's policy in that era was to assimilate the Indians, not to protect their native religions. Indeed, the local non-Indian population looked on the Taos Indians' secretive religious ceremonies at Blue Lake with a great deal of suspicion. Hagerman took stock of that local feeling against the Indians and assumed that part of the BIA's responsibility toward its Pueblo wards was to suppress their pagan rituals.[18]

The tribal leaders, getting nowhere with Hagerman, next took their case directly to Commissioner of Indian Affairs Burke. They wanted exclusive use of the area so they could keep it sacrosanct. Under Forest Service administration, non-Indians were grazing livestock, prospecting for minerals, and camping in the area around Blue Lake, polluting its waters. "This region is like a church to us," they wrote, "and if you look at it that way you will understand how deeply we feel." Burke forwarded their request to Secretary of the Interior Hubert Work, who relayed it to the Department of Agriculture. The reply was negative. "It is quite foreign to the policies of the Department of Agriculture, when once some land has been set aside as a National Forest, to allow it to be withdrawn completely and donated to a private purpose." Not only did the department want to avoid setting precedent by giving forestland back to the Indians, it also dismissed the tribe's religious imperative as a "private purpose."[19]

Despite those rebuffs, the Taos Indians did win a couple of concessions from the government at this time. First, negotiations between the tribe's attorneys and the Forest Service resulted in a Cooperative Use Agreement, signed September 28, 1927. The Forest Service pledged to protect the water supply from pollution and prohibit non-Indians from entering the area without prior written consent by the forest supervisor. The tribe, for its part, pledged to assist with fire suppression, provide salt licks for stock at suitable locations, and report all known cases of trespass. The agreement could be viewed as an early gesture toward comanagement; however, it left no doubt as to which party was in control, as it reserved the right of the Forest Service to take any measures deemed necessary to protect the forest.

The second concession involved Congress and the president. At the tribe's request, the Department of the Interior proposed legislation that would allow for a special executive order withdrawal of certain lands within the Carson National Forest for the protection of the Rio Pueblo headwaters. Congress passed the desired bill on March 27, 1928, and under its authority President Coolidge withdrew thirty thousand acres by executive order on July 7, 1928. Under the terms of the act, the secretary of agriculture was to promulgate regulations "to govern the use and occupancy of lands withdrawn."[20] As a result of those measures, the Blue Lake area was protected from mineral entry but not much else. To the tribe's dismay, the Forest Service promptly built a ranger patrol cabin near the lake, and in 1928 it authorized no fewer than one hundred parties to make recreational use of the area.[21]

The Forest Service insisted on administering the Carson National Forest for use. Forest managers could privilege one user group over another, but they could not allow one group to use a forest to the exclusion of all other groups. Forest Service officials found little reason to modify their stand on those principles in the 1930s when federal Indian policy swung in a new direction under the second President Roosevelt and the Indian New Deal. The test of Forest Service resolve came after the Pueblo Lands Board finished its work and Congress passed the act of May 31, 1933, which compensated the various Pueblos for their loss of lands. Section 4 of the act directed the secretary of agriculture to "designate and segregate" certain lands that the Taos Indians relied on for their water supply, livestock grazing, timber and wood for personal use, and "as the scene of certain of their religious ceremonials." Further, it stipulated that the secretary would grant the tribe, upon request, a permit to occupy and use the area for a period of fifty years. The way the act was worded, it left to the secretary of agriculture's discretion whether the occupancy and use privilege would be exclusive or not.[22]

Resolution of this vital question was prolonged. With Forest Service guidance, Secretary of Agriculture Henry A. Wallace designated the lands on the Carson National Forest that would be subject to the fifty-year permit. The Taos Indians found that the designated area was not extensive enough to protect the lake, and they petitioned Commissioner of Indian Affairs John Collier to get a bill passed that would increase the area by nine thousand acres. Collier tried. Though he got a total of three bills introduced in Congress, none was passed. So in 1939, Collier persuaded the tribe to apply for the fifty-year permit as the designated area was presently configured. Thus, the question of exclusive use finally came to a head more than six years after the law was passed.[23]

The Department of Agriculture's Acting Secretary Harry Brown took a hard line in staking out the Forest Service's position. Nothing in the 1933 act, he insisted, provided for the tribe's exclusive use. Absent that statutory directive, the Forest Service must abide by its policy of managing the forest for use. The permit would allow the tribe *free* and *prior* use, but not *exclusive* use. Whatever timber and grazing resources the tribe did not use, the Forest Service would make available for public use. The Forest Service would only prohibit recreational use during the short period each summer when the Indians occupied the area for ceremonial purposes. As for the tribe's use of the area for hunting and fishing, tribal members would be subject to regulations of the state of New Mexico like everyone else.[24]

Collier firmly believed that the fifty-year permit should give the Taos Indians exclusive use of the area (in part because the use was integral to the Pueblo land claims settlement, and the Taos Indians had yielded on other claims in order to have their way with the Blue Lake area). But in the high-level negotiations between Interior and Agriculture to hammer out terms of the permit, the Forest Service prevailed. Practically the only concession to the Indians was that the permit made no mention of state fishing and hunting regulations. After all its efforts, the tribe had only a use permit that it found practically worthless. Any pretense that the Indians' sacred Blue Lake would receive protection under some form of comanagement quickly vanished. Indeed, in the ensuing years the tribe watched helplessly as recreational interest burgeoned, livestock grazing increased, and the Forest Service even approved small timber sales in the area.[25]

Enter the Indian Claims Commission (ICC). The tribe looked to the new judicial body as its last resort. Having been let down once by the Pueblo Lands Board and a second time by the Forest Service, the tribal leadership was more determined than ever to win back ownership of the Blue Lake area. Before entering its claim with the ICC, the tribal council sought assistance from the Association on American Indian Affairs (AAIA). The president of the AAIA, Oliver La Farge, was a friend of the Taos Indians and a resident of nearby Santa Fe. Although La Farge was skeptical toward the tribe's goal of attaining land rather than money, he helped the tribe develop its case. The Taos Pueblo filed its suit with the ICC in August 1951. La Farge and the AAIA provided crucial financial and legal support as they shepherded the Taos Pueblo's claim through the hostile political environment of the termination era.[26]

The turning point in the Taos Pueblo's long struggle came in the 1960s when the tribe insisted on making its stand on grounds of protecting its religious freedom. Although tribal leaders had never ceased to emphasize that Blue Lake was their people's sacred area and therefore vital to their people's continued well-being, that message had repeatedly failed to impress Washington bureaucrats and politicians. Through the 1950s, tribal leaders worked to convince their own legal counsel that they must insist on the return of Blue Lake; it was imperative to the practice of the tribal religion and therefore vital for the survival of the tribe. Here was an argument that had never been used before in the annals of Indian land claim cases. At last, in the early 1960s, La Farge and the AAIA lawyers on the case came to agree that it was a fight they could win.[27]

In 1965, the AAIA published an eight-page booklet, *The Blue Lake Appeal*, aimed at rallying national public opinion to the Taos Pueblo's cause. At the same time, they launched a letter-writing campaign aimed at Washington lawmakers. Fortuitously, the ICC reached a judgment on the Taos Pueblo's case about the same time, generating more publicity. The ICC found that the U.S. government had illegally extinguished the Taos Indians' aboriginal title in 1906 and had failed to make amends through the Pueblo land claims settlement. It recommended a monetary award, the amount to be determined by a land appraisal. As expected, the Taos Pueblo announced it would not accept a monetary settlement of the claim.[28]

That set the stage for a final showdown on the matter in Congress. In the House, Congressman James Haley of Florida, chairman of the House Subcommittee on Indian Affairs, introduced a bill that would grant nearly fifty thousand acres to the Taos Pueblo. In the Senate, New Mexico's Senator Clinton P. Anderson introduced a similar measure. However, the senator did so "by request," indicating that his bill was pro forma to give the proposal a hearing on behalf of his constituents. Anderson was a Democrat, former secretary of agriculture under President Truman, and staunch friend of the Forest Service. As a powerful member of the Committee on Interior and Insular Affairs, he had no difficulty killing his own bill in committee.[29]

Anderson opposed transferring land from the Carson National Forest to the Taos Indians for three reasons. First, he had friends in the timber and mining industries and believed that the area should remain under multiple-use management by the Forest Service. Second, he thought that to settle an Indian claim by awarding land rather than money would set a bad precedent. Other tribes would demand the same and where would it end? Third, he did not accept the religious basis of the claim. He thought it was a smokescreen. Once the Indians acquired title, they would exploit the land for its resource values. In addition to those arguments, Anderson expected to prevail against the legislation based on the strong tradition in the Senate that no measure affecting a state would be passed over the opposition of a senator from that state. This last factor appeared to be decisive as year after year Congressman Haley would reintroduce the same bill in the House, while Anderson would offer a different version in the Senate that was patently unacceptable to the tribe.[30]

With the bill deadlocked in Congress, the Taos Pueblo took their case to President Nixon. The year was 1970; the Red Power movement had just appeared on the national stage, adding another dissonant sound of protest to the cacophony of radical movements rattling the Nixon administration. Indian militants were grabbing headlines with their occupation of Alcatraz Island in San Francisco Bay and their political theater at the base of Mount Rushmore. Nixon had decided to make a major speech on Indian policy, renouncing termination and embracing self-determination. At this propitious moment some of his close advisers brought the Blue Lake issue to his attention, pointing out that the Taos Indians had a great deal of public sympathy and were in no way connected with the militant groups. One adviser, Leonard Garment, noted that the Blue Lake case "has snowballed and is now the *single* specific Indian issue. . . . A new Indian policy needs a starting point. Blue Lake is just that—strong on the merits, and powerfully symbolic." Nixon decided to endorse the return of Blue Lake to the Taos Indians in his message on Indian affairs.[31]

With the president calling on Congress to pass the legislation, Senator Anderson could no longer prevent it. In December 1970, the Senate passed the House's bill on a vote of 70 to 12.

Ironically, Senator Anderson was on the mark when he argued that the return of Blue Lake to the Indians would be precedent setting. Afterward, many tribes did request land instead of money; some got their way, and others were denied. In 1970, Congress awarded the Yakama Tribe a twenty-one-thousand-acre tract, which was transferred from Gifford Pinchot National Forest to the Yakama Reservation. In 1975, Congress transferred 185,000 acres from Grand Canyon National Park and the Kaibab National Forest to the Havasupai Tribe. In 1988, Congress placed 11,905 acres from the Olympic National Forest in trust for the Quinault Tribe and designated another 5,460 acres on the national forest as a special management area. There were several other instances of land being transferred from the National Forest System to Indian tribes in settlement of land claims.

Sadly, some claim settlements have been held in limbo because the U.S. government insists on a monetary award while the tribe insists on getting the land back. The most famous example involves the Lakota claim to the Black Hills—another area that falls substantially within the National Forest System. In 1979, the U.S. Court of Claims made the largest monetary award in an Indian land claim case ever in *Sioux Indian Nations v. United States* to compensate the Lakota tribes for the illegal taking of the Black Hills in 1877. The Lakota refused the money, insisting that the Black Hills are sacred to them and nothing but the return of the land to tribal ownership will do. Thirty-odd years later the Lakota and the federal government remain at an impasse.[32]

CHAPTER SUMMARY

The termination era was a period of about a decade and a half in U.S. Indian affairs when Congress sought to extinguish the federal Indian trust relationship one tribe at a time. According to the policy, a tribe was ready for "termination" when its members were deemed to be well assimilated in the dominant society and no longer in need of BIA support services. The termination policy rejected the Indian New Deal's aims of tribal self-determination and cultural revitalization. Rather, it strove to complete the program of Indian assimilation that had reached its apogee under the allotment policy.

The termination era was both an end and a beginning. It was supposed to end the federal government's role of trustee and emancipate Indians from their status as wards, and for some tribes it truly did mark an end to the tribe's existence as a political and legal entity. At the same time, many tribes felt threatened and betrayed by the termination policy and fought to have it overturned. The rage that the policy engendered ultimately gave rise to a wave of Indian activism and a recommitment to Indian self-determination.

Two of the most controversial and precedent-setting episodes of the termination era each involved the Forest Service. The first episode concerned the Klamath Tribe in Oregon. The process of terminating the Klamath Tribe was so contentious that Congress lost its appetite for terminating other tribes. Most of the Klamath Tribe's forest was made into the Winema National Forest—the last time in the twentieth century that a tribal forest was converted into a national forest. The second episode involved the Taos Pueblo in New Mexico. The Taos Pueblo refused to accept a cash award for the loss of their sacred Blue Lake on the Carson National Forest, insisting they wanted the land back. The Forest Service fought the claim and ultimately lost. Neither episode endeared the Forest Service to Indian peoples, nor did it inspire much desire on the part of the Forest Service for reaching out to tribes.

6

FORESTERS AND INDIANS IN A TIME OF FERMENT AND RENEWAL

The 1970s

THE FOREST SERVICE BEGINS TO TRANSFORM ITSELF

B Y 1970, THE FOREST SERVICE had become a blend of old and new, tradition and innovation. It still retained much of the character that Gifford Pinchot had given the organization at the beginning of the century. Pinchot believed that the Forest Service's greatest strength was its foundation in scientific forestry. Three generations after Pinchot's time, it remained fundamentally an agency of professional foresters. By the Forest Service's own reckoning, college-educated foresters made up 16 percent of its total permanent workforce and 90 percent of its professional staff. No other land-management agency had an equivalent cadre of coprofessionals. In the National Park Service, for example, the management-track position of park ranger accounted for just 12 percent of full-time employees, and the park ranger profession did not cohere around a core discipline like forestry. Foresters still dominated the Forest Service from top to bottom even as environmentalists brought mounting pressure on the agency to take a more ecological, interdisciplinary approach to land management. The Forest Service leadership still subscribed to that central maxim of the Progressive conservation movement, which held that land-management decisions should rest with appropriate technical experts.[1]

There were also strong echoes of Pinchot and the Progressive era in the Forest Service's midcentury adoption of "multiple use." At the beginning of the twentieth century, Pinchot argued that conservation could be summed up in the phrase, "the greatest good for the greatest number over the long run," and he set out to make the Forest Service the champion of that idea. Pinchot strenuously insisted that national forests were for use. He had to combat the notion that the National Forest System would "lock up" resources and hinder economic development. As national forests were mostly in the West, the young agency depended on the support of Western senators and congressmen to survive. Pinchot won those senators' support by co-opting the opposition—particularly the western livestock growers who were accustomed to grazing cattle and sheep on public domain. Pinchot's Forest Service aimed at supporting local communities whose economies centered on use of the national forests.

Through the first half of the twentieth century, the Forest Service continued to operate in that vein, disarming its opponents by emphasizing use of the national forests for wood production, mining, grazing, and watershed protection as well as sport hunting and fishing and other forms of recreation. After World War II, the Forest Service gradually co-opted its critics in the timber industry by putting many more National Forest System lands to use for industrial forestry. And in the 1950s, amid burgeoning demand for outdoor recreation and mounting complaints by conservationists that logging on the national forests was going too far, it sought to deflect that criticism by giving more emphasis to recreation and wilderness preservation. Thus, even as conflicts between different uses intensified, the Forest Service made a convincing argument that it could successfully balance and even harmonize those conflicts. The capstone of its sales job for "multiple use" was the Multiple-Use Sustained-Yield Act of 1960, which directed the Forest Service to manage the national forests for five major uses (timber, range, water, wildlife, and outdoor recreation) without giving any one use priority. The law was practically a restatement of Pinchot's utilitarian philosophy updated to reflect contemporary demands on the National Forest System.[2]

Alongside those strains of tradition and historical continuity, the Forest Service also showed signs of an impending transformation. As historian Samuel P. Hays has shown so astutely in his history of the agency's first century, *The American People and the National Forests*, turning points in the Forest Service's evolution were never sharp. Shifts in the way the American public valued its national forests guided the Forest Service's evolution, and those shifts transpired across decades.[3] In the decades after World War II, growing public unease over the Forest Service's stepped-up timber program eventually forced the agency to abandon its traditional model of an industrial forest managed for maximum wood production and to accept a new model of land management based on principles of ecology. Public reaction to intensified road building and clear-cutting on the national forests found its sharpest expression in the Wilderness Act of 1964 and the National Forest Management Act of 1976. The Forest Service's transition from industrial to ecological forestry, meanwhile, commenced in the 1960s and finally culminated some thirty years later with its embrace of "ecosystem management."

The Forest Service undertook to transform itself through two main actions: public outreach and diversification of its workforce. Its public outreach initiative began with its new emphasis on land-use planning, which sought to bring the agency into closer dialogue with changing public values. Starting in the 1960s, the Forest Service began to promote land-use planning as a way to build public consensus and head off conflicts between forest users. Congress passed two acts in the mid-1970s that greatly amplified the role of planning in national forest management. The Forest and Rangeland Renewable Resources Planning Act of 1974 called for the Forest Service to develop a plan for sustainable use of forest and range on a national scale, the most robust exercise in long-range planning in its history. The National Forest Management Act (NFMA) of 1976 called for a more fine-grained approach as well, requiring the Forest Service to generate a separate forest plan for all national forests within ten years. While the agency had always prided itself on its outreach to local communities, the new planning process involved an unprecedented level of public input.[4]

As part of the planning effort, the Forest Service devised an administrative appeal process to accommodate public objections to its land-management plans and decisions. The number of lawsuits challenging the Forest Service's actions increased more than tenfold in the decade and a half before NFMA, and the agency wanted to hold down litigation costs by providing an effective mechanism for resolving disputes before they went to court. The administrative appeal process opened the door wide for conservation groups to tussle with national forest administration at the regional and local level. These groups filed hundreds of appeals concerning the draft forest plans, and these proved to be only a fraction of the volume of appeals that they dropped on the agency in subsequent decades. Responding to this bombardment consumed an enormous amount of staff time and resulted in battered morale. It seemed the agency was under siege. Furthermore, many administrative appeal cases ended up in court anyway. Some in the Forest Service came to believe the system was flawed. Others stood by it.[5]

Regardless of the efficacy of the Forest Service's planning and appeals processes, its overall effort to render decision making more open and democratic obviously departed from Progressive era tradition. Pinchot had formed the Forest Service around the precept that good land stewardship rested on placing the public trust in the hands of technical experts. Land managers could operate on their own merits, his thinking went, reconciling public needs and stewarding the natural resources according to their own scientifically informed judgment. As public trust in the U.S. government wilted in the face of the Vietnam War and the Watergate scandals, that old Progressive-era thinking became hopelessly outmoded. The Forest Service had to change with the times; the only question was to what degree.[6]

Around 1970, the Forest Service also began a concerted effort to diversify its workforce. This effort sprang from two different sources and actually involved two separate initiatives though they became, in fact, closely intertwined. One aimed at bringing more diverse expertise into the agency—adding more wildlife biologists, ecologists, hydrologists, and other specialists to the older contingent of foresters, range conservationists, and road engineers. The other initiative focused on hiring women and minorities in support of the federal government's affirmative action program. It is important to understand how the two separate initiatives were related, especially as the latter formed the seedbed for the development of the Forest Service's tribal relations program.

In bringing on board the so-called ologists—ecologists, hydrologists, geologists, archeologists, sociologists—the expectation was that the Forest Service would acquire a more interdisciplinary, holistic, ecological view of the forest. The more immediate justification for recruiting those people, however, came from the National Environmental Policy Act (NEPA) of 1969. NEPA introduced the interdisciplinary environmental impact statement (EIS) into federal land management. The Forest Service needed the ologists to ensure that it complied with the law. By and large, that put the ologists in a somewhat adversarial relationship with the foresters. Since their primary purpose was to advise forest managers about potential adverse effects of timber sales, road construction, and other actions that required compliance with NEPA, they could be viewed as a drag on the agency. The foresters and engineers were seen as the agency's "doers," while the wildlife biologists, ecologists, and archeologists were seen as the "constrainers."[7]

Since the Forest Service was being pounded by lawsuits and administrative appeals, the tension between old and new professional disciplines was fraught. As former chief forester Jack Ward Thomas explains it,

Foresters and engineers thought they worked for the Forest Service. Wildlife biologists and others of the "ologists" persuasion thought they worked for their profession. These professionals didn't have the same level of loyalty to the organization as they did to their profession—which they considered different things. Foresters and engineers, when I came into the agency, were the bosses. They were horrified by the mind-set of the "ologists." The old-line Forest Service guys would talk about the "good of the outfit." Many "ologists" were immune to such attempts at suasion and were more loyal to what they perceived as the tenets of the professions.[8]

The ologists found themselves being marginalized within a bureaucracy that was still broadly oriented to the timber industry. Even as Forest Service leadership sought to broaden the spectrum of biological and social scientists in the workforce, many in the middle and higher echelons of the organization reacted defensively to what, for them, was an unwelcome challenge to the traditional power structure. The ferment within the agency gave rise to such colorful pejoratives as "combat biologists" to describe those wildlife biologists whom foresters found to be unduly obstructionist, and "timber beasts" to describe those forest managers whom the biologists thought were blindly committed to the timber program.

The Forest Service's efforts to hire more women and minorities, meanwhile, started with the passage of the Equal Employment Opportunities Act of 1972, which mandated that the federal government would follow the Equal Employment Opportunity requirements set forth in Title VII of the Civil Rights Act of 1964.[9] At that time the Forest Service was one of the most white-male-dominated agencies in the U.S. government. In trying to diversify its workforce to resemble a cross section of American society, it had a lot of ground to make up. Because there was a dearth of women and minority job applicants coming out of the nation's forestry and engineering schools, efforts to diversify the professional staff were applied with extra vigor in the new discipline areas, particularly wildlife biology. The hiring trend widened the rift between old and new disciplines as one part of the professional staff acquired diversity and the other did not. Women and minority ologists faced off against a white male establishment of foresters and engineers that was widely perceived as old school, clannish, and bigoted. Conflicts in the workplace between "doers" and "constrainers" sometimes took on overtones of being something bigger or shadier. Retribution? Discrimination?

In 1972, Gene C. Bernardi, a research sociologist in the Pacific Southwest Forest and Range Experiment Station in Berkeley, California, sued the government for violating her civil rights. Hired in 1968, Bernardi entered federal employment with a master's degree and three years of professional experience working for the city of Berkeley. Repeatedly thwarted in her efforts to obtain either a promotion or pay raise, she alleged sex discrimination. Her case evolved into a class-action lawsuit on behalf of all women in the U.S. Department of Agriculture. The case was settled after the Forest Service agreed to a consent decree, finalized in 1981, that required the agency to accelerate the advancement of women and minorities into management and line officer positions.[10]

While Bernardi's case was being litigated in the 1970s, the Forest Service established a civil rights branch in the Washington office and mandated that each region adopt an affirmative action plan. Every region appointed a civil rights officer. The purview of the civil rights staff included looking out for the civil rights and interests of the agency's Indian employees, who by this time numbered several hundred men and women and made up about 2 percent of the workforce. Among other responsibilities, the civil rights officers were tasked to increase awareness of all agency personnel to Indian peoples' special relationship with the federal government. Here, springing up from the civil rights movement, was one tendril of the future tribal relations program.

In 1979, the regional forester for the Pacific Northwest Region established a Native American program, the first of its kind in the National Forest System. The program managers were Merle Hofferber, director of lands and minerals, and Bill Green, director of civil rights. What made this program distinct from the Forest Service's other affirmative action programs for women, blacks, and Hispanics was its outreach to tribes. It aimed to involve Indians in every program, benefit, and service that the Forest Service offered—not just employment and contracting opportunities but also access to special uses of the national forests. It sought to build relationships between the Forest Service and tribes for purposes of improving cooperation and coordination on land uses and resources planning as required by the NFMA—and in accordance with the newly enacted American Indian Religious Freedom Act (AIRFA).[11] Similar efforts were soon afoot in other Forest Service regions. In 1987, the agency's Service-wide Civil Rights Committee (SCRC) called on the Forest Service's leaders to take steps to improve understanding of the agency's unique responsibilities to Native American and Alaska Native communities. In an internal white paper, the SCRC stated that the Forest Service lacked clear recognition and definition of its role as a federal trustee for Native peoples, and it proposed that the Forest Service form a "process improvement team" to suggest ways to rectify that deficiency in the organization.[12] Springing from the Forest Service's civil rights program, the SCRC's call to action was likely the first time that anyone proposed anything like an internal, top-down review of Forest Service tribal relations.

Affirmative action provoked a backlash in the Forest Service just as it did elsewhere in American society. Disgruntled white males complained that the agency was trying to meet hiring "quotas" for women and minorities, thereby denying access to well-qualified white male job applicants. The same charge of "reverse discrimination" arose with respect to internal promotions. White male employees complained they were being passed over in the agency's rush to promote women and minorities into higher positions. Some grumbled about the "civil rights mafia." Meanwhile, civil rights staff heard complaints from Indians, women, and minorities of civil rights violations. For example, in the 1987 fire season, Indian and women fire crew members brought numerous complaints of racial and sexual harassment and abuse by their white male fire crew bosses. Chief F. Dale Robertson tasked the agency's SCRC to investigate the reports. Based on their findings, the deputy chief, State and Private Forestry, signed an action plan titled "Fire Model for Work-force Diversity." Robertson commended the plan and called on the Fire and Aviation Management Team, which was tasked with implementing it, to make annual reports on their progress to the SCRC.[13]

In 1988, Robertson renewed the Forest Service's commitment to affirmative action by issuing a statement, "Workforce 1995: Strength Through Diversity," that promised action in the five areas of recruitment, retention, upward movement, organizational culture, and public awareness. It acknowledged that progress from 1979 to 1988 was below target. (Minority employees composed 13 percent of the Forest Service workforce in 1988, whereas they made up 18.4 percent of the national civilian labor force. They held just 7 percent of professional jobs in the Forest Service compared with 12.5 percent of professional jobs nationwide.) Robertson set a goal of increasing the number of minority employees to one-sixth of the workforce by the year 1995.[14]

The premise of affirmative action is that individuals count. They create a synergy with the people around them that leads to social change. Profound change in the social makeup and orientation of a large organization like the Forest Service is not accomplished in a day or even in a year, but maybe in a generation.

Robertson saw that recruiting and promoting minorities in the Forest Service's lower echelons in the 1980s would help facilitate organizational change some ten, twenty, or thirty years later.[15] To take one example, Dan Meza, an O'odham, began working for the Forest Service as a seasonal firefighter in the 1970s and soon earned his way to a full-time engineering position on the Modoc National Forest in Northern California. There, in the 1980s, the forest supervisor began to assign Meza collateral duties in the civil rights arena in what was called the American Indian special emphasis program. Meza's specific responsibilities were in three areas: outreach to Indian communities, recruitment and retention of Indian employees, and cultural awareness training for Forest Service personnel. Over the next decade, Meza's collateral duties expanded more and more to working with Indian communities and tribal governments. In 2008, he took charge of the tribal relations program for the Southwestern Region, where eleven national forests work in partnership with fifty-five tribes. Meza's career illustrates how the civil rights movement and affirmative action formed one important strand in the evolution of Forest Service–tribal relations in the late twentieth century.[16]

THE RISE OF RED POWER

American Indians and Alaska Natives joined in the civil rights struggles of the 1960s, but with a difference. Their demands for better treatment usually centered on treaty rights or, if not actual treaty rights, their special concerns as indigenous people. In relation to the Forest Service, Native demands mostly had to do with resource use or resource protection. Most importantly, American Indians and Alaska Natives were at pains to remind everyone that they were not like other minorities who were demanding *equal* rights under the U.S. Constitution; rather, they were demanding recognition of their *special* rights under the federal Indian trust doctrine. Still, Indian activists identified with the civil rights goals of other minority groups. They drew inspiration from the black civil rights movement in particular, emulating its tactics of civil disobedience, confrontation, mass demonstrations, and use of the national media.

One of Native America's first civil rights actions took place in remote Barrow, Alaska. The Inupiat Eskimos who inhabit Alaska's Arctic coastline had long maintained the privilege to hunt and fish for their subsistence without federal regulation. In the 1950s, the U.S. Fish and Wildlife Service decided to challenge their privilege, and many Eskimos chose to flout the law rather than submit to regulation. In 1961, the issue came to a head when federal wardens booked two Inupiat men in Barrow on charges of possessing ducks in violation of the Migratory Bird Treaty Act. On the morning after the arrests, 138 Barrow Inupiats appeared outside the wardens' hotel, each one with a dead duck in hand, demanding his or her own arrest as well. This act of civil disobedience galvanized Eskimos across Alaska. It led to a meeting of Eskimo village leaders in Barrow four months later at which they requested that the government set aside most of the North Slope as an Eskimo hunting preserve. The show of unity formed an important precedent. In 1966, regional Native associations from all over Alaska came together to form the Alaska Federation of Natives to pursue a statewide Native land claim.[17]

Another important civil rights action by Native Americans occurred in the Pacific Northwest. In western Washington, Nisqually and Puyallup fishermen defied Washington state law to defend their tribes' 1854 treaty right to fish in common with non-Indians at all their accustomed places. At Frank's Landing on Puget Sound, they used nets in violation of state regulations. Courting publicity over the state's disregard of their treaty right, the Nisqually Tribe invited student activists in the National Indian Youth Council to join the fishermen protesters. When actor Marlon Brando came to the fishermen's support as well, the Puget Sound tribes succeeded in drawing the national media attention they were after. The media dubbed the protests "fish-ins," a clever wordplay on the student sit-ins that were then occurring on college campuses. By the late 1960s, the tribes had garnered enough support to bring a lawsuit against the state of Washington.[18]

In Minneapolis, Minnesota, where a large, urban, Indian community faced bitter poverty and discrimination in a ghetto known as "the reservation," a group of young militants formed the American Indian Movement (AIM) in 1968. One of AIM's first actions was to organize a "red patrol" in the ghetto for the purpose of protecting vagrants from acts of police brutality. AIM soon attracted Indian dissidents from various tribes and localities. As the organization grew, it forged a vision of Indian cultural revival and revolutionary action that was not specific to any single community, tribe, or treaty, but rather was self-consciously pan-Indian.

AIM was still focused on the ghetto in Minneapolis when a group of eighty-nine Indian activists from the San Francisco Bay area occupied Alcatraz Island on November 20, 1969. The group issued a proclamation listing several desired uses for the small island: a center for Native American studies to educate young Indian people about their history and culture, a Native American spiritual center for teaching them traditional medicine and religion, a Native American ecology center for training them in resource management, and the establishment of a Native American museum using existing buildings. The federal prison facility that dominates Alcatraz had been abandoned since 1963. Indian activists had been eyeing the island for several years and had made two previous landings. In an earlier action, the occupiers had made a far-fetched claim of ownership to the place under a provision of the 1868 Sioux treaty allowing Indians to take possession of abandoned federal lands. This time the group claimed Indian sovereignty over the island by right of discovery. That was not all that the group inverted for dramatic effect: it addressed itself "To the Great White Father and All His People" and promised to set up a Bureau of Caucasian Affairs.[19]

The Nixon administration treaded lightly, for the occupiers quickly gained sympathetic media coverage. Several famous actors and actresses went to the island with camera crews in tow to show their support for the activists. Although White House officials expressed interest in hearing the activists' demands, they also pointed out that the government had no legal basis on which to negotiate a land claim because the "Indians of All Tribes" entity was not a federally recognized tribe. Rather, officials requested that Indians in the Bay Area form a group that could negotiate on their behalf. When local Indians duly came together and formed the Bay Area Native American Council, the Nixon administration offered the group a $50,000 planning grant to study the Indian cultural center proposal. The gesture, however, failed to end the occupation of Alcatraz.[20]

The activists held the island for more than a year and a half. An organizational council assigned everyone jobs in security, sanitation, day care, schooling, cooking, and laundry. All decisions by the council were made by unanimous consent. But as the occupation lengthened, increasing turnover wore down the occupiers' morale. Richard Oakes, a Mohawk who became the group's leading spokesperson at the outset, departed early in 1970 after suffering personal tragedy when his young daughter fell to her death off a prison wall. Good self-governance gradually disintegrated into anarchy. Finally, media interest faded, and the activists' numbers dwindled away. In June 1971, White House aides decided the time had come to call in the federal marshals. The handful of activists who were still on the island submitted without a fight.[21]

FIGURE 16. Indian occupiers moments after their removal from
Alcatraz Island, June 11, 1971. *Left*, Oohosis, a Cree from Canada.
Right, Peggy Lee Ellenwood, a Sioux from Wolf Point, Montana.

PHOTO © ILKA HARTMANN, 2016

The Alcatraz occupation was still in its glory days when activists in the Pit
River Tribe decided to stage a similar takeover on public land in Northern California. Their grievance lay in the fact that the tribe sought a return of lands
taken in the 1850s. In a 1964 judgment, the Indian Claims Commission had
awarded the Northern California tribes money instead of land. Since then, the
Pit River Tribe had refused its share of the government's $29.1 million settle-
ment offer, holding to its claim of 3.5 million acres. In the spring of 1970, tribal
chairman Mickey Grimmell met with some of the organizers of the Alcatraz
occupation to discuss a protest demonstration. They formed a plan to occupy
a popular campground in Lassen Volcanic National Park just as it was set to
open for the summer season. As things worked out, however, the demonstrators altered their plan, taking their stand on the nearby Shasta National Forest

instead. The episode involved the Forest Service in its most significant confrontation with Indian activists in the era.[22]

Historian Sherry L. Smith, in her recent study of the Red Power movement, finds the differences between the Alcatraz occupation and the Pit River Indians' action instructive. "Indian activists who demonstrated in rural areas and who challenged the federal government's and/or corporations' use of federal lands that were not deemed 'surplus' faced a much more difficult climate and challenge. The odds, in fact, proved overwhelmingly against them."[23] The Pit River Indians of Northern California were too far removed from major media markets to get their story heard around the country, and they did not elicit much support from the local, non-Indian population. As a result, law enforcement came down hard on them.

On June 6, 1970, about two hundred Pit River Indians, including men, women, and children, arrived at the entrance gate to Lassen Volcanic National Park only to find their way barred by the superintendent and a line of U.S. marshals in riot gear. Evidently the Park Service had received a tip and was expecting them. Superintendent William Boyer denied the Indians admittance, commenting sympathetically, "You are a luckless people." Grimmell and the other organizers then improvised a plan B, leading the demonstrators to another campground owned by Pacific Gas and Electric (PG&E) located about eight miles away. Superintendent Boyer, concerned that they might return, took the precaution of postponing the opening of the park's north entrance until the following weekend.[24]

At the PG&E property, the activists were joined by Richard Oakes from Alcatraz together with some thirty hippies from a community called the Hog Farm. Grimmell made a speech in which he denounced the termination policy, reiterated the tribe's refusal of the Indian Claims Commission settlement, and demanded the return of the tribe's homeland. He also wanted reparations for all the damage and destruction done to the tribe and its land since the 1850s, and he called for a new birth of freedom for Indian culture and religion.[25]

A few days later, a strong force of Shasta County deputies and police officers went to the PG&E campground and ordered the Indians to leave. If they refused, the officers of the law warned, then they would be placed under arrest and charged with trespass at the request of PG&E. The Indians retorted that they would then bring suit against PG&E executives for trespassing on tribal land. Most of the Indians dispersed; a few were taken into custody. The next day about fifty activists returned to the campground. Law enforcement came back, too. Once more, most of the Indians left while a handful refused and got themselves arrested. After the second lot of demonstrators was booked, PG&E gave the order to drop all charges.[26]

Later that summer the group reassembled. This time the activists occupied vacant land on the Shasta National Forest near the intersection of two highways at a site called the Four Corners. Unlike PG&E, the Forest Service did not immediately move to disperse them. By fall, the group had established all-season living quarters in a Quonset hut and was preparing for a long occupation. By one newspaper reporter's estimate, they numbered about one hundred people. Someone decided—it is not known whether the decision originated in the Forest Service or from some other quarter outside the agency—that the Indians must now be evicted from the Four Corners camp. Regardless of who gave that order, what is clear is that Forest Service officials had to take responsibility for it, since the Indians were illegally camped on Forest Service land. Warrants were prepared charging the Indians with illegal timber cutting and insisting that they remove the Quonset hut. Fifty or more rangers were assembled for the impending law-enforcement action.[27]

On October 27, 1970, a combined force of Forest Service and Park Service rangers, federal marshals, and state troopers arrived at the camp and announced that the Indian activists must abandon the site. By one account, a spokesperson for the Indians said they would "have to be killed" first if the law officers expected to tear down their Quonset hut. According to park superintendent Boyer, who was there with three of his park rangers, the negotiations reached an impasse and the situation became very tense, with one activist displaying a gun and saying that someone would likely get shot. Suddenly all the officers went into action, using mace and billy clubs to subdue all the activists. Boyer himself disabled a number of individuals with mace. According to a newspaper reporter's account, the Indians fought back with bare fists, tree limbs, and planks of lumber. Indian women joined in the fighting. When it was all over a few people had sustained significant injuries and more than two dozen activists were under arrest.[28]

Considered up close, it would seem that when forest rangers and Indian activists engaged in a melee, then Forest Service–tribal relations had reached a point of complete dysfunction. But taking a longer view, the violent confrontation that occurred at the Four Corners on October 27, 1970, can be seen as the moment when the Forest Service became directly engaged in the civil rights struggles of the 1960s and 1970s. Indian activists' quest for Red Power was, at base, a campaign to reeducate the dominant society about Native America. Part of the Forest Service's process of transformation in the 1970s was to take a step back from the European form of scientific forestry and open itself to a range of new perspectives, including indigenous ones. It was an opening that Indian peoples would use to increasing advantage as tribes recovered some of their former authority over stewardship of natural resources in coming years.

The Red Power movement achieved few concrete victories. In terms of getting demands met, the occupations at Alcatraz and the Four Corners both ended in debacle. As consciousness-raising endeavors, it is much harder to measure their success. Undoubtedly, the Red Power movement's greatest success unfolded in the Pacific Northwest, where, as a result of the fish-ins, the U.S. Justice Department eventually brought suit on behalf of tribes in *U.S. v. Washington*. In 1974, Judge George Boldt gave the dominant society a huge jolt when he decided in favor of the tribes, interpreting the 1854 treaty language that protected the Indians' right to fish "in common" as meaning that the tribes were entitled to 50 percent of harvestable fish. As the volatile case went through a series of appeals, federal and state authorities wrangled over how the 50/50 allocation would be implemented. In 1979, the Supreme Court upheld the Boldt decision, forcing the state to accept tribes as comanagers of the fisheries. It was the single biggest gain on the tribes' long road back to sovereign control of their food sources.[29]

THE REBIRTH OF TRIBAL GOVERNMENTS

The strong commitment of modern tribal governments to natural resource management is rooted deep in the past. As one long-time biologist in tribal government remarked, "Native Americans have been directly dependent upon the well-being of fish and wildlife on their homelands since time immemorial. Their lives, movements, material needs, spirituality, and cultures have been, and continue to be, closely interwoven with the animals with which they share the land."[30] Whether the subject is fish, wildlife, water, or trees, these natural resources continue to lie at the base of virtually every tribe's economic, cultural, and spiritual existence. Even where tribal economies are now substantially integrated into the economy of the dominant society, tribal members often prize a job that is based outdoors and focused on resource management more than any other job on the reservation.[31]

Until as recently as the 1960s, policy makers did not think tribes were competent to manage Indian-owned natural resources held in trust by the United States. Under the policy of Indian self-determination, the U.S. government adopted laws and policies aimed at helping tribal governments take over programs administered by the BIA, including natural resource management. Both President Johnson's Great Society and President Nixon's strong support for Indian self-determination were instrumental in laying a foundation for the modern era of tribal self-governance.

The real cornerstone for building stronger tribal government was put in place with the passage of Public Law 638, the Indian Self-Determination and Education Assistance Act of 1975. Through a mechanism known as a 638 contract, a tribal government can assume responsibility for any program or service provided by the Department of the Interior. Federal funding for the program or service then goes to the tribe instead. "With regard to natural resource management," wrote the former technical services director of the Native American Fish and Wildlife Society, Patrick Durham, "this was a true turn-around point for tribes."[32]

The 638 contract provided a means for tribes to hire their own professional staffs and develop their own natural resource management programs. Before the 1975 law, tribal governments had to submit a prioritized list of programs to the BIA for potential funding. Only a limited number were approved. Given those constraints, natural resource programs took a back seat to social programs such as health care and housing assistance. As Durham has pointed out, "It was not a difficult decision for a tribal council to place medical care above a stream bank stabilization program or to let a Pacific lamprey eel restoration project be overshadowed by another program which supplied heating oil to the elderly during the winter months. With limited funding, it was a foregone conclusion that only the 'most important' initiatives would be fiscally addressed and through this imperfect system, this is exactly what occurred."[33] With the help of 638 contracting, tribal governments were enabled to invest in programs that not only met basic necessities but also spoke to the tribe's natural and cultural heritage. In a dozen years, tribal governments garnered more than a thousand 638 contracts nationwide. A considerable number of those involved various aspects of natural resource management. Tribal governments thereby acquired management authority over a substantial portion of Indian-owned lands that the Department of the Interior still held in trust.[34]

There were lingering problems with the 638 contracting mechanism. The accounting procedures for transferring federal dollars to the tribal governments

were so bound up in red tape that some tribes were discouraged from applying for them. Even after 638 contracts became operational, they were plagued
by charges of mismanagement, waste, and fraud. In 1987, the *Arizona Republic*
carried a series of articles on "Fraud in Indian Country," spotlighting some of
the problems. Congress held oversight hearings, which led to enactment of the
Indian Self-Determination Amendments of 1988. Title II of the act aimed to
expedite the process by which tribes could become self-governing. It called on
the secretary of the interior to name a handful of "Demonstration Tribes" to be
in the vanguard of this process. The law was further amended in 1994, introducing the "638 compact" for tribal self-governance.[35]

   While the Indian Self-Determination Act provided the legal underpinnings
for a rebirth of tribal self-governance in the last quarter of the twentieth century, each tribe's path to self-determination was unique. Often a tribe's political
development was influenced by the emergence of a new source of tribal revenue. Money mattered. Many tribes still lacked the financial resources to become
self-governing. Generally, the money that a tribe pulled in through a 638 contract was not sufficient to run a program. Tribal coffers had to supplement it.

   The relatively prosperous Confederated Salish and Kootenai Tribes (CSKT)
in western Montana were among the first tribes to take back control of their
natural environment. Their 1.3-million-acre Flathead Reservation includes
the southern end of the fertile Flathead-Mission Valley as well as the stun-
ning, precipitous western face of the Mission Mountains. In the early 1970s,
the tribal council passed ordinances asserting the tribes' right to exclude non-
Indians from hunting and fishing on the reservation and requiring that
non-Indians purchase and carry a recreation permit when on Indian lands. In
1979, the Salish and Kootenai established the 89,500-acre Mission Mountains
Tribal Wilderness. They sued the state for control of the southern portion of
Flathead Lake lying within the reservation and won. In 1982, they adopted the
most stringent air-quality standards, Class I, enforceable under the Clean Air
Act. In 1984, they declared their reservation a nuclear-free zone, barring all
shipment of radioactive materials into or across it.[36]

   The CSKT's drive for self-governance and greater environmental protection
gathered momentum in the latter half of the 1980s. A crucial step came in 1985
when the tribes negotiated a deal with the Montana Power Company for joint
operation of Kerr Dam, located at the outlet of Flathead Lake. Since the 1930s,
the tribes had received a modest income on the lease for the dam site. Now
they obtained $9 million in annual rent with an option to buy the dam after

FIGURE 17. View of Mission Mountains, Flathead Reservation, Montana

PHOTO BY JAIX CHAIX. COURTESY OF CREATIVE COMMONS

thirty more years. The new income was three times what the CSKT had been earning from timber sales, and the material increase in dam revenue came just as logging operations on the Flathead Reservation fell off sharply. The money from Kerr Dam helped immensely as the CSKT sought to take over more federal programs on the reservation. In 1988, they were selected to be among the demonstration tribes for testing the functionality of the revamped 638 contracting mechanism. Over the next few years, the CSKT assumed control over dozens of federal programs on the reservation. In 1995, they contracted with the BIA to take over the forestry program.[37]

In Arizona, the White Mountain Apache Tribe took a different path to self-determination. Under the leadership of its long-serving tribal chairman, Ronnie Lupe, the tribe sought to win control of the most important economic resource on the Fort Apache Reservation: the tribal forest. The quest began in 1964 with the establishment of a tribal sawmill operation, the Fort Apache Timber Company. Until then, timber operations on the reservation were dominated by Southwest Forest Industries, which paid the tribe for stumpage but did its milling elsewhere. The tribal enterprise added value to the resource by producing the milled lumber on the reservation, and in addition it provided good jobs and business management training for hundreds of tribal members. Once the tribal enterprise was secure, the tribe insisted that the BIA end its relationship with Southwest Forest Industries.[38]

But there was more to this story than earnings and jobs. The tribe also wanted to conserve its forest. Alarmed at the rate of cutting under BIA forest management, the tribe sued to get the harvest level reduced. It argued that the BIA's timber sales to Southwest Forest Industries were far in excess of sustained-yield management, and moreover, that the BIA's forest management did not respect the tribe's cultural and spiritual values associated with the land. Indeed, the tribal council believed the BIA had other, entirely nontribal interests in view; it found evidence that clear-cutting on the reservation was aimed in part at enhancing stream runoff for the benefit of downstream water users in the Salt River Project (the municipal water supply for Phoenix). As legal scholar Charles Wilkinson has stated, "The White Mountain Apache forests were caught up in the same mid-1960s dynamic that afflicted the Hopi's Black Mesa coal, the Tuscarora's Allegheny River, and many other tribal lands and waters: Heed the calls of the growing cities, develop the reservations, and to hell with the Indians."[39] In *White Mountain Apache Tribe v. Bracker* (1980), the court found that Southwest Forest Industries had severely overcut the tribe's forest and that the BIA had mismanaged the resource. After the court's decision, timber production on the Fort Apache Reservation was lowered from 90 million to 80 million board feet per year in 1981 and was further reduced to 68 million board feet by the early 1990s.[40]

Meanwhile, the tribe exercised its newfound sovereignty over the reservation's natural resources by turning to alternative sources of income. A new ski resort earned between $10 million and $15 million annually, other outdoor recreation services pulled in another $1.5 million, and grazing leases netted a further $5 million. By reducing its dependence on timber production, the tribe expected to conserve the forest in a way that better protected traditional values. To manage conflicts between forest uses, a Tribal Forestry Committee was charged with presenting a timber sale plan to tribal members on a yearly basis. If members could not reach a consensus about that year's plan, then it was referred to a five-person team composed of the chair of the forestry committee, the tribal forester, the forest manager, a wildlife biologist, and one member from the tribal council. The timber sale plan together with the team's recommendations were then put to the Tribal Council for a final decision.[41]

Tribal governments had to build their natural resource management programs from the ground up. The Quinault Tribe in western Washington launched its forestry program in the late 1970s by hiring a trio of PhDs in science from outside the tribe and giving them office space in a single-wide trailer. The CSKT hired their first full-time wildlife biologist in 1977, perhaps the first in that profession to be employed by a tribal government in all of Indian Country. The Nez Perce Tribe recruited its first three fisheries biologists in 1981. Typically, tribal governments had to hire outside the tribe to staff their natural resource departments, for in those years very few tribal members had the necessary professional training. But that began to change as tribal colleges established natural resource degree programs and state universities attracted more Indian students. A 1994 survey of tribal governments in the Pacific Northwest pointed to the growing opportunity for Indians with college degrees to find professional work in natural resources management on the reservation. By then, many of the tribes' natural resource departments already employed sizeable staffs: 110 on the Flathead Reservation, 31 on the Blackfeet Reservation, 74 on the Nez Perce Reservation, and 226 on the Colville Reservation.[42]

As tribal governments steadily built capacity in natural resource management in the 1970s and 1980s, they had to elbow their way to the table with state and federal land managers who were unaccustomed to working with them. State officials, in particular, were reluctant to share power with tribes, for state governments had long resisted the principle of tribal sovereignty because they considered it an affront to states' rights. More specifically, tribes' off-reservation hunting and fishing rights created a tangle of legal questions surrounding the doctrine of state ownership of fish and game. Nowhere was the tension between tribal and state governments more pronounced than in the Pacific Northwest, where the Boldt decision on treaty fishing rights led to the conclusion that numerous tribes and the state must comanage the resource. Within a few years of the 1974 Boldt decision, similar case law emerged concerning the treaty fishing and hunting rights of tribes in Michigan, Wisconsin, and Minnesota. (Many of the treaties made with tribes in those states dated from the same 1854–1855 period and carried very similar language concerning reserved hunting and fishing rights on ceded lands.) As the treaty rights clashed with state control over fish and wildlife, those states' natural resource departments refused to work with tribes until ordered to do so by the courts.[43]

Federal land managers hesitated to work with tribal governments, too, although for different reasons. They knew that most Indian lands were held in trust by the U.S. government, and they were used to thinking that the BIA was in charge of all natural resource matters involving Indian lands or treaty rights. For years, Forest Service officials assumed that their agency, being located in the Department of Agriculture, was one step further removed from the federal-Indian trust relationship than its sister land-management agencies in the Department of the Interior. Even as that notion became outmoded by the restoration of tribal sovereignty under the policy of Indian self-determination, those old habits of thought died hard. "'Isn't that a BIA thing?' is still heard occasionally," Patrick Durham observed in 1999 from his post as director of the Native American Fish and Wildlife Society, "although recent years have seen a dramatic increase in awareness of just exactly what the federal government's trust responsibility is."[44]

Tribes soon learned that if they were to gain an effective role in natural resource management, they must combine with other tribes and present a united front on issues of regional interest. The strategy was an outgrowth of Indian claims cases in which tribes often combined with one another to share litigation costs. One of the first new intertribal organizations was the Northwest Indian Fisheries Commission (NWIFC), which formed in 1975 in the wake of the Boldt decision. Representing twenty-three tribes, the NWIFC formed a platform for small tribes to pool their resources, hire fisheries biologists, and speak with one voice. In time, the commission operated hatcheries and laboratories where several dozen scientists conducted cutting-edge research. As mandated by the court, tribal and NWIFC personnel coordinated fish rearing, harvesting, and management with their counterparts in state government. They also worked with federal personnel on salmon habitat restoration projects on the national forests.[45]

Emulating the success of western Washington tribes, the Yakama, Umatilla, Nez Perce, and Warm Springs tribes formed a parallel organization in 1977 called the Columbia River Inter-Tribal Fish Commission. They were followed within a few years by the Michigan treaty tribes, who formed the Chippewa/Ottawa Treaty Fishery Management Authority, and the Chippewa bands in Minnesota, Wisconsin, and Michigan, who founded the Great Lakes Indian Fish and Wildlife Commission. All of these intertribal organizations carried out similar programs of research, policy analysis, and comanagement with state agencies.[46]

Four southeastern tribes came together in 1968 under the banner of "Strength in Unity" to promote tribal self-governance and Indian involvement at all levels of Indian affairs. Known as the United South and Eastern Tribes, the intertribal council grew to include twenty-six federally recognized tribes from Florida to Texas to Maine. Since 1975, it has been based in Nashville, Tennessee.[47]

Intertribal organizations took other forms besides regional consortiums. The Native American Rights Fund (NARF) was established so that tribes nationwide could obtain better representation in legal affairs. Founded in 1970, the nonprofit law firm was dedicated to the defense of Indian rights and tribal existence. Attorneys for NARF assisted in the lawsuits leading to the Boldt decision. Like other intertribal organizations, NARF took advantage of new networking possibilities arising from the computer age. It developed a national Indian law library that tribal attorneys could access via the Internet.

The Native American Fish and Wildlife Society was another organization that reflected the advancement of natural resource management on Indian reservations. Incorporated in 1983, its primary purpose was to bring together wildlife professionals working in Indian Country. Its membership was made up of BIA and tribally employed wildlife managers, technicians, and law enforcement officers from both tribal and nontribal backgrounds. Its mission was to assist tribes "to enhance, preserve, and promote the wise use of natural resources on tribal lands while keeping tribal interests in mind."[48]

In 1976, a number of timber-producing tribes formed the Intertribal Timber Council (ITC). A nonprofit consortium composed of tribes, Alaska Native corporations, and individuals, the ITC sought to facilitate cooperation between tribes, the BIA, and others interested in the management of Indian forests. With its headquarters located in Portland, Oregon, the ITC became a strong link between tribes and the Forest Service. It also became an effective advocate for tribes when Indian forest management issues came before Congress. When it was not facilitating and advocating for tribes in Washington, the ITC focused its efforts on the development of tribal forest industries, the support of Indian education in the natural resource professions, and the promotion of tribal values and perspectives in BIA forest management.[49]

The decade of the 1970s saw a sea change occur both in the Forest Service's organizational culture and in tribes and tribal governments. The Forest Service emerged from this era firmly committed to diversifying its workforce and to serving a more culturally diverse public. The two objectives, one internal and the other external, were in fact intertwined. Tribes, for their part, came out of the decade of the 1970s with a powerful new impetus to exert their tribal sovereignty in the natural resource management arena. When tribes demanded a role in natural resource stewardship, they not only addressed each tribe's desire for economic development and food security, they also spoke to each tribe's ancient connection to the land. Tribes' insistence on acquiring a greater voice in environmental affairs was tied fundamentally to their quest for cultural revitalization.

CHAPTER SUMMARY

The decade of the 1970s saw a dramatic change in the whole context of Forest Service tribal relations. On one side of the relationship, tribal governments acquired greater capacity and began to assert tribal interests in tribes' ancestral lands in ways that had not been possible before. On the other side of the relationship, the Forest Service's changing organizational culture made the agency more sensitive to tribal concerns as well as more receptive to Indians' different perspectives. Indian self-determination policy encouraged more dialogue between tribal governments and all federal land-managing agencies, not just the Forest Service. New environmental laws called for more dialogue.

The change in context owed much to the social ferment of the civil rights era. Indian activism drew some of its energy from the civil rights movement. Organizational change in the Forest Service got some of its steam from the overall push in American society to embrace cultural diversity. Affirmative action programs that were developed within the Forest Service for the benefit of Indian employees actually formed the seedbed for some of the Forest Service's earliest efforts to reach out to tribal communities and partner with tribal governments.

Yet American Indian and Alaska Native activists were quick to point out that their concerns were fundamentally different from the concerns of other minority groups because they were based on the special relationship that existed between them and the U.S. government. And their concerns were generally place centered, emanating from each tribe's cultural affiliation with its homeland.

7

BURIAL GROUNDS AND
RELIGIOUS FREEDOMS

The 1980s

THE EMERGENCE OF CULTURAL RESOURCE
MANAGEMENT IN THE FOREST SERVICE

T HE UNIFORMED RANGER is an icon of the National Forest System. The ranger is the boss on his or her district, and as the title "ranger" signifies, there is an expectation that nothing significant occurs on the district without the ranger learning about it. The ranger occupies the ground level of a paramilitary organization formed around line officers who are tiered in a clear chain of command. The chain of command starts with the chief and descends to the regional forester, then to the forest supervisor (the head official on each national forest), and finally to the district ranger. Until recently each line officer carried law-enforcement authority as well as administrative responsibility. (Now the law enforcement officer function is stovepiped directly from the field to a directorate in the Office of the Chief of the Forest Service.) The line officer's decision making is guided by an array of laws, regulations, and manuals, and when a situation arises where no clear guidance can be obtained from those, then the line officer must exercise his or her own best judgment unless the decision is directed from above.

The Forest Service's top-down command structure notwithstanding, it is a highly decentralized agency. Line officers at every level of the organization are given wide latitude to respond to local conditions. There is a strong institutional

FIGURE 18. Regional Forester Major Evan Kelly and Ranger
Clyde Fickes, ca. 1930. The modern forest ranger job is rooted
in a proud tradition of ranging the district on horseback.

COURTESY OF ARCHIVES AND SPECIAL COLLECTIONS,
MANSFIELD LIBRARY, UNIVERSITY OF MONTANA

bent toward working with local communities on and around the national forests. As a result, policies and procedures often develop at the forest supervisor
or district ranger level and percolate up through the organizational structure
rather than coming down from the top.

The Forest Service's initial efforts to institutionalize its relations with tribes
represented just such a decentralized, bottom-up formulation of policy. In
the 1960s and 1970s, line officers began choosing to deal with tribes primarily through their staff archaeologists. That choice reflected the Forest Service's
efforts to build a more professionally diverse staff and approach national forest
management in a more holistic, interdisciplinary fashion. Line officers assumed
that archaeologists (or in some cases, cultural anthropologists) were the best-
trained people to undertake tribal consultation. They assumed that tribes'

interests on the national forests were primarily of a cultural nature, more or less distinct from natural resource management.

Four laws mandate that the Forest Service shall consult with tribes on cultural resource matters. These laws are the National Historic Preservation Act (NHPA), the Archaeological Resources Protection Act (ARPA), the American Indian Religious Freedom Act (AIRFA), and the Native American Graves Protection and Repatriation Act (NAGPRA). The first one, the NHPA, was enacted in 1966. The Forest Service hired its first archeologist in 1967, and by the early 1980s it had professional archeologists or anthropologists on about half the national forests and a lead anthropologist in every region. The work of applied archeology and historic preservation on federal lands soon became known as cultural resource management, or CRM. Within the Forest Service, it was often called heritage management. Since the archeology and anthropology professions had a long history of working with Native American cultures, it is not surprising that the Forest Service turned initially to its archeologists and anthropologists to serve as tribal liaisons. For a period of about twenty years—from the late 1960s to the late 1980s—heritage or CRM programs were the principal arena of Forest Service tribal relations.[1]

Archaeology and tribal outreach were far from being a perfect match, however. While the archaeology profession may have been intrinsically curious and sympathetic toward Indians, it was also exploitative. In fact, the history of archaeology and anthropology in the United States is fairly entwined with the government's historic and now much maligned Indian assimilation policy. Historically, Indians often experienced the anthropologist as yet another emissary from the dominant culture betokening the white man's implacable opposition to their way of life. The Lakota writer Vine Deloria Jr. wrote caustically of anthropologists in his 1969 manifesto, *Custer Died for Your Sins*: "Indians have been cursed above all other people in history. Indians have anthropologists. . . . The fundamental thesis of the anthropologist is that people are objects for observation, people are then considered objects for experimentation, for manipulation, and for eventual extinction."[2]

Two modern CRM practitioners, Darby C. Stapp and Michael S. Burney, have provided a scholarly narrative of the long-running, problematic relationship between archaeologists, anthropologists, and Indian peoples in their book, *Tribal Cultural Resource Management: The Full Circle of Stewardship* (2002). They point out that the relationship between archaeologists and Indians in the 1970s was better than in earlier times, but it still carried a lot of baggage from the past.[3]

FIGURE 19. Major John Wesley Powell (1834–1902).
Veteran of the Civil War, explorer of the Colorado
River, and second director of the U.S. Geological Survey,
he served as first director of the Bureau of Ethnology.

PHOTO BY WELLS SAWYER. COURTESY OF
SMITHSONIAN INSTITUTION.

The origins of cultural resource management in the federal government actually can be traced back to the late nineteenth century, when archaeology and anthropology emerged as closely allied professional fields of study. The federal government became directly involved with the two academic professions through the founding of the Bureau of Ethnology in 1879 (renamed the Bureau of American Ethnology in 1894). Located in the Smithsonian Institution, the bureau employed a staff of ethnologists and archaeologists who conducted fieldwork among Indian tribes and at archaeological sites across the nation. They were collectors of artifacts as well as ethnographic information. In the name of science, they excavated Indian sacred sites and exhumed human remains, and without consideration of the Indians' point of view, the backrooms and cellars of the Smithsonian Institution became the new resting place for literally thousands of human skeletons or skulls.[4]

By the first decade of the twentieth century, professional archaeologists (most of whom were located in universities, not the federal government) were warning the public that many archaeological sites were being looted and destroyed by pothunters and vandals. They wanted a federal law to provide government protection of those cultural resources. The result was the American Antiquities Act of 1906, which authorized the president to set aside areas of the public lands as national monuments for the protection of historic and scientific objects. A few national monuments, such as Big Hole National Monument in Montana (established in 1910) came under Forest Service administration, and early Forest Service manuals actually addressed how those areas were to be protected. In 1933, all national monuments under Forest Service administration were transferred to the National Park Service (NPS).[5]

The Historic Sites Act of 1935 led to further federal involvement in historic preservation. The law declared that it was "national policy to preserve for public use historic sites, buildings, and objects of national significance for the inspiration and benefit of the people of the United States." It vested authority in the secretary of the interior, through the NPS, "to locate sites, conduct research, preserve data, and acquire property by condemnation or otherwise." The act influenced the later development of CRM in the Forest Service inasmuch as it established the NPS as the lead agency in this arena. It set up the Advisory Board on National Parks, Historic Sites, Buildings, and Monuments under NPS direction.[6]

With the passage of the National Historic Preservation Act of 1966, cultural resource management finally came into its own as a professional discipline centered in the federal government. The NHPA created the National Register of Historic Places (again, under NPS auspices) and mandated a system for evaluating and listing historic properties. As the law was first enacted, its Section 106 required federal agencies to consult with a State Historic Preservation Officer on any undertaking that would adversely affect cultural resources. The act was amended in 1992 to require federal agencies to consult with tribes as well as states.[7]

Evan DeBloois was among the early CRM practitioners in the Forest Service. Hired in 1970 to initiate an archaeology program for the Intermountain Region, DeBloois recalls that he began with an "academic" focus by setting out to identify important archaeological resources and develop a program to protect, preserve, and interpret them. Section 106 of the NHPA had not yet been translated into regulations, and federal undertakings with potential effects on cultural resources did not yet determine priorities. "We focused on the biggest and the best," DeBloois later recalled, "inventoried areas where we expected to find lots of sites, and developed research driven projects that were designed to generate scientific data about prehistoric resources."[8]

DeBloois had to change his approach after President Nixon issued Executive Order 11593 in 1971, which directed federal land-managing agencies to inventory historic and cultural resources on their lands and determine their eligibility for listing on the National Register. The expansive inventory process mostly hinged on Section 106 compliance—surveying in the path of bulldozers. Project-driven cultural resource surveys were often linear (e.g., following the course of a proposed road) and more or less scattershot from the standpoint of locating prehistoric artifacts. The emphasis of CRM for DeBloois—and for his counterparts throughout the Forest Service as well as in other federal land-management agencies—shifted from archaeology to historic structures. (Archaeologists, not historians, continued to dominate the field, however.) DeBloois remembered how Section 106 compliance came to control the Forest Service archaeologists' work plans: "Devoting resources to doing 'academic' research or research that did not contribute directly to 'project clearance' was inappropriate and for many years, unacceptable."[9]

Archaeologists composed one set of the myriad ologists that the Forest Service brought into the agency in the 1970s (see chap. 6). They were among the "constrainers" in the organization, holding the Forest Service accountable to environmental laws such as NEPA and NHPA. Mostly placed with recreation staffs in the organizational schemes of the forest supervisor and regional offices, they were not powerfully situated to influence Forest Service policy. Regarded with prejudice by the Indian community, they were in a tough spot to carry out the Forest Service's early efforts toward improving tribal relations.

THE SOUTHWEST AND THE ARCHAEOLOGICAL RESOURCES PROTECTION ACT

The Southwest, a region especially rich in archaeology because of its arid climate and sparse vegetation, became something of a proving ground for CRM on the national forests. The Southwestern Region hired its first CRM archaeologist in 1973. Judith G. Propper, regional archaeologist in the 1980s, wrote that the

CRM program in that region made slow but steady progress in its first decade. "The major focus of the program was on project compliance, specifically field surveys to locate cultural resource sites in advance of earth-disturbing projects," she wrote in a 1988 retrospective (echoing DeBloois's experience in the Intermountain Region). "The main outputs of the program were acres surveyed and sites located, and file drawers swelled with the accumulation of survey reports and site forms." One result of all the disparate Section 106 surveys was a realization that the Southwest's archaeological resources remained vulnerable to pothunters and vandals even as they were being inventoried. Indeed, pothunters baldly used the Freedom of Information Act to obtain site forms and learn the locations of recorded sites. Archaeologists and law enforcement officials, when they jointly investigated this problem, discovered there was a growing black market for prehistoric artifacts. Forest Service rangers could not possibly patrol thousands of newly identified cultural sites, and the Antiquities Act did not provide much deterrence against their plunder.[10]

The Antiquities Act had long made it a federal offense to take an "object of antiquity" from the public domain. But in a 1974 ruling by the Ninth Circuit Court of Appeals in *U.S. v. Diaz*, the court found that the act's wording as to what constituted an "object of antiquity" was unconstitutionally vague. The Ninth Circuit Court's decision in *Diaz* hobbled the Forest Service's efforts to prevent looting of Ancestral Pueblo ruins and other cultural sites in the Southwestern Region. Although federal prosecutors brought a handful of actions against pothunters in the mid to late 1970s, in every case they were strongly challenged on the basis of the *Diaz* decision. One time the government tried to prosecute the looters on charges of theft and destruction of government property, but the judge dismissed the case on the grounds that the government was misusing the law as a surrogate for the Antiquities Act to circumvent the Ninth Circuit's finding in *U.S. v. Diaz*. In another case, *U.S. v. Smyer and May*, the prosecution won, but the judge gave each of the two looters only a light sentence of ninety days in jail.[11]

These circumstances led Congress to enact the Archaeological Resources Protection Act of 1979. The main thrust of the law was to clarify what constituted an archaeological resource and prescribe stiffer penalties for violations. It directed federal land-managing agencies to treat the locations of sites as confidential information that was not to be released to the public. It required those same agencies to consult with Indians or tribes who had a direct stake in the archaeological resource either because they owned the land or had a cultural affiliation.

Chief John R. McGuire testified on the bill before a Senate subcommittee in May 1979. Others who testified at the hearing included attorneys, professors of anthropology, and private landowners. There were no tribal leaders or tribal spokespersons among the witnesses, although Leroy Wilder, general counsel for the Association on American Indian Affairs, testified. McGuire, in his testimony, highlighted the issues with looting in the Southwest as well as the need for confidentiality surrounding site locations. Federal land-managing agencies needed relief from the Freedom of Information Act, he told the senators, "to control the dissemination of such information to the public." Although McGuire could not have anticipated it, the same issue of confidentiality would arise with regard to Indian sacred sites during the next two decades.[12]

For resource protection, ARPA marked a step forward, but it did little to improve relations between archaeologists and Indian peoples. As written in 1979, the law defined an archaeological resource as "material remains of past human life or activities which are of archaeological interest . . . [which] shall include but not be limited to . . . human skeletal remains." Joe E. Watkins, the current chief supervisory anthropologist of tribal relations in the NPS and a Choctaw, observed some thirty years later that this language in the ARPA perpetuated the old scientific perspective on human remains that Indians generally found so offensive and disrespectful of their ancestors. When the ARPA was enacted, Indians had already begun to make their views on the excavation of burial sites known. Indeed, some tribes took the matter into their own hands by forming their own tribal CRM programs. The Navajos and the Pueblo of Zuni, both located in the Southwest, were two prominent examples of tribes who became active in archaeology during the decade. Given those developments, it was odd that the Senate committee did not hear the indigenous people's perspective in 1979.[13]

THE CONTENTIOUS ISSUE OF BURIAL REMAINS

Not infrequently, cultural resource surveys turned up human burial remains. When archaeological crews exhumed Native American grave sites, they exposed more than bones. The disturbance of long-buried human remains raised some highly sensitive cultural differences between Indian tribes and the dominant society and laid bare the fact that Western science practiced a double standard in its treatment of Native American and Caucasian human remains. The growing controversy in the 1970s and 1980s was by no means limited to national forestlands, but more than any other issue, it exacerbated the tension between Indians and Forest Service archaeologists. As Indians acquired a stronger political voice in American society, they sought redress through "repatriation" of burial remains. That meant defining which tribe had jurisdiction, or cultural patrimony, in each instance where a burial site was disturbed. Indian demands for repatriation soon extended to skeletal remains and funerary objects housed in museum collections. Those museum collections were widely dispersed all over the nation and in some cases were quite large, having been accumulated for more than a century. When museum collections were characterized by Indians as stolen property and sacrilegious to their belief systems, it made the problem both bigger and uglier, because it brought up sins of the past as well as present injustices. Charges of racial discrimination, both direct and implied, were a flashpoint for emotions for both Indians and the scientific community of archaeologists, anthropologists, and museum curators. The controversy over treatment of Indian grave sites and burial remains was one of the major drivers that pushed the federal government to adopt more rigorous forms of tribal consultation in the 1990s and after.

Nowhere did the treatment of Indian burial sites provoke more controversy than in California. The bleak history of Indian-white relations in that state formed an essential backdrop to developments in the 1960s and 1970s. A little more than a century before, in the early 1850s, California Indians had suffered the most sudden, brutal invasion of their country of any region in North America. Immediately following the Mexican cession of California to the United States at the conclusion of the Mexican-American War, gold was discovered in the Sierra Nevada. Adventurers poured in from all over the world. Historian Edward D. Castillo describes what happened next.

> Thinly spread government officials were overwhelmed by this unprecedented deluge of immigrants and all effective authority collapsed. Military authorities could not prevent widespread desertion of soldiers and chaos reigned. A virtual reign of terror enveloped tribesmen in the mining districts. Wanton killings and violence against Indians resisting miners developed into a deadly pattern. . . . Numerous vigilante type paramilitary troops were established whose principal occupation seems to have been to kill Indians and kidnap their children. . . . Nothing in American Indian history is even remotely comparable to this orgy of theft and mass murder.

Out of a Native population of perhaps one hundred thousand in 1849, an estimated two-thirds died in the first two years of the gold rush.[14] Mass burials resulting from this horrendous experience are found all over Northern California.

Indian treaty making and the federal government's reservation policy practically broke down when the government confronted the chaotic state of Indian affairs in California. Federal officials hurriedly negotiated eighteen treaties with approximately 125 tribes (fewer than half of all California tribes). Taken altogether, the eighteen treaties would have reserved approximately 9 million acres for Indian occupancy and use while providing the tribes with benefits and services for their ceded lands. But the treaties were never ratified. As Congress quickly granted California statehood, the U.S. Senate yielded to political pressure from the California state legislature not to ratify them. A legacy of those chaotic times is that many California Indian tribes today lack federal recognition. Even the federally recognized tribes have very little land in trust status. As a result, many California tribes have had to rely on national forests and other public lands as their primary traditional use areas.[15]

In 1963, the California state legislature found that California Indian culture was not "sufficiently understood" nor "adequately chronicled," and it directed the Department of Parks and Recreation to keep a record of archaeological sites throughout the state. In 1969, it came to light that a historic Yurok village site called Tsahpekw, located at Stone Lagoon in Humboldt County, was being looted by pothunters. In response, the Department of Parks and Recreation invited a team of archaeologists from San Francisco State University to excavate the site and salvage archaeological information before it was lost—even though the site was known to contain human burial remains.

As the archaeological dig went forward, local tribes complained to California Indian Legal Services, whose attorney wrote to the project leader requesting that the university team desist. Meanwhile, a small group of activists among the Yurok, Hupa, Karuk, and Wiyot tribes held meetings on how to stop the desecration of Indian burial sites. In 1970, the activists formed a nonprofit organization, the Northwest Indian Cemetery Protective Association (NICPA), and began publicizing their objections over the Tsahpekw archaeological dig. They soon succeeded in shutting down the project.[16]

For better protection of all Indian graves, NICPA lobbied the state government. The state legislature funded an investigative report on how well the state was preserving archaeological resources. The report revealed serious problems, including the disturbance of Indian burial sites, and recommended that the

FIGURE 20. Yurok plank house. The traditional dwelling of many Northwest Coast Indian peoples, it was built by lashing redwood or cedar planks to a wooden frame.

state appoint a Native American heritage commission to oversee their protection. In response to the report, and at the behest of NICPA, the state legislature imposed a moratorium on the disturbance of Indian burial sites that were less than two hundred years old.[17] NICPA also contacted federal agencies, and in 1973, it convinced the Corps of Engineers to abandon a dam project that would have flooded Indian burial sites. Buoyed by those successes, NICPA lobbied Governor Jerry Brown for stronger protections, and in 1976 the governor established the Native American Heritage Commission, charging it with the responsibility to identify, catalog, and protect Indian cultural resources.[18]

NICPA gave voice to Indian cultural perspectives that had long been overlooked or ignored by Western science. Archaeologists were used to respecting the sanctity of human remains in those cases where the identity of the individual could be established and there were surviving kin. Customarily, when human remains that dated to historical times were accidentally unearthed, and when they could be traced to a deceased individual through death records or a marked grave site, then they were reburied. Otherwise, human skeletal remains did not carry that same weight and were generally treated as fair game for scientific study, because in the Judeo-Christian tradition the human spirit had long departed them. Indian peoples tended to hold a different view; they perceived the bones themselves as having an inalienable spiritual dimension that continued to connect in some way with the deceased. Regardless of how old they were, the bones must be given proper respect or the bones' spirits would suffer. The distinction between historic and prehistoric times was insignificant in their view. It mattered not at all whether the identity of the individual was unknown.[19]

The clash of cultural values prompted a debate over ethics within the archaeology profession. Did archaeologists have an obligation to consult with Native Americans who were the biological and cultural descendants of the past residents of the sites they excavated? Some archaeologists argued unequivocally yes, while others questioned whether contemporary tribes could legitimately claim cultural patrimony over burial remains that dated back several centuries. Anthropologists had long embraced the standard that their fieldwork had to benefit the communities from which they obtained their data. Did that same ethical standard apply to archaeologists working on prehistoric sites? If a tribe objected to the excavation and study of prehistoric human remains, did the interests of science ever trump those concerns?[20]

Forest Service archaeologists were deeply involved in that debate because the Section 106 surveys that they oversaw so often ran across Indian cultural sites and because they themselves were in most cases the agency's tribal liaisons. Sonia Tamez began doing seasonal CRM work on national forests in California in the 1970s and was hired into a permanent position in the Forest Service in 1979. She brought to her job the dual perspectives of archaeology and cultural anthropology. Mainly on the basis of the latter, she was highly sensitive to contemporary Indian social and cultural values. Besides working in CRM, she served as a cultural anthropologist on environmental impact assessments and forest planning teams. She saw firsthand how archaeologists sometimes had to wrestle between their duty to consult with tribes and their desire to advance scientific knowledge in their discipline. "There were a lot of good archeologists who *did* work with tribes," she recalls. "But there were too many situations in which there was a lot of tension, particularly around burials and sacred sites, where there was a group of archeologists who would argue that the scientific value of burials outweighs the human rights associated with those burials." Tamez believed strongly that in such cases the agency needed to support the tribes' point of view. By the 1980s, Tamez was presenting to her colleagues that the whole CRM program needed to be overhauled to take account of tribal perspectives. The Forest Service needed to work in partnership with tribes to identify traditional values, and specifically it had to seek tribal input on prehistoric Indian cultural sites and artifacts, because those features obviously held cultural value for contemporary Indian communities. In so doing, the agency had to move away from the archaeologists' emphasis on material culture and look at the sociocultural values of Indian groups as well. "Anthropological models and methodologies are essential in order to identify both resources and values," Tamez wrote.[21]

THE FOREST SERVICE AND THE AMERICAN INDIAN RELIGIOUS FREEDOM ACT

At the same time that Indians pushed for protection of burial sites, they also sought federal protection for their sacred sites. Burial sites and sacred sites were, of course, closely related. For both, their significance was rooted in Native religion. When Indians sought to protect their sacred sites from intrusive construction projects or adverse land uses, non-Indians tended to misapprehend the Indians' concerns and show a dismissive attitude toward their values. To shake the dominant culture out of its complacency, advocates of sacred site protection often resorted to analogy. For example, when the Forest Service proposed an oil well development in the Blackfeet's sacred Badger-Two Medicine area, it was as if it had "set up a drilling rig in Mecca."[22] When a private landowner of Woodruff, Arizona unwittingly razed an ancient shrine of the Hopis, it was the equivalent of "Hopis going into Woodruff and bulldozing part of the Mormon church." If an oil company were permitted to drill in the Valley of the Chiefs (a place in southcentral Montana that is sacred to many northern plains tribes), it would be like "erecting an oil derrick in the Sistine Chapel."[23] Sam Cagey, a leader of the Lummi tribe of western Washington, protested a Forest Service plan to log in cedar groves that his people held sacred. "The forest is our temple," he said. "We don't question Salt Lake City's temple. We don't question the Vatican's temple. We don't want anybody to question how important nature is to us, because that's *our* temple."[24] Such analogies were somewhat strained, however, because Native American religions and the dominant culture held such different views of the land.

Native American religions were described as "nature-based religions," meaning that they were deeply imbued with a sense of the natural environment and physical geography that each tribe inhabited. Native American religions defined a Native people's connection to their ancestral homelands. In cultures based on oral tradition, sacred sites memorialized locations of historical significance in the life of the people, such as a place where the people had originated or had fought a battle. Or they were locations of spiritual power where tribal members or their religious leaders could best communicate with the spirit world through ceremonies and prayer. In the view of the religion, when such a place was desecrated or destroyed, the spirits departed from it. Since Native American religion was rooted in place, loss of a sacred site meant not only the loss of religious practice but the loss of belief as well. As one Indian religious teacher said, "Every society needs these kinds of sacred places. They help to instill a sense of social cohesion in the people. . . . A society that cannot remember its past and honor it is in peril of losing its soul."[25]

The dominant culture had its sacred sites as well, but in contrast to Native Americans, it had no such sense of deep time or rootedness in the natural world. "Protestant Christianity has been evangelical, transportable, Bible-based, and not rooted to a particular landscape," observes anthropologist Andrew Gulliford. "Europeans abandoned their cemeteries and cathedrals as they set sail for America. They crossed the water and then crossed the continent and reconstituted their religious communities by building new churches."[26] Whereas traditional Indians felt an obligation to care for the burial grounds and sacred places that defined their existence as a people, non-Indians were under no such cultural imperative.

Indians argued that federal actions leading to the destruction of their sacred sites or otherwise inhibiting their ability to practice their religion on public lands violated their religious freedom. They based their claim on two distinct legal theories. The first held that tribes, as sovereign entities, had a right and responsibility to look after the religious needs of their members, so when the federal government took actions tending to inhibit tribal members' practice of religion, then it breeched the government's trust responsibility to the tribe. The second legal theory held that any failure by the government to protect Indian sacred sites infringed on Indians' First Amendment right to the free exercise of religion. The two legal theories were potentially at cross purposes, since one focused on Indians' special relationship with the federal government and the other focused on their civil rights in common with all other U.S. citizens. The

Indian Civil Rights Act of 1968 specifically addressed that complex relationship, and a Supreme Court decision in 1974, *Morton v. Mancari*, appeared to reinforce the notion that Indians' religious freedom could be defended under both the trust doctrine *and* civil rights law.[27]

When Indians first started calling attention to their imperiled sacred sites, raising the question of the government's role and responsibility, Northern California once again was the scene of conflict that forced the issue. In the traditional culture of the Hupa, Yurok, Karuk, and Tolowa tribes, the role of a medicine person or "Native doctor" was hereditary. Future spiritual leaders were identified at a young age and had to undergo many years of education and training before they could assume their intended role. Their instruction by the religious elders began in the village and included a sacred indoctrination into various traditional ceremonies and dances. As the doctor apprentices matured, the center of their training moved from the village out to the surrounding riverine and coastal environments, then into the smaller mountain ranges, and finally to the rocky peaks of the Siskiyou Mountains. Two peaks were exceptionally important for their endeavors: Doctor Rock features an imposing forty-foot cleft boulder, and Chimney Rock stands at the crest of a curving, sawtooth ridge. When the apprentice doctors proceeded up those sacred peaks, they broke their journey at a series of small altars, each one attended by its own ceremony. On the summits of those peaks they completed the final stage of their enlightenment, seeking out peace, quiet, and a clear view over the distant landscape to receive their spiritual visions.

For the three tribes, the Siskiyou high country was the place where the religious leaders went to receive spiritual power and healing power for the people. They went to the mountains to gather herbs and to fast and pray in preparation for ceremonies involving the whole tribe. Those ceremonies usually featured traditional dances and regalia dating back hundreds of years, and the traditional elders stressed that the tribe must continue performing the dances and honoring the regalia at all cost. Thus, while few tribal members visited the sacred peaks themselves, they all recognized that the doctor's treks to the high country were essential to everyone's well-being. As Yurok Chris Peters said, "very few people venture to the sacred sites or participate in the high rituals, but the benefit of their participation impacts the moral and ethical foundation of the general population."[28]

The Siskiyou high country is part of the Six Rivers National Forest. In 1976, the Forest Service released the Blue Creek Unit Plan for a section of the forest, which proposed logging operations and road development in the area that the tribes considered sacred. The plan included paving a jeep road that ran within a half mile of Chimney Rock. The road improvement was part of a scheme to reroute and upgrade a through road called the Gasquet-Orleans Road, or G-O Road ("Go Road"). Indian individuals and several conservation groups filed an administrative appeal, complaining that the Forest Service had not given due consideration to effects on wildlife, plant species, cultural values, and water quality.[29]

Forest Service officials initially refused to take the Indians' complaint seriously, thinking that ceremonial use of the high country had virtually died out, or even if it did still occur, it was not something the Forest Service was required to protect under existing environmental laws.[30] However, that year the California state legislature passed the California Native American Cultural, Historical and Sacred Sites Act, which in effect called for government protections on the state level that would soon be mandated on a nationwide basis in the American Indian Religious Freedom Act of 1978. As the G-O Road was clearly turning into a test case with national significance, the Forest Service hired a consultant, Dr. Dorothea Theodoratus, to perform an ethnographic study. Her voluminous report, based on exhaustive review of ethnographic, historical, and archaeological sources and completed in 1979, strongly indicated that the Siskiyou high country did hold cultural significance for the tribes. After receiving the report, the Forest Service modified the Blue Creek Unit Plan to the extent of introducing protective zones around eleven identified sites. Then it denied the appeal.[31]

In the meantime, AIRFA became law in August 1978. In the run up to the bill's passage, the Forest Service raised concerns about how the legislation might lead to undue constraints on the use of public lands. According to Indian activist Suzan Shown Harjo, who was then doing a turn in the federal government as special assistant in the Office of the Secretary of the Interior, the Forest Service skated very near to outright lobbying against the bill (which would have been against the law). The agency provided information to Congressman Tom Foley, Democrat of Washington, who then went to the bill's sponsor, Congressman Morris Udall, Democrat of Arizona, and said he would oppose the measure unless Udall would publicly allow that his bill had "no teeth." Udall gave in to Foley's demand, stating for the record that AIRFA's intent was merely to express the "sense of Congress." Section 1 of the act did just that, while Section 2 directed federal agencies to review their policies affecting Indian sacred sites and religious practice in consultation with Native traditional religious leaders. The president was to report back to Congress on the findings of the policy review in one year.[32]

Harjo, in her position as special assistant, had the task of coordinating the multiagency review that the law mandated. She also produced the text of the final report together with Vine Deloria Jr., Walter Echo-Hawk, and a handful of others. She left the government the day after the report was delivered to Congress in 1979. Nine years later, she was called as a witness by the Senate Select Committee on Indian Affairs for its hearing on how to improve AIRFA. In her testimony, she gave a blistering account of the Forest Service's efforts not only to prevent AIRFA's passage but also to obstruct the policy review. It was, she said, the "least cooperative" among some fifty agencies that participated in the review after the law was passed.[33]

By then, Harjo had become executive director of the National Congress of American Indians (NCAI). She had an ax to grind against the Forest Service, for a decade had passed since the enactment of AIRFA, and the Forest Service's G-O Road still remained at the center of the debate over Indian sacred sites protection. That year, the Supreme Court handed down a decision in the G-O Road case that the NCAI and other Indian advocacy groups found very disappointing.

LYNG V. NORTHWEST INDIAN CEMETERY PROTECTIVE ASSOCIATION

The litigants in the G-O Road case spent five years in the administrative appeal process and finally lost their appeal in 1981. Two years later, they filed suit in U.S. District Court. The parties to the complaint were the Northwest Indian Cemetery Protective Association (the same group that had tussled with archaeologists over the treatment of Indian burial sites) together with four Indian individuals, six conservation groups, and two individual conservationists. Their complaint alleged that the Forest Service's Blue Creek Unit Plan violated the First Amendment, AIRFA, NEPA, NHPA, the Clean Water Act, the Wilderness Act, the National Forest Management Act, and the Multiple-Use Sustained-Yield Act and breeched the federal government's trust responsibility to protect Indian reserved fishing and water rights pertaining to the Hupa Valley Reservation.[34] They motioned the court to enjoin the Forest Service from carrying out its plan to construct the G-O Road and oversee logging in the

Siskiyou high country. The state of California filed its own suit against the Forest Service on similar grounds, and the two cases were consolidated for trial.

The Forest Service argued in defense of its actions, that it had faithfully complied with all environmental laws. It had performed the necessary impact assessments and had taken steps to mitigate adverse effects. In particular, it had consulted with the tribes on measures to reduce effects on archaeological resources in compliance with Section 106 of the National Historic Preservation Act.[35]

The court held for the plaintiffs on the First Amendment issue. The federal government appealed the case to the Ninth Circuit Court of Appeals, which upheld the lower court's decision. The government then pursued the case to the Supreme Court, which reversed in a five to three decision. In *Lyng v. Northwest Indian Cemeteries Protection Association* (1988), the high court found that the road construction would not prevent the Indians from free exercise of religion because it would not coerce individuals to "act against their faith." Moreover, the Supreme Court observed that AIRFA contained no protective cause of action, confirming that the statute had "no teeth."[36]

The *Lyng* decision appeared to be a major setback for the protection of Indian sacred sites. Harjo and other Indian activists interpreted the ruling by the conservative court as a provocation. For the next six years, they lobbied Congress to enact the necessary protective cause of action that was missing from AIRFA. Congress held hearings in 1988, 1992, and 1993, and it did pass amendments to AIRFA in 1994, but the new law addressed the use of peyote by the Native American Church, not the matter of protecting Indian sacred sites on public lands. Thus, Congress declined to give Indian sacred sites exclusive statutory protection, leaving it to the federal land-managing agencies to determine how those tribal interests would be protected.[37]

Some argued that the *Lyng* court was actually more sympathetic to the Indians' religion than its critics allowed. In the majority opinion, Justice Sandra Day O'Connor found that the "Government's rights to the use of its own land need not and should not discourage it from accommodating religious practices like those engaged in by the Indian respondents." Furthermore, the Forest Service had acted in accord with AIRFA when it commissioned a "comprehensive study of the effects that the project would have on the cultural and religious value" of the area.

If the Forest Service won anything by litigating the G-O Road case all the way to the Supreme Court, it was a hollow victory as far as the Six Rivers National Forest was concerned. Subsequent actions by Congress prevented the

Forest Service from constructing the G–O Road in spite of the court's decision. Through several cycles of appropriations bills, Congress explicitly prohibited the Forest Service from expending funds to build the road. In 1990, Congress passed the Smith River National Recreation Area Act, which expressly closed the Siskiyou high-country area to road development. Eventually the area became part of the Siskiyou Wilderness. Thus, Congress gave those particular sacred sites protection by indirect means. Ironically, the plaintiffs got what they wanted though they lost their argument in court.[38]

Law professor Marcia Yablon presented a case for "why *Lyng* was right" in a lengthy article published in the *Yale Law Review* in 2004. She argued that "judicial protection" for sacred sites would inevitably result in overly broad and general decisions, whereas federal land managers had access to both the local knowledge and discretionary authority to make proper "accommodations." The best way to protect sacred sites now and in the future, her critique suggested, would be through tribal consultation and administrative action.[39]

ADMINISTRATIVE ACTION IN THE AFTERMATH OF *LYNG*

By the time the *Lyng* decision came down, some federal agencies were already starting to take that more proactive administrative approach to sacred site protection that Yablon advocated. The NPS was first to take the initiative, beginning with questions being put to its leadership by national park managers in California in 1978 as they observed what was happening on the Six Rivers National Forest. The NPS produced its first iteration of a Native American policy later that year, acknowledging a need to grant Native Americans special privileges in national parks for the purpose of practicing their traditional religion. Hardliners in the NPS objected that the policy could put resources at risk, while the assistant solicitor for national parks worried that the policy might conflict with the First Amendment's prohibition against the federal government privileging any one religion over another. The NPS appointed a task force to consider the policy further. The task force came back with an even stronger position in support of allowing Indians special access to ceremonial sacred sites. Specifically, the policy allowed gathering of natural materials for ceremonial purposes as long as the activity did not adversely affect park resources, and it required consultation with Indian groups on interpretive materials and programs pertaining to their culture. At the same time, it affirmed that the NPS must retain full responsibility over its resource protection and interpretive programs (in other words, no comanagement). The task force report was still in review when Congress passed AIRFA.[40]

As a result of the AIRFA-mandated review, the NPS hired a cultural anthropologist, Dr. Muriel Crespi, to build an ethnographic program within the agency. Crespi fashioned two types of ethnographic studies for use in the field. One was a "rapid ethnographic assessment," which sought to assess effects of a proposed action on a park's Native American partners. The second was a "traditional use study" (or "ethnographic resource study") that aimed to be a more extensive investigation of a given park's indigenous residents or neighbors. By the late 1980s, the two types of studies were being pioneered in the Southwest and Alaska, respectively.[41]

Working concurrently on a parallel track, two other cultural anthropologists, Pat Parker and Tom King (a wife and husband team, one in the NPS, the other on the Advisory Council of Historic Preservation), developed principles and guidelines for a new type of historic property listing under the National Register of Historic Places. They called this new entity a "traditional cultural property" or TCP. The TCP was designed to recognize community values that were being overlooked by the usual methodologies employed by archaeologists and architectural historians doing CRM. An important precept of the TCP was that "a place can be eligible for the National Register based on its values in the eyes of a traditional community like an Indian tribe." The TCP designation was aimed primarily at addressing cultural sites that were important to Indian communities, but it was not exclusively for them. In 1990, Parker and King published their groundbreaking work in National Register Bulletin 38, *Guidelines for Evaluating and Documenting Traditional Cultural Properties.*[42]

Bulletin 38 provided a valuable tool for Forest Service archaeologists as they set out to document and assist with the protection of Indian sacred sites on national forests. It affirmed that TCPs could be "entirely natural places," without any cultural modification whatsoever, and that their significance to the Indian community need not be recognizable to the dominant society. It stressed that TCPs would be identified through consultation with communities. Most importantly, it stated that the significance of TCPs had to be understood with reference to the community's own perceptions of the place and its significance.[43]

Even before Bulletin 38 appeared, Forest Service cultural resource managers were following developments in the NPS closely. When the NPS finally produced its Native American policy in 1987 (defining how the agency would accommodate Native American use of national parks for traditional and religious purposes), forest planning coordinator Sonia Tamez remarked, "the NPS policy has set the pace for other agencies. The Forest Service will be expected to follow suit."[44]

Tamez was among six archaeologists and anthropologists from Arizona, New Mexico, and California who presented a paper on Forest Service tribal relations at a CRM symposium held at Grand Canyon in May 1988. Pending the adoption of a Native American policy for the whole Forest Service, Tamez and her colleagues offered a number of specific recommendations for addressing Indian interests on national forestlands. First, they pointed to the need for consistency across the agency in designating liaisons and establishing consultation protocols. Second, they called for sensitivity training sessions for Forest Service personnel at every level of the organization down to the ranger district office. Third, they touched on the need for confidentiality surrounding the identification of Indian sacred sites. Fourth, they wanted forests to consider waiving permit requirements for Indians to gather plant material for traditional use. And fifth, they looked to ethnographic studies as a means for identifying "base-line information on Indian uses of each Forest." It was a call for action to deepen the organization's commitment to tribal consultation, although it still envisioned CRM as practically the whole show for Forest Service–tribal relations.[45]

Disputes over Indian sacred sites still claimed more attention than anything else. There were perhaps sixty or seventy sacred-lands disputes simmering around the country, many of them located on national forests. In northern Arizona, a proposed uranium mine threatened devastation for the Havasupai's sacred Red Butte. In southern Arizona, plans to build a world-class astronomical observatory on the summit of Mount Graham would defile a sacred mountain of the San Carlos Apache. In northern Wyoming, the Forest Service and northern Plains tribes differed over how to manage the site of the Bighorn Medicine Wheel, a prehistoric stone circle located high in the Bighorn Mountains. As this impressive feature was already accessible to the public by a secondary highway, the Forest Service proposed to construct a visitor center at the site; the tribes wanted to keep it undeveloped. In Montana, the Forest Service and the Blackfeet tribe clashed over an area called the Badger-Two Medicine. The Forest Service proposed to step up oil and gas exploration in the area despite Blackfeet claims that it was sacred ground.[46]

FIGURE 21. Medicine Wheel, Bighorn National Forest, Wyoming. The feature sits at nearly 10,000 feet elevation on Medicine Mountain. Photo taken in 2008.

COURTESY OF FOREST SERVICE/WIKIMEDIA COMMONS

The Badger-Two Medicine was one place where Forest Service officials learned the necessity of consulting with tribes early and often if they were going to develop effective tribal relations. The area of approximately 123,000 acres lies on the east slope of the Continental Divide just south of Glacier National Park and southwest of the Blackfeet Reservation within the Lewis and Clark National Forest. In the mid-1980s, it was an area where multiple-use management was particularly divisive and challenging. As the area lies on the edge of the Overthrust Belt, energy companies saw it as a promising field for oil and gas development. However, as it also abutted Glacier National Park on the north and the Bob Marshall Wilderness on the south, wilderness advocates were keen to protect its natural, scenic, and recreational qualities, and they hoped to get Congress to designate it as wilderness. Also at that time, the NPS and environmentalists were in the process of developing public support for the idea that national parks such as Glacier required a protective buffer zone to preserve their ecological integrity. In the service of that idea, they prevailed on the Lewis and Clark National Forest to recognize a conservation imperative to protect the "Greater Glacier Ecosystem." As the Badger-Two Medicine was habitat to the grizzly bear, a threatened species, and as the Lewis and Clark National Forest was party to a newly formed interagency effort to recover a healthy population of grizzlies in the northern Rockies, the Forest Service came under strong pressure to make grizzly bear management its highest priority in the Badger-Two Medicine area. And finally, the interests of the Blackfeet tribe in the area were complex. Blackfeet traditionalists maintained that the rugged Badger-Two Medicine was their last refuge for making vision quests. Opposing the Forest Service's plan to permit more oil and gas exploration, they joined wilderness advocates in forming the Badger-Two Medicine Alliance. Others in the tribe were not averse to more drilling in the area if the tribe could some day reap an economic benefit in oil and gas royalties. They pinned their hopes for future tribal oil and gas revenues on a tribal claim that the Badger-Two Medicine really belonged to the tribe. The area, together with the eastern half of Glacier National Park, formed what was known as the "ceded strip"—a tract that the tribe had reluctantly given up under a controversial agreement with the U.S. government in 1895. Some tribal members disputed that the land had ever been sold, insisting that the terms of transfer had been for a fifty-year lease only. The festering issue of the ceded strip made it impossible for the Blackfeet tribe to take a unified position on the future of the Badger-Two Medicine.[47]

As the Forest Service went forward with plans to allow more oil and gas exploration, it contracted for archaeological surveys of proposed well pads and associated access roads to comply with Section 106 of the NHPA. The Section 106 survey was conducted in the mid-1980s without any meaningful input by the Blackfeet tribe. The archaeologist on the Lewis and Clark National Forest sent a letter to the Blackfeet cultural representative asking him to identify sacred sites on a map so that they could be avoided. The Blackfeet cultural representative thought it was an impossible request and did not reply. On the basis of the unanswered letter, the Forest Service decided that it had made a good faith effort to consult with the tribe. The Section 106 survey identified one Blackfeet cultural site, which was determined as not significant according to National Register criteria.[48]

FIGURE 22. Sawtooth Ridge, Lewis and Clark National Forest, Montana. This 1981 photo shows an area of the Rocky Mountain Front located about seventy miles south of the Badger-Two Medicine.

PHOTO BY G. E. GRUELL. COURTESY OF ARCHIVES AND SPECIAL COLLECTIONS, MANSFIELD LIBRARY, UNIVERSITY OF MONTANA.

In 1986, Blackfeet traditionalists formed the Pikuni Traditionalists Association and appealed the Forest Service's plan to permit more oil and gas drilling. Forest Supervisor James Overbay denied the appeal on the grounds that the Blackfeet were raising issues that were outside the scope of the Forest Service planning process. However, the appeal prompted the Forest Service to contract with the same CRM firm again to conduct a review of the ethnographic literature so that it could better understand Blackfeet use of the Badger-Two Medicine area. The Forest Service used excerpts of that study together with excerpts from the prior archaeological investigation report to prepare a discussion of Blackfeet use for a section of an environmental impact statement. The EIS was intended to fulfill requirements by NEPA, AIRFA, and other laws to consider effects of the proposed action on Blackfeet interests in the area. The Forest Service released the EIS in 1990—the same year that the NPS published National Register Bulletin 38 on traditional cultural properties. The Blackfeet appealed the EIS on the grounds that the EIS did not consider traditional cultural practices as defined in Bulletin 38.[49]

That sent the Forest Service back to its CRM consultants for yet another study, this one focused on Blackfeet traditional cultural practices. For the first time, ethnographic interviews were the primary goal of the research. As the project neared completion in the early 1990s, archaeologists Dr. Sally Thompson Greiser and T. Weber Greiser of Historical Research Associates ruminated on their experience for a special issue of *CRM*. "It seems obvious from this vantage point that the process was backwards," they wrote. "The archaeological studies would have benefited greatly from the context provided by the ethnographic literature review and the subsequent interviews with traditional Pikuni practitioners. Without the two ethnographic studies the archeologists operated in a cultural vacuum."[50]

Greiser and Greiser drew a number of lessons from the experience. First, an ethnographic study had to take into account many voices within the tribe: the tribal government, the traditional community, and even different factions within the traditional community. With such a welter of points of view, it could be difficult determining to whom the investigator was responsible. Second, the investigator (and the land manager) had to make allowances for dealing with an oral culture on its own terms. Rather than expect a tribe to put its review of a draft report in the form of written comments, it was better to schedule time to go it with tribal members in person. Tribal members simply could not feel comfortable commenting on sacred matters in writing. Accommodating tribal members' preference for oral communication should be part of the "good faith effort" required by law. Third, land managers had to recognize that traditional practitioners might refuse to divulge the information that the land managers wanted—such as specific site locations, details of how sacred sites were used, or how sites might be delineated with exterior boundaries on a map. By sharing such guarded information, traditional practitioners risked exposure of their sacred places and perhaps even a loss of their own spiritual powers. "To them, this is a no win situation," Greiser and Greiser observed. "If they don't tell, then there is no documentation of traditional cultural practices, and thus, nothing to protect. If they do tell, the mystery that sustains them is lessened if not lost."[51]

The years following the *Lyng* decision were both perplexing and stimulating for people working in the area of Forest Service–tribal relations. Forest managers and their tribal liaisons began to realize that tribal consultation had to involve much more than sending letters to tribal offices and checking a box when those letters went unanswered. Just what the Forest Service should do instead, and who would provide guidance and energy for that extra effort, remained to be seen.[52]

The conceptualization of the TCP as a type of property eligible for listing on the National Register offered one promising path for collaboration between tribes and the Forest Service. If Indian sacred sites could be duly identified and listed, then they stood a better chance of receiving the federal government's protection. When Congress amended the National Historic Preservation Act in 1992, it was another step forward for collaboration and Indian sacred site protection. Section 101(d)2 provided for tribes to assume all or any part of the functions of a State Historic Preservation Officer (SHPO, pronounced "Ship-O"). By 1996, a dozen tribes had formed their own Tribal Historic Preservation Offices, each one headed by a Tribal Historic Preservation Officer (THPO, pronounced "Tip-O"). Just as SHPOs had a national organization called the National Conference of State Historic Preservation Officers, the tribes had a national organization they called Keepers of the Treasures. The name was selected to reflect tribes' different perspective on historic preservation.[53]

As federal land-managing agencies turned to ethnographic research to improve their understanding of indigenous people's traditional uses and cultural needs on federal lands, they created more opportunities for collaboration between archaeologists and Native groups. As anthropologist Andrew Gulliford notes, "Archaeologists claim that they can understand prehistoric peoples from studying habitation sites, lithic scatters, and hunting camps. Alaska Natives and American Indians contend that archaeologists should consult them, too, because they can provide personal insight into the lifeways of their ancestors even if an archaeological site is thousands of years old."[54]

THE NATIVE AMERICAN GRAVES PROTECTION AND REPATRIATION ACT

While federal agencies and tribes wrestled with the problem of how to protect Indian sacred sites, a movement grew to obtain federal legislation addressing Indians' long-standing grievances over the treatment of Indian burial remains housed in archaeological collections all over the country. A major catalyst for the movement came when members of the Northern Cheyenne Tribe, investigating collections held at the Smithsonian Institution, found there were an estimated 18,500 human remains warehoused in that facility alone. Publicity of the finding shocked Indian people across the nation.[55]

As the movement for tribal repatriation of human remains gathered momentum, historical research began to expose a record of atrocities in the nineteenth century in the treatment of Indian dead. After the Sand Creek Massacre of 1864, for example, Colonel Chivington ordered his soldiers to decapitate the bodies of their Cheyenne and Arapaho victims so that the skulls could be sent back east for study of the crania. Historical research also brought to light a notorious surgeon general's order that specifically encouraged more of the same practice by the army. An estimated 4,500 heads were snatched from battlefields and burial grounds in the closing decades of the nineteenth century.[56]

While the desecration of fresh corpses ceased after the Indian Wars, the pillaging of Indian graves did not. During the 1930s, for example, a Smithsonian expedition landed at Larson Bay on Kodiak Island in Alaska and excavated an ancient burial ground located immediately adjacent to the Native village, taking more than eight hundred human remains without the village's permission. A half century later, the Smithsonian still retained those objects in wooden boxes in a dimly lit hallway, having repeatedly turned down requests by the village that they be returned for reburial.[57]

In reviewing this sordid history, some read the Antiquities Act of 1906 as being a piece with the "deplorable federal policy" that allowed Indian burial remains to be exploited for medical science. In practical terms, the Antiquities Act defined deceased Indians interred on federal lands as "archaeological resources," and treated those human remains as "federal property."[58] Walter R. Echo-Hawk, an attorney for the Native American Rights Fund and one of the leading lobbyists for legislative reform, remarked that when a person desecrated a white grave, the person was sent to jail, but for desecrating an Indian grave, "you get a Ph.D."[59]

Attorneys for the Indians argued that the protection of graves and the sanctity of human remains was well established in common law. The treatment of disinterred Indian dead as scientific specimens was a violation of human rights. Further, they argued that tribes had rights to repatriation as sovereign Indian nations: one of the basic attributes of tribal sovereignty was the right of tribes to govern domestic internal affairs of their members, and that included the relationship between the living and the dead. For the U.S. government to interfere with that relationship constituted a violation of the principle of tribal sovereignty. Attorneys also argued that repatriation was a treaty right: since the courts had found that an Indian treaty only granted rights from the tribe to the United States that were expressly stated in the treaty, and since no treaty expressly granted the United States the right to disturb Indian graves or expropriate Indian dead from ceded lands, then it followed that the signatory tribe reserved the right to repatriate and rebury the remains.[60]

In 1990, Congress enacted the Native American Graves Protection and Repatriation Act (NAGPRA). The law required federal agencies and museums, as well as state and local museums and educational institutions that received federal funding, to repatriate human remains, funerary objects, sacred objects, and objects of cultural patrimony to tribes at tribes' request. More than five thousand federally funded institutions and government agencies were affected. It laid out a set of legal standards and procedures for tribes and the holders of collections to follow as they undertook the repatriation. It established penalties for trafficking of all human remains except for remains that had been obtained with full knowledge and consent of kin or the culturally affiliated group.

The law represented a hard-fought compromise between Indians on one side and the archaeology academy, museums, and federal land managers on the other. As the law mainly dealt with the inventory and transfer of objects, the holders of the collections tended to view NAGPRA as a specimen of property law. However, Indian attorneys who worked on the bill saw NAGPRA as a piece of human rights legislation. Walter Echo-Hawk stated that Congress's intent was to address its trust responsibility to Indian tribes and people, and he quoted from the statute that it "reflects the unique relationship between the Federal Government and Indian Tribes and Native Hawaiian organizations." The trust element was important, Echo-Hawk observed, because "the trust doctrine has given rise to the principle that enactments dealing with Indian affairs are to be liberally construed for the benefit of Indian people and tribes—a canon of construction similar to that applicable to remedial civil rights legislation."[61]

The lawmakers recognized that the process of repatriation would be a long one. The collections-holding institutions had five years—until November 16, 1995—to complete their inventories. They were to produce those inventories in consultation with tribal governments and traditional leaders and a review committee appointed by the secretary of the interior. All funerary objects, sacred objects, and other items of cultural patrimony were to be divided into two classes: those items that were believed to have been placed with human remains at the time of burial or that were exclusively made for burial purposes, and those items that were not so associated. The latter, unassociated objects were then made subject to a four-step process to establish cultural patrimony for objects to be repatriated.[62]

NAGPRA gave the oral traditions of tribes equal footing with scientific evidence in meeting the test of cultural patrimony. For example, a tribe could claim prehistoric remains if tribal tradition held that its people had always lived in the place where the remains were found. "NAGPRA is unique legislation," Echo-Hawk wrote, "because it is the first time that the federal government and non-Indian institutions must consider what is *sacred* from an Indian perspective."[63] In 1994, *Science* magazine ran an article on the process of repatriation under NAGPRA with the title "An Anthropological Culture Shift." "A federal law that puts Native American rights and religion ahead of scientific curiosity is reshaping North American anthropology and archeology," the article headlined.[64]

As the painstaking process of repatriation began to unfold, it became evident that the law did not address reburial of human remains once they were repatriated. Tribes sought access to ancestral homelands on national forests for reburial. Eventually, the Forest Service would seek legislative authority to assist tribes with reburials. Before that legislative authority was obtained (in the 2008 Farm Bill), some national forests were already doing it.

One such reburial, on the Lassen National Forest in Northern California in the year 2000, had particular significance. Some ninety years earlier in 1911, a solitary, middle-aged man had emerged from hiding and visited a ranch in the foothills of the Cascade Mountains, revealing himself to be the last survivor of his tribe, the Yahi. The desperately lonely individual was soon brought into the sympathetic custody of a prominent anthropologist, Dr. Alfred Kroeber of the University of California, Berkeley. The Indian, unwilling to reveal his name, became known to the world as "Ishi"—the Yana word for "man" or "one of the people." For the remaining five years of his life, Ishi made his home at a museum in San Francisco, where he informed anthropologists and the public about his people's culture.[65]

After Ishi's death in 1916, his body was cremated, but his brain was sent to the Smithsonian, contrary to his own wishes. When this fact surfaced in 1998, a question arose as to what tribe could claim the remains, since Ishi was the last of his tribe. A Maidu woman stepped forward with the claim that she had some Yahi blood, and a delegation of Maidu and Atsugewi elders traveled to Washington to retrieve Ishi's brain and ashes from the Smithsonian. Upon their return to California, Maidu and Atsugewi tribal members buried the remains at an undisclosed location on the Lassen National Forest.[66]

CHAPTER SUMMARY

Forest archeologists were in the forefront of Forest Service–tribal relations in the 1980s. Mostly new to the Forest Service, they worked with tribal cultural committees and tribal archeologists who were usually new to tribal government as well. Together with other federal agencies, the Forest Service struggled to implement effective and consistent tribal consultation protocols in the changing political environment. In learning how to work with its new tribal partners, the Forest Service showed its penchant for taking a decentralized, bottom-up approach.

The 1980s were bookended by two critical laws affecting Forest Service tribal relations. The American Indian Religious Freedom Act (AIRFA) called on federal land-managing agencies to provide protection to Indian sacred sites. In practice, tribes were reluctant to share information about such sites, and federal land-managing agencies were loath to demarcate large areas and afford them strict protection. The Forest Service disappointed many tribes by its stand on construction of the G–O Road in Northern California. The Reagan administration litigated the case all the way to the Supreme Court. Tribes viewed the *Lyng* decision (1988) as a setback for Indian sacred sites protection on federal lands and a provocation to push Congress for a stronger statute.

The Native American Graves Protection and Repatriation Act (NAGPRA) required federal agencies and federally funded institutions to consult with tribes on collections containing funerary objects or human skeletal remains. After objects had been repatriated, many tribes requested the Forest Service's permission and assistance to rebury them on a national forest that lay within the tribe's ancestral homeland.

The 1980s proved to be a decade of trial and error for Forest Service–tribal relations as the two parties negotiated the sensitive terrain of burial grounds and sacred places.

8

THE NEW FORESTRY ON NATIONAL FORESTS AND RESERVATIONS

The 1990s

THE NEW FORESTRY AND THE SPOTTED OWL CRISIS

I N 1989, DR. JERRY FRANKLIN, professor of forestry at the University of Washington and chief instigator of a team of innovative Forest Service and academic scientists in the Pacific Northwest called the H. J. Andrews Ecosystem Research Group, published an article in *American Forests* titled "Toward a New Forestry." His article began with an epiphany: "For decades we thought we knew all that we needed to know about forests. But in fact our level of knowledge is remarkably superficial." Dr. Franklin referred to the state of knowledge concerning the remarkable old-growth Douglas fir forests of the Pacific Northwest—fecund, dripping with moss, and teeming with life in the forest duff. As just one example of the forest's amazing complexity, his colleagues had recently discovered a certain symbiotic association between fungi and tree roots that could not exist without the presence of a certain fungus-eating mole, because the mole actually dispersed the fungi spores through the process of defecation. Take away the mole, Franklin said, and the tree roots would soon be deprived of their subterranean fungus. Take out a forty-acre patch of Douglas fir forest by the usual practice of clear-cutting, and the mole would most likely vacate the area. The aim of the New Forestry was to comprehend such ecological relationships and make allowance for them, prescribing logging practices that would mimic nature and thereby maintain ecosystem complexity. Understanding ecosystem complexity was vital, for loss of complexity equated to loss of function, and ultimately it made the ecosystem more vulnerable to collapse.[1]

Traditional foresters were already aware of many of the concepts employed by the New Forestry, Franklin hastened to acknowledge. Nevertheless, the old school tended to be reductionist, turning everything into computations of board feet and sustained yield, or at best placing those quantifiable outputs alongside amenity values such as wildlife and recreation. The New Forestry aimed to address a far more encompassing set of values: preservation of biodiversity, protection of forest ecosystems from the stresses of acid rain and global warming, and prevention of habitat fragmentation on a landscape scale. At its core, the New Forestry called on the profession to take a step back and give due regard to the complexity of nature. It was not so much about new concepts as it was about a new outlook. Franklin closed his article with a plea to his fellow foresters: "Let us adopt a forest ethic. Let us approach forest ecosystems with the respect that their complexity and beauty deserve. And, considering our current level of knowledge, let us approach the forest with appropriate humility."

Humility, respect—those were Indian values. The New Forestry's holistic vision and circumspect approach to its own know-how appeared to be steering modern forest scientists in the direction of a Native American land ethic. Just as Stewart Udall had written in *The Quiet Crisis* a quarter century before, conservationists found themselves "turning back to ancient Indian land ideas. . . . recovering a sense of reverence for the land."[2] There was a touch of mysticism in the New Forestry's profound fascination with old-growth forest. Advocates for the protection of old growth even had a kind of totem animal, as author Steven Lewis Yaffee would soon point out with his aptly titled book, *The Wisdom of the Spotted Owl: Policy Lessons for a New Century*.[3]

However, the significance of the shift in values espoused by Franklin and his team should not be pushed too far. The New Forestry still had a manipulative, managerial intent. It offered a middle course between outright forest conversion (replacing old-growth stands with tree farms) and total, hands-off preservation. Its object was to develop methods of timber extraction that would meet society's continuing demand for wood products on one hand and satisfy the public's desire for preserving endangered species, old-growth forest, and aesthetic values on the other. While the conciliatory tone of the New Forestry held a certain appeal for environmentalists, Franklin made no bones about where he himself stood. Foresters and environmentalists, he said, "must learn to share the sandbox rather than divide it."[4]

FIGURE 23. Northern spotted owl. The endangered species was in the eye of the storm over
old-growth logging in the Pacific Northwest.

PHOTO BY JOHN AND KAREN HOLLINGSWORTH,
FOREST SERVICE. COURTESY OF FISH AND
WILDLIFE SERVICE/WIKIMEDIA COMMONS.

Franklin's article in *American Forests* appeared just as the conflict over
logging in the Pacific Northwest reached a climax. The crisis was long in
the making. The northern spotted owl was at the center of the crisis, though
everyone recognized that the larger issue was the future of old-growth forest.
Of greatest moment was what the Forest Service was doing with old growth
on the national forests. It came to light in the early 1970s that the northern
spotted owl nested almost solely in old-growth trees, and scientific and public
awareness of the ecological relationship between the owl and late-successional
forest ecosystems steadily grew over the next decade and a half. In 1989, an
environmental coalition led by the Sierra Club Legal Defense Fund sued the
Forest Service in federal court, asking for an injunction to stop all logging on

the national forests in western Washington and Oregon until the agency developed an owl management plan. Judge William Dwyer granted the injunction, suddenly bringing to a halt 140 planned timber sales. He also took the bold step of ordering the executive branch to form an Interagency Scientific Committee (ISC) for the purpose of writing guidelines for the protection of the owl and other old-growth-dependent species, stipulating that the injunction would remain in effect until the ISC completed its task and the court was satisfied that the agency was back on track in protecting the owl, as it needed to do under the National Forest Management Act (NFMA). At the end of 1989, Congress passed an appropriation bill that funded the court-mandated ISC. However, a rider was attached to the same bill that countermanded the judge's decision to the extent of allowing timber operations to go forward on 1.1 billion board feet of timber in old-growth forest.[5]

Those were the opening shots in a conservation battle that came to symbolize both a federal government in gridlock and a Forest Service in crisis. Not only had the Forest Service lost control of the situation, it was being batted back and forth like a shuttlecock between the federal courts and Congress. All three branches of government complained that one or both of the other branches were exceeding their powers. Meanwhile, the people of the Pacific Northwest were increasingly polarized. The slogan "jobs versus the environment" created a civic divide and split politicians into opposing camps. Owls were burned in effigy. Bumper stickers talked of exterminating owls and shooting environmentalists. One by one, lumber mills closed down and rural communities faced the threat of their own grueling form of extinction. While forest workers blamed environmentalists for destroying their livelihoods, environmentalists bemoaned the continuing uncertainty and turmoil.

For the Forest Service, the spotted owl crisis came after years of escalating conflict with the environmental movement. Indeed, the legal challenge to the Forest Service's timber sale plans in western Washington and Oregon in 1989 was reminiscent of the lawsuit that halted Forest Service timber sales on the Monongahela National Forest in West Virginia in 1975. In the earlier controversy environmentalists argued that clear-cutting contradicted the Forest Service's mandate to protect watersheds. The court agreed and enjoined the Forest Service from further use of that logging practice, and Congress passed the NMFA of 1976 to resolve the impasse. The NFMA was a compromise; it affirmed that the Forest Service could conduct timber sales on the basis of clear-cutting, but it also made the Forest Service more answerable to the environmental movement by instigating forest planning and an administrative appeals process. Historian Samuel P. Hays has characterized the long transition in national forest management after the NFMA as a time of "confronting the ecological forest." New public values and laws required the Forest Service to manage the national forests primarily for biodiversity rather than timber production, and the agency slowly pivoted to that different role as myriad problems such as the protection of the spotted owl cropped up.[6]

Hays and other scholars have noted that as the Forest Service performed its pivot, it had to appeal to different groups of forest users for political support. Political scientist William M. Salka described the Forest Service as being stretched between two key coalitions of supporters. The first coalition was the "commodity production coalition," consisting of timber companies, timber workers, and mill towns as well as local governments and members of Congress who were close to those timbering interests. The second coalition was the "amenity coalition," made up of environmental and wildlife groups, state and local fish and game management agencies, water quality agencies, and environmentally friendly members of Congress. Tribes, it needs to be pointed out, were not conspicuous in either coalition. Tribal interests in national forestlands were mostly something else again. Tribal interests did not mesh with the clusters of interests Salka was talking about. What is important to note here is that the Forest Service was trying to satisfy both the commodity and amenity coalitions at the very time that tribes were demanding to be heard as well. The spotted owl crisis compounded the Forest Service's difficulties. As Salka wrote, "the agency's external environment was in turmoil as competing conditions struggled to impose their policy preferences on an agency long accustomed to autonomy."[7]

Dr. Jack Ward Thomas, a scientist at the Pacific Northwest Forest and Range Experiment Station and another prominent proponent of the New Forestry, was appointed by the Forest Service to head the ISC demanded by the court. Thomas picked Franklin and other like-minded scientists to serve with him. But despite the team's scientific heft, it produced a report that was essentially political. Thomas's ISC aimed for a workable compromise, proposing that some old-growth areas be reopened to logging while other areas be retained for nesting habitat so as to give the northern spotted owl "a high probability of population viability." The Bush administration, insisting on higher timber targets, declined to implement the ISC plan in any case. The House Agriculture Committee then put together its own scientific panel, putting Thomas once again at the helm. The scientific panel presented a report similar to the ISC report while offering a range of options with escalating timber harvest levels and diminishing probabilities of success associated with each option. None of the options was selected. By the time the scientific panel completed its work, the 1992 presidential campaign was in progress, and the politics surrounding the spotted owl had become hopelessly deadlocked. Democratic candidate Bill Clinton, pointing to the crisis as a prime example of "Washington gridlock," promised if elected to call a "timber summit" that would clear the air and find a solution.[8]

On April 2, 1993, shortly after taking office, President Clinton convened the Pacific Northwest Forest Conference in Portland, Oregon. More than sixty people were invited to join the president and vice president in three roundtable discussions on the social effects, ecological and economic elements, and small- and large-scale solutions to the impasse. Among the participants were two Native Americans: Margaret Powell, owner of a small mill on the Hupa Valley Reservation, and Ted Strong, executive director of the Columbia River Inter-Tribal Fish Commission and a member of the Yakama tribe. Spokespersons for Pacific Northwest tribes commented that while they were glad to be represented, two seats at the conference table were no substitute for government-to-government relations.[9]

As the president and vice president listened and reacted to the roundtable discussions, the conference had the feeling of an informal arbitration hearing. It produced high hopes for a new spirit of collaboration. As it concluded, Clinton set a goal for the government to develop a regional forest plan in sixty days. The forest plan was to embody three main principles: it would protect old-growth ecosystems on a regional scale, it would provide a stronger framework for inter-agency cooperation, and it would be sensitive to local communities. The president appointed three interagency working groups to accomplish those goals.[10]

Jack Ward Thomas was tapped to lead the science group, which was called the Forest Ecosystem Management Assessment Team. The team included more than a hundred scientists, analysts, and technicians drawn from six federal agencies and several universities. This enormous team, working long hours in a rented auditorium, hammered out a thousand-page document that served as the scientific foundation for the Northwest Forest Plan. A draft of the plan was released in July 1993, and the court injunction was removed soon thereafter. Once the plan became final in December 1994, the administration claimed it was "the first regional land management plan to pass full legal muster."[11]

In the half decade from 1989 to 1994, the spotted owl crisis grew into a conservation battle such as the nation had never seen before. When it ended, ecosystem management (EM) emerged as the new paradigm for managing the national forests and indeed for managing all public lands. EM recognized the unity of humankind and nature and the interconnectedness of local economies and the natural environment. It accepted ecological complexity. Most of all, it insisted on taking a wider view of the landscape and working across jurisdictional boundaries. "This is a mind-wrenching thing to pull back and pull up and start to look at the world with a satellite view," said Thomas in 1992, "but that is how we're going to deal with it."[12] The Clinton administration underscored the dramatic new approach to public land stewardship when it selected Thomas to succeed F. Dale Robertson as chief of the Forest Service in December 1993. Although Robertson had articulated a change of direction for the Forest Service with his "New Perspectives" in the early 1990s, skeptics questioned whether Robertson's policy initiative went far enough. Thomas was truly a fresh face. He had been virtually unknown outside of the agency before his sudden rise to stardom in the spotted owl crisis. He was the first wildlife biologist as well as the first research scientist ever to occupy the office of chief forester, and his appointment was a political statement that the Forest Service had entered an era of reform.

Tribes were encouraged but not overly impressed by the federal government's move to ecosystem management. When Jaime Pinkham, president of the Intertribal Timber Council and a member of the Nez Perce tribe, was asked by a mostly non-Indian audience what he thought of EM, he gave a sardonic reply: "ecosystem management—it is about time you guys caught on."[13] In an article on Indian forestry in *Journal of Forestry*, Gary S. Morishima, a long-time technical adviser to the Quinault Nation, remarked, "Although this concept has recently become fashionable, Indian tribes had been practicing it for thousands of years before they were displaced from their territories."[14] Throughout 1993, *Indian Country Today* did not run a single article on the Forest Service's move to EM, though it kept up a drumbeat of stories on the Forest Service's mismanagement of Indian sacred sites.

A NEW DAY FOR INDIAN FORESTRY

While the spotted owl crisis drew the whole nation's attention and ushered in a new era in national forest management, few people were aware that a new day was dawning for forest management on Indian reservations as well. The signal event for tribal forest management was the passage of the National Indian Forest Resources Management Act of 1990 (NIFRMA). Tribes hailed the act as a long-overdue charter for Indian forestry. To be sure, the BIA had been conducting timber operations on Indian reservations for more than a hundred years before that. Congress had provided previous authorities for managing Indian forests under the Dead and Down Act of 1889, the Indian Appropriations Act of 1910, and the Indian Reorganization Act of 1934, to name only the principal statutes. Indeed, the last-named law mandated sustained-yield forestry on Indian lands many years before it was mandated for the National Forest System in the Multiple-Use Sustained-Yield Act of 1960. Nevertheless, by the time NIFRMA was enacted, Indians had become utterly dissatisfied with the state of BIA forestry, and they held Congress partly to blame for it. Don Peasley, president of the Intertribal Timber Council (ITC) and a member of the Colville Confederated Tribes, testified to the Senate Select Committee on Indian Affairs before the law was passed: "Presently, all that is guiding the Federal trustee in the management and protection of our forests are four laws that total two pages in length and the Snyder Act."[15] How was it that BIA forestry had fallen so short of tribes' expectations?

The answer lay in the fact that the BIA viewed the Indian forest as strictly a trust asset. As trustee, the BIA's fiduciary responsibility was to maximize revenue from the trust resource. Therefore, it managed the Indian forests almost exclusively for commercial timber production. When tribes began to reassert their sovereign authority over reservation resources in the 1960s and 1970s, they found that the BIA's focus on commercial timber values did not match their own forest values. Even though many tribes depended on timber operations to provide tribal employment and much-needed revenue for the tribal government, most timber tribes wanted to reduce the level of logging on their reservations in order to give more weight to ecological and aesthetic values. As tribal traditions and practices were revitalized, tribes wanted to protect their forests for a variety of traditional values: for places of worship; for gathering medicinal herbs, basket-weaving material, and other forest products used for traditional purposes; for supplying fuel wood for home heating; and for subsistence hunting and fishing. So they increasingly found that BIA's traditional focus on commercial timber operations failed to take account of their community needs.[16]

Tribes began to establish their own forestry programs in the 1970s. At first, the fledgling tribal forestry programs operated in cooperation with BIA forestry. It took several years before any of them were able to stand up as federally funded

638 contracts under the Indian Self-Determination Act. The Quinault tribe of western Washington started building its program in the 1970s under Buy-Indian contracts: the tribe would undertake a forest project such as reforesting a cutover area of the reservation, and BIA forestry would provide all technical specifications for the job, such as what kinds of species were planted, what amount of space was left between seedlings, and so on. While the Buy-Indian contracts gave the tribal forestry programs a foot in the door, tribal foresters found the BIA's oversight extremely burdensome. Gary Morishima remembered how the BIA obstructed his every attempt at innovation:

> I was unable to initiate programs to reduce wildfire hazards created by massive clearcuts and enormous accumulations of logging slash, plant seedlings from appropriate seed sources, prepare sites for reforestation while avoiding compaction of clay soils from scarification, improve log jams that impeded passage for salmon, and thousands of acres of once productive forestland that had remained brush fields for decades due to years of neglect, complete forest inventories, or gain basic information on the productivity and sensitivities of the soils found on the Reservation. In short, I had become appalled at the condition of the forests on the Quinault Reservation and frustrated that I couldn't get the BIA to recognize what to me was an obvious and compelling need for corrective action.[17]

As tribal forestry programs gained more professional expertise and financial support over the years, they were more inclined to challenge what they did not like about BIA forestry. The Hupa Tribe initiated a forestry program in 1972 and established an environmental department in 1980. The latter quarreled with BIA forestry over effects of logging on fish and wildlife habitat for some eight years until finally, in 1988, the Hupa Tribe was able to take over BIA's forestry and roads program under the Indian Self-Determination Act and stop the objectionable logging practice.[18]

Tribal and BIA forestry programs not only clashed over how to manage tribal forests, but they also fought over shrinking appropriations. As tribes sometimes opted to take over BIA forestry programs one piece at a time, the partnership between the BIA and tribes became fraught with petty quarrels over access to federal moneys and shifting responsibilities. In the 1980s, the ITC had to combat moves by Congress and the Reagan administration to cut BIA forestry budgets and interdict administrative fee deductions on tribal timber sales for deposit in the U.S. Treasury. Up till then, those fee deductions had been used to help fund tribal forestry programs.[19]

Finally, the ITC got the ear of the Senate Select Committee on Indian Affairs and its chairman, Republican Senator John McCain of Arizona. The ITC worked closely with Senate committee staff and Senator McCain to craft legislation that protected investments made in Indian forest management while promoting tribal self-determination and self-sufficiency. The legislation paralleled major statutes affecting the National Forest System, and the authors looked at the Forest Service as the prime example of another forestry organization. But the bill made no specific references to cooperation between tribes or the BIA and the Forest Service. That would await legislative action in the future. President George Bush signed NIFRMA into law on November 29, 1990.

Tribes were generally pleased with the law. One important innovation was that it specifically addressed both commercial forestlands and commercial woodland, the latter consisting of scrubby forestlands on which commercial timber species made up less than 5 percent of the crown cover. Woodland made up a substantial portion of all Indian forestlands, and it was important to many tribes that its woodland be recognized as a renewable, manageable resource. NIFRMA introduced forest management plans into Indian forestry but with an important difference: they were to be integrated with tribal resource management plans to ensure that tribal values were taken into consideration. Another important feature of NIFRMA was its provision for a periodic independent assessment of Indian forests. The first would be made in the ensuing year, and another would follow every ten years. The assessment would include a review of the funding, staffing, management, and health of Indian forests, offering comparison with public and private forests. Another benefit of the law was its provision for educational assistance that would allow tribes to train their young people in natural resource management.[20]

NIFRMA was a huge gain for Indian forestry. The difficult partnership of BIA and tribal forestry programs on Indian lands needed that overarching organic law to give it coherence and to provide credibility to Indian forestry alongside federal, state, and private forestry. Veteran BIA forester Bob Miller explained the need well when he said that BIA forestry's underlying problems "resulted from the fact we were a forest management organization wrapped inside a social services agency that was forever trying a new program it thought would help the Indian people. Forestry was often swept away in nebulous, trust related issues over which we had little control."[21] NIFRMA promised a greater level of congressional support and federal funding for Indian forests right then and into the future. Among Congress's findings and declarations in Title I of the act was that federal funding for management of Indian forestland was significantly below what they were for national forestland, Bureau of Land Management forestland, and private forestland. It appeared as though Congress intended to close that gap in the coming years.

The Indian Forest Management Assessment Team (IFMAT), which commenced its independent study of Indian forests in 1991 and made its report to Congress in 1993, drew further attention to the disparity in funding levels. IFMAT reported that Indian forests received just one third of the dollars per acre that the federal government invested in national forest management. IFMAT recommended that Congress increase the annual appropriation for Indian forestry from $66 million to $187 million, which would put its forest planning and management budget on par with that of the Forest Service.[22]

Over the next several years Congress did narrow the gap in dollars-per-acre appropriations, but it was not clear whether the increases for Indian forestry were aimed at putting it on a road to parity with the Forest Service. The comparison of BIA and Forest Service appropriations overlooked important differences between Indian forests and the National Forest System. Indian forestlands were not subject to the rigorous forms of environmental impact assessment, public review, and administrative appeal that attended the Forest Service's management of national forestlands. Indian forestry faced far less litigation. Furthermore, tribal governments kicked in substantial amounts of money from their own coffers for tribal forestry, matching federal dollars one for one in some cases. While some viewed that financial contribution by the tribes as wrong because Indian forest management was the federal government's trust responsibility, others considered it in a more favorable light as part of the progression toward tribal self-sufficiency. It was a hard call because the line between federal trust responsibility and tribal self-sufficiency was constantly shifting.

By the time the second ten-year assessment of Indian forests was completed in 2003, the federal funding gap was reduced by half. On a per-acre basis, federal funding for Indian forestry rose from one-third to two-thirds of the amount spent on national forest management. But again, the comparison tended to ignore underlying differences. One reason the gap narrowed was

FIGURE 24. Forest inspection on the Flathead Reservation, Montana, during the Intertribal Timber Council annual meeting, 2006. Facing camera is Fred Clark, Citizen Potawatomi, then Forest Service regional social scientist for the Eastern Region.

COURTESY OF DALE KANEN

because federal funding for the National Forest System was cut substantially over the ten-year period. The other reason was that the federal government significantly increased spending on forest fire management during the decade, and a portion of those moneys went to Indian forestry. Absent those factors, Indian forestry's gains were modest.[23]

Even if the comparison of Forest Service and BIA forestry budgets gave only an approximate idea of their relative strength and effectiveness, the fact that the IFMAT reviews, the ITC, and various tribal spokespersons focused attention on the comparison year after year was significant. It showed that Indian forestry now had a place at the table with federal, state, and private forestry—and it was not looking for crumbs but demanding its fair share of federal dollars.

THE FOREST SERVICE APPOINTS A TRIBAL RELATIONS COORDINATOR

In January 1988, the U.S. Department of Agriculture and the U.S. Department of the Interior entered into an Agreement in Principle, which recognized that the two agencies had a common objective to promote the highest and best use of Indian lands. Pursuant to that ideal, Chief of the Forest Service F. Dale Robertson decided to bring a Native American into the Forest Service headquarters staff to advise on how the Forest Service could improve its relations with tribes. His choice for the position was Robert Tippeconnie, forest supervisor on the Coronado National Forest. Tippeconnie was offered a two-year position as staff assistant to the deputy chief for State and Private Forestry, Allan J. West. He was to travel around the nation, meet with tribal representatives, canvas Forest Service people in the field who had experience working with tribal governments, and advise the Forest Service's senior leadership on whether it should establish a permanent office of tribal relations at the national level.[24]

Tippeconnie brought an interesting background to his new assignment. Born into the Comanche tribe and raised on the White Mountain Apache Reservation, he was certainly at home talking with Indian people. As supervisor of the Coronado National Forest, he had also learned a bit about power politics in the nation's capital. In the years immediately before his appointment as tribal relations coordinator, he was embroiled in one of the Forest Service's biggest controversies involving an Indian sacred site. The controversy revolved around plans to build a massive astronomical observatory on the summit of Mount Graham, a prominent peak in southern Arizona and one of the Western Apache's four holiest mountains.

Behind the plans for the world-class, $200 million observatory was a powerful consortium of research institutions headed by the University of Arizona with support from the Smithsonian Institution and the Vatican (whose own Vatican Observatory had relocated most of its field operations from Castel Sandolfo, Italy, to southern Arizona in 1980 to get away from light pollution). In 1982, the consortium proposed an expansive development that would virtually blanket the mountain's top one thousand feet of elevation, and they lobbied for the inclusion of their project in the Coronado National Forest management plan.

The summit of Mount Graham is home to the southernmost subspecies of red squirrel in North America. The Mount Graham red squirrel, first described in 1894, occurs nowhere else but on this "sky island" in the southern Arizona desert. Quite apart from the Western Apache's concerns about their sacred mountain, environmentalists opposed the observatory on the grounds that its construction would threaten the extinction of the Mount Graham red squirrel. The proposed 3,500-acre site would take out a substantial portion of spruce-fir forest crowning Mount Graham's high summit, which was critical habitat for this isolated and unique population of red squirrel.[25]

Confronted by environmentalists and the strong arm of the Endangered Species Act on the one hand and powerful development interests with solid backing from Arizona's two senators on the other, Tippeconnie sought compromise. He revised the plan for the observatory so that it would have a much smaller footprint, with five telescopes instead of eighteen. He detached the plan for the observatory from the rest of the forest management plan so that it could be cleared through a separate environmental review process. In 1988, Congress authorized the construction of the observatory on the basis of those narrower parameters under a special exemption to the Endangered Species Act. The observatory was built in the early 1990s after Tippeconnie took up his new responsibilities in Washington as tribal relations coordinator.[26]

Ironically, Tippeconnie gave short shrift to the religious concerns of the Western Apache while he was forest supervisor. In the mid-1980s, his office sent a letter to the tribal council of the San Carlos Apache informing the tribe of the proposed development and inviting comment. There was no reply, and that was the extent of the forest's tribal consultation. In October 1986, the Coronado National Forest issued its draft environmental impact statement (DEIS) containing the brief statement that "No Indian Tribes have come forward with information on potential impacts to their religious use of Mount Graham at this time."[27] In 1987, the Department of the Interior found the Forest Service's DEIS "inadequate" and advised the agency to address Native American religious concerns more fulsomely, as directed by AIRFA. Tippeconnie chose not to pursue it. In 1988, the tribe was still reticent to take an official stand on the issue, although tribal members joined with environmentalists in opposing the development soon thereafter. In a 1993 interview with a reporter for the *Phoenix New Times*, Tippeconnie said that he had been well aware in the 1980s that many traditional Apaches considered Mount Graham to be sacred, but he also understood that they would be reluctant, if pressed, to describe their feelings to non-Indians.[28] It was the same conundrum that the Forest Service faced elsewhere: how was the federal land manager to protect a Native American religious site when the religious practitioners did not want to disclose any information about it?

The answer was to strengthen the agency's commitment to tribal consultation and raise the level of trust between Indians and federal land managers. Tippeconnie's first objective in his new position as tribal relations coordinator was to raise the agency's awareness about its trust responsibilities to Indian peoples and strengthen its institutional commitment to government-to-government relations. To that end, he developed the Forest Service's first statement of Indian policy, consisting of four points:

1. Maintain a governmental relationship with federally recognized tribal governments.
2. Implement our programs and activities honoring Indian treaty rights and fulfill legally mandated trust responsibilities to the extent that they are determined applicable to National Forest System lands.
3. Administer programs and activities to address and be sensitive to traditional Native religious beliefs and practices.
4. Provide research, transfer of technology, and technical assistance to Indian governments.

The policy was introduced together with supporting materials into the Forest Service Manual as Section 1563, Tribal Relations, under Title 1500, External Relations. That gave it official weight. But to give the policy wider notice, Tippeconnie advertised it in a letter-size, eight-leaf pamphlet printed on yellow cardstock under the title *Forest Service Native American Policy—Friends and Partners*. The publication was distributed in 1990.[29]

Friends and Partners began with a message from the chief. Robertson sincerely desired to bring about change. As he indicated elsewhere, his views on enhancing tribal relations were similar to his views on affirmative action. There was strength in cultural diversity. There was value in tapping into Native Americans' different thinking and outlook.[30] "The opportunities are at hand. . . . It is time to visit, meet, and walk the land together. The rewards of these actions should benefit us all."[31]

Friends and Partners used similar phrasing where it amplified on the policy's third point concerning traditional Native religions. The Forest Service needed to "walk the land with Native Americans to gain an understanding and appreciation of their culture, religion, beliefs, and practices. We must identify and acknowledge these cultural needs in our activities. We consider these values an important part of management of the National Forests."[32]

As Tippeconnie traveled around the country, he saw an urgent need for a tribal relations specialist to be stationed in each regional office. The task of educating the workforce and changing the organizational culture far surpassed anything he might be able to accomplish by himself. Consistent with the Forest Service's historic tendency toward decentralization, he pursued the staffing issue with each regional forester separately and got a variable response.[33]

The Pacific Northwest Region, the first region to appoint a full-time tribal relations liaison, hired Les McConnell from the BIA in 1990. McConnell had a background in natural resource management with a focus on fisheries and treaty-reserved fishing rights. He brought to the position a strong legal understanding of the federal government's trust responsibilities, which he had learned through his work for the BIA. He also brought a sympathetic understanding of the Pacific Northwest tribes' extensive treaty-reserved rights. Of some three dozen federally recognized tribes in the Pacific Northwest, two dozen had reserved rights to take fish at usual and accustomed places and hunt, gather, and graze livestock on open and unclaimed lands.[34]

The Pacific Southwest Region (California) followed close behind its northern neighbor, establishing a full-time tribal liaison position in 1992. The person selected was Sonia Tamez, a midcareer Forest Service employee who had been serving in that capacity on a part-time basis for several years already, first as a specialist in CRM, then as a forest planner. Tamez's experience with Forest Service–tribal relations was quite different from McConnell's, because California Indians were beset by quite different circumstances, both present and historical. Relatively few California tribes had reserved treaty rights, or even reservations; many lacked federal recognition, and a large proportion relied on national forest and BLM lands for traditional use. The Native American Heritage Commission, a state organization, had a memorandum of understanding with the Forest Service (signed in 1990) and was actively engaged with Indian-public land issues. For these reasons, Tamez took a broad view of federal responsibility that was less sharply drawn around Indian trust assets and treaty rights.[35]

The Alaska Region appointed its first Alaska Native liaison, John Foss, in 1992. Foss, who was an archeologist on the Tongass National Forest before becoming the Alaska Native liaison, concentrated on the Southeast Alaska region while Fred Clark, archeologist on the Chugach National Forest, gradually moved into tribal relations work as well over the next three years. In terms of budget and staff, the Alaska Region was (and still is) the smallest of the nine National Forest System regions, so the fact that it was one of the first to fund a tribal relations position was an indication of the importance of Native issues there. "In Alaska, 15 percent of the population is native—that's huge," said Clark later. "Everything about Alaska is flavored by the indigenous experience. All those lands that the Forest Service has on the Tongass and Chugach forests— those are the native lands of the indigenous tribes." Partly because the Alaska Region is so small, the tribal relations program and the heritage program have remained closely aligned there.[36]

The fourth region to create a tribal liaison position was the Northern Region (Idaho and Montana). There, the position started out in the civil rights program before eventually being transferred to State and Private Forestry. Ira Jones was employed in the late 1980s as an affirmative action specialist. As a Nez Perce, he knew how important treaty rights were in the region. (As in Washington and Oregon, reserved rights cover enormous areas of ceded territory in Idaho and Montana.) With Tippeconnie's encouragement, he put more and more of his efforts toward educating the agency about treaty rights. Starting in 1991 and continuing for the next two years, he helped put on three big treaty rights workshops at different locations in the region for forest supervisors, district rangers, other interested federal employees, and tribal representatives. Each workshop drew three hundred to four hundred people. The workshops were a combination of education and training, giving the participants an opportunity to meet one another and practice collaborating.[37]

The remaining regional offices were slower to develop a tribal liaison position. Some started out with half-time appointments. Pat Aguilar served as a tribal liaison in the Intermountain Region (Utah and Nevada) in the mid-1990s. In 1998, the Southwest Region (Arizona and New Mexico) hired its first tribal relations specialist, Dorothy FireCloud. An enrolled member of the Rosebud Sioux Tribe, she held a degree in law from the University of New Mexico and was a member of the New Mexico bar since 1991. Before joining the Forest Service, she worked for the U.S. Department of Justice, the BIA, and the Pueblo of Zuni as a water rights specialist.

Susan Johnson, a plant pathologist and entomologist in the Rocky Mountain Region (Colorado, Wyoming, and the central plains states), was asked to work on specific tasks for the tribal relations program because of her personal knowledge and interest in Indian affairs as an enrolled member of the Three

Affiliated Tribes. But it was not until 2000 that she changed jobs and became that region's tribal relations specialist.[38]

Tippeconnie remained in the post of national coordinator until 1997, at which time he retired from the Forest Service and went to work for his tribe. Over the years, colleagues marveled at his energy in conducting a one-man show as program administrator, recruiter, educator, adviser, and Forest Service ambassador to tribes. Through his nine years of service in that position, he stressed the need to implant tribal relations specialists in all the Forest Service regions rather than establish a tribal relations staff in the Washington office. It was a significant choice of emphasis reflecting the agency's historic bent toward decentralization.

Tippeconnie could not ignore the call for a more fulsome national policy manual, however. As the Forest Service regions became more and more involved with tribal issues, they took different approaches on numerous matters where the agency needed to have consistency. Short of forming a new staff group in the Washington office to develop national-level policy, Tippeconnie tried to address this problem by asking the tribal relations specialists in the regions to get together and produce a desk guide for use throughout the National Forest System. The document became popularly known as the "Yellow Book" because of its yellow cover. First produced in the mid-1990s, then revised and expanded for a large printing in April 1997, its formal title was *Forest Service National Resource Book on American Indian and Alaska Native Relations.*

The book began with a thirty-two-page overview of the history of federal Indian policy. Oriented to the interests of the land manager, it included such useful features as a recitation of why Indian Country in Alaska differs from Indian Country in the Lower 48 and a chronological table of major statutes affecting American Indians and natural resources. The next forty pages were divided into four sections corresponding with the four points of the Forest Service's Indian policy. Each one took the reader briskly through the pertinent laws, legal cases, and federal policies. Several appendices took up the final twenty-five pages, the last one being an alphabetical listing of the 543 federally recognized tribes.[39]

The Yellow Book was significant because it not only provided a helpful digest of information for line officers, but it also constituted a first attempt by the Forest Service to bring about greater consistency in the way the nine regions dealt with tribal issues. The effort to achieve greater consistency across such a decentralized agency as the Forest Service was not without tension.

Several individuals who worked on the first draft asked to be removed from the team when they found that the Washington office was making extensive changes to the document that they did not agree with and could not approve. At least one of the book's key contributors requested to have his name removed from the list of authors after he saw the final version.

Still, one of the benefits of producing the Yellow Book was that it became an enormous team-building exercise, welding a diverse group of individuals who were scattered among different regional and local offices all around the country into one committed staff.[40] Several individuals who helped produce the Yellow Book subsequently worked together on the Forest Service's National Tribal Relations Program Task Force in the year 2000, ushering in the agency's national tribal relations program at the turn of the century. That protracted team effort, which culminated with the establishment of a tribal relations directorate in the Washington office, is the subject of the next chapter.

CHAPTER SUMMARY

During the 1990s, both the Forest Service and tribal governments went through further dramatic changes. The Forest Service adopted ecosystem management (EM) as a new paradigm for land stewardship. With the shift to EM, the agency signaled that it was adopting a less commodity-oriented, more holistic view of the environment. It was rebalancing the scales of multiple-use land management to give more weight to emerging values such as biodiversity, ecosystem resilience, and Indian sacred sites. Leading foresters began to talk about the need for "humility" in doing scientific research, "respect for nature," and a "forest ethic." The agency culture was changing in ways that made it more respectful of indigenous peoples' perspectives on the land.

Tribal governments continued to build capacity. Tribes with significant forest resources took over forestry on the reservation from the Bureau of Indian Affairs. The National Indian Forest Resources Management Act of 1990 provided a new charter for Indian forestry. The law established standards for tribal forest plans, provided education assistance for tribal members, and promised periodic review for the purpose of bringing Indian forestry up to par with federal forestry. As tribal governments began to do forestry on reservations, it set the stage for cooperative forestry between the Forest Service and tribes.

The Forest Service appointed a national coordinator for tribal relations in 1988, and over the next nine years he oversaw the development of a tribal relations staff in the Forest Service regions. While the Forest Service tribal relations program was gestating at the regional level, the first statement of national policy appeared in 1990 in a short booklet with the title *Forest Service Native American Policy—Friends and Partners*. It was followed in 1997 by a desk guide popularly known as the Yellow Book.

9

ELEVATING THE TRIBAL RELATIONS PROGRAM

IN SEARCH OF A NATIONAL PROGRAM

IN 1995, THE FOREST SERVICE'S Pacific Southwest Region hosted a national meeting on tribal relations in San Francisco. The regional program managers shared information and talked about a national strategic plan. They formed a consensus that the program needed a director and staff in Washington to bring greater attention to tribes' issues. Some argued that they needed leadership from above for development of new legislation and national policy. They pointed to differences in policies and practices from region to region and outright gaps in legislative authorities for some of the things that the agency was already doing.

An example of the need for new legislative authorities and policy could be found in the Forest Service's follow-up actions under the Native American Graves Protection and Repatriation Act (NAGPRA). Five years out from the passage of that law, tribes began to request the assistance of the Forest Service for reinterring human burial remains on national forestlands. Tribes obtained the bones of their ancestors from distant museums and wanted to put the bones to rest in their ancestral homes. NAGPRA addressed repatriation of human burial remains but was silent on the matter of reburial. It fell to district rangers and forest supervisors to decide how to respond to tribes' requests. Should it be permitted? If so, then what were the appropriate measures for confidentiality and protection of burial sites? Should the arrangements for reburial be strictly between the Forest Service and the tribe, or should they also involve the museum or university that originally excavated and removed the bones from national forestlands? Where was the funding for costs of reburials? (Costs were not incidental; usually the Forest Service provided transportation and other logistical support to bring elders and other tribal members to a remote location for the reburial ceremony.) These were very emotional, highly sensitive issues. The Forest Service could not be arbitrary or capricious. As more and more line officers dealt with this issue, they insisted on the need for policy to ensure consistency.[1]

Another example of a pressing need that argued for elevating the tribal relations program within the agency was in the area of cooperative forestry. Under existing law, the Forest Service could make grants for cooperative forestry to state and private forestry but not tribal forestry. As tribal governments built capacity and took over forestry on reservations from the BIA, the new tribal forestry programs began looking to the Forest Service for cooperative assistance. The Intertribal Timber Council (ITC) led on this issue, pointing out to tribes and the Clinton administration that the Forest Service could be doing more to help tribes compete for cooperative education grants and other types of federal assistance. The law had to be changed, and the Forest Service's cooperative assistance mission needed to be broadened to include outreach to tribes.

Reburials and cooperative assistance to tribal forestry were two prime examples among myriad issues that became more pressing as the decade advanced. Comparison of the two examples is instructive, as the first related to tribal interests on the national forests and the second related to tribal interests on reservations. Put another way, the two issues concerned two different divisions in the Forest Service organization: national forest administration and cooperation with state and private forestry. The regional tribal relations program managers were familiar with tribal concerns in both arenas, although in most cases their experience was more embedded in national forest administration. Chief Robertson highlighted the importance of cooperative assistance to tribal forestry when he appointed Robert Tippeconnie national coordinator in 1988 and placed him under the deputy chief of State and Private Forestry.

A central question facing the tribal relations program then, as it sought elevation within the agency, was where to locate the office of tribal relations in the Forest Service organization. When the regional tribal program managers worked as a team on the Yellow Book in the mid-1990s, they carefully described their program's complicated placement relative to cooperative forestry and national forest administration.[2] Indeed, they noted that tribal issues were not limited to those two main divisions of the Forest Service organization but extended as well to forest products research, the agency's third main mission area. Some tribes were in communication with Forest Service research stations, which were outside the National Forest System and managed by station directors who reported directly to the chief of the Forest Service. Clearly, wherever an office of tribal relations might reside in the organization, the tribal relations staff would need to work across several deputy areas.

The biggest challenge in elevating the tribal relations program to the national level was money. The program had to claim a bigger piece of the Forest Service budget. The Forest Service, even more than most other federal land-management agencies, faced pressure to downsize at the end of the 1990s. Nowhere in the organization was there more pressure to downsize than in the Washington office. To establish a new director position and staff group in the agency headquarters in a time of government downsizing meant to sacrifice other priorities and take money from other programs. The regional tribal relations program managers were seasoned enough to know that they would need to move their request all the way up the bureaucratic chain to the chief, breaking past a cordon of deputy chiefs and associate deputy chiefs in the Washington office who, guarding their own budgets, would be resistant to the tribal relations initiative.[3]

THE WESTERN STATE FORESTERS WEIGH IN

In 1996, Joe Mitchell became the national coordinator for tribal relations, replacing Robert Tippeconnie. Mitchell was a Forest Service career professional in natural resource management. As a member of the Cherokee Nation, he also developed an interest and specialization in Forest Service–tribal relations, holding two different posts in the agency's civil rights program before becoming national coordinator. The first of those assignments was in the Rocky Mountain Region, and the second was in the Washington office. When he was offered the position of national coordinator, Mitchell was back in the Rocky Mountain Region working as a natural resource manager. He agreed to head up the tribal relations program on the condition that he could work remotely from his office in Fort Collins, Colorado.

Serendipitously, Mitchell's Colorado location placed him near the Denver-based Council of Western State Foresters (CWSF) and therefore near Mit

Parsons, the Forest Service's liaison to the CWSF and a person with connections to the Forest Service leadership team in Washington. Parsons held a doctorate in fisheries and wildlife science and had an extensive background in legislative affairs. With an office in the regional office in Denver, he reported to the regional forester and the chairman of the CWSF. In his role as liaison to the CWSF, he kept his ear to the ground for trends and developments in western forestry. Since taking the position in 1992, he had observed the growth of tribal forestry programs on reservations and the tribes' increasing vigor in asserting their interests on national forests. When Joe Mitchell became national coordinator, the two men began discussing the need to elevate the tribal relations program to the national level. Since Mitchell served under the deputy chief of State and Private Forestry and Parsons worked with state foresters through the CWSF, they were in agreement that the initiative ought to go up the chain through the deputy chief of State and Private Forestry. The problem, they both knew, was that the initiative must have state foresters' support to get traction inside the Forest Service. Parsons thought the CWSF was an ideal forum in which to work the issue.[4]

Established in 1967, the CWSF was a regional organization dedicated to creating one clear voice for western forestry. A major goal of the organization was to forge the seventeen western states into a bloc for purposes of influencing the Forest Service's cooperative forestry program and budget. The Forest Service's assistance to state forestry programs amounted to well over $100 million per annum. State forestry agencies were very interested in Congress's annual appropriations for the Forest Service not only because those appropriations acts contained moneys for cooperative forestry but also because they shaped other Forest Service priorities. For example, western states were keenly interested in Congress's annual appropriations for wildland fire suppression. As costs of wildland fire suppression rose precipitously in the 1990s in the face of climate change and other factors, the CWSF and the Forest Service formed the Western Forestry Leadership Coalition, a group composed of all state foresters and Forest Service regional foresters and station directors located within the seventeen-state region, to manage the West's shifting priorities.[5]

Western state foresters were not known for their support of tribes. Being part of state governments, state foresters often dealt with the tension between states rights and tribal sovereignty. Moreover, they did not want to compete with tribes for federal dollars. Nevertheless, western state foresters respected the rising tribal forestry programs, especially those belonging to the so-called timber tribes (tribes with significant commercial forest resources). They were increasingly mindful of the need to cooperate across different land ownerships on transboundary forest issues such as wildland fire management and ecosystem health, partnering with all comers. Parsons thought the western state foresters could be persuaded to support making tribal relations a higher priority and that their support would be key in moving the initiative up the chain.[6]

Meanwhile, Parsons saw an opportunity to engage the right people in the Washington office when his friend Phil Janik became deputy chief of State and Private Forestry in January 1998. Janik, as regional forester in Alaska since 1994, had an excellent grasp of many aspects of Forest Service tribal relations, Parsons believed. His knowledge base included direct involvement in Alaska's important and unique federal subsistence management program. In view of his Alaska experience, Janik was sure to understand the importance of establishing a more robust tribal relations program in the agency. Janik was well respected in the agency for his successful handling of the second-generation forest plan for the Tongass National Forest. The plan was considered state of the art, a model of consensus building. Parsons was confident Janik would put his shoulder to the wheel on tribal relations. His confidence in Janik rested in part on their personal relationship; they were old buddies from their student days at the University of Montana (Classes of '66 and '67), and they had remained close friends ever since.[7]

In January 1998, Parsons and Mitchell prepared a memorandum for Janik about the need to improve tribes' access to the Forest Service's cooperative forestry programs. As the ITC had been pointing out for some time, federal moneys for cooperative forestry were funneled through the Forest Service to state agencies and private landowners with none going to tribes except for a tiny fraction that tribes secured by way of the states. Although the need to share those federal moneys with tribes was just one aspect of Forest Service–tribal relations, it was the most sensitive issue as far as state foresters were concerned. Parsons thought the state foresters would be broad minded.[8]

Janik tentatively endorsed the initiative, but in floating the idea to western state foresters he met with resistance. A few state foresters took the position that tribes had no business requesting a share of the Forest Service's cooperative assistance to state and private forestry since they received federal dollars and assistance through the BIA. States already shared the pie forty-four ways with other states, Gary L. Hergenrader, Nebraska's state forester, pointed out. "There are 556 tribes that want to be treated like states. For state and private forestry programs this could mean dividing the budget into 600 pieces."[9]

Colorado's long-serving state forester, James Hubbard, who was at that time on temporary assignment to the Forest Service as staff assistant to Deputy Chief Janik, opposed the tribal relations initiative. When Mit Parsons raised the matter with Hubbard early in 1998, Hubbard candidly informed him that he would try to talk Janik out of it. After his conversations with Janik, however, it was Hubbard who changed his mind. Hubbard's conversion was important not only then but for the future, since he would later come back to the Forest Service and eventually move into Janik's position as deputy chief of State and Private Forestry. One thing the Forest Service stood to gain by taking strong action on this issue, Hubbard pointed out to his fellow state foresters at the annual meeting of the CWSF the following year, was an opportunity to work constructively with the Senate Committee on Indian Affairs. He did not need to remind everyone how the Forest Service had taken a licking from the Senate committee over its management of Indian sacred sites.[10]

Janik made tribal relations one of his top issues. He placed it fifth in a list of thirteen issues in a summary document entitled "Forest Service Action Strategy for State and Private Forestry Services," which he cosigned with acting deputy chief Janice McDougle, James Hubbard, and assistant deputy chief Larry Payne on March 27, 1998. The summary statement on tribal government relations read, "Federally recognized Indian tribal governments have a unique relationship with the United States Government. The S&PF Deputy Chief offers to lead coordination of a Board of Deputy Chiefs to improve these relationships, pursue partnerships, provide research and technical assistance, and establish exchanges of information."[11] Over the next year, Janik and Parsons talked with western state foresters one by one to garner support. A vital point was that Congress had enacted the Cooperative Forestry Assistance Act of 1978, the main authority for state and private forestry, when tribal forestry did not yet exist. Now the tribes were doing their own forestry, and they were intent on changing the law. It was far better for the Forest Service and the states to be proactive than to be passive or obstructionist.[12]

At the CWSF annual meeting in May 1999, which took place in Anchorage, Alaska, the western state foresters were asked to go on record in favor of elevating tribal relations in the Forest Service. Janik was not there, having just been tapped by Chief Michael Dombeck to take the job of chief operating officer and help Dombeck meet the demands of the Clinton administration to downsize the agency. In Janik's place was acting deputy chief Janice McDougle, soon to be named deputy chief. McDougle informed the gathering that tribes were already asking Forest Service assistance with preparation of tribal forest plans, as mandated by the National Indian Forest Resources Management Act. The larger timber tribes were producing their plans with tribal moneys, but the smaller timber tribes needed help. The plans were costing about $35,000 apiece. It was a "heads up," McDougle told the state foresters. Tribes were undoubtedly going to start getting federal dollars that had gone exclusively to state agencies in the past.[13]

As Janik and Parsons had been priming state foresters on this matter all year, members were restrained in their comments. The western state foresters agreed that they needed to recognize tribes' empowerment in natural resource management as an "emerging trend." The CWSF passed the suggested resolution, and a committee met in August to finalize the plan, which was published in September 1999. The plan included a strong statement of intent to improve partnerships between state and tribal forestry and between the Forest Service and tribal governments.[14]

THE NATIONAL TRIBAL RELATIONS PROGRAM TASK FORCE

Later that year, Janik expressed concern to Parsons that the initiative appeared to be leaderless again and grinding to a halt. He told Parsons he was considering forming a task force to keep it going. Parsons replied, "Phil, it is absolutely needed." Parsons thought they needed help from the tribal relations specialists in the regions. Janik suggested that Parsons organize a team, divide it into a handful of work groups, and oversee the effort. Parsons was eager to participate, but he thought the task force should be led by someone in the Senior Executive Service, a person with enough stature to impress the deputy chiefs and associate deputy chiefs in the Washington office. Janik decided to appoint Brad Powell, regional forester in the Pacific Southwest Region, to head it up. Powell had previously served under Janik as a forest supervisor on the Tongass National Forest, so Janik trusted him. Moreover, Powell had a good working relationship with his tribal liaison, Sonia Tamez, who was already outspoken on the need to elevate tribal relations in the agency.[15]

Janik wanted a diverse team with ample experience in the field. The task force came to include thirteen people including Powell. They were a mix of line officers and subject specialists in the Forest Service as well as two individuals from outside the agency (Arch Wells from BIA and Gary Morishima from the ITC). Among the subject specialists were experts in tribal relations, heritage, lands, and timber. Six different regions of the National Forest System were represented as well as the Washington office. There were eight men and five women.[16]

Janik formally commissioned the National Tribal Relations Program Task Force in October 1999. He informed Powell that he wanted the task force to report to the Forest Service leadership by early summer 2000.[17]

In June 2000, after eight months of almost monthly meetings of the whole team, Powell and Tamez presented the National Tribal Relations Program Task Force findings to the Forest Service leadership. Besides the chief and deputy chiefs and associate chiefs, the audience included some of the key program directors in the Washington office. As was usual for such a presentation, everyone was briefed in advance so that there would be no fireworks. Materials were circulated beforehand, deputies met with their teams to review them and discuss their concerns, and then they came to the meeting with direct questions and issues. As Parsons later recalled the tenor of the meeting, the task force findings were politely received. The deputies and associate deputies made some requests for clarification, but they found no major stumbling blocks.[18]

Nonetheless, it was a hard-hitting report. Its thesis was that the Forest Service had formed practices and policies for accommodating the panoply of tribal interests on national forests without due guidance from the top. These practices and policies were at best inconsistent, at worst outmoded. In the words of the executive summary, the task force recommendations provided "a strategic focus for addressing pervasive problem areas that require definitive action to strengthen government-to-government relationships between the FS and Indian Tribes."[19]

The National Tribal Relations Program Task Force report started at the top with a recommendation to the chief that he issue a chief's order to the whole Forest Service. The order would identify the specific obligations of the agency to the fifty-two tribes with treaty-reserved rights in ceded lands, and it would address its obligations under the U.S. government's trust responsibility to all 558 federally recognized tribes. A nine-page draft of such an order, which fulsomely addressed the major issues, was included in the appendixes.

The next set of recommendations dealt with tribal consultation and coordination. Despite President Clinton's strong message on government-to-government relations delivered in April 1994, the Forest Service and other federal agencies continued to struggle with the precise meaning of tribal consultation as they sought to engage with tribal governments in different contexts.

In what specific instances should consultation be initiated? Who should it include? When was it complete? Line officers required more guidance, and the task force recommended revisions to Forest Service Manual 1563 (tribal relations) as well as revisions to the various Forest Service manuals on planning, recreation, heritage resources, timber management, and special forest uses so as to cross-reference applicable tribal relations policy.

The task force recommended internal monitoring and periodic review of Forest Service–tribal relations. Monitoring would cover all tribal consultation, including compilation of data on all incidence and disposition of issues and concerns raised by tribal governments. Periodic review would include some form of reporting on changing levels of tribal participation in Forest Service programs and tribal uses of national forests. These internal assessments would also track the numbers of Native Americans and Alaska Natives employed in Forest Service operations.

Other recommendations by the task force included appointing a tribal relations director and staff in the Washington office, establishing higher standards for tribal relations program managers in the regional offices, and training regional foresters, station directors, area directors, forest supervisors, district rangers, and appropriate staff across all deputy areas that were involved with tribal governments.

The task force defined six issues to be addressed through "issue-specific" reforms. The first involved the ability of Indian tribes to obtain special forest products for traditional cultural use. For some items, such as basket-weaving material, no fee or permit was required for noncommercial use. But for other items, such as cedar logs, they were. Besides that inconsistency, traditional-use forest products raised other issues. Were these items reserved by treaty? If a tribe did not have treaty rights, should it still have free use of forest products for traditional cultural uses?

The second issue, related to the first, was the ability of tribal governments to access existing forest products programs alongside other governments (federal, state, and local agencies). The Forest Service often received requests to provide forest products to tribes for nontraditional use, either free of charge or without competitive bidding. Other federal, state, and local agencies made the same requests and were able to obtain the products under certain authorities. The task force recommended a combination of administrative and legislative changes to remove the inequities.

The third issue involved tribes' requests for temporary closure or exclusive use of areas on national forests so that they could practice traditional cultural rites. Tribes' need for privacy was in conflict with recreational use of those same areas by the general public. Tribes also objected to requirements that they pay fees or get permission to have ceremonies on their aboriginal lands. The task force recommended a mix of administrative, policy, and legislative actions aimed at affording tribes those use and occupancy privileges in a way that was consistent and fair to the general public.

The fourth issue concerned the need to improve tribes' access to the Forest Service's myriad agreements and acquisition programs that formed a part of national forest administration. Once again, seemingly antiquated regulations and legislative authorities barred tribes from engaging in the kinds of partnerships that the Forest Service encouraged with state and local entities. The task force found that there was "much confusion about different programs and authorities." Tribes and the Forest Service were "unclear about the availability of FS grants and contracts." These problems needed to be addressed through a combination of administrative, policy, and legislative changes.

The fifth issue, tribes' access to state and private forestry programs under the Cooperative Forestry Assistance Act, fell squarely within the Forest Service's Division of State and Private Forestry. The problem was twofold: (1) tribes did not have access to federal assistance on the same basis as state and private entities, and (2) tribes did not receive equivalent levels of assistance through the BIA. The task force recommended reforms that would integrate tribes into the Forest Stewardship Program. A critical piece of that process would involve working with the ITC and other intertribal organizations to ensure that tribal needs were duly reflected in budget requests for the Forest Stewardship Program. The goal was to increase overall appropriations for cooperative forestry so that tribal, state, and private forestry needs were all accounted for.

The last issue addressed in the task force report was reburial of Native American human remains on national forests. Although the Forest Service allowed reburials of Native American remains on national forestlands when they were originally disinterred from those lands, there was no national policy that addressed funding and other specific issues associated with the reburials. The task force report noted that while NAGPRA addressed repatriations, it was silent on reburials of human remains. "NAGPRA compliance is very emotional, highly sensitive, and a high priority among Tribes," the report explained.

The task force recommended development of national policy guidelines on reburials to provide consistency as well as funding.

The task force deliberately left one major issue out of its report: management of Indian sacred sites on national forestlands. Task force members decided the issue was too big to tackle in their allotted timeframe. They believed it was necessary to get a stronger framework for tribal relations in place and then grapple with sacred sites policy.[20]

The task force's report identified so many problems needing to be addressed, it would be easy to overlook the positive message at the heart of the program. Tribes were the Forest Service's natural allies. "Tribes have been culturally tied to the land and its resources for thousands of years. Their traditional knowledge and continuing contributions to the body of scientific information can improve management of the Nation's resources. . . . Conservation of the Nation's resources has been part of tribal stewardship for generations." These were familiar ideas that had been expressed before. Yet they were more compelling than ever in the present setting. Several individuals among the Forest Service leadership emphasized that they wanted to change the overall tenor of Forest Service–tribal relations from a focus on differences to a new spirit of collaboration.

THE NATIONAL TRIBAL RELATIONS PROGRAM IMPLEMENTATION TEAM

A few months before the task force completed its work, Joe Mitchell stepped aside as coordinator and moved to Tahlequah, Oklahoma, on a detail to write a forest plan for the Cherokee Nation. He never returned. Carol Jorgensen, another member of the task force and a seasoned expert in tribal relations in the Forest Service's Alaska Region, took Mitchell's place for a couple of months; then Dorothy FireCloud, another member of the task force, took a turn after her. When it was clear Mitchell was not coming back, the deputy chief asked Jorgensen to accept a permanent appointment. Since there was still no national office of tribal relations, Jorgensen's leadership marked a time of transition between the coordinator role that Tippeconnie and Mitchell each held and the subsequent appointment of a program director with a staff. Jorgensen's official title was Tribal Relations Program Manager.

Amid the confusion surrounding Mitchell's departure, Phil Janik sensed that the tribal relations initiative might falter. Even though the task force report had been accepted by the Forest Service leadership, none of the deputy chiefs was anxious to assume responsibility for implementing it. Neither he nor Chief Dombeck had time to take it on, the two being immersed in budget performance review at the behest of the Clinton administration. Then came the extremely close, tangled presidential election in November 2000 followed by weeks of uncertainty over which candidate had won, Vice President Al Gore or Governor George W. Bush. Once the issue had been decided in favor of the Republican candidate, there was an impulse to wait and see what the new administration would do when it took power in January. In the interim, Janice McDougle moved from deputy chief of State and Private Forestry into Janik's office, and Dombeck appointed Michael T. Rains in her place. Janik admonished Rains not to allow the tribal relations initiative to fizzle. Soon after stepping into his new job, Rains announced that he was establishing the National Tribal Relations Program Implementation Team to complete the necessary staff work to carry forward the recommendations in the task force report.[21]

The implementation team bridged a period of indecision surrounding the 2000 election. Carol Jorgensen served in the Washington office from September 2000 until September 2002, carrying the tribal relations initiative forward into the Bush administration. Six months into Jorgensen's two-year tour, Chief Dombeck retired, and the Bush administration selected Dale N. Bosworth to be the next chief of the Forest Service. Half a year after Dombeck's departure, Rains stepped down as deputy chief of State and Private Forestry, and Bosworth appointed Joel Holtrop to take his place. While the presidential election of 2000 and the change from Democratic to Republican control of the executive branch did cause the tribal relations initiative to be delayed, ultimately the new administration supported it.

Jorgensen, as tribal relations program manager, played an important role through this pivotal time. Born in southeast Alaska, she was Tlingit and a member of the Eagle/Killer Whale Fin of Klukwan. After spending part of her youth in Minnesota, she entered government service at the age of seventeen as an employee of the Central Intelligence Agency and for several years lived internationally with her first husband, a member of the foreign service, in Bolivia, Austria, and Afghanistan. In 1975, she returned to Alaska, took a job with Sealaska Corporation, and married her second husband, an Inupiat Eskimo from Kotzebue. She worked several years for the Alaska Department of Fish and Game's Subsistence Division, then did a turn as mayor of Pelican in the early 1990s, and then was recruited to work for the Forest Service as coordinator for the regional subsistence council. Later she served as a district ranger on the Hiawatha National Forest in Michigan for a few years before returning to Alaska in the late 1990s to become deputy forest supervisor on the Tongass. In 2009, she died suddenly at the age of 63, still much beloved and admired by her former colleagues in Forest Service–tribal relations.[22]

Despite her proven track record as a capable administrator, Jorgensen soon found herself isolated in the Washington office. Her leadership style was "positive, soft, careful," Susan Johnson later stated. "She had a soft style, collaborative—not a table pounder." Jorgensen sent out a questionnaire to seventy Forest Service employees, including seven regional foresters, asking for input on a variety of issues, including the utility of having an office of tribal relations at the national level. She and the National Tribal Relations Program Implementation Team conducted focus group meetings with key officials in the Washington office. Some found Jorgensen's measured approach to building a new program unsettling. In the cut and thrust between senior-level bureaucrats in the thirty-thousand-strong Forest Service organization, the things that really mattered were dollars and fulltime equivalent positions (FTEs), or personnel. Some who came to oppose Jorgensen still thought of the tribal relations program as a civil rights initiative, and they questioned why Indians should have special treatment over other minorities. Her major opponents were individuals who had a wealth of knowledge about how to fight budget battles in Washington and relatively little experience working in the regions or on the national forests. They well knew that the federal government had a special relationship to Indians based on the Indian trust doctrine, but they lacked the perspective, for example, of having worked with tribes to protect treaty rights on national forestlands. Many senior-level bureaucrats in the Forest Service had spent so much of their career in Washington they did not fully appreciate how tribal issues intersected with the Forest Service's core mission of environmental stewardship. They resisted the tribal relations initiative on grounds that the Forest Service had more pressing needs.[23]

Jorgensen asked FireCloud to accept a six-month detail in Washington to help her move the tribal relations initiative forward. Jorgensen made FireCloud team leader of the National Tribal Relations Program Implementation Team. FireCloud set it up to mirror the structure of the task force. She divided the team into work groups to address each of the dozen issues in the task force report. The implementation team convened in March 2001, and it worked through the dozen issues over the next twenty-four months. It practically

FIGURE 25. Dorothy FireCloud, Sicangu Lakota,
Forest Service tribal liaison for the Southwest Region

PHOTO BY GARY CHANCEY.
COURTESY OF FOREST SERVICE.

replicated the decision-by-committee workflow of the task force. Work group
leaders reported to the team at regular meetings about once per month.[24] The
team-centered approach had a somewhat tribal flavor, and as many of the team
members were themselves members of tribes, they were obviously comfortable
with it. Three team members, Dorothy FireCloud, Sonia Tamez, and Susan
Johnson, had by this time forged exceptionally strong collegial relationships
with one another. They were passionate and committed.

In the spring of 2002, while the implementation team was still at work on its
overall recommendations, Jorgensen and FireCloud sent a memo to the chief
specifically about creating an office of tribal relations. In response, Bosworth
directed them to prepare a proposal for the Forest Service's national leadership team. The national leadership team usually consisted of the chief, associate chief, deputy chiefs, and associate deputy chiefs, and it met regularly in

the Washington office. On June 8, 2002, Jorgensen and FireCloud made their presentation, reporting that the initiative to form an office of tribal relations found "overwhelming support" among Forest Service employees, tribal leaders, and other federal land-managing agencies whom they had queried. They presented a preferred plan and two alternative plans. The preferred plan would establish a new directorate headed by a member of the Senior Executive Service. The directorate would be funded at the level of twelve FTEs. Besides the director, there would be two deputy directors and nine support staff including an attorney specializing in Indian law. The alternative plans indicated how the directorate might be staffed with fewer FTEs. One alternative had eight, the other six.[25]

In the lead-up to the June meeting, Joel Holtrop, deputy chief of State and Private Forestry, emerged as the new office's strongest advocate. At the meeting, he laid out four points as to why it should be placed under State and Private Forestry. In essence, it would accentuate shared interests between the Forest Service and tribes rather than points of conflict.[26]

Some of the associate chiefs argued against creating an office of tribal relations, citing the Forest Service's budget squeeze. They noted that all those FTEs would have to come from somewhere else in the organization. Investing in a national-level office with so many staff was not worth the investment, they said, when the work of tribal relations was mostly happening in the field and was already being handled at the regional level. A single national coordinator was sufficient, they argued. It was a credit to the Forest Service that the program was decentralized and focused in the field, and it should stay that way.

For Chief Bosworth, the budget was indeed a looming consideration, but the arguments for elevating tribal relations were more compelling. As was the case when any program was elevated, the cost of additional staffing in the Washington office had to be weighed against the benefits that would accrue from giving the program that higher profile. There would be technical benefits: a stronger ability to develop national policy and achieve consistency, a national-level platform from which the Forest Service could engage with national-level Indian organizations such as the NCAI. And there would be the overarching benefit of elevating the importance of tribal relations in the Forest Service mindset. To Bosworth, that was the most important consideration. Based on his own experience in the field, the Forest Service could be doing much more to partner with tribes, fulfill its trust responsibilities, and cultivate better relations.

"Philosophically we are in the same place with tribes," Bosworth noted, when he recalled this decision several years later. "We want to manage these lands for future generations and that is very much part of the culture of the Indian people." The Forest Service was "missing out on a lot of advice from tribes." As for protecting Indian sacred sites on national forestlands, those were places that the dominant society might not deem sacred but could still value as wilderness or otherwise set aside. "There is this natural tie between the Forest Service and Indian culture," he explained, "and we weren't capitalizing on it. So [I thought] maybe this could help."[27]

On July 17, 2002, Chief Bosworth announced his decision. The Office of Tribal Relations (OTR) would be established with an initial staff of six FTEs "with possible expansion later based on monitoring and evaluation," and it would be located in the Division of State and Private Forestry.[28] Bosworth agreed with Holtrop that there were good reasons to keep the tribal relations program under State and Private Forestry rather than under national forest administration. Although the National Tribal Relations Program Implementation Team wanted it to be located in the Office of the Chief, Bosworth believed that that would be counterproductive. As chief, he already supervised all the regional foresters, station directors, and deputy chiefs plus some other national programs such as law enforcement. When it came to budget decisions and ordering the Forest Service's priorities, he could not advocate for the tribal relations program and listen to everyone else, too. Rather, the tribal relations program needed to have its own deputy chief advocating for it.[29]

At an award ceremony held in September 2004 to recognize outstanding individuals for their help in creating the OTR, Chief Bosworth was honored together with six American Indians. In presenting the award to Bosworth, Assistant Secretary of Agriculture Mark Rey praised his record in building strong relationships with tribes going back to his tenure as a deputy regional forester. Jorgensen also received an award, as did her long-serving predecessor in the position of national coordinator, Robert Tippeconnie.[30]

Jorgensen resigned from her position in the Washington office in September 2002 to become director of the U.S. Environmental Protection Agency's American Indian Environmental Office. To fill the void, members of the National Tribal Relations Program Implementation Team took turns taking temporary assignment to the Washington office, "keeping the seat warm," as one said. First Dorothy FireCloud, then Sonia Tamez, then Susan Johnson, then Gary

Harris, each did a stint. Usually these were 120-day tours. Dale Kanen served as acting director for two months in the spring of 2003. Mit Parsons took the last turn as acting director from June 1, 2003, through the end of the year. Finally, Kanen was appointed OTR director and started on duty on January 1, 2004.[31]

When the National Tribal Relations Program Implementation Team concluded its work in March 2003, its members were pleased overall with what they had accomplished. True, the staffing of the OTR was not as robust as desired. Some of the dozen issues raised by the task force still required resolution by legislative action. Another issue, the potential establishment of a National Tribal Leaders Advisory Council, still needed the chief's attention. Yet the team had succeeded in developing new policies, regulations, and training programs to address everything else on the task force's agenda. "It was an exciting time," FireCloud later recalled. "The amount we got done was amazing for the amount of people we had."[32]

SETTING UP THE OFFICE OF TRIBAL RELATIONS

The OTR's first director, Dale Kanen, is an enrolled member of the Tlingit and Haida Tribes of southeast Alaska and is Dog Salmon/Raven through his mother. Speaking of his background, Kanen said that the village of Shakan, the home of his mother's people, was wiped out in the 1930s after federal marshals arrived in a couple of large boats and ordered all the inhabitants, including some thirty school-age children, to relocate to Klawock. The brutal order was given in the name of providing the group with schools and a path to assimilation. As a result, Kanen's mother spent her early childhood in Klawock. Kanen's father was a non-Indian, and Kanen grew up mostly in Anchorage and Maryland, often quite removed from his Native heritage.

In the mid-1990s, Kanen became a district ranger on the Tongass National Forest and took up residence in Craig, not far from his ancestral home. There, he had the thrill of being a line officer and working with his grandmother's relatives to manage the area. It was an "interesting social experiment," he later remarked. "I may have been the first line officer in the Forest Service . . . who was actually put back in what I'd call my maternal spawning habitat."[33]

Those unusual circumstances notwithstanding, Kanen's experiences as a line officer ultimately shaped how he approached management of the tribal relations program after he became OTR director in 2004. Through his readings on Indian law and his own dealings with the handful of Alaska Native communities on his ranger district, he came to believe that the relationship had to be based on a foundation of government-to-government relations. It followed that Forest Service–tribal relations had to revolve around direct communications between the line officer and the tribal government. The role of the tribal liaison, in his view, was to facilitate those communications and step back as soon as communications were effective. Many of the regional tribal liaisons were reluctant to step back, being too eager to maintain those relationships with the tribal governments themselves. In many cases, Kanen believed, the tribes did not really want to talk to the liaisons; rather, they wanted to talk directly to the federal officials in charge. "The tribes get this government-to-government thing better than some of our tribal liaisons did," Kanen maintained. Whether that was accurate or not, Kanen's assessment of the regional tribal liaisons' limitations did not endear him to them.[34]

Kanen had two rocky years as OTR director. One of his objectives was to fashion the regional tribal relations program managers into some kind of team even though they reported to the regional foresters, not to him. Sometimes those individuals disagreed with his views, which he misconstrued as insubordination. Lines of communication between the OTR and some of the regions broke down. To try to make amends, Kanen contracted with an outside firm often used by the Forest Service to conduct teambuilding sessions, but the effort fell flat.

Meanwhile, Kanen was trying to build up the OTR staff and secure those six precious FTEs before any were taken away. In the course of hiring and mentoring the new staff, he experienced disappointing delays, dysfunction, and turnover, and he barely succeeded in filling four positions by the time he left. He was overwhelmed by the job and could not find enough hours in the day or days in the week to get it all done. He met with tribal leaders in national organizations such as the NCAI, but by some accounts he did not represent the Forest Service well in those venues.[35]

Kanen did not have sufficient experience to navigate the complex divisions of responsibility in the Forest Service organization. When he was still green in the job, he tried to send some carryover moneys out to one of the regions to help with a tribal issue on a national forest. Holtrop nixed it, saying that State and Private Forestry's relationship to the National Forest System was advisory only—it did not deliver moneys to the national forests. The incident added to Kanen's growing sense that OTR was located in the wrong division. If he could only advise regional staff, and if he could not deliver moneys to the field, then what good was it to be under State and Private Forestry? All he could see was that tribes and the OTR were at the bottom of the pecking order in that division. "Anybody who is going to survive in state and private forestry had better be taking care of the needs of the fifty state foresters," Kanen later remarked.[36]

Despite Kanen's many trials and tribulations in setting up the OTR, there were a few bright spots. One of those was the OTR's involvement in setting up the Hall of Tribal Nations in the Yates Building, the location of the Washington office since 1990. It happened that the creation of the OTR came just months in advance of the grand opening of the Smithsonian Institution's National Museum of the American Indian and a year in advance of the celebration of the Forest Service's centennial. The coincidental timing of those two gala events presented an opportunity to highlight Forest Service–tribal relations and the new OTR. The idea developed to create an exhibit called the Hall of Tribal Nations on the Yates Building's fourth floor. The exhibit space was to center on a long, wide hallway in the historic Romanesque building, well lit by tall arched windows down one side together with a foyer area right outside the Office of the Chief.[37] The OTR was tasked to take the lead in developing the exhibits.

Edie Morigeau spearheaded the effort. A teacher by background and a member of the Confederated Salish and Kootenai Tribes in Montana, Morigeau came to the OTR on a temporary detail to develop a staff training course on tribal relations. While she continued with that assignment, she also put together the Hall of Tribal Nations. She began by consulting with Smithsonian curator George P. Horse Capture on ideas about how to incorporate the Forest Service's concepts into museum-quality displays. Then the exhibit began to take shape around the twin themes of partnering and strength through diversity. When completed, it showcased a wide variety of the Forest Service–tribal partnership activities in the nine regions.[38]

Two displays stood out. The Forest Service contracted with a tribal artist through the Salish and Kootenai College in Montana to design and fabricate three metal sculptures. These were displayed outside the Office of the Chief. And Morigeau worked with Alaska Region to select a carver to design, carve, paint, and ship a totem pole to commemorate the story of the Civilian Conservation Corps and the Forest Service's ongoing relationship with Native villages in southeast Alaska. The thirteen-foot totem pole was dedicated on September 22, 2005.[39]

While the Hall of Tribal Nations was still in development, the Forest Service hosted an open house, "Celebrating the Partnerships Between the Forest

Service and Indian Tribes," on September 22, 2004. The OTR invited more than two thousand people, including representatives of all federally recognized Indian tribes, tribal college presidents, state foresters, congressional delegates, U.S. Department of Agriculture officials, and representatives of Indian organizations. Chief Bosworth presided over the event, which focused on the Hall of Tribal Nations and included traditional Native American foods, flute music, and storytelling.[40]

Another bright spot in Kanen's two years as director of OTR occurred in connection with the Forest Service's establishment of a forester liaison position and research center at the College of Menominee Nation. In the Washington office, Kanen went to meetings of the research station directors to discuss how the OTR might assist the research stations in partnering with tribes to acquire traditional ecological knowledge. The issues were complex, and much

FIGURE 26. 2004 award ceremony for Gary Morishima, consultant to the ITC, for assisting in the establishment of the Office of Tribal Relations. *Left to right*, Associate Chief Sally Collins, Chief Dale Bosworth, Deputy Chief Joel Holtrop, Gary Morishima, OTR Director Dale Kanen.

to his chagrin, the OTR proved to be too short handed to deliver much assistance. Yet to Kanen's way of thinking, the agency needed to get people on the ground in places like the Menominee Reservation to make a difference. He was delighted when Holtrop returned from the Menominee Reservation with newfound respect for what that tribe had to offer, and he was hopeful that the agency was moving in the right direction.[41]

In April 2006, Kanen resigned and took a position as tribal liaison for the Northern Region in Missoula, Montana. After a little more than two years in the capital city, he and his wife decided they needed to get back to quieter living out West.[42]

NEW LEGISLATIVE AUTHORITIES

The National Tribal Relations Program Task Force and the National Tribal Relations Program Implementation Team identified a half dozen issues where the Forest Service needed to pursue new legislative authorities.[43] As soon as the task force completed its report in 2000, the ITC went to work on drafting legislation and urging Congress to enact it. The support of the ITC was important because the Forest Service, as a federal agency, was prohibited by law from lobbying Congress on its own behalf.[44]

The ITC had a bill written by May 2001. Its title was "Tribal Governmental–U.S. Forest Service Collaborative Relations Act," and it addressed all six outstanding issues. Significantly, the ITC's bill gave precedence to cooperative forestry assistance. The bill's "Title 1: Cooperative Programs" would have given the secretary of agriculture authority to work directly with tribes just as the Forest Service did with states. The language stated that "the Secretary may provide financial, research, technical, educational and related assistance to Indian tribes," and the title went on to list many specific purposes.[45]

In the summer of 2001, the ITC's lobbyist Mark Phillips managed to bring draft legislation to the attention of both the Senate Committee on Indian Affairs and the Senate Committee on Agriculture. As a result, Senator Patty Murray of Washington and Senator Tom Daschle of South Dakota, both Democrats, introduced all of the provisions into the Senate version of the 2002 Farm Bill. Significantly, the U.S. Department of Agriculture made no objection to the cooperative forestry provisions. The Senate passed the bill with all the provisions intact, but when the bill went to a conference between the two chambers,

House members in the conference committee insisted on jettisoning the entire forestry title from the bill. The farm bill is an omnibus bill in the name of food and agricultural policy, which Congress traditionally enacts about once every four to five years. As the farm bill is carefully crafted so as to get a solid, winning coalition behind it, the sacrifice of the forestry title in the 2002 farm bill came as a sharp disappointment to the ITC, the tribes, and the Forest Service.[46]

After the Forest Service published and distributed the implementation team's report in August 2003, the decision was made to pursue the desired legislation through the administration. During the fall and winter, the Forest Service prepared a legislative proposal and sent it up the chain of command through the undersecretary and secretary of agriculture to the Office of Management and Budget (OMB) for inclusion in the president's FY 2005 budget for the U.S. government. The legislative proposal cleared all hurdles and was submitted to Congress with the president's budget in February 2004.[47]

The legislative proposal that the Forest Service sent forward through the administration contained just four of the six issues identified by the tribal relations staff. It omitted the issues involving equal access to federal programs by tribal governments and delivery of cooperative forestry assistance to tribes—the items that were in Title 1 of the ITC's bill. In effect, the omission preserved the states' advantage over tribes in accessing federal moneys through the Forest Service. It is not clear whose directive it was to cut those items—whether it came from within the Forest Service or from the undersecretary of agriculture. In an undated, anonymous memo, a source who was close to the tribal relations staff informed an Indian leader of these developments, evidently with the hope that it would trigger another legislative proposal. Referencing the ITC bill's Title 1, the anonymous memo concluded, "This language is desperately needed in order for the FS to truly carry out its mandate to work on a government-to-government relationship with Tribes." No further legislative proposal emerged, and the legislative package henceforth included just the four remaining items.[48]

Secretary of Agriculture Mike Johanns transmitted the legislative proposal to Congress in 2004. As the Forest Service was prohibited by law from lobbying members of Congress, it attracted little notice and did not get a hearing. The administration submitted it again in 2006. The second time, the legislative proposal picked up sponsors, one from each party, in both houses, but neither the House bill nor the Senate bill reached a vote on the floor. Finally the ITC and the NCAI came forward to support it in the next Congress. The

Food, Conservation, and Energy Act of 2008 was enacted on June 18, 2008, the Democrat-controlled Congress overriding a veto by President Bush.[49]

In the 628-page act, Title VIII, Subtitle B, "Cultural Heritage and Cooperation Authority," contained the four new legislative authorities that the Forest Service had pursued for nearly a decade. A briefing paper prepared by the OTR announced that the provisions "strengthen the Forest Service's commitment to Tribes by providing needed legal authority to improve government-to-government relationships."[50] As the Forest Service proceeded to implement the new legislative authorities, it marked the final completion of the national tribal relations program initiative that had begun with the appointment of the task force in 1999.

CHAPTER SUMMARY

The push for an office of tribal relations came primarily from the regional tribal relations program managers and line officers who saw the need to elevate tribal relations in the Forest Service organization and culture. The push came secondarily from tribes and intertribal organizations. The initiative was consistent with presidential directives calling for federal agencies to improve government-to-government relations with tribes, but it remained up to the Forest Service to decide how and when to establish the Office of Tribal Relations (OTR). The Council of Western State Foresters provided critical support.

The National Tribal Relations Program Task Force, which was operational from the fall of 1999 through the spring of 2000, gave clear focus to the initiative to elevate tribal relations in the agency. The National Tribal Relations Program Implementation Team carried the initiative forward from the closing months of the Clinton administration through the early years of the Bush administration. Despite concerns that the initiative would be derailed by the change of administrations, it found a strong champion in Chief Bosworth. The OTR was formally established in 2004. Four legislative needs identified by the task force were finally met with passage of the 2008 Farm Bill.

10

TRIBES AND THE HEALTHY FORESTS INITIATIVE

THE HEALTHY FORESTS INITIATIVE

I N 2000, CATASTROPHIC wildfires in the West captured the nation's attention. In May, a prescribed burn in Bandelier National Monument, New Mexico, flared out of control and swept into the town of Los Alamos, destroying 235 homes and threatening the U.S. Department of Energy's nuclear weapons lab. Later in the summer, enormous wildfires scorched areas of western Montana and Idaho. By mid-August, forests were burning in many parts of the West, and the nation's firefighting capabilities were stretched so thin that it had to call on the help of fire crews and soldiers from Canada, Mexico, Australia, and New Zealand.[1]

The shocking severity of the fire season led to the preparation of a National Fire Plan by the secretaries of agriculture and the interior in the fall of 2000 and then to the Ten-Year Comprehensive Strategy one year later. The Council of Western State Foresters was heavily involved in the latter effort, and states and tribes were asked to provide input. In essence, the Ten-Year Strategy directed federal resources toward reducing fuel loads on national forest and Bureau of Land Management (BLM) lands wherever communities were at greatest risk from wildfire. It gave special attention to the urban-wildland interface. States and tribes helped compile a list of over twenty-two thousand threatened communities. The strategy aimed to build collaboration at the national, regional, and local level so that future wildfires would be less destructive of lives and property.[2]

The summer of 2002 proved to be another hot, devastating season of wildfires. In June, the Hayman fire near Colorado Springs, Colorado, grew into the largest recorded fire in the state's history and claimed the lives of five firefighters. That same month, the Rodeo-Chediski fire in Arizona burned nearly half a million acres, destroyed more than four hundred homes, and took the life of firefighter Rick Lupe, an Apache. By late summer, with another monster fire ablaze in Oregon, the season was shaping up to be as destructive and costly as the earlier one. Not since the big fire season of 1988—the year of the Yellowstone fires—had the West's forest fires attracted so much public attention.[3]

The 2000 and 2002 fire seasons seemed to confirm that the nation's forests were out of whack. True, the immediate cause of the fires' unusual destructiveness could be attributed to adverse weather conditions—abnormally high

FIGURE 27. Fire fighters on the Hayman Fire in Colorado, June 11, 2002. Photo by Michael Rieger.

COURTESY OF FEDERAL EMERGENCY
MANAGEMENT AGENCY/WIKIMEDIA COMMONS

temperatures, drought, lightning storms, and wind. Yet there appeared to be underlying causes that portended more big fire seasons in the future. Were the adverse weather conditions a product of global warming? Were the western forests becoming more flammable because of widespread beetle infestations? Were fires becoming more frequent as a result of the spreading urban-wildland interface?

One prevalent theory was that nearly a century of fire suppression had interrupted fire-dependent cycles of natural succession, causing a buildup of small-bore trees and underbrush that would normally be kept in check by frequent, low-intensity fires. In other words, fire suppression had had the unintended long-term consequence of "fuel loading." When foresters and others talked of "reducing fuel loads" in the forest, they referred to clearing the forest of an unnaturally dense understory to make the forest less flammable.

During the height of the 2002 fire season, President Bush visited the giant Biscuit Fire on the Siskiyou National Forest in southern Oregon, where he announced his "Healthy Forests Initiative" to accelerate efforts to reduce fuel loads in the nation's forests. In short order, three separate bills were introduced in the House. On September 5, 2002, Republican Congressman James V. Hansen of Utah, chairman of the House Committee on Resources, gaveled into session a hearing on the president's initiative, starting a debate that would stretch for over a year and culminate in passage of the Healthy Forests Restoration Act (HFRA). Bush signed the bill into law on December 3, 2003. It was the first major piece of legislation on national forest management in over three decades.

Title I of the HFRA, the vital piece, provided for fast-tracking fuel reduction projects on some 20 million acres of federal lands that were deemed most at risk for conflagration. It charged the secretaries of agriculture and the interior with establishing a new administrative appeals process for these projects, and Congress appropriated $760 million per year for the next five years for the agencies to administer them.

The Healthy Forests Initiative and the HFRA sharpened the debate over what was causing the increasing severity of forest fires in the West. Some scientists cautioned against overgeneralizing about fuel loading. Fire suppression had had a marked effect on specific forest types, such as ponderosa pine forest in the Rocky Mountain states, where natural succession was shaped by a fire regime of frequent, low-intensity fires. It was much less significant for other forest types such as subalpine forest in the Rocky Mountain states or Douglas fir forest in the Pacific Coast states. Furthermore, the historical record of fire suppression should not be exaggerated, they said, noting that the policy did not become truly effective until the 1930s and was replaced by prescribed burning on the national forests in 1978; therefore, the effect on fire ecology was mainly limited to about fifty years, not the whole past century.[4]

Environmental groups contended that the HFRA's emphasis on fuel reduction projects was misguided, and worse, it was disingenuous. Fuel reduction in the name of protecting communities from wildfire was a subterfuge for stepped-up logging on federal lands. The urgency in fast-tracking these projects—circumventing the usual environmental review process—was a strategy for weakening environmental protections. Bush's opponents in the environmental community contended that the very name "Healthy Forests Initiative" was devious, being an example of the administration's outrageous doublespeak: whoever is *not* in favor of healthy forests, say *aye*!

The heated rhetoric around the HFRA was largely of the administration's own making. In pushing the measure, the administration and its Republican allies in Congress advanced the thesis that "radical environmentalists" had so abused the Forest Service's administrative appeals process that forest managers could no longer do their jobs. As authors Jacqueline Vaughn and Hanna J. Cortner show in their book, *George W. Bush's Healthy Forests: Reframing the Environmental Debate*, the Bush administration's attack on environmentalists largely succeeded in "changing the narrative" from a broad examination of forest fire ecology to a narrow focus on the Forest Service appeals process, which they claimed had been hijacked.[5]

Given the complexity of the appeals process, data could be variously interpreted. In 2001, Republican Congressman Larry Craig of Idaho requested the General Accounting Office (GAO) to determine how many fuel reduction projects on the national forests that were funded in Fiscal Year 2001 had been appealed. The GAO made an analysis of Forest Service data and put the number at just 20 out of 1,671 projects, or about 1 percent. Later, the Forest Service released a statement that in fact 48 percent of such projects had been appealed. Following the president's announcement of the Healthy Forests Initiative, Chief Bosworth's public remarks in support of the initiative helped steer the conversation about wildfire into a technical debate over whether the Forest Service appeals process needed reform.[6] Meanwhile, Republican Senator John Kyl of Arizona focused intensely on a fuel reduction project that had been held up on the Apache-Sitgreaves National Forest in 2001, which lay in the path of the Rodeo-Chediski fire the following year. "Ground crews estimate that as much as 90 percent of the trees that were to be treated under the plan are now destroyed," he told readers of the *Arizona Republic*.[7] He implied that the Center for Biological Diversity, the appellant in this instance, was responsible for the "waste" of so much burned timber if not for the fire itself.

Indians were on both sides in the debate over the Healthy Forests Initiative. Tribes had a stake in seeing the Ten-Year Strategy implemented expeditiously, as many of their own communities and resources were at risk. Moreover, they saw an economic opportunity in the movement to develop markets for the small-diameter trees and woody biomass that were removed in forest thinning operations. An editorial in the *Fort Apache Scout* was perhaps a typical reflection of Indians' pragmatic thinking on the Healthy Forests Initiative. Noting that spotted owl habitat on thousands of acres was being destroyed by fire, the writer commented that it was better to allow short-term harassment of wildlife by fuel reduction projects than to allow long-term damage by habitat loss. "It is better that a bald eagle nest be disturbed briefly by mechanical thinning than obliterated by wildfire."[8]

Others expressed a deep mistrust of the Bush administration's environmental agenda. An example was Tanya Lee's opinion piece in *News from Indian Country* titled "From the Redwood Forests to the Gulf Stream Waters." Lee characterized the Healthy Forests Initiative as being part of a larger attack on environmental protections, a piece with the administration's similarly deceptive "Clear Skies Initiative," and ultimately aimed at privatization of the commons. Suggesting that the Bush administration's attack on environmentalists was equally an attack on Indian values, she wrote: "The passing of the 'commons'— those essentials for life on earth that according to Western law from its beginnings and Indigenous ethics for millennia 'belong' to everyone and therefore to no one—into private hands is perhaps the most dangerous and alarming development in modern history."[9]

When President Bush launched his Healthy Forests Initiative in August 2002, he reached out to tribes by inviting the president of the Intertribal Timber Council (ITC), Nolan C. Colegrove Sr., to meet with him and the secretaries of agriculture and the interior in Oregon, where he made the announcement. Over the next year, the ITC maintained a neutral stand on the initiative while following it closely. No tribal leaders or representatives of Indian organizations testified in congressional hearings on the legislation, but the ITC nevertheless managed to get one significant provision added to the law. Section 303 provided assistance to tribes for protecting watersheds on Indian reservations.

Under its terms, the Forest Service was to provide technical and financial assistance to tribes for the purpose of building their capacity to protect water quality and enhance watershed forestry. Congress appropriated $2.5 million for each of the next five years for forest health work on Indian lands. Beyond that one special consideration, Congress sought to include tribes in HFRA's collaborative framework. In the law's six titles and twenty-nine pages, "Indian tribes" appeared no fewer than sixteen times.[10]

Some hoped that the HFRA would serve as a vehicle for developing new Indian-owned small businesses on reservations, capitalizing on a long tradition of Indian participation in wildfire management. Since the 1950s, Indians had served in disproportionately high numbers on fire crews deployed on public and Indian lands. Indian firefighters were especially prominent in the Southwest, where the hard-working "Red Hats" of the Mescalero Apache tribe were legend.[11] Under the HFRA, the Small Business Administration contracted with the Intertribal Information Technology Company, a firm based in Albuquerque, New Mexico, to develop and train twenty Indian-owned forest restoration companies.[12]

The late summer and fall of 2003 was another bad fire season, especially in Southern California, where fires raged across 600,000 acres, taking several lives and destroying more than a hundred homes. Numerous small Indian reservations lay in the path of destruction. Altogether, 30,000 acres of tribal land were burned, 11 reservations were evacuated, 2,750 tribal members were dislocated, and 2 people died on the Barona Reservation. A few small reservations were totally burned over. Without exception, the big fires that swept across Indian reservations all began on adjacent federal lands, some on national forests.[13]

The fires in Southern California spurred final passage of the HFRA. The stricken Southern California tribes, together with the ITC, complained that the law was discriminatory. While Congress appropriated hundreds of millions of dollars for fuel reduction projects on federal lands nationwide, it provided nothing for reducing fuel loads on Indian lands. The law had nothing for the Southern California tribes who had just been victimized.[14] Representative Richard Pombo of California, a Republican, came to the tribes' support. In February 2004, he introduced the Tribal Forest Protection Act (TFPA). The bill provided for tribally initiated forest health projects on adjacent federal lands. The intent was to give tribes an opportunity to protect Indian forest and rangelands from losses like those that occurred in 2003 by restoring adjacent federal lands that posed a fire, disease, or other threat to the Indian reservation.[15]

The TFPA was enacted with bipartisan support. While the HFRA met with profound public skepticism, the TFPA did not attract that kind of scrutiny or opposition. Pombo, the bill's principal sponsor and certainly no friend of environmentalists, reached out to Senator Diane Feinstein of California, a Democrat, to introduce the legislation in the Senate, so as to make the bill bipartisan and allay environmentalists' suspicions. Some tribes voiced concerns that the bill's focus on "adjacent" federal and tribal lands was too narrow, and the ITC sought to get it amended. In spite of the ITC's efforts, the language in the act remained fairly clinical, confining the legislation's geographic scope to certain lands "bordering or adjacent to the Indian forestland or rangeland under the jurisdiction of the Indian tribe."[16]

After the bill was passed, tribes and the ITC worked with the Forest Service to define what "adjacent" meant. Although Forest Service officials did acknowledge that "adjacent" could be interpreted as "proximate" or "nearby" and not just "adjoining," no such allowance was entered into the Forest Service manual for implementing the TFPA. Some tribes were discouraged, concluding that the Forest Service was not serious about facilitating projects under the TFPA.[17]

From the Forest Service's standpoint, the major limitation of the TFPA was its stipulation that projects must be initiated by tribes, not by the federal agencies themselves. To work around that stipulation, the Forest Service and the BLM held a series of workshops to inform tribal foresters about the act and offer training on how to initiate a project. The Forest Service's Pacific Southwest Region organized the first workshop. Tribal liaison Sonia Tamez met with several Southern California tribes that were among the legislation's original backers, and after a promising start, those meetings led to a statewide workshop in cooperation with the ITC and the BLM. More than a hundred people attended, including tribal government representatives, traditional practitioners, Regional Forester Jack Blackwell, and BLM State Director Mike Pool. Blackwell assured the tribal participants that the TFPA had the warm support of the chief of the Forest Service as well as the Forest Service's timber management staff back in Washington. Following the workshop, three California tribes submitted proposals, and all three proposals were accepted.[18]

Even as the Forest Service sought to encourage use of the TFPA through workshops, however, tribes ran into difficulties of their own. First, there was the problem of adjacency: at least two tribes submitted proposals that failed to meet the test. Moreover, tribes hesitated to enter into the morass of National Environmental Policy Act requirements and red tape associated with undertaking a project on federal land. One tribe proposed doing forest restoration work on the Sequoia National Forest only to find its proposal ensnared in the public review process involving the preparation of a new forest plan.[19]

The Forest Service tried to remove some of those impediments by using stewardship contracts as a vehicle for implementing TFPA. "Stewardship contracts" were authorized under the 2003 appropriation act, and like the TFPA, their aim was to support efforts to reduce fuel loads and wildfire risks on public lands. Stewardship contracts were aimed specifically at engaging local communities in forest thinning, brush clearing, and other types of forest work. Stewardship contracts were supposed to be relatively easy to work with, but they required their own set of standards that were confusing in their own right. Their main feature was that they allowed the Forest Service (and the BLM) to trade goods for services. The cash value of forest material removed in a forest thinning project, for example, could be used as an offset against labor costs. In some instances, this goods-for-services provision of stewardship contracting worked well for tribes interested in proposing projects under the TFPA, and in other instances it did not. Six years out from the act's passage, the Forest Service began working on another form of contract to use in its place.[20]

By then, the Forest Service, tribes, and the ITC all expressed disappointment over the number of TFPA projects that had actually gotten off the ground. After eight years, only six projects had been successfully implemented. An analysis done by the ITC in collaboration with the Forest Service and the BIA identified four major problems with the implementation. These were lack of training on the TFPA and federal-Indian relationships, inadequate agency funding for tribally proposed projects, frequent turnover in staff, and the cost and legal hurdles posed by federal administrative processes.[21]

WOODY BIOMASS UTILIZATION

Forest thinning projects in the early 2000s spurred consideration of how to dispose of huge quantities of small-diameter trees and brush in the depressed lumber and pulpwood market. The Forest Service conducted research on converting sawmills and pulp mills into power-generating plants using the material as feed stock for electric power production. The concept was to form an industry based on the supply of harvested small trees and brush which had no commercial value for the wood products industry but could be of value in the evolving energy market. The new economic enterprise was called "woody biomass utilization."

A number of timber tribes with struggling sawmill operations were keenly interested in this development. The Confederated Tribes of the Warm Springs Reservation in Oregon was one such tribe. In the wake of the Healthy Forests Initiative, it decided to experiment with the new technology involved in this form of energy production and to partner with the Forest Service so as to have an ample supply of woody biomass beyond what the tribe harvested on the reservation. The Forest Service viewed it as a pilot project for developing similar partnerships with other tribes.

The 640,000-acre Warm Springs Reservation lies east of the Cascades in central Oregon. Four national forests either border the reservation or are located nearby. The Warm Springs, Wasco, and Northern Paiute who make up the Confederated Tribes altogether number about four thousand members. Logging and manufacturing of lumber have long been mainstays of the tribal economy. In 1967, the tribes purchased Jefferson Plywood Corporation and established Warm Springs Forest Products Industries (WSFPI). In recent years, WSFPI has harvested about 42 million board feet of timber per year. The tribally owned company sells some of the annual harvest from the reservation on the open market and processes most of it in the company mill. The mill produces Douglas fir, white fir, and ponderosa pine framing and industrial lumber and timbers.[22]

Like other mills in the interior West, the mill on the Warm Springs Reservation faced declining prospects in the twenty-first-century global timber market. Rising production and transportation costs placed the mill at a competitive disadvantage with mills located closer to markets or sea shipping. To keep their reservation-based logging and milling operation economically viable, the Confederated Tribes of the Warm Springs Reservation looked to biomass energy production as a way to subsidize milling equipment upgrades and transportation costs.[23]

In 2004, the tribal government approved a three-phase plan put forward by WSFPI to refurbish and expand the lumber manufacturing plant into a combination mill and biomass power plant. The first phase was to replace the cogeneration power plant's old 1927 boilers. The second phase involved replacing the condensing turbine with an extraction turbine. Together with the new boiler, the different turbine was projected to produce six megawatts of power, supplying the energy needs of the lumber mill plus a modest surplus that the tribes would sell to their current energy supplier, PacifiCorp. The third phase

FIGURE 28. View of Mt. Jefferson from the Warm Springs Reservation, Oregon. The volcanic cone straddles the boundary of the reservation, the Willamette National Forest, and the Deschutes National Forest.

PHOTO BY LYN TOPINKA. COURTESY OF U.S. GEOLOGICAL SURVEY/WIKIMEDIA COMMONS.

contemplated expansion of both the energy plant and the lumber mill, with the potential of producing fifteen to twenty megawatts of power both for internal use and sale. According to plant manager Larry Potts, the biomass plant would then produce enough power to supply electricity to fifteen thousand homes.[24]

In 2005, the Confederated Tribes of the Warm Springs Reservation completed phase one of their project and obtained a grant from the Forest Service to assist with phase two. The grant was a maximum award of $250,000 under a $4.4 million grant program for woody biomass utilization, which was authorized under the HFRA beginning in that year. As the Forest Service's own general announcement indicated, the tribes' grant was "intended to help improve utilization and create markets for small-diameter material and low-valued trees removed from hazardous fuel reduction activities."[25]

Looking ahead to phase three of their project, the Confederated Tribes of the Warm Springs Reservation entered a memorandum of understanding (MOU) with the Forest Service and the BLM to secure a long-range supply of feedstock for their biomass plant. Under the MOU, the Forest Service and the BLM jointly agreed to offer residual woody biomass (piled slash and brush) from approximately eight thousand acres per year of thinned or treated forest. The MOU was signed in January 2006.[26]

The project took another step forward with an assist from the American Recovery and Reinvestment Act (ARRA) of 2009, the economic stimulus package that Congress and the Obama administration put forward in response to the financial crisis in 2008. The Warm Springs Tribes secured a $5 million award in September 2009. The money represented about one-fifth of a total estimated cost of $25 million to bring the biomass energy plant on line.[27]

Uncertainties surrounding the biomass energy market delayed the project's completion, however. Although federal subsidies had encouraged the tribal government thus far, it hesitated to invest more in the project lest those needed subsidies should melt away. The tribal government sought more concrete assurance of a continuous supply of feedstock. Beyond the MOU, it wanted a ten-year stewardship contract with the Mount Hood, Deschutes, and Ochoco National Forests and the BLM. The stewardship contract would accomplish hazardous fuel reduction and ecosystem restoration—central goals of the Healthy Forests Initiative—as well as protect tribal assets and enhance cultural resources, namely by restoring huckleberry production. The tribal government argued that it needed the stewardship contract in order to obtain financing (it sought to obtain a $15 million loan from the state of Oregon) and a power sales agreement with PacifiCorp.[28]

The Forest Service hesitated to enter a stewardship contract until the Confederated Tribes of the Warm Springs Reservation made more progress with the $5 million ARRA grant. Through 2010, the tribal government refused to authorize further investment of tribal funds in the project. At the start of 2011, the Forest Service sent a letter to the tribal government requesting that the unspent ARRA funds be returned to the Forest Service while the tribe worked on an alternative plan to utilize the funds for forest health and wildfire prevention. The tribal government responded with a request that the funds be permitted to go to refurbishment of the existing boiler and other improvements short of bringing the power plant on line. In the third quarter of 2012, the Forest Service approved the request, and work finally went forward as described. At last report, new conveyors and a transformer were in service and a fuel shed was under construction.[29]

Despite project delays, both the Confederated Tribes of the Warm Springs Reservation and the Forest Service remained positive. To put the project in perspective, it was one of 64 projects recognized under the Forest Service's Woody Biomass Utilization Grant program; it was the only such project involving a tribe; and relative to other projects it was "very large," with the initial grant of $250,000 representing just 1 percent of the anticipated total project cost. Because of the economic downturn in 2008, especially in the housing industry, many wood processing companies had to curtail operations. The Confederated Tribes of the Warm Springs Reservation was far from being the only grant recipient to experience delays in bringing its biomass power plant on line.[30]

THE PROPOSAL TO ESTABLISH A NATIONAL TRIBAL LEADERS ADVISORY COUNCIL

Even before the ITC partnered with the Forest Service on implementing the TFPA, it began to work closely with the agency on a range of other matters. Nolan C. Colegrove Sr., a member of the Hupa tribe and president of the ITC from 2001, was a strong advocate for deepening tribal forestry's relationship with the Forest Service. Under Colegrove's leadership, the ITC worked with Forest Service staff during 2001 and 2002 to develop the desired authorities to go into the next farm bill. The ITC participated in the agency's effort to elevate the tribal relations program through its representative on the National Tribal Relations Program Task Force, Gary Morishima. In 2003, Colegrove invited the Forest Service to attend the annual meeting of the ITC executive board and give the members a briefing on what was happening. Deputy Chief Holtrop accepted the invitation and met with the ITC board in Cherokee, North Carolina, in June. The timing was auspicious. The Forest Service was about to establish the Office of Tribal Relations. It had just obtained a new authority to enter stewardship contracts for carrying out fuels management on national forestlands, and there was an expectation that the new form of contracting would be a handy vehicle for expanding the Forest Service's cooperative work with tribes. The Healthy Forests Restoration Act was nearing passage. Holtrop closed his PowerPoint presentation with a slide of forested mountains and a caption "The Time Is Now!" The pitch underneath read, "Increased opportunities for FS to collaborate with Tribes regarding stewardship contracting, fuels management and other strategies of mutual interest and benefit for future generations."[31]

Colegrove shared Holtrop's enthusiasm. He touted the deepening relationship between tribes and the Forest Service in his president's message in annual reports for 2003, 2004, and 2005. Among Colegrove's most ardent hopes was that tribes would soon be able to share traditional ecological knowledge with the Forest Service in order to improve stewardship on national forestlands in the tribes' ancestral areas.[32]

At the meeting in Cherokee, the ITC and the Forest Service joined forces in working to bring about a National Tribal Leaders Advisory Council. The ITC's Gary Morishima and the Forest Service's Mit Parsons were tasked with preparing a joint memorandum that would set forth alternatives for how to structure such a body.[33]

Reporting back two months later, Parsons and Morishima recommended structuring the advisory committee around a core membership of fewer than twenty people who would have the capacity to involve others on an ad hoc basis. Parsons and Morishima envisioned that the body would be cochaired by the chief of the Forest Service and a tribal leader who would be selected by the other members. The advisory council would meet a minimum of three times per year in January, May, and September, with the May meeting to focus on tribes' priorities for the Forest Service tribal relations program. Cochairs would set the agenda for the other meetings. Meetings would be open to participation by elected officials of tribal government unless closed by the call of the cochairs, and it would strive for consensus.[34]

Selecting the tribal representatives for the advisory council would be a challenge. How could the tribal participation be structured so as to reflect the diversity of tribes without being so large as to be unwieldy? How could so many tribes select such a small number of members to represent them? Parsons and Morishima offered three options for how to structure the tribal side of the advisory council. Option one was the formula recommended in the implementation team's draft charter, which provided for two representatives from tribes located in each of the nine Forest Service regions, with tribes in each region deciding on the method of selection. Parsons and Morishima did not endorse this option because the number of members (eighteen) and the method of selection both seemed unworkable. They recommended that the tribal participation be a mix of representatives from intertribal organizations and individual tribes and that the method of selection would consist of the chief of the Forest

Service selecting ten individuals from a list of nominations submitted by the tribes and tribal organizations. In their option two, five of the ten would come from a core group of intertribal organizations: the ITC, the National Congress of American Indians (NCAI), the Alaska Federation of Natives, the American Indian Higher Education Consortium, and the Intertribal Agriculture Council. In their option three, there would be no such restriction. Federal participation, meanwhile, would consist of eight core members: the chief, the associate chief, the deputy chiefs for State and Private Forestry and National Forest Administration, the OTR director, one regional forester, one ex officio Indian law specialist from the Office of General Counsel, and the BIA chief forester.[35]

The Forest Service gave the OTR the task of forging a consensus among tribes on how to bring the advisory council into being. The OTR conducted tribal consultations and listening sessions at numerous locations across Indian Country and met with various intertribal organizations, including the NCAI and the United South and Eastern Tribes. After two years of these deliberations, the Forest Service convened an ad hoc working group of tribal leaders and intertribal organization representatives in May 2006. This group revised the draft charter, whereupon the OTR sent it out to tribes for a final 120-day review period ending on February 1, 2007. OTR director Fred Clark, who came into that office at the end of 2006, expressed hope in his first quarterly report that the advisory council would be inaugurated by July 2007.[36]

However, that year the effort to establish a National Tribal Leaders Advisory Council foundered. On August 29, OTR director Fred Clark attended a meeting with Chief Gail Kimbell and her leadership team and discussed what course to take. At that time, Kimbell supported the establishment of an advisory council. The leadership team envisioned a body that would include fifteen tribal delegates and five Forest Service delegates convening on a regular basis. But three months later the proposal was dead. The ostensible reason given by the Forest Service for its abandonment was that tribes could not agree on how to structure tribal participation.[37]

Perhaps, too, Chief Kimbell's decision to nix the advisory council related to structural challenges then facing the Forest Service. Around the same time that the Forest Service leadership team weighed in for the last time on the proposal to establish an advisory council, it was also formulating a plan to trim operating budgets for the Washington office and the regional offices by 25 percent or more in three years—a structural change dubbed "the Forest Service Transformation."[38] Furthermore, earlier that year the Division of State and Private Forestry launched what it called the "State and Private Forestry Redesign." There were several elements to Redesign that ranged from fine grained to grandiose. It addressed everything from the technical systems for contracting and allocating funds for cooperative forestry to the overarching question of how cooperative forestry could best assist in restoring healthy forests. At its core, Redesign was a reflection of the Bush administration's intent to help states acquire a larger role in public land management. The Forest Service's attention to Redesign in 2007 tended to stir up old jealousies between tribal and state foresters, creating a climate that was unfavorable for bringing the National Tribal Leaders Advisory Council to fruition.

When the ITC learned about the Redesign initiative, council members were concerned that state foresters seemed to be exerting undue influence on the Forest Service. ITC president Nolan C. Colegrove Sr. wrote to Deputy Chief James Hubbard in April 2007 requesting a meeting at the earliest possible time to discuss the Redesign. "We understand that the National Association of State Foresters (NASF) has been involved in this effort," Colegrove noted. "We appreciate that the NASF has a long-standing relationship with the Forest Service and has a vested interest in evaluating and updating the Forest Service programs in which they participate. However, our review of the Redesign materials we have just recently received indicates the initiative expects to reshape the entire Division of State and Private Forestry, including its focus, goals and priorities. If that is the case, entities other than NASF should be involved in the discussions." Colegrove suggested that the Forest Service invite the ITC to participate in those discussions. He went on to remind Hubbard of the effort still underway to establish a National Tribal Leaders Advisory Council, and he asked Hubbard to revisit the ITC's earlier suggestion that the Division of State and Private Forestry change its identity to state, private, *and tribal* forestry.[39]

In response to Colegrove's letter, Deputy Chief Hubbard dispatched Larry Payne to brief the ITC executive board on the Redesign at the ITC's annual board meeting in Cherokee, North Carolina. He also requested OTR director Clark to participate in internal discussions about the Redesign. But Hubbard did not reply directly to Colegrove's remarks about the need to establish a National Tribal Leaders Advisory Council, nor did he address the ITC's suggestion that State and Private Forestry be renamed. Rather, he used the opportunity to explain to Colegrove his own vision and expectations for the Redesign. He viewed the reform of the system as a necessity in light of reduced federal funding, and he was enthusiastic about the potential to turn it to advantage in producing more effective results on the landscape. A key point was that state foresters actually supported the Forest Service's move to introduce a more competitive process for awarding funds based on regional priorities rather than state shares. "The Forest Service *must* be able to demonstrate how it is delivering public benefits of national scope and importance through a more coherent and integrated suite of federal programs," he emphasized. Though the Redesign would begin to go into effect in 2007, he anticipated that the new approach would be refined over a period of years.[40]

Hubbard then provided his view of the Redesign's implications for tribes. "The Office of Tribal Relations (OTR) correctly pointed out that this change could affect Tribal lands that are an important and productive part of the landscape. The Board of Directors [of State and Private Forestry] added OTR to the deliberations. Many other partners are also part of the landscape, therefore, the State Foresters are looking at how to better use funds provided from current appropriations to reach further. It is our expectation that Tribes and other stakeholders and partners will engage at the local level during the State assessment and response plan processes."[41] Hubbard made no mention of tribal consultation in his letter to Colegrove despite his acknowledgement that "this change could affect Tribal lands." Clearly, the Forest Service viewed the Redesign as essentially an internal matter, notwithstanding the strong involvement by NASF.

The new system for allocating cooperative forestry dollars did not encourage much tribal participation, at least in the early going. In 2008, the first year in which a portion of funds were allocated to competitive projects, tribes figured in just three out of 124 projects nationwide. In terms of money, just 15 percent of cooperative forestry funding, or $19.5 million, was reallocated toward competitive projects. Those funds leveraged nearly $23 million in matching funding from state agencies and partner organizations, of which a little over $375,000 came from tribes.[42]

CHAPTER SUMMARY

As wildfires grew more frequent and costly around the beginning of this century, the American people were drawn once more into a national debate over the condition of the nation's forests and forest policy. Like earlier debates in the 1970s, 1980s, and 1990s over clear-cutting, timber management, and the protection of old-growth forests, the politics of forest policy reform in the early 2000s were controversial and divisive. Tribes engaged in the latest round of discussion and reform more than they had in earlier ones, though they still felt marginalized after Congress passed the Healthy Forests Restoration Act in December 2003. They were only partly satisfied after Congress passed the Tribal Forests Protection Act in 2004.

Using new legislative authorities contained in those two acts, the Forest Service sought to partner with tribes on a variety of forest management projects on both federal and Indian lands. The principal areas of cooperation were in fuel reduction projects, watershed protection, and woody biomass utilization.

11

VALUING THE SACRED

TOWARD A SACRED SITES POLICY

A S TRIBES AND the Forest Service strove to build stronger collaborative relations, the sacred sites issue remained perhaps the most intractable and emotional problem still to be addressed. Protecting Indian peoples' spiritual connections to the land went to the very heart of the nation's commitment to help Indian cultures survive. Congress took an important step toward protection of Indian sacred sites when it enacted the American Indian Religious Freedom Act (AIRFA) of 1978. The law states, "henceforth, it shall be the policy of the United States to protect and preserve for American Indians their inherent right of freedom to believe, express, and exercise the traditional religions ... including but not limited to access to sites." But the Supreme Court decision in *Lyng v. Northwest Indian Cemetery Protective Association* (1988) tended to vitiate AIRFA as a legal basis for protection of these areas (see chap. 7).

Thereafter, tribes sought further legislation that would give them the needed "cause of action" to defend their sacred sites in court. Democratic Senator Daniel Inouye of Hawaii tried to pass such a law in the early 1990s, but its prospects faded after the Republican landslide in the midterm congressional elections of 1994. As Indian rights activist Christopher Peters of the Seventh Generation Fund wrote, "the 1994 change of leadership in the House of Representatives suddenly [made] the Congress a resolutely conservative body with an agenda that had little room for legislation that might interfere with the economic development of natural resources."[1]

In 1996, President Clinton signed Executive Order (EO) 13007, Indian Sacred Sites. EO 13007 directed federal land-managing agencies to (1) accommodate ceremonial use of Indian sacred sites by Indian religious practitioners, (2) avoid adversely affecting the physical integrity of such sacred sites, and (3) maintain confidentiality of information about them when appropriate. Further, EO 13007 required federal land-managing agencies to develop procedures for implementing the order. Within one year, the agencies were to report to the president on what they had accomplished.

At that time the Forest Service had not yet appointed its National Tribal Relations Program Task Force, and Chief Dombeck had other priorities for his leadership team. When the year was up, the Forest Service's associate chief Dave Unger duly notified the White House's Domestic Policy Council of the Forest Service's intent to comply with EO 13007. But in fact the Forest Service made no real effort to develop a sacred sites policy for another five years. When the National Tribal Relations Program Task Force took up its work in 2000, its members decided not to touch the sacred-sites hot potato, thinking it could distract from the task force's other initiatives.[2]

Finally, in September 2002, Deputy Chief Joel Holtrop appointed the Sacred Sites Policy Development Team, charging it with responsibility to develop policy and guidelines to address EO 13007 as well as AIRFA and other relevant statutes. The team of nine people included five Forest Service specialists in tribal relations or heritage management, one tribal elder from the Pine Ridge Reservation, one specialist in tribal relations from the National Park Service, one attorney from the Office of General Counsel, and one Forest Service line officer. Heading the team was Susan Johnson, tribal liaison in the Rocky Mountain Region. The team traveled around Indian Country and held dozens of listening sessions with tribal elders, tribal leaders, and Native religion practitioners to obtain insights into how Indian sacred sites on national forestlands could best be protected. After more than two years of effort, Johnson and other team members presented their findings orally to the Forest Service leadership in August 2005. Johnson submitted a final report the following spring.[3]

The Forest Service leadership suppressed the report and ignored its recommendations, choosing to defer action on a national-level sacred sites policy yet again. Johnson recalls that when she took copies of the completed, spiral-bound report with her to Washington—this was several months after her oral presentation to the leadership team—the sight of the bound reports elicited some sharp questions. Had the report already been published and distributed without the Washington office's approval? Why was there a Forest Service logo and date on the cover? "It wasn't received like we thought it would be," she recounted a few years later. "We were very surprised." Her superiors informed her that the Forest Service would not promulgate a new policy accompanied by such a long report. They raised a number of specific objections to the report, the principal one being that it made too much use of information provided in listening sessions without providing documentation to back up its assertions. Looking back on it, Johnson believed that the team's decision to respect confidentiality by not recording the listening sessions was "one of the downfalls of our report."[4]

Other circumstances combined to defeat this effort. Although Deputy Chief Holtrop called for the report in the first place, he was not well briefed on its progress by the new Office of Tribal Relations (OTR) owing in part to the breakdown in communications between OTR director Kanen and the field (see chap. 9). Furthermore, when Johnson reported to the Forest Service leadership team in August 2005, Holtrop was then transitioning from deputy chief of State and Private Forestry to deputy chief of National Forest Administration, and the Forest Service leadership team was ambivalent about whether he was still the appropriate executive, in his new position, to lead the effort. Holtrop himself was leery of moving the policy initiative forward at that time in view of the current political climate surrounding the issue. Among his colleagues, there was a feeling that the report would not be well received by the political appointees in the Department of Agriculture, and to push it forward regardless of its likely reception carried the prospect of an "epic fail" that would result in a long-term setback for the Forest Service.[5]

Indeed, the timing of the sacred sites report could not have been more awkward for the Forest Service. A lawsuit involving an Indian sacred site on the Coconino National Forest in Arizona—the Snowbowl ski resort on the flank of the San Francisco Peaks—was just then acquiring notoriety in the national media. At issue was a plan to use treated sewage effluent to make artificial snow. Tribes alleged that to spray the artificial, impure snow on the ski slopes would be to desecrate their most sacred peak, which they would find devastating. Not since the G-O Road case in the 1980s did the Forest Service receive such a public-relations goose egg over management of an Indian sacred site. When Johnson delivered her team's sacred sites report, the judge in the Snowbowl case had just made his ruling. Although he decided in the agency's favor, the case was still an embarrassment. Forest Service officials anticipated that the decision would be appealed to the U.S. Ninth Circuit Court of Appeals and then possibly to the Supreme Court. One internal e-mail that circulated at this time offered the dour prediction that "it could take a couple of years for this case to finally be resolved."[6] As in the earlier G-O Road case, the Forest Service would ultimately win its case in the court of law while losing in the court of public opinion.

SNOWBOWL

The Snowbowl lawsuit was brought by thirteen Southwest tribes against the Forest Service for authorizing expansion of an existing ski area located in the San Francisco Peaks near Flagstaff, Arizona. The Hopi and Navajo had sued over the same development years before, in 1981, to stop an earlier expansion. Then, they had claimed that the development would violate their First Amendment right to the free exercise of religion, since it would impair their ability to pray and conduct ceremonies on the sacred peaks as well as to collect sacred objects that were essential to the performance of their religious practices. The judge in that earlier case had ruled in favor of the Forest Service, finding that the ski-area expansion would not prevent the Indians from going elsewhere on their sacred peaks to practice their religion. What distinguished the second round of litigation from the first was that the second ski-area expansion called for the making of artificial snow using reclaimed wastewater. The thirteen plaintiff tribes complained that the Forest Service's decision to expose the area, including its plants and springs, to treated sewage would have a "devastating effect" on the tribes' ability to practice their religion and historic culture. Even though the Forest Service reached its decision only after holding numerous meetings with tribes and the general public, nonetheless, from one point of view, its action to permit the snowmaking plan to go forward was egregious. The difference in values could not have been more stark. As one journalist summed up, the Forest Service had approved "the use of treated sewage to make snow on a mountain considered sacred to southwestern Indian tribes."[7]

The Forest Service argued in its own defense that it had outlined the ski-area expansion in the Coconino National Forest Plan, that it had run the plan through all the procedural requirements of the law, and that the planned development

FIGURE 29. San Francisco Peaks

PHOTO BY TYLER FINVOLD. COURTESY OF CREATIVE COMMONS.

answered to a desired public use of the forest that was consistent with the Forest Service's mission to manage for multiple use. Without the expansion and the addition of artificial snow-making equipment, the ski area would likely not remain economically viable. There was no room for a compromise, the then forest supervisor Nora Rasure explained after the event; the Forest Service had to decide whether the ski area would continue or not. She thought of the forest plan as "the contract we have with the public for how lands will be managed." When she considered the fact that to accommodate the tribes' religious views would likely cause the ski area to fail, she decided that her responsibility to the public trust had to come first. "It was one of my hardest decisions and even this many years later it is hard thinking about it. You have to weigh different cultures, and to have to make a decision about that is pretty difficult."[8]

In January 2006, Judge Paul G. Rosenblatt issued his sixty-two-page opinion in the Snowbowl case. He found that the Forest Service properly observed all of the procedural requirements during its deliberations, including preparation of an extensive environmental impact statement (EIS). The plaintiffs appealed, and in March 2007 a three-judge panel of the U.S. Ninth Circuit

Court of Appeals reversed the lower court's decision, finding that the survival of the ski area did not constitute a "compelling interest" that would cause the Forest Service to interfere with the tribes' free exercise of religion. The U.S. Department of Justice, on behalf of the Forest Service, petitioned the ninth circuit to rehear the case en banc, or by the whole panel of judges—an unusual request reserved for cases of particular complexity and significance. The court granted the request for rehearing, and in December 2007, eleven judges decided to reject the analysis by the three-judge panel and affirm the decision by Judge Rosenblatt. In the latter opinion, the judges referred to Supreme Court decisions on the question of what constitutes a "substantial burden" for the free exercise of religion. While the judges acknowledged that the use of treated wastewater to make artificial snow for the ski runs would violate the plaintiffs' religious beliefs, they said it would not measure up to a "substantial burden" under Supreme Court precedent. The plaintiffs appealed once more. In June 2009 the Supreme Court refused to hear the case.[9]

Most Indian rights activists found the verdict disappointing but no surprise. Indeed, the Snowbowl case reinforced the point they had been arguing ever since the *Lyng* decision: Congress needed to pass a stronger law to protect Indian sacred sites. In March 2002, the National Congress of American Indians, in collaboration with the Seventh Generation Fund, Native American Rights Fund, United South and Eastern Tribes, and the Association on American Indian Affairs, hosted a summit meeting of traditional and tribal leaders in Washington, DC, to form a strategy for sacred lands protection. Out of this meeting came the Sacred Lands Protection Coalition. The following November, the coalition conducted a national gathering in San Diego attended by Indian traditional religious leaders and practitioners as well as tribal representatives, cultural specialists, and attorneys. The gathering reached a consensus "to begin an organized effort to halt private and governmentally-sponsored development that will threaten or destroy sacred places." The greatest need, the coalition affirmed, was to obtain a sacred-places cause of action—a federal law with teeth. "All the other religions have several doors to the courthouse," declared the coalition's spokeswoman, Suzan Shown Harjo. "We do not have even one door. Native Americans need protection for our places of worship and for our exercise of religious liberties, too. It is grossly unfair that we do not have them."[10]

In 2004, the Senate Committee on Indian Affairs held an oversight hearing on AIRFA. Harjo, as well as Walter Echo-Hawk Sr. testified on the need for new legislation. "It is good to have Federal Executive orders and Federal land use changes and some consultation," Echo-Hawk said, "but at bottom what is needed is a cause of action statute to level the playing field." Harjo was more caustic. "We have no way of getting into court on this matter. The Federal agencies know that. That is why they are pretty cavalier about ignoring what we have to say about access and protection of our sacred places on what they view as their land."[11]

Deputy Chief Joel Holtrop testified on behalf of the Forest Service at this hearing. He reviewed the Forest Service's responsibilities toward Indian sacred sites under AIRFA as well as the National Environmental Policy Act, the Native American Graves Protection and Repatriation Act, the National Historic Preservation Act (NHPA), and the Archaeological Resources Protection Act. He listed the four statutory authorities for cultural resources management that the Forest Service was seeking in the next farm bill. He reported on the Forest Service's recent establishment of the Office of Tribal Relations and its current deployment of a task force to develop a national sacred sites policy. The major point to his testimony was that Congress did not need to provide Indians with a "cause of action" to protect their sacred sites on the national forests. "Mr. Chairman," he respectfully concluded,

> the religious freedom of American Indians is and will continue to be an important factor in our management of the National Forest system lands and all Forest Service programs. The agency has made great strides to increase awareness of all Forest Service employees of the agency's responsibilities to Indian tribes. The Forest Service is eager to work with Indian tribal governments. Together, we can take appropriate actions to support the religious beliefs and practices of American Indians on National Forest system lands.[12]

In spite of Holtrop's upbeat prognosis, Indian rights activists and the Forest Service continued to hold opposing views about the need for new legislation to protect Indian sacred sites on the national forests.

CAVE ROCK

One reason the problem was so intractable was that every situation was unique. Tribes might find the Forest Service to be unhelpful in one set of circumstances and find it to be their friend in another. While the Navajo and Hopi and other Southwest tribes finally lost their bid to protect what was sacred to them on the

Coconino National Forest, the Washoe tribe of Nevada had a different experience with the agency when it came to protecting Cave Rock, a landform on the edge of Lake Tahoe. In the latter case, the Forest Service used the NHPA to protect tribal interests and close the area to recreational use. A group called the Access Fund sued. Ironically, the Ninth Circuit Court of Appeals made a final ruling in the Cave Rock dispute in the same year that it decided the Snowbowl case. In the Cave Rock case, Indians' religious freedom actually won in court.[13]

Cave Rock is a granite massif that juts out into the deep, blue waters of beautiful Lake Tahoe. Twin highway tunnels penetrate the center of the rock, and a blasted-out shelf left by an older, abandoned highway route still runs like a waistband around the outside of the rock formation. Despite those conspicuous cultural modifications to the landform, when the Washoe tribe asserted its need to protect Cave Rock as a sacred site in the early 1990s, it accepted the highway tunnels as an accomplished fact and directed all its angst toward rock climbers. Rock climbers were attracted to two large caves above and below the level of the highway. Starting around 1990, climbers began building climbing routes with fixed anchors and bolts, and making staircases in the rock for easier access to the caves. Acting without permission from the Forest Service, they even paved one cave floor. As the Washoe tribe perceived the rock climbers' actions as desecrations of its sacred site, it pressured the Forest Service to ban all recreational activity.[14]

The Forest Service's former tribal liaison for the Pacific Southwest Region, Sonia Tamez, says her agency "made a strong effort to engage the tribe" on this issue, while the tribe for its part was very effective in conveying its traditional values and needs to the agency. The dialogue led to the conclusion that Cave Rock must be recognized as a traditional cultural property and protected under the NHPA. "It took three forest supervisors and many years to get to that point," Tamez recounted. Maribeth Gustafson became supervisor of the Lake Tahoe Basin Management Unit in July 2000 and reached the bold decision to ban recreational use of Cave Rock for the protection of its cultural and religious values. The decision flew in the face of the Forest Service's strong tradition of multiple-use management. Moreover, Gustafson issued her record of decision in 2003—two years into the Bush administration in a political climate that was decidedly unfriendly toward restrictions on public access. "Nobody thought we could do it," Tamez recalled. "The Washington office didn't think so." When the decision was challenged in court, people thought "we would never win." All the cards were stacked against them. The Justice attorney assigned to the case had

FIGURE 30. Cave Rock, Tahoe National Forest, California

COURTESY OF CREATIVE COMMONS

never tried another case like it before. Once they were at trial, a tribal member confided to Tamez that the judge was not perceived to be a friend to the Washoe tribe. But to many people's surprise—perhaps even their own—they did win. The attorneys for the rock climbers appealed the case to the Ninth Circuit Court, and the Forest Service won there, too.[15]

The two courts' decisions set important precedents. First, the district court accepted the Forest Service's contention that Cave Rock qualified for protection as a traditional cultural property under the NHPA. It was the first time the Forest Service used the NHPA to protect an Indian sacred site, and its effort was vindicated. The appellate court then took up the Access Fund's contention that by protecting the Washoe tribe's sacred site and banning climbers the Forest Service was violating the Establishment Clause of the First Amendment—the clause that prohibits the government from creating an official or established church, privileging one religion over another, or favoring believers over nonbelievers. The court rejected the Access Fund's argument and found that the Forest Service's protection of Cave Rock was consistent with First Amendment freedom of religion protections. Although the climbing ban was instituted to protect Washoe religion, the court pointed out, it was also done to protect a culturally, historically, and archaeologically significant site. In the end, the Cave Rock case was a win for the Washoe tribe and a win for those who argued that the Forest Service had the ability to protect Indian sacred sites using the legal authorities and discretion currently at its disposal.[16]

A NATIONAL SACRED SITES POLICY AFFIRMED

During the presidential election campaign in 2008, Democratic Party candidate Barack Obama addressed the issue of Indian sacred sites in his Native American policy platform, pledging his support for Native American religious freedom, cultural rights, and sacred places protection. While Native Americans usually voted Democratic, the Obama campaign sought to increase Native American voter turnout. In the run-up to the election, political analysts observed that the Native American vote could potentially determine the outcome in several swing states, including New Mexico, Nevada, Colorado, and Wisconsin. The Native American vote was credited with having already won a handful of Democratic seats in the U.S. Senate in the midterm elections of 2002 and 2006; then, practically for the first time in U.S. history, it was courted in a presidential race.[17]

After the election, Native Americans insisted that President Obama deliver on his campaign promises or risk losing their support. One of his sharpest critics was Suzan Shown Harjo, the long-time leading activist on Indian sacred sites protection. Harjo seized on Obama's campaign pledge to demand that the administration send a bill to Congress for the protection of sacred places, and by the middle of Obama's first term she was lambasting the administration for not having done so. When Obama endorsed the United Nations Declaration on the Rights of Indigenous Peoples, Harjo applauded him but pointed out that he thereby committed the U.S. government to do much more in defense of sacred lands. When Obama met with a dozen tribal leaders at the White House in 2010, Harjo publicized the fact that the first leader to speak, a Navajo, talked about the desecration of the San Francisco Peaks and the destruction of other sacred sites. Through her nonprofit organization, the Morning Star Institute, Harjo initiated an annual event called National Sacred Places Prayer Days. Held over a three- or four-day period around the summer solstice, the prayer gatherings took place in the capital and at numerous sacred places across the nation. The event grew year by year, attracting the support of national Indian organizations such as the National Congress of American Indians (NCAI) and the Native American Rights Fund.[18]

While the Obama administration showed no more interest in pursuing new sacred sites legislation than the previous administration had, it did move forward purposefully and methodically to improve sacred sites protection under existing law. In 2010, Secretary of Agriculture Tom Vilsack directed the Forest Service to work with the U.S. Department of Agriculture's Office of Tribal Relations to complete the task of fashioning a national policy on Indian sacred sites. (The USDA Office of Tribal Relations, not to be confused with the Forest Service Office of Tribal Relations, was established in 2009. It was headed by Janie Hipp, the secretary's senior adviser on Indian affairs.) Vilsack's directive specifically called on the Forest Service to conduct further listening sessions in Indian Country and find out how it could do a better job of accommodating and protecting sacred sites while simultaneously pursuing its multiple-use mission. This time, the Forest Service committed senior-level staff to the effort. Deputy Chief of National Forest Administration Joel Holtrop and Deputy Chief of State and Private Forestry James Hubbard worked on it alongside Janie Hipp. Led by Fred Clark, director of the Forest Service OTR, a core team of tribal relations and heritage program specialists did the spade work, compiling public and tribal consultation comments, drafting recommendations, and writing the report.[19]

The final *Report to the Secretary* came together over a two-year span. The first year was devoted to gathering information. The team sought input from Native Americans and Alaska Natives as well as Forest Service employees. It used teleconferences and surveys as well as going into the field to conduct listening sessions. It attended more than fifty meetings in Native communities. The team also conducted a comprehensive review of current laws, rules, regulations, and policies pertaining to sacred sites. At the end of the first year, a draft report was distributed to all federally recognized tribes and Alaska Native corporations for comment. The second year was spent in tribal consultation on the recommendations of the report. In all, the Forest Service reached 125 tribes through face-to-face meetings and received input from an additional twenty-two tribes and intertribal organizations through correspondence. The level of effort by Forest Service senior executives, together with the close involvement of the USDA Office of Tribal Relations, were unprecedented in the history of Forest Service–tribal relations.[20]

The report was basically conservative in its thesis. It argued that the Forest Service could succeed in protecting Indian sacred sites on the national forests by operating within its traditional framework of multiple-use management under existing legal authorities. Yet the report promised much more in its overall tone. It contended that greater consistency across the National Forest System would improve the level of trust and foster stronger collaboration between Forest Service personnel and tribes. Staff training would raise forest managers' awareness and increase their competence in making use of the considerable "discretion" they already had at their disposal.[21]

The report looked to EO 13007, Indian Sacred Sites, as "currently the clearest federal policy on sacred sites." While observing that numerous Indians and Alaska Natives had concerns about the definition of sacred site contained in EO 13007, the report nevertheless cited it as the most authoritative definition currently available, that being "any specific, discrete, narrowly delineated location on Federal land that is identified by an Indian tribe, or Indian individual determined to be an appropriately authoritative representative of an Indian religion, as sacred by virtue of its established religious significance to, or ceremonial use by, an Indian religion; provided that the tribe or appropriately authoritative representative of an Indian religion has informed the agency of the existence of such a site." A key feature of this definition, the report noted, was that sites could only be identified by Indians, not the federal land manager. This was one of the ways in which an Indian sacred site differed from a traditional cultural property listed under the NHPA.[22]

The *Report to the Secretary* was unveiled by Secretary Vilsack at Obama's fourth annual Tribal Nations White House Conference on December 5, 2012. At the same time, Vilsack announced that he had joined with the secretaries of defense, energy, and the interior and the chairman of the Advisory Council on Historic Preservation in signing a memorandum of understanding (MOU) for interagency coordination and collaboration in the protection of Indian sacred sites. Not since AIRFA was enacted in 1978 had the federal government made such a concerted effort in defense of Native religions. The MOU called on the participating agencies to establish a working group and develop an action plan aimed at improving protection and Native access to Indian and Alaska Native sacred sites located across all four agencies' managed lands.[23]

Neither the Forest Service's *Report to the Secretary* nor the interagency MOU called for any immediate actions, such as land orders or promulgations of policy. Rather, they were statements of intent. Even the Action Plan, which followed from the MOU and was released on March 5, 2013, consisted entirely of procedures that the government would follow to bring about better sacred sites management. Still, the unveiling of the two documents together, the impressive display of interagency coordination, and the decision to announce these things at a gathering of some five hundred tribal leaders at the White House were all calculated to raise expectations and summon commitment and support. At the unveiling, Vilsack stated, "The President is insistent that these Sacred Sites be protected and preserved: treated with dignity and respect. That is also my commitment as Secretary of USDA. I know my fellow Secretaries share in this commitment. We understand the importance of these sites and will do our best to make sure they are protected and respected."[24]

The response by tribal leaders appeared to be mostly one of wait and see. At the NCAI annual conference in October 2013, held in Tulsa, Oklahoma, Harjo led a symposium on sacred sites protection where she continued to criticize the federal government as before, complaining that its oversight of sacred sites was lacking and uneven. On the other hand, when tribal leaders convened for the fifth annual Tribal Nations White House Conference in November 2013, the participants gave the administration a pass on sacred sites in favor of addressing other matters.[25]

In the spring of 2013, the NCAI submitted comments in response to the Obama administration's EIS for the Keystone XL Pipeline Extension project. The Obama administration's vigorous pursuit of domestic energy sources raised concerns among many tribes, since their sacred places frequently stood in the path of new energy development schemes. The proposed Keystone XL Pipeline project alone, which extended from the Montana-Saskatchewan border all the way to Texas's Gulf Coast, threatened to disturb innumerable burial grounds and sacred sites within the ancestral homelands of many Plains Indian tribes. Since the Keystone XL Pipeline Extension would cross the U.S.-Canadian border, the U.S. Department of State was in charge of the presidential permitting process. The NCAI, in its comments on the EIS, recommended that the Department of State review the recently released Forest Service report on sacred sites to gain an understanding of how the project would affect Native cultures. The admonishment by NCAI was a pointed reminder that the Obama administration still had a long way to go in implementing a comprehensive and uniform policy for the protection of Indian sacred sites.[26]

As the Forest Service proceeded to apply the new national policy guidelines on the ground, it did so in the context of recognizing that many tribal leaders would still prefer to have new legislation to augment AIRFA, NHPA, and other existing laws. Those who advocated legislation insisted that the law could be carefully crafted to resolve the constitutional dilemmas posed by AIRFA and the Indian Civil Rights Act of 1968. Some argued that the underlying problem with the existing legal framework was that it put too much emphasis on Indians' individual rights (as U.S. citizens) when Indian cultures sought to emphasize responsibilities and duties rather than rights. In that regard, it was notable that the Forest Service report on sacred sites leaned toward EO 13007, with its focus on tribes, rather than AIRFA, with its focus on individual rights. The Forest Service report upheld the view that protection of Indian sacred sites had to be case-specific and nuanced, bringing to bear two principles of law that were potentially at odds: Indians' fundamental right to practice their religion on one hand, and the federal government's trust responsibility to tribes on the other.[27]

Among those with hope for the future was Larry Heady, tribal relations program manager in the Forest Service's Eastern Region. A member of the Delaware tribe, Heady had thirty-five years of experience in the Forest Service in law enforcement and tribal relations. One of the things the new policy guidelines set out to do, Heady said, was give Forest Service line officers "a sense of equal value." When a commodity-driven proposal had potential to affect an Indian sacred site, then the values of that Indian sacred site were of equal worth to the other values that were driving the proposed action. To embed that idea in Forest Service culture was the challenge of today and tomorrow, Heady said, but he believed it was truly happening. "This concept of equal value for something that is sacred" was foreign to most line officers, but they were learning. And furthermore, they were "recognizing that an Indian sacred site does not only hold value for Indian people; it should hold equal value to the American public—that the site is revered for whatever reason."[28]

Heady's thoughts echoed the observation made a half century earlier by Secretary of the Interior Stewart Udall, that conservationists were coming to appreciate the Indians' "land wisdom." His thoughts also embodied the observation made a quarter century earlier by Chief Robertson that there was strength in diversity.

CHAPTER SUMMARY

Protection of Indian sacred sites remained the most intractable and emotional feature of Forest Service–tribal relations. Besides the obvious conflict between sacred values and other land uses, there were more subtle tensions involved as well. Who got to decide whether a place was sacred? The tribe or the individual traditional practitioner? And if a public agency was responsible for protecting it, then how could it protect the confidentiality—even secrecy—surrounding many religious rites? Indian activists tended to seek legislation on this issue; federal officials generally eschewed new legislation in favor of developing a more effective regulatory framework.

The Snowbowl case, litigated through the 2000s, was a constant source of friction between tribes and the Forest Service. Tribes held that the administrative decision by the forest supervisor on the Coconino National Forest did not go far enough in protecting sacred values. Although the Forest Service won in court, the case was an embarrassment because it seemed to undermine the Forest Service's contention that it could adequately protect sacred sites under existing law.

The Cave Rock case presented a contrast with the Snowbowl case. In the Cave Rock case, the Forest Service sought to protect an Indian sacred site through an administrative action under the NHPA. An opposing user group sued, and the Forest Service won in court here, too, but this case constituted a win for the tribe and the cause of Indian religious freedom. In contrast with the Snowbowl case, this one reinforced the argument that federal land managers could protect Indian sacred sites under existing law.

The Obama administration made a concerted effort to strengthen Indian sacred sites protection through interagency coordination and improved administrative policy. A long-awaited report by the Forest Service was released in conjunction with the interagency memorandum of understanding, forming a promising foundation for anticipated reforms in federal management of sacred lands.

12

LESSONS FROM ALASKA

OUT OF ALASKA

FOREST SERVICE TRIBAL relations evolved in a different legal and historical context in Alaska, and they still have a somewhat different character today. Nowhere else in the United States do the indigenous people constitute such a large minority of the population, and nowhere else are Native issues so prominent in state and local affairs. On the massive Tongass National Forest in Southeast Alaska, forest officials have cooperative relationships with nineteen Tlingit and Haida villages ensconced within the exterior boundaries of the forest. On the smaller Chugach National Forest, which wraps around Prince William Sound on the Gulf of Alaska, forest officials have relations with the Kenaitze Indian Tribe and a handful of other Native communities that are similarly located within the exterior boundaries of the forest. Native corporation lands selected by Alaska Natives under terms of the Alaska Native Claims Settlement Act (ANCSA) are interspersed throughout the two national forests. Subsistence use, as provided for under the Alaska National Interest Lands Conservation Act (ANILCA), is a federally managed Native use on all federal lands in Alaska, including national forestlands. Deputy Regional Forester Ruth Monihan said that the national forests are "interwoven" with the local communities and indigenous cultures in Alaska to a degree not seen anywhere else in the National Forest System. "When we get new people coming from outside, and when they realize how interwoven Native issues are, that is one of their 'aha' moments," she remarked.[1]

Despite its uniqueness, the Forest Service's Alaska Region offered valuable lessons for the agency as it implemented a system-wide tribal relations initiative at the start of the new century. Although much of the Alaska experience was not applicable to the rest of the National Forest System, nevertheless the Alaska Region's close involvement with Native communities and issues made it a valuable resource to the larger Forest Service organization. After the Forest Service elevated the tribal relations program to the national level, the first three individuals to head the program all came out of the Alaska Region. Carol Jorgensen and Dale Kanen each had roots in Alaska Native communities. Fred Clark, who became director of the Office of Tribal Relations (OTR) in 2007, served, like Jorgensen and Kanen, on the staff of the Anchorage-based, multiagency Federal Subsistence Board. The Alaska experience shaped each one's professional outlook, and each one, in turn, was placed in a position to shape the Forest Service's tribal relations program at the national level.

The very term *Alaska Native* calls for definition. The indigenous peoples of Alaska, Alaska Natives comprise three main ethnic groups: Indian, Eskimo, and Aleut. Generally, the term is capitalized to convey that Alaska Natives have legal standing as a group, which is similar but not identical to the legal standing of Native Americans. Congress has been strongly inclined in recent times to include Alaska Natives with Native Americans under the single umbrella of the federal-Indian trust relationship. Because of Alaska Natives' long history of being treated apart from federal-Indian relations, however, many legal differences remain.

When the United States purchased Alaska from Russia in 1867, the United States treaty with Russia did not extinguish the use and occupancy title of Alaska Natives. U.S. courts subsequently found that because the treaty of 1867 was silent on this matter, it left Alaska Natives with "possessory rights" in the land equivalent to aboriginal title held by American Indians. But long before those court opinions came about, the federal government settled on a course of "benign neglect" toward Alaska Natives whereby it was assumed that missionaries would see to their assimilation wherever white settlements might spring up in that remote northern territory. Alaska Natives, therefore, were not subjected to the pressures of treaty making, land cessions, and confinement on Indian reservations that framed U.S.-tribal relations for most Indian peoples in the Lower 48. As a result, Alaska Natives have no treaty rights today.

Conflicts between whites and Alaska Natives over aboriginal title and land use did not get Congress's attention until the 1930s and 40s, and even then, Congress chose to postpone resolution of the issue of aboriginal title, passing the Tongass Timber Act of 1947 to clear the way for land-use development regardless of the Native land claim (see chap. 4). So it was not until after Alaska achieved statehood and began to select state lands from the public domain as provided under the Alaska Statehood Act that the Native land claim once more became urgent. In the 1960s, Alaska Natives from around the state came together and formed the Alaska Federation of Natives (AFN) to press their case in the media and directly with Congress and federal administrators. When enormous oil reserves were discovered on Alaska's North Slope, the matter acquired added urgency. In 1971, under strong urging by the Nixon administration, Congress enacted ANCSA. The law extinguished aboriginal title, allocated $965 million in startup capital for a system of Native corporations created under the act, and authorized the Native corporations to select 44 million acres of public domain, or about 12 percent of the state's land area, for economic development and subsistence use.

FIGURE 31. Secretary of the Interior Walter Hickel and Alaska Native leaders, 1970. The Alaska Native claim movement culminated with the passage of the Alaska Native Claims Settlement Act the next year.

For a fuller description of this complicated law, it is pertinent to quote the Forest Service's previously mentioned sourcebook on American Indian and Alaska Native relations, popularly known as the Yellow Book:

> ANCSA in some respects was a treaty—a law—with the U.S. Government. In return for a grant of title to about 44 million acres and other benefits for Alaska Natives, the act extinguished aboriginal title to the remaining lands Alaska Natives traditionally used and occupied. However, Congress wrote the act to deliberately exclude traditional features of treaties.
>
> - It excluded reserves of land for exclusive use and occupancy, termed "reservations" in the Lower 48.
> - It made provisions for addressing the Bureau of Indian Affairs (BIA) or their delegated trust responsibilities for Indian-owned land and resources.
> - Alaska Natives were not signatories to the act: American Indians were signatories to treaty documents negotiated by the U.S. before 1871.
>
> The resolution of ANCSA provided a battleground for two dissimilar value systems—that of the Alaska Natives, whose tribal perspective viewed land and its resources as something of value to be passed on to future generations of tribal members, and that of Congress, which viewed Native corporation land as an asset that could be sold or even lost in risky commercial ventures.
>
> Nonetheless, ANCSA provided for the grant of title to about 44 million acres to the Alaska Natives and provided for continued efforts to protect Native subsistence rights (Conference Committee Report).
>
> ANCSA is the product of two Federal Indian policies:
>
> - The Termination Policy of the 1950's
> - The Self-Determination Policy of today
>
> While the language speaks of self-determination, the overall goal of ANCSA was termination and assimilation. Alaska Natives were given full control over their land and money; however, Congress assigned control not to tribal governments, but to State-chartered Native corporations.
>
> Federal courts generally support the special political status of Alaska Natives. However, complexity, ambiguity, and contradiction have not been eliminated from Indian law and policy. Even where policy seems consistent, there is still room for dispute.

Given the ambiguity of the record and political resistance to claims of "sovereignty" in Alaska, Alaska Natives have turned to practical political and social actions to strengthen their special status and cultural identities. Alaska Natives' special status is ultimately a political question, not a legal one, in which status depends less on what Federal policymakers say, than on what Alaska Natives choose to do.[2]

The Native corporations established by ANCSA were of two kinds: regional corporations and village corporations. The state was divided into twelve Native regions based on the Native population's traditional patterns of land use and occupancy. Each Alaska Native was made a shareholder in both a local village corporation and a regional corporation, and the $965 million settlement was distributed among just over two hundred village corporations and thirteen regional corporations (one per region plus one for Alaska Natives living outside of Alaska). Each of the twelve regional corporations in Alaska was allowed to select lands that were suitable for economic development. In many parts of Alaska, that meant lands with valuable mineral deposits. In Southeast Alaska, the Native regional corporation selected valuable timber lands on the Tongass National Forest. At the same time, each one of the village corporations was allowed to select lands within a certain distance of the village. The intent was for village corporations to select lands primarily for the purpose of subsistence, although that was not a requirement. ANCSA provided for an orderly process of land selections so that village corporations, regional corporations, and the state would all receive their turn. Inevitably, the process became more complicated and drawn out when it was actually carried out on the ground. Land exchanges stemming from ANCSA were still in progress forty years later.

One major cause of delays in the land selection process was that ANCSA practically ignored calls by the environmental movement to protect wildlands in Alaska. Americans' interest in the Alaska wilderness burgeoned during the 1960s and 1970s in part because the scramble for lands and North Slope oil made it apparent that the nation's "last great wilderness" was a perishable asset. Soon after passage of ANCSA, environmentalists mobilized the Alaska Coalition, and the battle was on. Blueprints for a comprehensive Alaska conservation lands bill were drawn and redrawn. The National Park Service, the Forest Service, and other federal agencies jockeyed for position to get their appropriate share of the public domain. After a decade of political fighting, ANILCA was passed in 1980.

Unprecedented in its sweep, the law established eleven new units in the National Park System and a similar number of new national wildlife refuges. The Forest Service was the big loser: ANILCA added no new lands to the National Forest System, although it did give the Forest Service jurisdiction over two new national monuments carved out of lands in the Tongass National Forest—a dubious consolation prize. It was revealing of the agency's low standing with environmentalists in the 1970s that it received nothing in the scramble for wild Alaska.

Instead, the Forest Service had to stand by while the state of Alaska and Native corporations resumed making their land selections, dismembering parts of the Tongass and Chugach national forests in the process. Each Native village on the Tongass National Forest was to select 23,040 acres of national forestland. Each Native village on the Chugach National Forest was to select 69,120 acres. Altogether, the two national forests stood to lose a million acres. A contemporary report, *The Forest Service in Alaska* (1980) gives a flavor of the agency's determination to deal with the Native land selections with grace:

> The period between passage of the act [ANCSA] and final conveyance of selected land is a challenging one to both the Native corporations and the Forest Service. Although ANCSA provides the authority for continued management of the national forests by the Forest Service before conveyance to the Natives, it also provides for "maximum participation by the Natives in decisions affecting their rights and property." The corporations, in their efforts to protect the present and future interest of their stockholders, can legitimately question past management decisions made by the Forest Service and current efforts to fulfill contractual obligations.
>
> Certainly problems will continue to arise until land title conveyances are complete. Thus, we are committed to support and assist Native corporations in their land claims and to encourage conveyances as rapidly as possible.[3]

As the Tongass and Chugach National Forests became riddled with enclaves of Native corporation lands, the Forest Service modified its forest plans accordingly. Sealaska, the Native regional corporation of the Tlingit and Haida people of Southeast Alaska, commenced commercial logging operations in the late 1980s. A few village corporations did as well. The Forest Service provided some technical assistance to these entities. The irony is that the Native villages had been there all along, yet the Forest Service had previously given them little attention. The land base gave these communities new visibility. The Forest Service had a strong tradition of supporting nearby rural communities whose economies depended on use of national forestlands, and henceforth it drew on that tradition to forge better relations with the Native communities on the Tongass and Chugach National Forests.

SUBSISTENCE

In the decade-long campaign for an Alaska conservation lands bill, a major policy question arose over how the federal government would protect Native subsistence hunting and fishing on federal lands. While ANCSA extinguished Native aboriginal title, the Conference Committee Report accompanying the law stated that Native subsistence uses on federal lands would be protected. The idea slowly formed that subsistence hunting and fishing must be differentiated from sport hunting and fishing and that the former activity must be given priority in resource management. Early versions of the eventual 1980 act pointed to how the federal government intended to protect subsistence. In 1978, the state of Alaska passed a subsistence priority law aimed at meeting the anticipated federal requirements. ANILCA Title VIII largely predicated federal protection of Native subsistence on the willingness of the state of Alaska to play ball with the federal government and do the right thing by subsistence users. In deference to Alaska's state constitution, Title VIII defined subsistence users as rural Alaskans, both Native and non-Native, regardless of ethnicity. However, it did make one narrow but crucial distinction between Native and non-Native subsistence users in declaring that subsistence use was "essential to Native physical, economic, traditional, and *cultural* existence and to non-Native physical, economic, traditional, and *social* existence." Title VIII also referred back to ANCSA and its implicit guarantee to protect Native subsistence. By so doing, it made ANILCA a piece of Indian law, and it made the protection of subsistence a federal trust responsibility.[4]

It still remained for the state of Alaska to define a subsistence priority in state law. Alaska's 1978 law did not define the subsistence user; it only defined subsistence as "customary and traditional uses of . . . wild, renewable resources for direct personal or family consumption." That meant that anyone in Anchorage who wanted to fill his or her freezer with wild game could claim to be a subsistence user. Alaska Natives who lived in remote areas of the state were placed in the same pool of hunters with urban dwellers, competing for the same limited supply of game. That was hardly a subsistence priority. Under pressure from the federal government, the Alaska legislature amended the law in 1986 to conform with ANILCA Title VIII and its definition of subsistence use as a rural preference. That led advocacy groups representing urban hunters and fishers to challenge the constitutionality of the state law. In 1989, in *McDowell v. Collinsworth*, the Alaska Supreme Court struck down the law. When the Alaska Department of Fish and Game averred that it could not distinguish rural subsistence users from other groups following the *McDowell* decision, it became evident that the state would not meet the federal government's requirements for protecting subsistence use.[5]

Reluctantly, the federal government moved to implement the subsistence priority on its own. The task involved setting up an interagency regulatory apparatus that would essentially duplicate what the state did but come to different decisions on who was eligible for subsistence, how many moose or caribou could be harvested in a given area, and so on. It created a wasteful and contentious dual management structure under which the federal government regulated subsistence wildlife harvests on some 200 million acres of federal lands while the state retained authority on the remaining 125 million acres of state and private lands. Anticipating that it would only be a temporary regime until the state amended the law, the federal agencies underestimated the costs involved, and so they saddled themselves with a far bigger job than they had budgeted for. Fortunately, they got another bite at the apple when the federal government took over management of subsistence fishing in navigable waters some ten years later. Having shorted themselves of money to manage subsistence in land areas, federal subsistence managers made sure to request much more funding when navigable waters were added to the mix.[6]

When the federal government took over subsistence management in 1990, it gave the Forest Service an opportunity to work with Native communities in important new ways. The Forest Service now joined with four other federal agencies, all in Interior—Fish and Wildlife Service (FWS), National Park Service (NPS), Bureau of Land Management, and Bureau of Indian Affairs—in striving to understand, protect, and monitor Native subsistence use.

The Federal Subsistence Board was made up of the head official in Alaska for each of the five federal agencies. The board met just twice yearly, once for wildlife and once for fish. The board had a technical staff of about fifty people, most of whom came from FWS and NPS. The FWS established an Office of Subsistence Management and took the lead in organizing and hosting the biannual meetings of the board. The meetings took place in Anchorage, where the four Interior agencies were located. The Forest Service alone was based in Juneau, a two-hour airplane ride away. Forest Service officials such as Dale Kanen and Fred Clark, who served on the Federal Subsistence Board technical staff, spent most of their time either out in the Native villages gathering information and hearing the concerns of the subsistence users themselves or in the Forest Service's regional office in Juneau communicating over long distance with the rest of the technical staff on the Federal Subsistence Board.[7]

Although subsistence had been much debated and analyzed over the previous twenty years, it was still very much a confounding subject in 1990. The Forest Service's Yellow Book (1997) gave considerable space to explaining Alaska Native subsistence rights. "Subsistence has many definitions depending on whom you speak to and in what context," it began. "To the Western/European culture, subsistence means the gathering and preparation of resources for nutritional purposes. To others, it represents a lifeway. To Alaska Natives, subsistence represents the very core of their existence as a people. It is a spiritual, cultural, physical, and economic means of continuing their heritage. It is the essence of their being."[8]

Carol Jorgensen, who served as assistant forest supervisor on the Tongass National Forest in the 1990s and who was Tlingit, wrote a particularly lyrical description of subsistence that the Forest Service published in 2001. It read in part, "Native people see subsistence as the very essence of their souls, the tapestry of their culture; it is how we communicate to one another, how we take care of one another, how we set up relationships between clans or groups of different villages. It is health, happiness, well being, love, communication and complete interaction of many things. It goes far beyond food."[9]

Discussion of subsistence could be polarizing. Non-Natives sometimes based their understanding on a dictionary definition of subsistence as the minimum requirements of food and shelter to sustain life; therefore, it seemed, the subsistence priority should be limited to poor people who were in dire need. The confusion gave rise to a "subsistence-as-welfare" concept that Native people found insulting. Some Natives countered by suggesting that the term should be replaced with an appropriate Native word—one that would translate as "our way of life" or "our way of being." (The Forest Service assisted with one such effort: an ethnographic study of Tlingit and Haida subsistence in the 1980s that originally took the title *The Subsistence Lifeway of the Tlingit People*. Revised and reprinted in 2006, it received the new title Haa Atxaayí Haa Kusteeyíx Sitee: *Our Food Is Our Tlingit Way of Life*.) The basic breakdown in understanding stemmed from two widely divergent cultural visions, wrote Thomas Thornton, a professor of anthropology in Juneau. There was "a Native one based on cultural identity, customs, and traditional values, and a non-Native one based on individual rights and economic need."[10]

Dale Kanen, who represented the Forest Service on the technical staff of the Federal Subsistence Board from 1991 to 1995, recalled some of the cases of subsistence use that were brought to the board's attention and led to a broader view of subsistence management. There was the case of the Aleut hunter of Kodiak Island who took a brown bear without having a state tag. In the Native culture it was presumptuous to declare one's intention to hunt a brown bear. "The tradition was that you just said, 'I'm going for a walk,' and as you went out the back door you picked up your rifle and headed out. And then after you shot the bear you buried the skull facing east." The state had a problem with that because it wanted the skull for measurement and record keeping. It was managing the brown bear as a population for trophy hunters. The Federal Subsistence Board ruled that an Aleut subsistence hunter did not have to bring back the skull nor did he have to obtain a permit beforehand. Then there was the case of a Tlingit hunter from Angoon who shot some twenty to thirty deer by himself. It was brought to the board's attention that that was not unusual in the subsistence economy, where a village community of perhaps 500 people might have just a few hunters who would typically do most of the hunting for the entire village. After a large take like that, the hunter would distribute the meat to the rest of the community.[11]

Some Forest Service officials believed their agency was better prepared than the FWS or the Park Service to grasp what subsistence really meant to Native communities. The Forest Service was first to recognize that subsistence management was less about sustaining wildlife resources than it was about sustaining cultures. With the agency's long tradition of caring about local communities, Forest Service officials—even those who were trained in the biological sciences—could approach subsistence management from a more sociological perspective.[12]

Besides its traditional orientation to local communities, the Forest Service brought other strengths and advantages to its participation on the Federal Subsistence Board. The Forest Service's tradition of being a decentralized agency served it well in this context. Whereas the other four agencies had to work their policy initiatives up a chain of command to Washington and ultimately clear whatever they did with the Office of the Secretary of the Interior, the Forest Service's Alaska Region did not have that level of oversight. It was freer to respond to local conditions. In the early years, at least, the Forest Service was out in front of the other agencies in asserting a subsistence priority. From the standpoint of the Tlingit and Haida, the Forest Service was the only agency on the Federal Subsistence Board that gave much attention to Southeast Alaska.[13]

A major innovation by the federal subsistence program was the establishment of ten regional councils in 1992. The regional councils were composed mainly of traditional elders and Native community leaders; as time went on, rural non-Natives participated as well. The goal of the regional councils was to bring these knowledgeable representatives of the subsistence users into dialogue with federal subsistence managers. The state of Alaska had attempted a similar structure in the early 1980s but had decided that it was too expensive to continue. To make them more functional, the federal government appointed six regional coordinators who facilitated council meetings and activities. The Federal Subsistence Board used the regional councils in two ways: to gather public testimony on community subsistence needs and to review the accuracy of technical, biological, and ethnographic information developed by the board's technical staff. In more than 90 percent of cases where the regional councils advised the board on a need for regulatory changes, the board adopted the recommendations. The regional councils represented one of the first efforts to institutionalize the collection and implementation of traditional ecological knowledge.[14]

Another important development in the federal subsistence program was the use of agreements with Alaska Native organizations to comanage certain fish and wildlife species. Federal land managers had authority to make these arrangements under both ANILCA and the Marine Mammal Protection Act (1972). By the end of the 1990s, more than $2 million had been invested in ANILCA Section 809 cooperative agreements with several Alaska Native organizations. For the Forest Service's part, the cooperative agreements dealt mainly with monitoring of salmon fisheries. In 2005, the Forest Service Alaska Region had twenty-two contracts with fifteen tribes totaling $1.5 million. The contracts dealt with tending weirs, counting salmon, monitoring harvests, and capturing traditional ecological knowledge. The various studies assisted managers in determining allocations between subsistence fishing in salmon streams and commercial fishing in nearby open waters. In 2009, the Forest Service contracts with tribal organizations supported some sixty jobs in a half dozen Native villages.[15]

For all of the positive developments in Forest Service–tribal relations that occurred under the federal subsistence program, many would say that the Alaskan subsistence issue grew more and more intractable as the years passed. From the Alaska Native perspective, the fundamental problem was that the dominant society treated subsistence as a mere subset of fish and wildlife management. Funding for the program was below par, and subsistence users were continually on the defensive in fish and game allocations. It was disappointing that the state of Alaska still remained at odds with ANILCA Title VIII more than twenty years after the *McDowell* decision.

Some held that Congress had erred in the first place by defining subsistence use as a rural preference. "We don't know what rural means," explained sociologist Bob Schroeder, who worked for the Subsistence Division in the Alaska Department of Fish and Game for many years before transferring to the Forest Service. It was impossible to define *rural* because it meant different things in different contexts: rural electrification, rural school districts, rural living. Some Native villages were at risk of losing their rural status because they were being engulfed by predominantly non-Native communities. The village of Saxman, for example, was becoming a suburb of the adjacent town of Ketchikan. Native subsistence users rightly pointed out that they had little or no control over non-Natives' in-migration to their communities.[16]

Two major critiques of the Alaskan subsistence issue were made in the 1990s. The first was a study by the state-appointed Alaska Native Commission, which filed its three-volume report in 1994. The second appeared as a collection of articles in a special issue of *Cultural Survival Quarterly* in 1998. Both critiques offered bleak assessments. More recently, Secretary of the Interior Ken Salazar stirred another round of interest when he declared the federal subsistence law "broken."[17]

There was one point that everyone agreed on. Alaska Native communities needed to be empowered. Hopelessness and despair were the communities' worst enemies. Unfortunately, past government policies had too often contributed to a debilitating sense of dependency and disempowerment. The Alaska Native Commission report in 1994 put it most forcefully:

> Whether in the area of economic development or social "advancement," the impact of government on the villages during the past quarter-century, while often

materially beneficial in content, has been destructive in process. The federal government appears to have believed that "development"—social, political, economic and cultural—is something that can be done to one group of people by another.[18]

The way out of the quagmire would be found through Native village self-governance.

GOING GOVERNMENT-TO-GOVERNMENT WITH ALASKA NATIVES

Most Alaska Natives do not belong to "tribes" in the same way that most Indians in the Lower 48 do. The nearest equivalent to the tribe is the village. Most Alaska Natives think of the village as the political unit that best defines their group's relationship to the dominant society. In Alaska, tribal governments are in reality village governments. While these Alaska Native communities now carry the political and legal status of being federally recognized tribes, it was not always so.

During the Indian New Deal, the Roosevelt administration encouraged Native villages to form village councils under terms of the Indian Reorganization Act. Many did. These were so-called IRA governments, which were given standing under the federal Indian trust doctrine. Yet when Congress enacted ANCSA, it sidestepped those IRA governments and established Native village corporations. As noted earlier, ANCSA vested the village corporations with power to make land selections for the village and to use those landholdings in whatever way they chose. ANCSA empowered the Natives by making them shareholders in the corporation, but in so doing it disempowered the traditional councils and IRA governments. Because of that action and ANCSA's express purpose to extinguish aboriginal title, the law is often characterized as a termination act. It is a strange legacy, because not long after Nixon signed ANCSA into law, he repudiated the termination policy and declared his administration's support for Indian self-determination. Every president since Nixon has upheld the principles of tribal sovereignty and government-to-government relations as vital elements of Indian self-determination policy. Consequently, Alaska Natives entered the modern era of self-determination with two contending, federally imposed systems of self-governance: the IRA governments dating from the 1930s and 40s, and the Native corporations established under ANCSA.

In the 1970s and 1980s, the state of Alaska generally treated the ANCSA corporations as de facto substitutes for the tribal governments and adhered to the view that ANCSA had terminated the federal trust relationship with Alaska Native tribes. Even as the rest of the nation turned away from the termination policy, the state of Alaska refused to recognize Alaska Native tribes as legal entities and opposed efforts to empower their traditional and IRA governments. The Reagan and first Bush administrations did not contest the state of Alaska's position, but they did not renounce the federal government's trust relationship with Alaska Natives either. The Alaska Native Commission described the federal government's position in those years as walking "a non-existent fine line."[19]

The Clinton administration reaffirmed that the federal government recognized the tribal sovereignty of Alaska Native communities. On October 21, 1993, Secretary of the Interior Bruce Babbitt published a list of 226 federally recognized tribes in Alaska. The great majority of entries in the list were villages or communities. All were either IRA governments or traditional councils, quite distinct from the village corporations set up under ANCSA.[20] On April 29, 1994, President Clinton declared his administration's commitment to Indian self-determination in a speech to Native American and Alaska Native leaders, and afterward he issued a memorandum to all heads of federal agencies in which he laid out specific steps for strengthening government-to-government relations with tribal governments. While the presidential order applied to all federally recognized tribal governments throughout the United States, Alaska Native leaders had particular reason to be pleased about it.[21]

In 1995, Alaska's Senator Ted Stevens, a Republican, attached a rider to an appropriations bill that required federal agencies to treat the ANCSA corporations on the same basis as federally recognized tribes. In effect, the Stevens rider reasserted the state's position on ANCSA without contesting the Clinton administration's position. As the Forest Service and other federal agencies duly began to strengthen communications with the ANCSA corporations, some tribes objected. From their standpoint, the government-to-government relationship was based on the principal of tribal sovereignty, and the ANCSA corporations must not be treated as sovereign entities. The Forest Service, for its part, agreed to the distinction but also aimed to comply with the law; therefore, henceforward it *consulted* with tribal governments and *shared information* with the ANCSA corporations. A very fine line again.[22]

Since the Clinton years, the Forest Service's Alaska Region has made exceptional efforts to develop effective government-to-government relations with Alaska tribes. One example is found in the internal protocols that Forest Service tribal relations specialists and line officers follow whenever they do tribal consultation. Every act of consultation is summarized and logged in a database to make an official record of the consultation process. The consultation database was started in 2005 on a system-wide basis, but budget cuts soon caused it to fall by the wayside in other regions. The Alaska Region, meanwhile, stuck with it and made it an effective tool. Rangers are instructed to use it. Judges have been known to request those records as evidence that the tribal consultation occurred.[23]

Lillian Petershoare, who directed the tribal relations program in Alaska starting in 2004, observed that the success of the Forest Service tribal relations program largely depended on the level of engagement by the regional foresters and the Forest Service leadership team in Washington. Without their endorsement, the program could not be successful. She saw that principle in action in the way the regional forester and forest supervisors in Alaska model their tribal relations to the district rangers. Whenever they held a meeting with tribal leaders, they made a meeting summary and sent it to all line officers. When forest supervisors conducted a monthly conference call with tribal leaders, they made minutes, documented all of their follow-up actions, and copied everything to their district rangers, demonstrating for them the importance of tribal consultation.[24]

The singular event in Forest Service–tribal relations in Southeast Alaska in recent times was the Acknowledgement Ceremony, which occurred in 2008. In their meetings with the Forest Service, the Tlingit and Haida Indians had their own protocols, one of which was to remember their ancestors. Again and again, they reminded Forest Service officials of a past grievance that the agency had never apologized for. They referred to the removal of fish camps and smokehouses at countless locations all over the Tongass National Forest. From the 1930s through the 1960s, rangers had burned down those camps and structures whenever they found them unoccupied. To the Tlingit and Haida people, the Forest Service's unilateral action in discouraging Indian use of those sites was one egregious example of the dominant society's broad assault on their culture that had occurred over the past several generations. In the early to mid-2000s, when Forest Service officials heard that grievance repeated over and over again,

FIGURE 32. New footbridge and trail crew near Angoon, Tongass National Forest, Alaska. *Left to right*: Tribal liaison Donald Frank, Angoon trail crew leader Aaron McCluskey, Youth Conservation Corps member (and tribal member) Roger Williams, Admiralty Island National Monument ranger Chad Van Ormer.

PHOTO BY TRAVIS MASON-BUSHMAN. COURTESY OF FOREST SERVICE.

they came to realize that some kind of acknowledgment was necessary. Tribal liaison Petershoare, who is Tlingit, helped them reach that understanding.[25]

Petershoare's direct involvement began after she attended a meeting with tribal leaders to promote an initiative by the chief of the Forest Service to establish a national tribal leaders committee that would form a liaison with the Forest Service leadership. The Tlingit and Haida leaders who were at the meeting expressed consternation: how could they be expected to favor such a plan when the Forest Service had not yet apologized for its past wrongs? Petershoare responded that the Forest Service had undertaken to research the historical record on the smokehouse removals and that she would inform them of the progress of the research effort. By then, John Autrey, the tribal relations specialist and former archaeologist on the Tongass National Forest, had completed a white paper that documented the smokehouse removals on Prince of Wales Island. Petershoare shared the white paper with tribal leaders Rob Sanderson of Hydaburg and Richard Peterson of Kasaan. Afterward, with the regional forester's concurrence, the three of them formed a committee to plan an acknowledgment ceremony. Regional Forester Denny Bschor supported it even though some directors in the Washington office advised against it.[26]

Sanderson urged that the acknowledgment cover not just the Tlingit and Haida communities on Prince of Wales Island but all the tribes in Southeast Alaska. Peterson, who was president of the Organized Village of Kasaan, agreed but emphasized that many tribes had suffered the grievance and each one must be allowed its own space to accept an apology. Moreover, their people's two moieties, the eagle and the raven, must each be given a say in it as well. After careful consideration, it was decided that the acknowledgment ceremony would happen over two days: on the first day, a formal acknowledgement by the Forest Service leaders that the wrongs had been committed, and then, on the second day, a potlatch where the leaders of the eagle and raven clans would present their response. Each tribe would be made to understand that the acknowledgment ceremony opened the door for an apology. Any tribe that so wished could then work with the ranger district in its area to obtain an apology directed specifically to that tribe.[27]

As part of its preparation for the acknowledgment ceremony, the Forest Service consulted with all nineteen federally recognized Native communities located within the Tongass National Forest. Petershoare worked closely with three traditional elders—one from each of the three affiliated tribes, the Tlingit, Haida, and Tsimshian—to determine how the Forest Service could observe proper protocols. She was assisted, too, by Dr. Walter Soboleff, a beloved Tlingit elder and spiritual leader of Juneau who was nearing his 100th birthday. (He was born in the same year that Theodore Roosevelt proclaimed the Tongass National Forest.) The Forest Service commissioned Indian carvers to craft two ceremonial staffs for presentation to the eagle and raven clans.[28]

The acknowledgment ceremony took place in April 2008 at the seventy-third General Assembly of the Central Council of Tlingit and Haida Indian Tribes of Alaska. The meeting was attended by some three hundred elders and other tribal members from all Tlingit, Haida, and Tsimshian tribes participating in the General Assembly. Speaking to the large gathering, Regional Forester Bschor said, "I am here today to stand before you and acknowledge that these things happened, that the Forest Service, in its efforts to manage uses of the

Tongass National Forest, did burn and remove many fish camps, cabins, and smokehouses that once belonged to Alaska Native families and clans."[29] After the Forest Service officials spoke, Soboleff was the first among the Indian leaders to reply. Petershoare later recalled that the feeling of relief in the hall was palpable when Soboleff said, "Of course, we will forgive them."[30] Following him, the three tribal elders each spoke. They followed his lead, but dwelt more on the hardships that had followed from the Forest Service's actions. On the second day of the ceremony, Forest Supervisor Forrest Cole presented the ceremonial staffs to former president of the Central Council Edward Thomas on behalf of the ravens, and to Richard Peterson, president of the Organized Village of Kasaan, on behalf of the eagles. Thomas then explained that the intent of the ceremony was to open the door for interested tribes and ranger districts to pursue further actions for healing at the local level. In fact, Peterson had already initiated such action for his local tribe. He and Sanderson were working with the Thorne Bay Ranger District on Prince of Wales Island to reestablish a fish camp and smokehouse at the mouth of the Karta River. (The project subsequently became part of a Forest Service–sponsored culture camp for Native youth, and it soon led to similar projects on the Sitka and Petersburg-Wrangell ranger districts.)[31]

The acknowledgment ceremony proved to be an enormous boon for Forest Service–tribal relations in Alaska. It established a foundation of trust and immediately ushered in a new phase in the evolving collaborative relationship between the Forest Service and Native communities. Once again, the Forest Service and the Indians had been hindered from working together constructively by the gulf that existed between their two different perceptions of Forest Service–tribal relations in the past. Things had occurred that were practically forgotten in the Forest Service but that still felt raw in the hearts and minds of the resident Indians. The outrage that the Tlingit and Haida expressed over the smokehouse removals from the 1930s to the 1960s was analogous to the anger that the modern Blackfeet had over the taking of their sacred Badger-Two Medicine area more than a century ago or the bitterness that the Leech Lake Band of Ojibwe continued to vent over the confiscation of their forestlands in 1902. In the case of the Tongass National Forest, it was particularly telling that the agency had to perform historical research in the files to confirm that the Indians' claims of past wrongs had indeed happened. The agency's institutional memory did not even extend as far back as the 1960s.

One positive development that followed directly from the acknowledgment ceremony was the creation of the Alaska Tribal Leaders Committee. Alaska

Native leaders were aware that the Forest Service had attempted to establish a national tribal leaders committee but that the proposal had fallen flat: getting hundreds of different tribes to form a committee that was reasonably small yet still representative of their diverse interests had proven too unwieldy a task (see chap. 10). In a conference call with Chief of the Forest Service Gail Kimbell, Woody Widmark of the Sitka Tribe of Alaska and Sasha Lindgren of the Kenaitze Indian Tribe proposed that the idea was still worth trying at the regional level in Alaska. Kimbell agreed, and Petershoare was tasked with developing a proposal and a plan.

The Forest Service was somewhat surprised a few months later when tribal leaders, including Widmark, asked the Forest Service to run the first election for the leadership committee. The agency had expected to contract for that service, and it took the request as a sign of growing trust. The election results were gratifying. All twelve of the federally recognized tribes on the Chugach National Forest and fifteen out of nineteen tribes on the Tongass National Forest participated. The new Alaska Tribal Leaders Committee (ATLC) consisted of four tribal delegates, two tribal alternates, the regional forester's team, and a representative of the Pacific Northwest Research Station and one alternate.[32]

FOR THE CHILDREN

Under the Obama administration's Great Outdoors initiative, the Chugach National Forest was designated a "Children's Forest" in 2010. The Tongass National Forest was designated a Children's Forest the following year. Those designations helped the Forest Service's Alaska Region obtain grants for a host of youth programs aimed at encouraging young people to find better health and enjoyment through organized outdoor activities. Most of the youth programs went hand-in-hand with the Alaska Region's growing outreach to Native villages. Increasingly, Forest Service rangers, biologists, and archaeologists worked with Native youth on a variety of projects that benefited both the national forests and the Native communities. Regional Forester Beth Pendleton was a strong supporter of the Children's Forest initiative and contended that Native youth engagement was vital to national forest administration in Alaska. "I am thinking about our future workforce," she said.[33]

Although each youth program was a modest endeavor by itself, the cumulative, long-term effect held promise. Working with a handful of teenagers at a time, Forest Service rangers involved the youth in service projects, such as tree planting or trail work, taught them about the forest environment, and exposed them to the possibility of future careers in the Forest Service. Some projects had a component of cultural revitalization. One project with the Douglas Indian Community, for example, brought together five youths and five elders for several weeks of activities including gathering traditional foods and traveling to historic sites. Other projects focused on job training for Southeast Alaska's burgeoning tourism industry. Regional Forester Pendleton cited the recent work of a ranger in Ketchikan, whose project with the nearby Indian village was to build a new community building and chef school with the object of training youths in food preparation and cultural interpretation so they could work on cruise ships and in visitor centers.[34]

Pendleton observed enormous changes in Southeast Alaska since her first time in Alaska in the mid-1990s when she worked with then Regional Forester Phil Janik on the Tongass National Forest's revised *Land and Resource Management Plan*. At that time, the local economy was still depressed after the closures of the two pulp mills at Ketchikan and Sitka that had been in operation since the 1950s. In 2012, massive, ten-story cruise ships, docking two or three in a row along the Juneau harbor front, dominated the view from Pendleton's third-floor window in the Federal Building, while Juneau's downtown streets pulsed with teeming humanity as the cruise ship passengers periodically debarked and circulated through the souvenir shops. And in spite of the tremendous social and economic problems that still plagued the Alaska Native population, there were strong signs that the Native culture would survive. In 1982, Sealaska Corporation and its cultural arm, the Sealaska Heritage Institute, organized a biennial Tlingit and Haida festival called the Celebration. Thirty years on, the Celebration had grown into the largest cultural activity in Alaska, drawing more than two thousand dancers. Dressed in traditional regalia emblazoned with clan crests, they perform over a three-day period.[35]

For many years, Forest Service archaeologists in the Alaska Region have enjoyed unusually strong interest and support from the indigenous people. Mark McCallum, heritage program manager on the Tongass National Forest, attributed the good record of collaboration to a combination of the archaeologists' own enlightened approaches to community relations—for instance, going into the village schools and sharing their findings with the tribes—and the Native peoples' own avid interest in contributing their efforts and local knowledge to Western science. Indeed, archaeologists' findings sometimes bolstered

FIGURE 33. People of the Tongass

COURTESY OF FOREST SERVICE

Native pride in being the area's first colonists, McCallum noted, providing a sort of validation of their claim to long-time occupation of the land and countering racist attitudes that they have long endured from some of Southeast Alaska's white communities.[36]

As proof of the Alaska Region heritage program's record of good tribal relations, Forest Service archaeologists pointed to the excellent collaboration they enjoyed with Native groups on Prince of Wales Island over the major discovery made there in On Your Knees Cave in 1996. During a Section 106 survey in connection with a timber sale, researchers found ancient skeletal remains. Terry Fifield, archaeologist for the Thorne Bay Ranger District, immediately shared the discovery with the Native community. By knowing the Native community and respecting Native sensibilities at the very outset, Fifield and his team were able to kindle a cooperative research project to excavate the site and learn the age of the skeletal remains. The bones and associated stone tools recovered from the site proved to be about 10,300 years old. It was one of only a few dozen Paleo-Indian skeletons known to science and the oldest one ever found in Alaska. The cooperation surrounding this major find contrasted sharply with the bitter controversy over repatriation that sprang up around the so-called Kennewick Man, another Paleo-Indian skeleton discovered in Washington State that same year.[37]

In 2007, the Thorne Bay Ranger District returned the bones to the Native community and the twelve-year-long project concluded with a two-day festival and reburial attended by tribal members and Forest Service representatives. Dr. Sherry Hutt, national director of the Native American Graves Protection and Repatriation Act (NAGPRA) program in Washington, congratulated both parties on their successful repatriation: "Your actions are a model for NAGPRA performance, but the highlight is the lasting relationships that are certain to come from the respectful way in which this matter was handled." Sealaska Heritage Institute and the Tongass National Forest, together with the University of Colorado and the National Park Service, produced a documentary film about the discovery titled *Kuwóot yas éin (His Spirit Is Looking Out from the Cave)*.[38]

CHAPTER SUMMARY

Forest Service–tribal relations are different in Alaska from those in the Lower 48, owing mainly to the absence of reservations and treaties and the legacy of the Alaska Native Claims Settlement Act, which was enacted to form a partial substitute framework for federal-Native relations there. Despite its many differences, the Alaska Region has had a significant influence on Forest Service–tribal relations outside of Alaska. Outstanding features of Forest Service–tribal relations in Alaska include federal subsistence management and close connections between the national forests and Native communities.

13

THE NEZ PERCE TRIBE AND THE FOREST SERVICE

A Case Study

CALL HOME

IN 1989, NEZ PERCE forester Jaime Pinkham, at age 33, was considering going home to his tribe. After four years of schooling in forestry at Oregon State University followed by eight years working for the Washington State Department of Natural Resources and two years for the Bureau of Indian Affairs forestry, he was anxious to apply his education and experience to the natural resource challenges on the Nez Perce Reservation. He was weighing an offer by his uncle, Allen Pinkham Sr., who was then chairman of the Nez Perce Tribal Executive Committee, to serve the tribal government as its natural resource manager. He was in the throes of making his decision when his uncle stopped by his office in Portland one afternoon and tossed a *Lewiston Tribune* on his desk, saying, "are you willing to deal with this?" The headline announced that LSD was making a comeback on the reservation. His uncle's meaning was clear: if he wanted to head up the tribal government's natural resource program, then he had to understand that working for the health of the land was part of working for the health of the tribe. One could not flourish without the other.[1]

Jaime Pinkham accepted the challenge. In 1990, he took over direction of the tribal forestry program, and two years later, he won election as the tribe's first natural resource manager. He joined a rapidly expanding tribal government that devoted a generous one-third of its annual budget to natural resource management and employed some three hundred people in natural resource jobs by the end of the decade. Yet the economic conditions among the tribe of about three thousand people were austere. Unemployment on the reservation stood at 64 percent. About three-fourths of people of working age earned less than $7,000 per year. Much of the population divided its energies between the depressed local capitalist economy and a shadow "Indian economy" that was based on subsistence hunting and fishing, huckleberry picking and gathering of other edible wild foods, and resource sharing. The tribe retained control of just 12 percent of lands within the Nez Perce Reservation, the rest having been lost as a consequence of allotment. Thus, the tribe pursued natural resource management against a backdrop of tribal impoverishment and land loss. As Pinkham would testify to a Senate subcommittee a few years after his return to the reservation, "Fish, game and plants that are our traditional foods and medicines continue to be critical for human subsistence."[2]

The political, economic, social, and environmental conditions on the Nez Perce Reservation in the 1990s flowed from the tribe's two-hundred-year history of relations with European Americans and the U.S. government. The Nez Perce, like so many other tribes, has forged a modern relationship with the Forest Service against a devastating background of near extinction in earlier times. The following sketch of Nez Perce tribal history affords a synopsis of Forest Service–tribal relations from the standpoint of one tribe—from first contact with European Americans through several generations of land loss and cultural assault to the modern era of cultural revitalization and resurgent tribal sovereignty. It provides a more vivid picture of the devastating consequences of allotment and the seeds of mistrust toward the Forest Service that were sown in the early part of the twentieth century. It presents an outstanding example of how treaty rights frame so much of Forest Service–tribal relations in the present era.

TREATY RICH AND LAND POOR

The Nez Perce was once a wealthy tribe favorably positioned for trade between buffalo-hunting peoples roaming the valleys and plains west of the Bitterroot Mountains and coastal and riverine peoples dwelling on the lower Columbia River. Divided into several bands associated with specific areas, the Nez Perce collectively occupied a large geographic province of about 13.5 million acres encompassing all of north-central Idaho and parts of Washington and Oregon.

Lewis and Clark thought the tribe numbered perhaps four thousand to six thousand people in 1805.

In the Walla Walla Treaty of 1855, the Nez Perce Tribe ceded 5.5 million acres and retained a core reservation in Idaho of 8 million acres. As was characteristic of the several treaties negotiated by Governor Isaac Stevens of Washington Territory in 1854–55, the Indians reserved the right to hunt, gather, and pasture livestock on all "open and unclaimed lands" within the ceded area, as well as the right to fish "in common" with non-Indians at all usual and accustomed fishing places.

After gold was discovered in north-central Idaho in 1860, the federal government brought strong pressure on the Nez Perce to make another treaty and cede most of their remaining territory. The Nez Perce bands were divided over what to do. In the Nez Perce Treaty of 1863, the Nez Perce chiefs who signed agreed to cede all but 750,000 acres of the 8-million-acre 1855 reservation. Other chiefs refused to sign or to acknowledge the cession. Those bands became known as the "nontreaty Nez Perce." In 1877, war broke out between them and the United States. The nontreaty Nez Perce were pursued in a fighting retreat from north-central Idaho through western and central Montana nearly to the Canadian border, where they at last surrendered. The 1863 treaty and the 1877 war left the Nez Perce tribe bitterly divided.[3]

The allotment era saw a further drastic reduction of the Nez Perce land base. Two years after Congress passed the General Allotment Act of 1887, the government sent Special Agent Alice Fletcher to the reservation to implement the process of assigning parcels of land to individual tribal members. After issuing 1,905 allotments of 80 and 160 acres apiece, much of the 750,000-acre reservation was deemed to be "surplus" land under the terms of the act. Consistent with the allotment policy, the government coerced tribal leaders into signing an agreement in 1893 whereby the tribe sold about 542,000 acres to the United States for $1,626,222. Those lands were then opened to white settlement under the Homestead Act. Finally, when the government began converting the trust patents on individual Indian allotments to fee status in the early twentieth century, a further loss of lands ensued as Nez Perce sold their fee allotments to whites or lost them through failure to pay property tax. By 1982, Nez Perce allottees owned just 51,067 acres, or less than a third of what they had started with at the beginning of the century.[4]

At the end of this calamitous experience of land loss, tribal leaders remarked that the Nez Perce tribe, relative to other Pacific Northwest tribes, was "treaty

FIGURE 34. Nez Perce powwow, 1904

COURTESY OF IDAHO STATE HISTORICAL SOCIETY

rich and land poor."[5] The tribe's treaty-reserved rights on ceded lands extended to five different national forests, while its treaty-reserved fishing rights gave it a hand in both the Columbia and Snake River basins. Yet the tribe's land base had shrunk to less than 1 percent of what it had been a century and a half earlier. Tribal leaders considered how the tribe might press its far-flung treaty rights to compensate for the fact that non-Indians now owned most of the land within the Nez Perce Reservation.

THE EARTH IS MY MOTHER

The Nez Perce tribe, it must be emphasized, never abandoned its heritage of caring for the forests and rivers and animals. This is a point that contemporary

Nez Perce well remember. While Pinkham was natural resource manager, he always began his public pronouncements by quoting one of the Nez Perce leaders in 1877: "The Earth is part of my body. . . . I belong to the land out of which I came. The Earth is my mother."[6] The chiefs who negotiated the treaties of 1855 and 1863 were careful to reserve the tribe's fishing, hunting, and gathering rights, and tribal leaders strove to preserve that legacy through the dark times of the allotment era.

Even as they faced subjugation by the superior power of the U.S. government, the Nez Perce retained a measure of tribal control over some forestland, resisting the central thrust of federal Indian policy to "detribalize" Indians and make them into freeholders of agricultural land. Article 8 of the 1863 treaty reserved all timber within the bounds of the reservation for the tribe's exclusive use except for the small amount of timber the government would need for constructing its own buildings on the reservation. A generation later, when tribal leaders negotiated the 1893 agreement on the cession of unallotted "surplus" lands, they reserved 32,030 acres of those lands from sale, insisting that they be held in trust as tribal timber reserves. The scattered reserves were intended to provide fuel wood and construction material for the Nez Perce allottees as they proceeded to build their new frame-style houses. The tribe also obtained two portable sawmills in the mid-1890s, which were used to mill lumber for allottees who were engaged in home construction. The mills moved from timber reserve to timber reserve on the Nez Perce Reservation, staying in nearly constant operation over the next decade. Thus, the Nez Perce remained committed to tribal control of the forest resource even as they adopted American patterns of wood production and utilization.[7]

The Nez Perce resisted moves by the Forest Service in 1908–9 to take on management of the tribe's forest resources. When news arrived on the reservation of the January 22, 1908, cooperative agreement between the Department of the Interior and the Department of Agriculture, which provided for the Forest Service to take charge of management of Indian forests, a group of tribal members wrote to the commissioner of Indian affairs in protest. "Considering the many promises the Government has broken with us in the past," they wrote, "we now have many grave apprehensions that our timber lands will be taken away from us."[8]

In spite of those concerns, the superintendent of the Nez Perce Reservation, the forest supervisor of the Clearwater National Forest, and the district (regional) forester developed a plan for implementing the cooperative agreement on the Nez Perce Reservation and sent it to Washington for approval in January 1909. Among other provisions, it would have allowed the Forest Service to issue grazing leases and make timber sales to non-Indians on the Nez Perce tribe's timber reserves. Tribal members would be given preference in timber sales over nontribal members provided they could meet the highest bid. Ostensibly, the Forest Service would be generating tribal income on resources that would otherwise go to waste. But as applications from white settlers for timber and stock range on the Nez Perce Reservation poured into the Clearwater National Forest supervisor's office, it was obvious that the plan was motivated by other considerations. Forest Supervisor F. A. Fenn urged that the plan be approved without delay "in justice to the white settlers and the community as a whole." The plan was never put into effect because Interior officials at higher levels soon scuttled the whole cooperative agreement between Interior and Agriculture. Before the proposed plan for the Nez Perce Reservation was completely withdrawn from consideration, though, the reservation superintendent called a tribal council meeting in June 1909. The council was almost unanimous in opposing the sale of any timber or the leasing of any land. In fact, the council went on record stating that it did not want the government to exercise any authority over its timber reserves other than to prevent nontribal members from trespassing.[9]

The Indian Appropriations Act of June 25, 1910, established a Forestry Division in the Office of Indian Affairs so that the Department of the Interior could manage Indian forests and sell Indian timber without help from the Forest Service. Even so, the Nez Perce remained hostile to federal administration of tribal timber reserves. The tribe accepted fire protection, but it resisted the Forestry Division's efforts to make commercial timber sales without tribal consent. The Forestry Division, for its part, insisted on having that authority in order to operate efficiently. The power struggle between the tribe and the Indian Service continued for several years, culminating in an appeal by the Nez Perce to the Board of Indian Commissioners for support. That last move seemed to provoke the Department of the Interior into finally taking decisive action in defiance of the tribal council. The secretary of the interior had authority to act unilaterally under the 1910 law. Overruling the tribal council and ignoring the Board of Indian Commissioners, Interior officials approved the reservation's first large timber sale to Craig Mountain Lumber Company in June 1918.[10]

Thereafter, BIA forestry acted with more or less impunity in administering timber sales. Over the next four decades, BIA forestry managed the Nez Perce forest resource according to sustained-yield principles. Allotments and tribal timber reserves were combined into management units for purposes of making timber sales and planning cutting cycles. Proceeds from timber sales on tribal land were generally divided three ways: 8 percent deducted for administrative expenses and paid to the U.S. Treasury, another portion deposited in the U.S. Treasury for the benefit of the tribe, and the remainder paid out to tribal members in per capita payments.[11]

In 1961, the Nez Perce tribe adopted new bylaws and formed a new government, the Nez Perce Tribal Executive Committee (NPTEC). Among NPTEC's first actions to regain the initiative in natural resource management, it contracted with Ernest Wohletz, dean of the College of Forestry of the University of Idaho, for a study of the current forestry program on the Nez Perce Reservation being run by the BIA. Not surprisingly, Wohletz found the existing program inadequate. The so-called Wohletz plan of 1963 proposed a more robust tree-planting program, a shorter cutting cycle, and a larger annual allowable cut—in short, more intensive timber management. Now the shoe was on the other foot. The Nez Perce wanted the BIA to produce more commercial timber and stumpage returns from the tribe's meager land base.[12]

Meanwhile, the Nez Perce joined with other Columbia Basin tribes in suing the government for failure to protect treaty fishing rights. The case helped set the stage for the famous Boldt decision in 1974, which recognized that treaty tribes had an equal role with the states in managing fisheries. In response to that decision, the Nez Perce joined with three other tribes in forming the Columbia River Inter-Tribal Fish Commission (CRITFC) in 1977. CRITFC's principal focus was (and is) on restoring salmon. One major concern is the effect of hydroelectric dams on salmon runs. Another is the effect of timber operations on salmon spawning habitat in upper watershed areas. Settlement moneys were put to fish tagging and monitoring and other research, hatchery production, and stream rehabilitation. As part of the overall settlement, the tribe began to receive more than $4 million annually from Bonneville Power Administration for salmon habitat restoration. The Nez Perce tribe, being located farthest inland of the four CRITFC tribes, was most interested in exploring options for bringing back salmon populations in upper watersheds.[13]

The Nez Perce tribe now had momentum from both the Boldt decision and the Indian Self-Determination Act, and so the tribal government, which had no more than a handful of employees when the decade began, was able to start building the capacity to undertake modern natural resource stewardship. In 1977, NPTEC made a 638 contract with the government for forest development work on the reservation—mostly tree thinning and tree-planting projects—and it hired a forestry technician, Roger van Houten, to lay out areas and plans for work crews, which were composed entirely of tribal members. In 1981, NPTEC initiated its own fisheries program (distinct from the tribe's participation in the CRITFC program, which was centered in Portland, Oregon), and the following year it established a natural resources program. By the end of 1982, it had a technical staff of eleven: one in forestry, three in fisheries, and seven in natural resources. The three programs were housed in the planning branch, which had a total of nineteen employees.[14]

BIA foresters worked with the tribal government to produce a forest management plan for the Nez Perce Reservation in 1982. The plan put new emphasis on "tribal values." It stated that the tribe's forest resources had "an important historic, religious, and cultural tie to the forebears of the present Nez Perce people." At the same time, the plan gave plenty of attention to sustained-yield forest management. It pushed market-oriented and science-based forest values that the tribe had absorbed from the dominant culture—tribal values of a nontraditional or "progressive" nature. Furthering the aim of the Wohletz plan of 1963, it strove to increase tribal revenues through more intensive tree farming. New silvicultural practices would produce "a more useful forest than nature [could] and . . . in far less time," the plan said.[15]

Besides wanting to find an appropriate balance between traditional and commercial uses of the forest resources, the tribe's main interest in forestry at that time was to recover tribal sovereignty over forest management. Over the next five years, it took over the BIA forestry program piece by piece. The transition was contentious and fraught with personality conflicts, but the tribe's efforts were unstinting. On October 1, 1987, it assumed responsibility for the entire forest management program except fire control, which remained part of an agreement between the BIA and the state of Idaho administered out of the Boise Interagency Fire Center. In 1989, the Nez Perce forestry program had a budget of $648,423 (about half of which came through its 638 contract) and a staff of eleven. The work covered timber sale and permit administration, forest presales, silviculture, forest development, management, inventory, planning, some elements of fire management, forest pest management, trespass, and communications. Arguably, the tribe had not been able to exercise so much influence over its forest resources since signing the Treaty of Walla Walla in 1855.[16]

About the time that Jaime Pinkham went to work for NPTEC, the tribal leadership made a strategic choice. It could litigate with the federal government

FIGURE 35. Nez Perce woman digging camas roots, 1960. An important traditional food source, a woman could collect about one bushel of camas roots from one-half acre in one day.

COURTESY OF IDAHO STATE HISTORICAL SOCIETY

for damages relating to its treaty rights in ceded territory, or it could seek a cooperative role in the management of federally owned lands in the tribes' ceded area. Considering that the ceded area overlapped no fewer than five national forests, there seemed to be more opportunity in taking the latter course. Some pointed out that tribal leaders in the early 1990s were seventh-generation descendants of the treaty signers. Nearly 140 years had passed since the Walla Walla Treaty of 1855. According to the Indians' mythology surrounding seven generations, the seventh one is a generation given to healing. By joining with the Forest Service and other federal agencies in doing conservation work, the Nez Perce tribe would be using its sovereign power for healing. Through a new conservation partnership, it would not only strive to heal the land but also to heal its troubled relationship with the U.S. government and the dominant society. The seventh generation would finally heal the tribes' old wounds dating from the historical period when the treaties and the War of 1877 had nearly rent the tribe in two.[17]

In 1992, the Nez Perce tribe signed a memorandum of understanding (MOU) with five national forests establishing a Forest Service liaison position with the tribe. The number of forests has since fluctuated up and down; today the MOU is with the Nez Perce-Clearwater, Payette, Boise, Wallowa-Whitman, and Umatilla National Forests. The cluster of national forests straddles the administrative boundaries between three regions of the Forest Service: the Northern, Intermountain, and Pacific Northwest regions. The first person appointed to the liaison position was Allen Pinkham, the former NPTEC chairman. The Forest Service provided funding for the position while the tribe provided administrative support. It was the first full-time tribal liaison position in the Forest Service dedicated to one tribe.[18]

Around the same time that the Forest Service and the Nez Perce Tribe entered the MOU, the Forest Service's tribal relations specialist in the Northern Region, Ira Jones, organized a treaty-rights workshop in Clarkston, Washington. Jones later recalled that he took the idea to his superior, Deputy Regional Forester John Hughes, who was "very supportive" and "the key person to make it happen." Regional Forester John Mumma gave the workshop the final go-ahead. Framed around discussions about the contemporary meaning and significance of the Nez Perce treaties for national forest management, the workshop was attended by some three hundred to four hundred Forest Service employees who were spread over three Forest Service regions. The following year, Jones held a second workshop in Polson, Montana, that focused on the Flathead Treaty of 1855. Then, in 1993, Jones put on a third and final workshop on the Nez Perce treaties again. Indian law professor Charles Wilkinson participated in the third workshop. He was impressed by both the size of the attendance and the "interest and sincerity" of all those he met.[19]

The establishment of the liaison position and the treaty workshops marked a new beginning for the Forest Service's relations with the Nez Perce tribe. It was not long before the relationship was put to the test. That test involved Idaho's most contentious environmental issue in recent times: the effort to reestablish a viable population of gray wolves in the state after an absence of this animal for sixty years or more. Abruptly and dramatically, the Nez Perce tribe was engaged in a joint project with the federal government that would soon encompass a few million acres of national forestlands located many miles outside the Nez Perce Reservation.

BRINGING BACK THE WOLF

A few years into the wolf recovery effort, when wolf numbers were trending up and the tribal government was becoming confident of eventual success in the project, Jaime Pinkham talked about its significance for the Nez Perce people.

> The Nez Perce Tribe and the recovery of [the wolf] has created a mirror, and our taking a leadership role in the recovery effort has added new dimensions.
>
> The trailblazers cleared a path out West to tame the frontier and bring order to the wilderness. Obstacles and threats to settlement needed to be eliminated. The grey wolf, and the Nez Perce, were both seen as obstacles and subsequently, we were both dispossessed. Our history resembled one another and today the reflection of our journey remains. Through our leadership role in the reintroduction of the grey wolf in Idaho, we along with the wolf, continue our recovery, to once again be occupants upon lands that we were removed from, to regain our rightful place spiritually, socially, and politically.[20]

Keith Lawrence, a wildlife biologist employed by NPTEC, recalled how the reintroduction of the wolf energized tribal members, prompting "questions about all kinds of things." For example, "if people had historically gone on a vision quest and received the wolf as their *wiakin*, could they still do that if there were no wolves?" In his view, it contributed in no small measure to a cultural rebirth and renewed sense of self-identity among the tribe. Pete Hays, a former NPTEC chairman, likened the reestablishment of the wolf in Nez Perce country to a "conversation that had been interrupted and had been restored."[21] There was an unusual kinship between Nez Perce and wolf; each had been persecuted and driven off the land. For the Nez Perce to help bring back the wolf offered a way for the tribe to bring back itself.

The wolf has long had a powerful hold on the imaginations of non-Indians as well. Long feared by rural folk, maligned in nineteenth-century literature,

and despised by open-range cattle and sheep growers, the wolf was extermi-
nated in Idaho and throughout the West when the region became settled.
Federal wildlife officers, operating in support of the livestock interests, actually
aided in the wolf's destruction in the early 1900s. Public attitudes toward this
storied animal began to change around the middle of the twentieth century,
and when Congress passed the Endangered Species Act in 1973, the gray wolf,
which then survived within the continental United States only in northern
Minnesota, was immediately listed as endangered.

The U.S. Fish and Wildlife Service (USFWS) moved slowly on developing a
recovery plan for this controversial species, correctly anticipating that successful
implementation of the plan would depend almost entirely on local politics and
public opinion. The recovery plan, as first released in 1987, called for the establishment of viable populations in Idaho, Montana, and Wyoming. The goal for
recovery would be to have a minimum of ten breeding pairs in all three states
for three consecutive years. Beyond that tristate goal, the situation facing wolf
recovery in each state was unique. In Montana, the wolf population would be
reestablished through natural migration of wolves out of Canada. In Wyoming,
it would be reestablished through human-assisted reintroduction of wolves in
Yellowstone National Park. In Idaho, it was found that migration of wolves out
of Canada would take a very long time, so the plan was modified in 1990 to
include human-assisted reintroduction there as well. But unlike the situation
in Wyoming, where the USFWS had a large area of federal land in Yellowstone
National Park and a willing partner in the National Park Service, there was no
equivalent federal protected area or partner in central Idaho, so the USFWS
sought the cooperation of the Idaho Department of Fish and Game (IDFG).[22]

Idaho stock growers as well as many sport hunters and guides strongly
opposed the wolf reintroduction. In deference to those interests, the state legislature passed a law prohibiting the IDFG from participating in the wolf recovery effort. The political maneuvering around this issue continued for several
years as Idaho tried to put forward alternative plans that would allow the state
a certain latitude to destroy wolves when they preyed on livestock. The state
also wanted to define the wolf in Idaho as an "experimental population" and to
lower the standard for when it would be considered recovered.

Around the same time that the Nez Perce tribe entered an MOU with the
national forests, it began talks with the USFWS about taking the partnership
role that would otherwise be assumed by the state. The tribe found itself in the
position of power broker: it strengthened the hand of the USFWS to stand fast

against the state's efforts to weaken the wolf recovery plan, and it offered the state an acceptable alternative to complete federal domination of the recovery effort. In January 1995, NPTEC submitted its formal proposal to cooperate with the USFWS on the wolf recovery effort, and in March 1995, after the Idaho legislature voted down another alternative plan, the USFWS accepted the tribe's offer.

Patrick Impero Wilson, a professor of political science at the University of Idaho, examined the politics surrounding the wolf reintroduction in Idaho and found that state legislators were willing to take the surprising step of handing the state's role to the tribe for three reasons. First, by passing the responsibility off to the tribe, the state government left Idahoans in a stronger position to litigate against the wolf recovery effort. Second, in light of the Republican victories in the 1994 midterm elections and the conservative agenda put forth in House Speaker Newt Gingrich's "Contract with America," conservative state legislators calculated that the wolf recovery effort in Idaho would add grist to the mill for amending the Endangered Species Act in the U.S. Congress. Third, the Nez Perce tribe gave states' rights champions a peculiar out. Even though states' rights champions were usually antagonists of tribal sovereignty and the federal-Indian trust relationship, in this case they were inclined to see the Nez Perce as "a local actor and therefore more acceptable to state interests than USFWS."[23] Perhaps, too, some in state government were betting against the tribe's ability to succeed. As one tribal wildlife biologist remembered, it seemed to him that state legislators and bureaucrats were probably whispering among themselves, "Give it to them—they might just fail."[24]

The plan called for the capture and release of fifteen radio-collared wolves in central Idaho in the first year and further introductions of fifteen more wolves each year for five years. This was modified to just one more introduction of twenty wolves in the second year for a total of thirty-five individuals. The tribe's role was to track the wolves' movements and monitor how they were doing, alert livestock owners to the wolves' presence in their area, follow up on incidents of wolf depredation of livestock, and undertake public education about the wolf recovery project. The tribe entered the fray with a modest allocation from the USFWS of $150,000 for the first year.[25]

The Forest Service stepped up to help the tribe. As the tribe's employees went to work on monitoring the wolves' movements through the mountainous hinterlands of central Idaho, the Forest Service made its summer crew housing available to them, gave them air transport into remote locations, offered them emergency use of its radio frequencies, and helped with other logistics. The tribe prepared a weekly bulletin on the location of wolves, aiming to build confidence in the livestock industry that wolves would not ravage livestock. The Forest Service assisted the tribe in that effort by setting up a phone tree for disseminating the weekly bulletins. The tribe communicated its information to county sheriffs, stock growers' associations, local media, and extension agents, who then passed the information to area ranchers. In that way, ranchers received wolf information from trusted local sources. The Forest Service facilitated face-to-face meetings between the tribe and the holders of national forest grazing allotments. When a rancher reported loss of livestock, the USFWS would investigate whether it was a wolf kill. If it was, then Defenders of Wildlife reimbursed the rancher. The wolf recovery effort involved numerous partners. In that team effort, the Forest Service demonstrated to the tribe that it could be a "really good friend."[26]

After so many years of controversy leading up to the wolf recovery effort, the reintroduction proved remarkably successful. In its third year, there were fifty-five wolf pups born in the state. Within a decade, the wolf population expanded into most of the available habitat in the state, and total numbers rose to an estimated 850 animals. Wolf depredations on livestock did occur, but they were not unmanageable. There were funding challenges, however. The Endangered Species Act requires that recovery efforts be funded through annual appropriations, and the USFWS was not able to maintain the level of funding for the tribe that it started with in 1995 in spite of the fact that the task of monitoring only grew more complicated as the population expanded. The tribe turned to the BIA and other organizations for help but was unsuccessful. Meanwhile, the state legislature kept pressure on the federal government and the tribe to continue rigorous monitoring.[27]

The state of Idaho looked ahead to the wolf's delisting, when it expected to take back responsibility for wolf management. Jaime Pinkham opposed that move. "We brought the wolf population back to the status where it could be delisted and there's a great deal of pride in what the tribe has been able to do," he said in 1999. "We don't want to see the program taken away and given to somebody else. We want to make sure we have a major hand in the management of wild wolves even after delisting." Eventually the tribe and the state worked out a deal by which the tribe would continue to monitor about half the wolf packs in Idaho through a five-year transition period that followed the wolf's delisting.[28]

The Nez Perce saw the tribe's participation in the wolf recovery plan as a test of its ability to comanage wildlife resources in its ceded area, just as it was already comanaging fisheries in the Columbia and Snake River basins. The tribe was anxious to show that it could perform scientific research and monitoring in line with federal and state programs and that it could partner with federal and state agencies. One tribal official stated, "We wanted to show that cooperative arrangements work." Another said, "we've worked long and hard to position the tribe to take part in resource management activities." The refusal by the state of Idaho to cooperate in wolf recovery had "allowed the tribe to move from the back to the front of the room."[29]

The tribe's move "to the front of the room" was consistent with its desire to reclaim its traditional role as the guardian people of the land, or, in the more modern sense, to assume its rightful place as a steward of ecosystem restoration. At the same time that the tribe worked on wolf recovery, it engaged with the Forest Service and other agencies on planning for the return of the grizzly bear to the Selway-Bitterroot Wilderness Area. This area, too, lay inside the Nez Perce ceded area and many miles outside the Nez Perce Reservation. The tribe's decision to pursue cooperation rather than litigation was predicated on allowing it the opportunity to have a more expansive outlook embracing all of Nez Perce aboriginal territory, not just the few remnants of land within the Nez Perce Reservation that were still in Indian ownership. And that expansive geographic outlook meant, in turn, that the tribe was charting a course that would come closer and closer to comanagement of national forestlands.

A DEEPENING PARTNERSHIP

The Nez Perce Tribe and the Forest Service proceeded to cooperate on a wide range of resource management issues and activities, including fish and wildlife habitat improvement, cooperative law enforcement, cooperative fire management, cooperative watershed management, joint staff training workshops, and year-end wrap-ups of the collaborative relationship. One unique and very successful collaborative enterprise involved interpretation for the Nez Perce National Historical Trail, which stretches along the 1,200-mile route of the journey taken by Nez Perce bands in the War of 1877. The Forest Service is the lead federal agency administering the national trail in partnership with the National Park Service (NPS) and the Bureau of Land Management (BLM).

The tribe works primarily with the Forest Service on interpretation for the trail, while it has a similar relationship with the NPS in connection with the Nez Perce National Historical Park, a unit of the National Park System.[30]

Points of friction remained, however, and it was in dealing with those difficult issues that the nature of the relationship was most fully illuminated. The first major issue came about when the Forest Service began charging user fees at public campgrounds on the national forests. New regulations in the 1980s called for a user fee of $5.50 per day per campsite, ostensibly to defray costs associated with upgrades to the campground water systems. The regulations also imposed a stay limit of fourteen days to prevent recreational vehicle users from "homesteading" in the public campgrounds. Tribal members felt offended that they were being required to pay fees and limit their time at camping sites that their ancestors had used since time immemorial. As the number of complaints rose, the tribal government took up the matter with the Forest Service, requesting that the Nez Perce be allowed free use of those sites.

Initially, the Forest Service took a hard line. Tribal members should have to abide by the same rules as the general public, officials said. To grant the Nez Perce people special privileges on the national forests would be to create a distinction based on race, violating the equal protection guarantee under the U.S. Constitution. The tribe could not claim the privilege as a treaty right, Forest Service officials argued, because the Walla Walla Treaty of 1855 did not expressly reserve a right to free camping. If the Forest Service were to concede that such a treaty right was implicit, then what would the Nez Perce demand next? And if it entered such an agreement with the Nez Perce Tribe, where would it lead with other tribes who claimed treaty rights on national forestlands? The regional forester of the Northern Region asked the Office of General Counsel in the Department of Agriculture for a legal opinion, and the opinion upheld the Forest Service's position.[31]

Indian law professor Charles Wilkinson blasted that legal opinion in an article in *Idaho Law Review* in 1997. Wilkinson inferred from the opinion that its author probably knew little about Indian law, because the opinion failed to cite the two most germane Supreme Court cases, *United States v. Winans* (1905) and *Tulee v. Washington* (1942). Both cases happened to deal with the Yakima Treaty of 1855, another Stevens treaty with language on reserved rights very similar to that in the Nez Perce treaty. In the *Winans* case, the high court found that the treaty "was not a grant of rights to the Indians, but a grant of rights from them—a reservation of those not granted." The court went on to state that the Indians' right to resort to fishing places was part of the Indians' possessory rights in the land, which were "not much less necessary to the existence of the Indians than the atmosphere they breathed." The tribe's off-reservation rights were equivalent to property rights, so every one of the tribe's usual and accustomed fishing places had attributes of a property right.[32]

The *Tulee* decision addressed whether the state of Washington could require a member of the Yakama tribe to pay for a fishing license to fish in state-controlled waters. The court held that while the license fee might be an indispensable tool for sustaining the state's conservation program, Yakama tribal members must be held exempt from the fee charge. The 1855 treaty "forecloses the state from charging the Indians a fee of the kind in question here."[33] The facts of the case in *Tulee* were a close match with the situation in the Forest Service campgrounds. The main difference was that *Tulee* dealt with a fishing license fee, not a public campground fee. The Nez Perce request for a waiver of the campground fee assumed that the tribe had a right to free camping that was implicit with their rights to fishing, hunting, and gathering. Considering *Winans* again, that was hardly a stretch.

In the year that Wilkinson published his article, the Forest Service was already taking another look at the issue of waiving the campground fee for the Nez Perce. James Caswell, forest supervisor on the Clearwater National Forest, felt the tribe should be accommodated. He saw that the Forest Service's intransigence was undermining the relationship. Furthermore, he made a practical argument for changing the policy. Those who worried that Nez Perce tribal members would use more than their share of public camp sites really had nothing to worry about, because Nez Perce hunting, fishing, and gathering activities mostly occurred at different times of year from non-Indians' recreational activities. Caswell brought the other forest supervisors around to his point of view. In 1998, the tribe finally got what it wanted, an MOU with the Forest Service exempting tribal members from recreation use fees and length-of-stay limits on national forest campgrounds in Nez Perce ceded territory.[34]

After the campground MOU was implemented, the Nez Perce requested that tribal members also be allowed to cut firewood on the national forests free of charge. This time, forest supervisors were more obliging. Each national forest implemented a free, personal-use permit system that was available to tribal members only. The personal-use permit existed alongside a commercial permit system that allowed anyone, Indian or non-Indian, to cut firewood for resale for a small fee. The commercial-use fee permit set limits on the quantity and sale value of the firewood. Any woodcutting that exceeded those limits required a process of advertising and competitive bidding for commercial timber sale. If tribal members cut wood for other than personal use, they had to obtain the applicable commercial permit in the same way as a nontribal member.

Nez Perce tribal members found the Forest Service's permit system somewhat confusing and thought there were inconsistencies between national forests, so the tribal government requested the Forest Service to review its policy. Five forest supervisors jointly reviewed the policy and found no appreciable differences between national forests; however, they offered to accommodate the tribe by sending a representative from each forest to meet with tribal members who planned to cut firewood in the coming year, issue them the proper permit, and answer questions. This conciliatory offer was made in 2006, eight years after the Forest Service had changed its position on campground fees.[35]

It would be a mistake to view the tribe's requests for free use of campgrounds and free access to firewood as motivated solely by economics. In 1996, the regional forester of the Southwest Region had argued that free camping privileges for the Nez Perce would constitute "an unsustainable and unsupportable expansion" of the tribe's off-reservation treaty rights, implying that the Forest Service would be granting the tribe something it did not already have. The Nez Perce people saw it the other way around: the imposition of a user fee threatened to cut them off from making traditional use of the forest. It is important to recognize that tribal members' fishing, hunting, and gathering activities brought traditional foods and medicines into the community that were not just of economic value but vital to tribal members' physical and spiritual health, too. As people of the land, their bodies were genetically predisposed to respond well to a diet of local foods and to suffer various ill effects on a diet of non-Native foods. Obesity, heart disease, and diabetes were all too prevalent in the population. It was just as Jaime Pinkham said in his congressional testimony: "Fish, game and plants that are our traditional foods and medicines continue to be critical for human subsistence."[36]

After the free-use issue, the second point of friction between the Nez Perce and the Forest Service arose over management of bighorn sheep. Traditionally, the animal was an important resource for the Nez Perce people. They built stone blinds for hunting the animal and stone corrals for capturing and containing them. They used its curved horns to make bows and its thin, tough hide for clothing material. At one time, bighorn sheep may have been more plentiful than deer or elk, but numbers were brought low in the period of white

FIGURE 36. Bighorn sheep. The Nez Perce Tribe
is partnering with the Forest Service and others
to restore this culturally important animal on
national forest lands within the tribal homeland.

PHOTO BY JEREMY WEBER. COURTESY
OF CREATIVE COMMONS.

settlement. Following decades of gradual increase, bighorn sheep started on a
decline throughout the intermountain West in the 1980s. In the Salmon River
Canyon west of the Nez Perce Reservation, the bighorn sheep population
dropped from around four hundred to one hundred head. In 2004, the tribe
appealed the Payette National Forest's land-management plan on the basis that
it did not provide for viable populations of bighorn sheep. The tribe decided to
make it a priority to halt the decline and restore herd sizes to a level where they
could be hunted again. They saw their interest as a cultural imperative and a
treaty right.[37]

Research indicated that the probable leading cause of bighorn sheep decline
was from transfer of disease from domestic sheep occupying the same range.
To bring the wild sheep back, it would be necessary to curtail domestic sheep

grazing wherever the two species mingled. In the steep canyons of central Idaho, where bighorn sheep move up and down the river corridors, it would be difficult to keep the populations separate without making a drastic reduction in grazing use of the national forest.

The tribe's appeal was carried up to the chief of the Forest Service, who agreed with the tribe and remanded the Payette National Forest's plan to the region with the conclusion that domestic sheep grazing allotments must be reduced. The tribe requested that it be granted cooperator status as the Forest Service walked the plan through the National Environmental Policy Act process. Three other tribes—the Umatilla, Bannock, and Duck Valley Paiute—as well as the states of Idaho, Washington, and Oregon, followed the Nez Perce in making the request. The planning effort was then expanded to include the Nez Perce National Forest and the BLM as well. It was an unusual effort: federal land managers of two agencies sitting down with representatives of seven other sovereign governments. The Idaho Woolgrowers Association fought back, and there was a series of legal battles. Finally, a revised plan was completed in 2010 that called for phasing out domestic sheep grazing on seventy thousand acres, roughly a 70 percent reduction in grazing use of the national forest. Although the Forest Service was now solidly with the tribe on this issue, together they faced more challenges as woolgrowers tried to block implementation of the plan through court injunctions and even a rider on a bill passed by Congress in 2011 that would have the Forest Service slow the process. In June 2012, the tribe joined in a lawsuit as an amicus curiae to prevent the Forest Service from backing off the grazing reduction according to the rider.[38]

Today the Forest Service views its relationship with the Nez Perce Tribe as an outstanding success story in the annals of Forest Service–tribal relations. Although the relationship was not a happy one in the past, the two have forged a close, effective partnership in recent times. The Forest Service has held it up as a model for how it would like to do business with other tribes. At the same time, the Forest Service admits that it cannot appoint a tribal liaison to every tribe. Other tribes in the region caution the agency against lavishing praise on a single tribe simply because the relationship is a cordial one.[39]

The Nez Perce Tribe has a different perspective. Jaime Pinkham informed a Senate subcommittee at a hearing in Grangeville, Idaho, that "the terms of our relationship with the Forest Service is not as a neighbor nor a special interest group. It is expressly outlined by treaty and subsequently affirmed by the President, past and present, and the Forest Service itself. The tribal–Forest Service relationship requires interaction at a national and field level. Field activities are coordinated with three of their regions which include independent forests that are further subdivided into districts. The relationship extends beyond resource management and protection to include employment, training, and education. As a result, the Tribe is thrust into a tremendous workload trying to respond to actions and inquiries from the various administrative levels of the agency."[40]

That was in his written statement. In oral testimony, Pinkham reminded the panel of another crucial point. "The Nez Perce people are here to stay. We will not sell our land during wavering economic times and relocate our operations elsewhere. Our ancestors and our culture [are] committed to the land upon which we live."[41] His point applied with equal force to all of the Forest Service's partnering tribes.

CHAPTER SUMMARY

The Nez Perce Tribe collaborates with the Forest Service on salmon habitat restoration, wolf recovery, and myriad other resource management issues on five national forests in north-central Idaho. The tribe views the partnership as a way to assert tribal sovereignty over a broad area of its aboriginal territory and revitalize its relationship with the land. The Forest Service views the partnership as a model of what it would like to do with other tribes.

The case study not only highlights this important contemporary relationship, it also reminds us that tribes and the Forest Service have different stories about the past and different perspectives about the journeys that brought them together. While the Nez Perce Tribe only took over the BIA forestry program on the reservation in the 1980s and only began to work directly with the national forests in the early 1990s, the people have been caring for the land for countless generations.

14

THE TWENTY-FIRST-CENTURY PARTNERSHIP

TRIBAL SOVEREIGNTY, CONSULTATION, AND COMMUNICATIONS

THE RELATIONSHIP BETWEEN the Forest Service and tribes is, in essence, about coming to grips with tribal sovereignty. Tribal sovereignty is the inherent power of indigenous peoples to govern themselves within the larger nation. It is not a power or right that was bestowed on tribes by the national government at some time in the past. Rather, it is a power that indigenous peoples hold intrinsically and have never surrendered. It is elemental. When non-Indians think about tribal sovereignty in the contemporary world, they usually conceive of it as a political abstraction. If they have any direct experience with it at all, it is apt to be through the narrow, political mechanism of government-to-government relations. Government-to-government relations are a formalized, even ritualized, way for one sovereign power to communicate with another. Most Indians, on the other hand, have a far more direct and encompassing view of tribal sovereignty. They tend to conceive of it in more emotional terms. For them, tribal sovereignty is a life force that survives as long as their people survive as a distinct cultural entity.

Take the example of the Karuk Tribe of Northern California. The Karuk inhabit a mountainous terrain in the northern part of the Six Rivers National Forest. Although federally recognized since the 1980s, the tribe has no designated reservation. It owns a few parcels of land totaling less than a thousand acres. It partners with the Forest Service for the protection of its homeland in the upper Klamath River watershed. Some years ago, when the Forest Service began spraying herbicides to control spotted knapweed and other invasive plants, the Karuk saw the poisons in the environment as a threat to their cultural survival. Alarming data pointed to a decline in female fertility and an increase in miscarriages in the population. Consequently, the Karuk found it imperative to stop the Forest Service's use of herbicides, and they approached the issue as a matter of tribal sovereignty. The tribal council passed a resolution declaring that the Karuk Tribe was a "historic sovereign aboriginal People" and that it was dedicated to preserving the ecological integrity of the watershed; therefore, it opposed any and all use of pesticides in the area. A letter from a tribal member to the Forest Service put the case this way:

> I guess it's easy for such a large organization to ignore such a small group of people. But it is not as easy for us to ignore the Forest Service when its actions cause such terrible damage to us. There are only 800 of us left. When we lose one baby, it is the same proportion as if you [non-Indians] lost 275,000 babies. The herbicide spraying is clearly threatening our very survival as a people. Our cultural group is already endangered enough as it is.[1]

As the writer well knew, sovereignty's most fundamental property is the power to protect. Take that away, and the sovereignty is compromised.

Tribal sovereignty remains an elusive concept for the dominant society to grasp. Yet the concept is far better understood today than it was in the past. Tribes have managed to inform the general public of their sovereign rights through hard-fought political and legal battles as well as through public education and on-the-job training. The Forest Service's tribal relations personnel have worked long and patiently to educate line officers and staff within the agency. Gary Harris, a thirty-two-year veteran of the Forest Service who finished out his career as tribal liaison in the Pacific Northwest Region in 2011, said that Forest Service personnel have a much greater awareness of tribal sovereignty today than they had even a decade ago. Back then, he said, there was still a prevailing attitude of "why are we giving all of this to the tribes?" Now, the Forest Service's rank and file have a better appreciation of what Indian peoples lost through the course of history and what they retained rights to as tribal entities.[2]

As discussed in earlier chapters, various statutes enacted since the 1970s require federal agencies to canvas tribal governments about tribes' sovereign concerns through the formal process of tribal consultation. *Tribal consultation* is a term of art used for describing government-to-government negotiation or dialogue between sovereigns under the aegis of the federal-Indian trust relationship. Tribal governments had to find ways to cope with the sheer volume of requests for tribal consultation. As a practical matter, tribal representatives could not respond to every request for comment, much less offer confidential information or commit to a policy when they were being asked to do so in the name of the whole tribe. Tribal governments had to perform a kind of triage to decide which requests for tribal consultation needed attention when every single one signified a challenge, at some level, to the tribe's sovereignty.

Federal agencies learned how to consult with tribes through much trial and error. Slowly they came to see that they needed strategies for making their efforts results driven, meaningful, and systematized.[3] In 2009, President Obama issued a Memorandum to Heads of Executive Departments and Agencies on Tribal Consultation, which directed "complete and consistent implementation of Executive Order 13175." The referenced order was President Clinton's directive in 2000 to all agency heads to develop policies and procedures for effective tribal consultation. Clinton's directive was a repetition of a memorandum he issued in April 1994 following a meeting with tribal leaders. And that presidential directive followed earlier pronouncements on government-to-government relations by the Reagan and Bush administrations. Clearly, tribal consultation has traveled a long road from the early years of Indian self-determination to the present.

In response to Obama's 2009 memorandum, Secretary of Agriculture Vilsack committed the U.S. Department of Agriculture (USDA) to improving government-to-government relations with tribes. He formed an Office of Tribal Relations (OTR) in the Office of the Secretary, brought in a whole new staff, and appointed a new special assistant to the secretary, Janie Hipp, to head it up. In the Obama administration's first term, the USDA consulted with tribes on more than one hundred new rules and regulations.[4]

As part of that USDA initiative, the Forest Service embarked on its first national-level tribal consultation at the end of 2009. The matter it put to tribes was no small item: it was the Forest Service's proposed new land-management planning rule, the federal regulations by which the agency developed forest plans to comply with requirements under the National Forest Management Act (NFMA) of 1976, the Multiple-Use Sustained-Yield Act (MUSYA) of

1960, and other laws. The Forest Service still operated under its 1982 planning rule, having attempted and failed to implement a new planning rule in 2000. Without strong direction and support from the USDA's new Office of Tribal Relations, it is doubtful the Forest Service would have made its debut in national-level tribal consultation with such a vital piece of Forest Service policy at stake. In mid-December 2009, Deputy Chief Holtrop notified tribal governments that the Forest Service was initiating the process to promulgate the new planning rule. "The USFS is committed to government-to-government consultation on agency policy that could have an impact on Tribes," Holtrop wrote to tribal leaders. "When a proposed planning rule is available next fall, information will be sent out to the Regional Foresters and Forest Supervisors for consultation purposes. Tribes can request government-to-government consultation with their local line officer."[5]

The Forest Service's first national-level tribal consultation met with mixed success. It began with a three-hour conference call in which the Forest Service leadership connected with an unknown number of participants through a total of eighty phone lines. Then the Washington office staff put together a national road show to explain the proposed new planning rule and hold listening sessions around the country. From region to region, tribes' willingness to come together for government-to-government consultations varied considerably. In California, tribal representatives appeared at a central location in ample numbers. But in the Northern Region, when the team held a meeting at the regional office in Missoula, Montana, only one tribal person attended. The lone individual was a staffer for the Coeur d'Alene Tribe of Idaho, and he drove two and a half hours to find himself attending a meeting with thirty Forest Service officials. Following that awkward meeting, the team modified its approach; continuing onward to Alaska, it took its road show to each tribe. When it was all over, many tribal leaders praised the Forest Service for the degree to which the agency engaged tribes in the process.[6]

In 2011, the OTR added a national-level consultation schedule to its website. By May 2014, a total of twenty-four tribal consultations were completed, two were in progress, and another six were pending. National-level tribal consultations dealt with all kinds of changes to Forest Service policy and procedures: modification of the administrative appeal rule, preservation of paleontological resources, invasive species management, aerial application of fire retardant, wilderness management, and so on. Sometimes a regional issue with a great deal of tribal interest, such as bighorn sheep management in the Intermountain West, was elevated to a national-level tribal consultation. Ironically, some in the Forest Service and many in tribal governments now complained of "consultation fatigue." (The Forest Service was not the only federal agency trying to do more tribal consultation; tribes were getting requests from all directions.) A year and a half into it, OTR director Fred Clark wrote, "We all learned many lessons about consultation overload and made attempts to combine, bundle, and otherwise streamline the consultation process without shortchanging our Tribal partners on what the Agency learns from these interactions. We also experimented with greater collaborative processes and focused pre-consultation efforts that have proved invaluable."[7] Even as tribal consultation at the national level became more commonplace, it continued to evolve.

From the standpoint of most tribes, consultation with the Forest Service on national policy issues was a welcome development as far as it went. But tribal participants stressed that the long-distance call-ins were no substitute for face-to-face dialogue. The national-level consultations, or "listening sessions" as they came to be known, often began with reminders and admonishments by the tribes that consultation still needed to occur at the regional and local level to enable them to develop personal relationships and a level of trust. The venue was particularly ill suited for eliciting input from tribal elders.[8]

Forest Service officials concede that face-to-face dialogue is still the preferred method of consultation at the regional and local levels. Not only are face-to-face meetings vital for building trust, they are also important for bringing action on things that most need it. Both sides are trying to move past the days when the Forest Service sent out impersonal "Dear Tribal Leaders" letters without much confidence that they would be answered, and tribes responded in kind. Forest Service tribal liaison Larry Heady advises line officers, "If you think this has tribal implications then walk it over or pick up the phone and call the chairman." Part of developing a relationship is acquiring a good grasp of what the other party cares about.[9]

For many years past and still today, the most frequent complaint by tribes about the consultation process concerns the high turnover of Forest Service personnel. Line officers transfer from position to position and place to place frequently, because that is part of the Forest Service's culture for developing a loyal, career-committed workforce. While there is turnover of tribal executives, too, the newly appointed Forest Service officials come from a much bigger pot. Unfortunately for tribes, each new line officer with whom they deal has to be educated about the tribe's standing and special concerns. The Forest

Service's main answer to the problem is more training in tribal relations. Still, no amount of training can build the knowledge base that is desirable for a line officer to engage effectively with any given tribe in any given region. That only comes with experience on the ground.[10]

More and more often, the government-to-government consultation process has led to a memorandum of understanding (MOU) or a memorandum of agreement (MOA), which helps to formalize consultation protocols. Whereas an MOU is a statement of shared understanding, an MOA goes further to ensure that specific steps are followed, sometimes including reimbursement of travel expenses and other costs, such as compensating elders for their time. A recent study found that tribes with a consultation protocol in place generally believed it was critical to fostering a strong government-to-government relationship.[11]

Outside of the formal government-to-government relationship, another kind of interchange occurs at annual conferences and symposia. The Intertribal Timber Council began sponsoring an annual symposium in 1976. The symposium is designed to facilitate communication about forest management practices between tribes, federal agencies, private industry, legislative bodies, and academia, and it gives federal and tribal foresters a valuable opportunity for exchange. A more recent venue is one called "To Bridge A Gap." Initiated in 2001, the annual conference is specifically aimed at strengthening relations between the Forest Service and federally recognized tribal governments. It started as a local meeting between Oklahoma tribes and the Ouchita and Ozark-St. Francis National Forests, and it was so successful that it grew into a national conference. Each year it is cohosted by a different tribe and the Forest Service. In 2010, more than three hundred representatives from tribes in Oklahoma, South Dakota, California, Arizona, Idaho, Louisiana, Minnesota, Montana, New Mexico, and Texas, and national forests across the nation attended the conference in Tulsa, Oklahoma. Over the years, many federal, state, and local agencies as well as academic institutions and nongovernment organizations have attended. Tribes have found it to be a valuable opportunity to meet directly with land managers who care for cultural and natural resources within the tribes' aboriginal homelands.[12]

COOPERATIVE EDUCATION

In recent times, the Forest Service has formed connections with a handful of Indian institutions of higher education. Forest Service involvement with these institutions takes the form of classroom instruction, employee recruitment, and joint research and symposia. Two of the more robust connections are with the Haskell Indian Nations University in Lawrence, Kansas, and the College of Menominee Nation in Keshena, Wisconsin.[13]

The connection with Haskell began in the late 1980s when the Forest Service and the BIA jointly established a natural resources instructor position for purposes of instruction and recruitment. Since 1990, Forest Service employee Bill Welton has held the position, fulfilling both functions. For several years, funding for the instructional part of his job was provided by a consortium of federal agencies, including the Forest Service, the Natural Resources Conservation Service (NRCS), the Environmental Protection Agency, the Bureau of Land Management (BLM), the U.S. Geological Survey, and the National Park Service. Welton taught courses in forestry, soils, integrated range management, sustainable watersheds, and botany, and outside of the classroom he served as field supervisor for students working on a variety of contract jobs such as forest inventories of Indian lands in Kansas and Oklahoma and biological inventories for National Park System units in the Colorado Plateau region. Since his retirement in 2010, Welton has continued teaching as an adjunct professor with funding by the NRCS, while the recruitment office at Haskell has been maintained under separate staffing with funding by the Forest Service and the BIA.[14]

The Forest Service's relationship with Haskell developed out of a combination of Chief Robertson's commitment to bring more Indians into the Forest Service and the Department of Agriculture's longstanding tradition of providing support to land-grant colleges. The origins of the relationship underscore again how the Forest Service tribal relations program, in its early stages, was strongly linked to the Forest Service's civil rights and affirmative action programs. Soon after Robertson became chief in 1988, Secretary of Agriculture Richard Lyng appointed him head of a department task force to address the Department of Agriculture's historical neglect of the so-called 1890 schools. The 1890 schools are a group of eighteen historically black colleges that were founded under terms of the second Morrill Act of 1890. Consistent with the "separate but equal" doctrine of U.S. race relations of that period, the 1890 law allowed the Southern states to establish separate agricultural colleges for whites and blacks. Although the federal law subsidized the 1890 agricultural colleges with cash instead of land grants, the state schools were meant to parallel the land-grant colleges formed under the first Morrill Act of 1862. Southern state legislatures did not provide the black land-grant schools equal funding, however, and the Department of Agriculture, for its part, came to focus its grant support and recruitment efforts on the larger, better-funded, predominantly white agricultural schools to the exclusion of the 1890 schools. So Robertson's charge in 1988 was to establish belated connections between the department and those eighteen historically black land-grant institutions. The initiative came as part of the Department of Agriculture's effort to recruit more blacks and other minorities into its workforce, which was then the least racially diverse department staff in the federal government.[15]

Robertson quickly realized that the department's outreach to the 1890 schools charted a course that the Forest Service ought to follow with Indian colleges, too. As he later remarked in a 1999 oral history interview, "natural resource management is a natural choice for Indians [attending college]." Robertson saw an opportunity for the Forest Service to recruit more Indian college graduates using the peculiar legislative authorities that applied to the USDA and state agricultural schools. Fortuitously, Haskell's administrators were coming to the same idea from the opposite direction; they were looking for a federal partner to help the school prepare its students for federal jobs in natural resource management.[16]

Although Haskell was not then part of the land-grant college system, it was another institution whose history reflected the nation's heritage of racially segregated schools. Haskell was founded in 1884 as a boarding school for Indian youths. First known as the United States Indian Industrial Training School, its mission was to assimilate its pupils into the dominant society by taking them away from the tribe and teaching them skills for a new way of life off the reservation. In 1887, the name of the school was changed to the Haskell Institute. By the middle of the twentieth century, most Indian boarding schools were shut down, but the BIA transformed the Haskell Institute from a high school into a two-year college, the Haskell Indian Junior College, and integrated it into the emerging tribal college system. In 1993, it became a four-year institution and was renamed the Haskell Indian Nations University.

The tribal college system arose as the BIA Indian schools went away. Whereas the former BIA schools were associated with assimilation policy, the new tribal colleges were a reflection of Indian self-determination policy and the revitalization of tribal cultures. The first tribal college opened in 1968 on the Navajo Reservation, and several more were established in the 1970s. The Elementary and Secondary Education Reauthorization Act of 1994 designated twenty-three tribal colleges as land-grant institutions. Today there are thirty-seven tribal colleges and universities with a total enrollment of approximately thirty thousand students. According to the website of the American Indian Higher Education Consortium, "These academically rigorous institutions engage in partnerships with organizations including the U.S. Department of the Interior, the U.S. Department of Agriculture, the U.S. Department of Housing and Urban Development, the National Science Foundation, the National Aeronautics and Space Administration, and universities nationwide to focus on issues such as climate change, sustainable agriculture, water quality, wildlife population dynamics, and diabetes prevention."[17] Clearly, the tribal colleges are helping to create more opportunity for young Indian people to find careers in the federal government and in federal land-management agencies in particular.

The Forest Service's relations with the College of the Menominee Nation reflect a newer set of ideals at play in Forest Service–tribal relations. The

FIGURE 37. Youth Conservation Corps (YCC) on the Black Hills National Forest. Through a partnership between the Forest Service, National Park Service, and the Cheyenne River, Standing Rock, Rosebud, and Yankton Sioux tribes, the YCC crew performs wetlands restoration work on the national forest.

PHOTO BY GARY CHANCEY. COURTESY OF FOREST SERVICE.

partnership is an affirmation of shared values about land stewardship. The goal of the partnership is to cultivate a type of forest management that is good for both the national forests and tribal communities with the hope that from those labors will come a stronger Indian presence in the Forest Service. "You can have all the recruiters you want, but if you're not doing research or forest management that's of much interest to the tribal community, then the recruitment is not really going to do very much," commented Mike Dockry, the Forest Service liaison to the College of the Menominee Nation, in 2013. Dockry is an enrolled member of the Citizen Potawatomi Nation and holds a PhD in forestry from the University of Wisconsin. The new thinking on building diversity in the workforce, he said, "flips that whole idea of recruitment on its head. We need to have a core mission accomplished in ways that highlight projects that tribes are interested in."[18]

The Menominee Nation boasts of a unique history of sustainable forestry. In the mid-nineteenth century, Chief Oshkosh advised his people to practice a kind of sustained-yield logging by starting at one end of the reservation and cutting down only the sick and mature trees. A generation after Oskkosh was gone, tribal leaders prevailed on Congress to enact legislation that would allow the tribe to establish a commercial forest industry. The 1890 statute provided for the creation of a tribal forestry enterprise and mandated a maximum allowable cut of 20 million board feet. With that, the Menominee tribe initiated what would become the longest-running record of forest inventories and harvest data for one locale found anywhere in the nation.[19]

Proud of their success in forestry and committed to drawing lessons from the ecology of the Menominee Reservation that could be applied to their social landscape as well, the Menominee Nation founded the College of Menominee Nation and the Sustainable Development Institute in 1993. The Forest Service was interested in the Menominee Nation's indigenous perspective and holistic vision as well as its long history of forest management. In 2003, the agency and the tribe signed an MOU to establish a Center for First Americans Forestlands. In 2005, Forest Service employee Mike Dockry entered on duty as liaison. The center's mission is "to synthesize the best practices of forest ecology, utilization, and American Indian expertise and apply this knowledge to sustainable forestry practices and sustainable development."[20]

From its inception, the partnership has been oriented toward two-way information sharing and learning. The center hosts numerous technical workshops and conferences that bring together tribal officials, students, community members, and tribal, state, and federal natural resource managers in a "non-contentious space for dialogue." Topics have included forest management planning, invasive species, green design and construction, and Forest Service tribal consultation, among others. As a meeting place of Native knowledge and Western science, the College of the Menominee Nation has attracted considerable interest from indigenous peoples in Latin America and elsewhere around the world.[21]

In 2013, Dockry cited the recent workshops held on the emerald ash borer as an illustration of how indigenous perspectives and Western science come together. The emerald ash borer is an invasive species of Asian beetle that is wiping out ash trees in the eastern United States. The ash is held sacred by many tribal cultures. One tribe holds that their people came from the ash. For some indigenous communities, its likely disappearance will have a profound cultural effect. Dockry said that the workshops brought a new level of understanding for non-Indian biologists who were unaware of the tree's cultural significance for tribes.[22]

The wisdom to be found on the Menominee Reservation comes from age-old traditional practice and observation combined with more than a century of applied scientific forestry. Former OTR director Dale Kanen remembered that when he first began hearing the Forest Service discuss "adaptive management," he thought the approach sounded somewhat akin to traditional ecological knowledge, or the oral traditions about a given place held by the indigenous people. Adaptive management comes from the idea that foresters cannot say with certainty what a given silvicultural treatment will result in, so they will predict, practice, and observe, and if the results are different from what was predicted, then they will modify the silvicultural treatment. Kanen noted, "That's different from saying we're going to look at everything under the microscope and come up with a perfect recipe based on good science." When the Forest Service first described its adaptive management policy, Kanen recalled that he almost laughed. "Because I thought, 'wow, you could have gone to the tribes in your neighborhood and got a lot of this stuff right away.'" Kanen broached the usefulness of Native knowledge with a few of the senior foresters in the Washington office. "It may take us forever to know all the various basic dynamics between the microbes in the soils and the birds living in the tops of the trees," he would later explain. Rather than investing so much time and money in that trial-and-error form of scientific management, he wanted the agency to consider "taking a short cut" by talking with "the elders in the neighborhood."[23]

In 2003, Deputy Chief Holtrop and Associate Deputy Chief Kent Connaughton went to the Menominee Reservation to attend a dedication for the new Center for First Americans Forestlands. The forest manager for Menominee Tribal Enterprises, Marshall Pecore, gave them a tour. And as Pecore explained the history of the forest, Holtrop and Connaughton began to see what Kanen was driving at. "The forester talked not from a file that he kept in his office," Kanen remembered years later, "but talked from what his grandfather and father had taught him about prescriptive practices that had been done fifty or a hundred years ago, [pointing out] 'this is the stand today,' and 'this is what you get.' And they started to see. You can't get this [level of understanding] with a person who has worked in a dozen places across the country, but when you have a people who are so tied to a particular piece of real estate and it's been handed down for generations, you can get their very effective type of adaptive management based on those time-proven observations and history that the scientific approach might not allow you to get without decades of research."[24]

When the Forest Service and tribes consulted in 2011 on the Forest Service's proposed new planning rule, tribes made the same argument that Kanen did. The Forest Service got the message and inserted a provision into the planning rule for gathering traditional ecological knowledge, or what it calls "Native knowledge." Under the new rule, its planning teams will inquire with tribes as to whether they have Native knowledge to contribute to each forest plan. The rule was published, and tribes accepted it.[25]

On a visit to the Menominee Reservation in 2005, Chief Bosworth praised Menominee forestry and expressed confidence in the Forest Service partnership with the college: "The long-term hope of this partnership is that we can share knowledge with the Menominee, that we can learn from the many, many years of tribal knowledge that they have about managing forests." And he added his hope that the Forest Service would make similar connections with other tribes.[26]

INTEGRATING TRADITIONAL ECOLOGICAL KNOWLEDGE INTO NATIONAL FOREST MANAGEMENT

Traditional ecological knowledge refers to indigenous people's inherent appreciation of the cycles, fluctuations, and ecological relationships in nature that comes from close observation and habitation of an environment over hundreds of years. The term *traditional ecological knowledge*, or TEK, first came into wide use in the 1980s. Although TEK has been put forward as a vital complement to

Western science, professionals in applied ecology and natural resource management have been slow to accept its relevance to their work.[27]

Many tribal foresters have an ardent desire for TEK to become broadly integrated with science-based forest management. In 2004, ITC president Nolan C. Colegrove Sr. commented to his fellow tribal foresters on the promise and challenge of accessing TEK for modern forestry: "The difficulty is that a lot of our traditional knowledge is oral traditions. That's hard to compare to science, because science always wants to prove something, wants to be written down, and has to be researched. And there is that gap there that we are having a problem bridging." Colegrove was hopeful that tribes were turning a corner on this matter and would find increasing opportunity to share TEK with the Forest Service and other land managers.[28]

The Forest Service's Larry Heady described the opening for TEK from his own perspective and that of the agency: "One thing we are recognizing now is that there is some real value in using traditional ecological knowledge along with Western science to develop best management practices. . . . Western science is fact-driven and really has no soul. Maybe it has no ethic. The marriage between Western science and TEK brings a soul with it. It brings that element to our knowledge base that is driven by a land-use ethic that has been in place for 10,000 years."[29] Heady cited the Forest Service's new planning rule as Exhibit A of how the agency was repositioning to integrate Native knowledge into its management philosophy. He emphasized that it would take time for TEK to work its way into the agency culture, but the framework was being put in place to accomplish it.

There were precedents. Perhaps the earliest example in which federal land-management agencies sought to integrate TEK with Western science in any sort of robust fashion was when the Federal Subsistence Board was set up in Alaska in the early 1990s. Although the Federal Subsistence Board managed fish and wildlife resources rather than forests, it made a strong effort to obtain TEK and assimilate it with Western science in order to develop policy that was both enlightened about local ecology and culturally sensitive. As TEK began to be recognized around the world, the subsistence management regime in Alaska was seen as one important laboratory for observing how it was being collected and used. The Forest Service's Fred Clark teamed with Helga Eakon, a Yupik Eskimo who worked for the Fish and Wildlife Service, in presenting the work of the Federal Subsistence Board at international conferences.[30]

California is another part of the country where federal land managers and scientists have been interested in TEK for some time now. Over the past two decades, they have developed an appreciation for the enormous role Indians had in shaping the natural environment of pre-Columbian California—and the TEK that still encompasses that. M. Kat Anderson is an ethnoecologist with the USDA Natural Resources Conservation Service located at the University of California, Davis. In 2005, she published a major work on the subject, *Tending the Wild: Native American Knowledge and the Management of California's Natural Resources.* The book's thesis is that California's indigenous peoples, through thousands of years of occupation, "very purposefully harvested, tended, and managed the wild." They practiced an earlier form of resource management that maintained certain vegetation types in an early stage of succession, promoted habitat heterogeneity, and increased biodiversity. She gives numerous examples of California plants that coevolved with their human cultivators. She advocates more use of TEK in modern resource management. "Learning about the ways in which the indigenous people of California appropriated plants and animals for cultural uses while allowing them to flourish can help us to change the ways in which we interact with nature today," she writes. "We can begin to see the possibility of becoming part of localized food webs once again, being full participants in nature, and restoring and reinhabiting damaged lands."[31]

From interviewing many Native elders and traditional gatherers, Anderson gained insights into contemporary Indians' views on public land stewardship and wilderness. The views she describes are pertinent to how Forest Service traditional gathering policy has developed in California in the present century. She writes,

> Interestingly, contemporary Indians often use the word *wilderness* as a negative label for land that has not been taken care of by humans for a long time, for example, where dense understory shrubbery or thickets of young trees block visibility and movement. A common sentiment among California Indians is that a hands-off approach to nature has promoted feral landscapes that are inhospitable to life. . . . California Indians believe that when humans are gone from an area long enough, they lose the practical knowledge about correct interaction, and the plants and animals retreat spiritually from the earth or hide from humans. When intimate interaction ceases, the continuity of knowledge, passed down through generations, is broken, and the land becomes "wilderness."[32]

When Indians sought to protect their traditional gathering activities from interference by Forest Service regulations, they were asserting not only an economic interest but a cultural imperative. No wonder, then, that for many of them the idea of having to obtain a permit for "personal use" rankled.

The Maidu Stewardship Project, located on the Plumas National Forest in Northern California, provided one opportunity for California Indians and the Forest Service to collaborate on ecological restoration based on traditional gathering or the Indians' approach to "tending the wild." A group of Mountain Maidu proposed the project in 1997, and the following year the Forest Service selected it as one of twenty-two National Pilot Collaborative Stewardship Projects for demonstrating innovative approaches to resource management. It is the only one of the stewardship projects nationwide to feature the use of TEK. The project area spans approximately 1,500 acres of cutover and grazed valley floor situated between 3,600 and 4,600 feet above sea level. The Maidus' plan was to reintroduce a variety of cultural plants that were missing from the area and cultivate them according to traditional methods, such as pruning willows to produce straight stalks for basket-weaving material and digging some camas bulbs for food while leaving others to ensure a constant supply. Their plan also called for regular use of fire to reduce underbrush and restore a diverse assemblage of plants and animals. Key elements of the Maidu Stewardship Project included demonstration of TEK by the Maidu, monitoring of changes in vegetation by the Forest Service, and reduction of hazardous fuels to protect the nearby town of Greenville. The expectation by both parties was that the project would "weave culture and science together to create a healthy landscape."[33]

The Maidu Stewardship Project inspired much interest when it was inaugurated. Ethnoecologist Kat Anderson and the Forest Service's tribal relations coordinator Joe Mitchell both expressed hope that the blend of Forest Service and Maidu prescriptions in one closely studied area would reveal how the ecosystem responded to different treatments and would be a pilot for more such efforts. Unfortunately, it was hard to sustain that level of interest. The greatest challenge, the Forest Service's project manager wrote, was "integrating Forest Service processes and procedures with the Maidu proposal."[34]

The Maidu proposed a ninety-nine-year project—not an unreasonable idea from the standpoint of a people who have occupied that place since time immemorial. Bound by budget considerations, the Forest Service agreed to fund the stewardship project for ten years and then reevaluate it. A Forest

Service science team met twice with the Maidu cultural team in May 2002 and October 2003. To monitor changes in vegetation, a series of quadrats and transects were laid out, and a class of Maidu college students was enlisted to collect data. Then the project began to wind down. A "final report" on the project in May 2004 concluded on a note of realism. "These things take time. Building common awareness of plants and plant attributes between variously trained people including, at the foundation of the project, an entirely unique culture (Maidu) will not be completed in one meeting or even two."[35]

CONFLICTS OVER SPECIAL FOREST PRODUCTS

The Forest Service has regulated the gathering and harvesting of noncommercial timber products for many years. Originally, it regulated only the gathering of firewood and pinecones and the harvesting of Christmas trees. In the 1980s, it began to address the collecting of other "special forest products" such as salal and fern plants sold in floral shops and matsutake mushrooms used in Japanese cuisine. By the late 1990s, medicinal plants such as ginseng and St. John's Wort were in great demand, and the agency was issuing special forest products harvesting permits valued at some $3.3 million annually.[36]

The Forest Service recognized a responsibility to regulate special forest products not just for their commercial value but also for their ecological value as part of the forest ecosystem. As demand for such resources grew, forest managers discovered that they had little or no idea of those various resources' abundance, nor could they say how much harvesting of them was sustainable. In some cases, forest managers recognized that rising demand for special forest products threatened to infringe on Indian treaty rights covering those same resources. In the Pacific Northwest, for example, where huckleberry harvesting by non-Indians encroached on Indians' traditional use of the national forests, the Mount Hood National Forest entered a MOU with the Confederated Tribes of the Warm Springs Reservation to protect the tribes' interests in specific areas. This measure was reminiscent of the Handshake Agreement between the Forest Service and the Yakama, which dated from the 1930s.[37]

Tribes had mixed reactions to the Forest Service's move to put more stringent controls on harvests of special forest products. On one hand, tribes readily saw the need to protect those resources from destructive types of harvesting by non-Indians. On the other hand, they opposed being regulated themselves. The strength and tenor of tribal opposition varied according to whether a tribe's claim was based on traditional use or actual treaty right and whether or not the tribe was federally recognized. Those differences between tribes tended to be regional, with the result that the various Forest Service regions took different approaches to Indian use of special forest products. By the first decade of the twenty-first century, the regional variations across the National Forest System were creating tensions of their own.

The Pacific Northwest Region was ahead of other Forest Service regions in trying to reach an accommodation with tribes. It had to be, because Pacific Northwest tribes were politically savvy about asserting their treaty-reserved rights to carry on traditional gathering activities in their ceded territory. There are thirty-six federally recognized tribes in the Pacific Northwest, and twenty-four tribes have treaty-reserved rights to hunt and gather off reservation. When Les McConnell was hired in 1990 as the region's first tribal liaison, tribes were already asserting their right to gather firewood on national forestlands without having to pay fees. Having worked for the BIA on Pacific Northwest fisheries issues, McConnell recognized that the tribes were making legitimate requests. Working with forest after forest and responding to tribe after tribe, he pushed for the fee waivers and got them. An especially memorable case involved the Winema National Forest in southern Oregon, which entered an MOA with the Klamath Tribes in 1999. The Klamath Tribe of Oregon was terminated in 1954, and the Winema National Forest was established with lands of the former Klamath Reservation (chap. 5). The Klamath Tribes (Klamath, Modoc, and Yahooskin tribes) won back federal recognition in 1986. The MOA allowed tribal members to set up camps and gather firewood anywhere on the national forest within the former reservation. "One of my first tasks," McConnell recalled, "was to educate forest supervisors that this kind of collecting is based not only on treaties, but for those tribes that do not have treaty rights, it is based on their culture. What I was saying is that all tribes need to have access regardless of whether they have treaty rights."[38]

McConnell wrote a desk guide about the Pacific Northwest tribes' reserved rights on ceded lands, reaching for a policy that would be applied consistently across all the national forests in the region. It was "an eye opener for the agency," he said. But as the Pacific Northwest Region's practice of accommodation came to involve larger volumes of cordwood and other kinds of resources, the Washington office and the Office of General Counsel (OGC) began to push back. Then, around 2003, the Elwha Tribe requested permission to harvest a large cedar tree on the Olympic National Forest with which to make a canoe. The single tree was worth several thousand dollars. The forest supervisor was willing to issue a permit but not to waive the charge. McConnell objected, and the matter was referred to the OGC. This time, McConnell was overruled. The OGC lawyer's argued that the treaty did not explicitly refer to cedar trees, so there was no treaty right. And since there was no treaty right, the Forest Service had no legal authority to waive the fee for the Elwha Tribe. McConnell shot back that the OGC lawyer's notion that treaty-reserved rights had to be spelled out item by item in the treaty was a patent misinterpretation of Indian law. Furthermore, McConnell said, the Forest Service had no authority to collect money from a tribal government. They were still arguing over it when McConnell retired in March 2004.[39]

A second Forest Service region where tribes sought relief from special forest products permitting was the Pacific Southwest Region (California). In contrast to the Pacific Northwest tribes, California tribes mostly based their demands on traditional-use rights, not treaty rights. Two intertribal organizations were staunch supporters of California Indians' rights to practice traditional gathering on national forestlands. The first was the California Indian Basketweavers Association (CIBA), formed in 1992 to preserve basket-weaving traditions. It had a particular interest in protecting basket weavers' access to basket-weaving material on public lands. The second was the California Indian Forest and Fire Management Council (CIFFMC), formed in 1994 to promote sound wildland fire management. The CIFFMC had a special focus on cultural burning.[40]

"Cultural burning" refers to the use of prescribed fire to mimic aboriginal burning practices with the intent of restoring ecosystems that contain culturally important species. Probably no other place in pre-Columbian North America was so culturally modified by fire as California was, so the connections between wildland fire management and traditional gathering are particularly strong there. The past century of fire suppression has produced a more forested, less savannah type of landscape, with the result that many of the indigenous peoples' traditional dietary staples, such as acorns and juniper berries, are much less plentiful now than they were in the nineteenth century. Tribes generally favor a type of wildland fire management that will bring back more oak savannah. Merv George Jr., forest supervisor for the Six Rivers National Forest and a member of the Hupa Tribe, confirms the very real connections between wildland fire management and traditional gathering when he says, "I'm married to a basket weaver, and when I go home I get lobbied very hard to implement more prescribed burning." George himself spent nine years as director of the CIFFMC before joining the Forest Service.[41]

Starting in 1999, the Forest Service consulted with California tribes to develop a framework for improved government-to-government relations and stewardship of culturally significant plants on a statewide level. The effort began with a summit meeting attended by representatives of thirty-three tribes and eleven national forests held on the Mooretown Rancheria. After numerous listening sessions and consultations over the next four years, it concluded with a pronouncement on Native American relations folded into the Sierra Nevada Forest Plan Amendment, issued in January 2004.[42] In this landmark accord, Regional Forester Jack Blackwell pledged the agency to an impressive set of commitments relating to Indian traditional gathering on the national forests. The commitments included:

- Tribal consultation regarding wildland fire management and the development of fire protection plans for Indian reservations and rancherias
- Integration of traditional Indian land-use practices in national forest planning
- Integration of traditional Indian vegetation management strategies into ecosystem restoration activities and participation with tribes and intertribal organizations in ecosystem stewardship projects
- Consideration of the relationship between fire management and culturally significant plants
- Tribal consultation regarding noxious weed management programs
- Inclusion of culturally significant species in monitoring protocols
- Protection of appropriate access to sacred and ceremonials sites and traditional tribal use areas[43]

TOWARD A TRADITIONAL GATHERING POLICY

Shortly after the Pacific Southwest Region pronouncement was published, the Washington office issued a draft national policy on special forest products that threatened to undermine what the regional forester promised to the California tribes. Rather than protecting Native access to culturally significant plants, the Washington office appeared to be moving in the direction of classifying culturally significant plants along with other botanical resources as "special forest products" subject to permits and fees. One reason California Indians found the proposed policy to be so threatening was that a large percentage of them did not have standing as members of federally recognized tribes; therefore, they had little prospect of being exempt from federal regulations. Moreover, the majority of California tribes had no land base; they had to have access to public lands to practice their cultural traditions. The Pacific Southwest Region relayed those concerns back to the Washington office, insisting that the draft policy was not responsive to traditional gathering needs in the region.[44]

After the flare-up over the draft national policy, the CIBA pushed for stronger protections for traditional gathering on public lands in California. Regional Forester Blackwell and BLM state director Mike Pool convened a Gathering Policy Working Group composed of Forest Service and BLM personnel and representatives of CIBA and CIFFMC. Holding listening sessions around the state, they developed input from more than 250 participants. Indians in the northern and southern halves of the state were divided over whether traditional gatherers should have to hold a free-use permit or prove tribal membership if challenged by a ranger. After a year and a half of effort, however, the working group crafted a reasonable degree of consensus. On November 29, 2006, the regional forester and the BLM state director signed the Interagency Traditional Gathering Policy, which assured that traditional gatherers and basket weavers in California would have free access to gather material on lands managed by the two agencies.[45]

Meanwhile, the Washington office moved forward on the more restrictive national policy. In October, the proposed rule was published in the *Federal Register* for public comment. The California tribes were prepared for it and came to the defense of the regional policy. Other tribes were inspired by the show of strength of California's traditional gatherers. One hundred and fifty letters poured into the Forest Service from tribal leaders and spokespersons all over the country.[46]

The tribes' criticisms generally clustered around three main objections. First, treaty tribes—especially those in the Pacific Northwest—argued that the rule infringed on their treaty rights. Although the proposed rule made an exemption for treaty tribes, it asserted that the "Regional Forester may set conditions on the harvest, as necessary to protect the product as a sustainable resource, or to otherwise protect the forest." The Quinault Indian Nation objected to this language most forcefully, saying that it purported that the Forest Service had the power to limit a treaty right. Only Congress could limit or abrogate Indian treaties. The attorney for four other western Washington tribes took a similar line to the Quinault, insisting that the Forest Service could only impose such a limitation "in the face of specific congressional authorization or a demonstrable conservation necessity."[47]

Another major objection was that the proposed rule approached Indians' traditional gathering too narrowly within a treaty-rights framework. Its effect would be to privilege treaty tribes over all other tribes. The Cowlitz Indian Tribe in the Pacific Northwest made its concerns clear on that score. "The Cowlitz Tribe is federally recognized but never signed a treaty. This should not mean that Cowlitz people are hampered in gathering traditional resources. Nor should it cause the Tribe to be regarded differently than 'Treaty Tribes' for special products gathering.... Our Tribe requests equal and fair regulations among all Federally Recognized Tribes on this matter."[48]

Connie Reid, archeologist on the North Kaibab Ranger District of the Kaibab National Forest in Arizona, objected on the same grounds. "There are a number of tribes in the U.S. that do not have treaty rights, yet have viable ancestral claims to specific lands managed by the USDA Forest Service," she wrote. Indeed, to underscore what an arbitrary distinction that could be, she noted that most tribes in her own Southwest Region were "executive order tribes," having been established on executive order reservations in the last three decades of the nineteenth century after the treaty-making period ended. Her forest had established MOAs with neighboring tribal governments to allow traditional gathering within their former homelands. "To exclude the non-treaty tribes that have already been formally recognized through MOA's and other agreements would disrupt current practices on many Forests and likely strain government-to-government relationships," she stated. The proposed rule would be "a step backwards for us."[49]

A third main objection to the proposed rule revolved around the terms *commercial use*, *personal use*, and *cultural, ceremonial, and/or traditional use*. Just what made a gathering activity "commercial" or "noncommercial?" Just what would a person need to do to claim an activity as "personal use?" Many Indians knew from bitter experience how labels such as "personal use" would intrude on their privacy or embarrass them later. In a joint letter, four spokespersons for the Yavapai-Apache Nation movingly described their objections to the Forest Service's wish to impose further regulation.

On several occasions in the past our Elders have actually had permits or permission to gather personal amounts of plant materials used in crafts and as traditional medicine(s), but they have been nonetheless confiscated by overzealous FS cops. This discourages and embarrasses our Elders to the point of making them reticent to go back out. So because of your agencies' lack of communication and occasionally insensitive responses on the ground to matters of small consequence some of our fragile traditions are compromised as a result. This is why we are concerned about more regulations, which are vague in general and poorly thought out in particular with regard to Native American sensibilities.[50]

Altogether, the comments from Indian Country on the proposed regulation of special forest products filled two large three-ring binders. Few other matters of Forest Service policy drew such widespread interest from tribes. Many tribal leaders felt consternation, therefore, when the Forest Service published a final rule in December 2008 that looked much like the one they had reviewed the previous year. Had the Forest Service ignored the tribes' comments? The notice in the *Federal Register* explained that the final rule moved the regulations on the sale of special forest products from the Timber Management regulations to a new part in the Code of Federal Regulations. That was owing to the fact that the 2008 Farm Bill, enacted six months earlier, gave the Forest Service authority to dispose of trees and other forest products without charge to tribes for traditional and ceremonial purposes. Relieved that it had finally obtained that long-sought legal authority, the Forest Service rushed to complete the process of getting the rule in place in the closing weeks of the Bush administration. As soon as Tom Vilsack entered office as the new secretary of agriculture in January 2009, he was hit with a barrage of tribal protests over the new special forest products rule. The Obama administration rescinded it along with a handful of other questionable rules that the Bush administration had promulgated at the eleventh hour. On Vilsack's direction, the Forest Service announced that it would reevaluate after a further round of comment.[51]

Eventually, based on further review of the tribes' concerns, it was decided to split the rule into two parts, one specifically addressing the treaty-reserved right of tribes to obtain trees and other forest products for traditional and ceremonial use (as authorized by the farm bill), and another aimed at reconciling the Indians' interest in maintaining their traditional gathering activities with the public interest in protecting the resource and regulating commercial

FIGURE 38. Jicarilla Apache Butterfly dancers at the Wilderness50 Conference, Albuquerque, New Mexico, 2014.

PHOTO BY DIANE KRAHE AND THEODORE CATTON

harvests of special forest products. In other words, one set of regulations would deal with tribes as sovereign entities, and the other set would deal with Indians as individual users. Four years later, both sets of regulations were wending their way through the more rigorous process of tribal consultation put in place by the Obama administration.[52]

NEW FACES

The start of the year 2014 marked the ten-year anniversary of the establishment of the Office of Tribal Relations. It also marked the passage of a quarter of a century since Chief F. Dale Robertson brought Robert Tippeconnie into the

Washington office to serve as national coordinator of tribal relations, the real beginning of the Forest Service's tribal relations program. Back in 1988, Robertson tried to envision what the Forest Service's relationship with tribes would look like a generation hence. Besides giving support to the tribal relations program at the top, he called for change from the bottom as well, stressing the agency's need to recruit more American Indians and Alaska Natives into the outfit. It was part of his affirmative action program called "Strength through Diversity." Now that a generation has passed, some of those individuals who began their Forest Service careers during Robertson's tenure are running tribal relations programs or serving as line officers. Those new faces are mostly leading the charge as the Forest Service moves forward to redeem the agency's trust responsibility and protect American Indian and Alaska Native reserved rights on national forestlands.

One of those new faces is OTR director Fred Clark. Clark is a Citizen Potawatomi. Born in Kansas, he was raised in rural Idaho and Montana. After graduating from the University of Idaho, he worked as an archaeologist at various places in the Pacific Northwest as well as California, Costa Rica, and Alaska. He worked for the BIA in Alaska for three years and then completed a master's degree in public administration and anthropology at the University of Alaska Anchorage. While still enrolled in the graduate program, he was hired as an archaeologist by the Chugach National Forest. While he was working on the Chugach from 1991 to 1995, his job gradually changed from archaeologist to archaeologist/tribal relations program manager. From 1996 until 2002, he was the subsistence coordinator for the Southeast Alaska Federal Subsistence Advisory Council. From 2002 to 2006, he was the regional social scientist for the Forest Service Eastern Region, with his home in Milwaukee.[53]

In 2006, Clark became the second director of OTR. When he started in the job, the OTR was operating at just half strength. His first task was to get the staff group up to its full complement of six fulltime equivalent positions. After consulting with his predecessor, he decided on a new model for how to organize the group: he and an assistant would handle operations and administration and there would be two specialists in natural resources and two specialists in cultural resources. Soon he had very capable people working in all of those positions.[54]

Clark is an enthusiastic, upbeat, and inclusive program director. Communications are the heart and soul of the program, and since 2008 the OTR has been advertising what it and the tribal relations programs in the regions do through an attractive newsletter as well as an informative website. The OTR website is replete with scores of uploaded documents that are pertinent to Forest Service–tribal relations. The document directories are kept current to be maximally useful to the OTR's many clients. Besides directing the OTR staff and providing leadership for the national program, Clark has devoted much effort over the past four years to assisting with the Forest Service's strong initiative to perform national-level tribal consultation on a whole range of Forest Service policies.

Clark's most recent initiative (as of 2014) is to oversee the revision of FSM 1560 and FSH 109.13, the Forest Service tribal relations manual and handbook, respectively. The revisions reflect three major developments that have occurred since these documents were first produced in 2004: first, the four new authorities that the Forest Service acquired with passage of the 2008 Farm Bill; second, the new direction provided by the Forest Service report on Indian sacred sites and the interdepartmental MOU on sacred sites; and third, the commitment to Native knowledge contained in the Forest Service's new planning rule. Together, these represent a sea change in how the Forest Service intends to partner with tribes. The focus is now on making the ideal into a reality.

Soon after Clark took the helm at the OTR, there was significant turnover of tribal relations staff in the regions. Nearly all of the old hands who served on the National Forest Tribal Relations Program Task Force retired or left the Forest Service. New people came into those positions: Dan Meza in the Southwest Region, Larry Heady in the Eastern Region, Alan Dorian in the Southern Region, Cheryl Vanderberg in the Northern Region, Waldo Walker in the Pacific Northwest Region, and Robert Goodwin in the Pacific Southwest Region. A substantial majority of the individuals who work in tribal relations, both in the regions and the OTR, have American Indian or Alaska Native heritage. The integration of tribal people into the Forest Service that began in the 1980s still continues a generation later, bringing more diverse perspectives and gradual transformation.

Nowadays a considerable number of Forest Service line officers claim Native heritage as well. One notable appointment occurred in September 2009 when Nolan C. Colegrove Sr. was named new district ranger of the Orleans Ranger District on the Six Rivers National Forest in California. Colegrove needed no introduction to the local Indians as he was himself a member of the Hupa Valley Tribe. Besides serving as president of the Intertribal Timber Council from 2001 to 2009, he was a twenty-four-year veteran of working for the Hupa Natural Resources Department Forestry Division and was the tribe's forest manager for most of that time. The Hupa Valley Tribe welcomed Colegrove's appointment to the Forest Service and the local ranger district, as they had been plagued by the Forest Service's high turnover, having formed new relationships with four district rangers and five forest supervisors over the past decade and a half. Starting in August 2014, Colegrove reported to a new forest supervisor for Six Rivers National Forest: fellow tribal member Merv George Jr.[55]

In October 2011, Arthur "Butch" Blazer, a Mescalero Apache, became deputy undersecretary for natural resources and the environment and boss to Forest Service Chief Tom Tidwell. Blazer is a twenty-seven-year veteran of the BIA and former New Mexico state forester. During his tenure as state forester under Governor Bill Richardson, he chaired the Council of Western State Foresters. He is a past member of the Mescalero Apache Tribal Council and a cofounder of the Native American Fish and Wildlife Society. As of this writing, Blazer was actively engaged in the interdepartmental initiative to improve Indian sacred sites protection.

CONCLUSION

THE HISTORY OF Forest Service–tribal relations lies at the confluence of Indian history and conservation history. Major currents in Indian affairs and federal conservation are the forces of change that have shaped the development of Forest Service–tribal relations from the beginning of the twentieth century to the present day. This study has identified a number of separate tributaries coming into that stream of history, for example, the unique federal-indigenous experience in Alaska. It may be useful, in concluding, to step back and take a longer view of the historical forces that have been at work in shaping this important relationship. If we think about the history of Forest Service–tribal relations as a river, we might say that there is an upper stretch, which started at the beginning of the twentieth century and took us down to about the year 1970. And there is a lower stretch, which started in about 1970 and has brought us down to the present.

THE UPPER RIVER

In that upper stretch, or over that earlier stretch of time, the thing that mattered most was land. Two major developments in the late nineteenth century, the making of the allotment policy and the setting aside of public lands for conservation, formed the essential conditions for Forest Service–tribal relations.

Forest Service rangers worked for an outfit that prided itself on being at the cutting edge of the conservation movement. That meant defending the idea of public land ownership to the American public; protecting resources from theft, abuse, and destruction; and facilitating use of the national forestlands in ways that supported local communities while conserving the resources for future generations. The Forest Service worked with ranching communities and stock growers who were interested in operating grazing leases on the national forests. It cooperated with game protection associations and state wardens to restock game populations on the national forests. Forest rangers were not friendly to Indians who went on the national forests to do traditional hunting and gathering because they viewed the Indians as poachers hunting without state licenses and as firebugs who were apt to set fire to the woods.

Indians, meanwhile, were undergoing the traumatic and ruinous effects of allotment. Tribe by tribe, they were forced to consent to the breaking up of their remaining tribal lands into individual allotments and to the sale of their "surplus" lands on the reservation so that they could be opened for homesteading by non-Indians. Most tribes had had just a few decades to adjust to reservation life before they saw their remaining tribal lands further diminished or lost altogether. Not even their allotments were secure; soon those began to get sold off as well. The allotment era proved to be the last stage in more than a century of Indian land loss.

Against such a backdrop of catastrophe, many tribes found the making of national forests and national parks to be yet another form of land taking by the dominant society. The Pillager Band of Ojibwe lost control of their tribal forest when Congress turned it into the Minnesota National Forest by statute in 1902. While such takings were rare, other national parks and national forests were established in areas that tribes had ceded by treaty or agreement with the understanding that they would be able to continue using those lands as long as they remained open and unclaimed. More often than not, Indian peoples found they were no longer welcome in those reserves. Their off-reservation treaty rights carried little weight in the years that followed the U.S. Supreme Court decision in *Ward v. Race Horse* (1896).

The conservation movement began as a check on the national land policy of selling the entire public domain into private ownership. It was ironic that the U.S. government was experimenting with public forestry at the same time that it was selling off tribal forests. Yet the leaders of the conservation movement saw no contradiction between their effort to retain some of the public domain in permanent public land status and the U.S. government's drive to break up all remaining tribal lands into individual ownerships. Pinchot and other conservationists of his time saw no future for tribally held forests because the policy of the U.S. government was to break up tribes and assimilate Indians into American life on the basis of individual U.S. citizenship. J. P. Kinney, the long-time head of the Branch of Forestry in the BIA, intended no irony when he gave his history of the Indians' landed heritage the title, *A Continent Lost: A Civilization Won*.

The tribes' bitter experience with land loss and persecution in the first third of the twentieth century cast a pall over Forest Service–tribal relations throughout those years and through much of the middle third of the century as well. To be sure, there were instances of positive interaction and cooperation: the Tlingit-Haida totem pole restoration project, the Yakama Handshake Agreement, the Menominee tribal forestry enterprise. Yet there were also instances of Forest Service assault on Native land uses and values: destruction and removal of Tlingit and Haida smokehouses and cabins on the Tongass National Forest, discord with the Taos Pueblo over the return of their sacred Blue Lake, a violent clash with the Pit River Indians over a land claim on the Shasta National Forest.

Tribes began to acquire a stronger political voice in those middle decades of the century through tribal revitalization initiatives under the Indian New Deal, through the NCAI and other national organizations, and by virtue of some large cash settlements that they were awarded under the Indian Claims Commission. But Indian peoples remained by and large the most marginalized minority group in the United States. Much of tribes' political energies in the 1940s and 1950s were focused on warding off the threat of termination.

THE LOWER RIVER

The big change in Forest Service tribal relations started around 1970. The upper waters flowed on, but now the character of the river began to change.

Now the thing that mattered was Indian self-determination, and the key development was the rebirth of tribal governments. Once tribes were able to discredit the termination policy and get the federal government firmly behind Indian self-determination, they proceeded to press their tribal sovereignty in areas where their sovereign rights had long been denied. It then became just a matter of time until tribes began to assert their interests in the management of public lands, including the National Forest System.

A concomitant effect of the rise of tribal governments was that tribes gradually took control of their own forest resources from BIA forestry. As tribal forestry programs became well established in the 1990s and 2000s, it followed that the Forest Service mission to provide cooperative assistance to state and private landowners should be expanded to include the tribes.

The decade of the 1970s was a turning point for the Forest Service, too. With the rise of the environmental movement, the Forest Service could no longer stay the course of managing the national forests for intensive forestry and commercial timber production. The public demanded that it give more consideration to other uses of the national forests, including recreation and protection of fish and wildlife habitat. New environmental laws and regulations mandated that the agency manage the national forests with greater consideration for rare and sensitive species, air and water quality, and cultural resources. To meet all of these new demands, the Forest Service began to hire wildlife biologists, ecologists, hydrologists, and archaeologists. As these new agency scientists challenged the foresters' traditional management practices, it became a time of ferment and change in the Forest Service culture.

The Forest Service helped itself in this process by actively taking part in the federal government's affirmative action initiatives. Starting the decade as one of the most white-male-dominated federal agencies, it recruited women and minorities in disproportionately high numbers to establish a more culturally diverse workforce relatively quickly. To help manage this tumultuous process, the agency established a strong internal civil rights program. The agency's first systematic outreach to tribal communities came as an offshoot of its internal civil rights program. The ferment within the agency culture, and more specifically the hiring of a handful of interested tribal people who were willing to work in key positions, helped the tribal relations program take off in the late 1980s and early 1990s.

The history of the Forest Service tribal relations program over the past twenty-five years is largely about the process of building an institutional framework within the agency. First, the Forest Service had to build a core professional staff and develop core policies and guidelines. Then, it had to elevate the program by establishing the Office of Tribal Relations in the Washington office. After that, it pursued new legal authorities, which it got in the 2008 Farm Bill. And most recently, it included consideration of Native knowledge in the new planning rule. All the while, it has been doing more training for line officers and other key personnel. Getting the institutional framework into place is a necessary part of changing the agency culture on tribal relations.

As the Forest Service's culture has been evolving over the last four decades, it has become increasingly receptive to Indian perspectives. With its growing emphasis on ecological complexity and the protection of biodiversity, the Forest Service's approach to managing the national forests has come closer to the Indians' spiritual approach to caring for the land.

Dale Bosworth, the former chief of the Forest Service, said it best when he explained his reasons for deciding to establish the Office of Tribal Relations. There was a "natural tie" between the agency and the indigenous people that was getting overlooked, Bosworth said. The Forest Service had been managing the national forests for about a hundred years, whereas the Indians had occupied the land for about ten thousand years. From his perspective in 2003, the Forest Service's relationships with tribes did not appear to be as strong as they could be or should be. The Forest Service was missing out on a lot of advice from tribes. "There may be something they know that could be helpful to our work."

Indeed. In navigating the next stretch of river, the challenge will be making use of that Native knowledge.

ACKNOWLEDGMENTS

I WOULD LIKE TO express my gratitude to all the people who helped in making this book. Fred Clark, director of the Forest Service Office of Tribal Relations, conceived of the study, and I owe him huge thanks for bringing me to the project. Lincoln Bramwell, chief historian of the Forest Service, was closely involved from the first meeting and shared Fred's and my enthusiasm for framing this administrative history broadly. Sonia Tamez, retired tribal liaison for the Forest Service Pacific Southwest Region, was instrumental in putting Fred and me together, and she warmly supported our efforts all the way through.

Many people in the Forest Service and tribal governments gave generously of their time in interviews. Their names are listed at the start of the bibliography. I want to express special thanks to four of these individuals: retired tribal liaison Les McConnell and retired special assistant to the deputy chief Mit Parsons for providing very extensive follow-up in multiple emails, retired director of the Office of Tribal Relations Dale Kanen for taking two full mornings with me and sharing documents, and retired deputy chief Joel Holtrop for writing the foreword.

I am indebted to several people for reading and commenting on the manuscript. Besides all the before-mentioned people, I received constructive criticism from Gary S. Morishima, consultant to the Intertribal Timber Council; Trudy Tucker, deputy director of the Council for the Interpretation of Native Peoples; Bill Welton, adjunct professor at Haskell Indian Nations University;

Dorothy FireCloud, superintendent of Montezuma Castle National Monument and Tuzigoot National Monument, and Ilka Hartmann, photographer.

Mike Turek, tribal liaison on the Six Rivers National Forest, gave me valuable pointers and friendly encouragement. I first met Mike in about 1995 when he was working on his book with Robert H. Keller Jr., *American Indians and National Parks* (University of Arizona Press, 1999), and we have corresponded over the years. I have always thought of the present study as being essentially a companion work to the one by Keller and Turek.

I wish to thank Kristen Buckles, acquisitions editor at the University of Arizona Press, for taking an interest in the project at an early stage and patiently seeing it through to completion, and Steve LaRue, copyeditor for the press, for his marvelous skill and attention to detail.

I had the pleasure of meeting Melody Remillard and the rest of the staff at Grey Towers National Historic Site through a Grey Towers Scholar-in-Residence Fellowship in spring 2013. The grant afforded me the opportunity to spend a month at the historic Pinchot family estate in Milford, Pennsylvania. Built in the style of a French chateau, Grey Towers was the name the Pinchot family gave to their Gilded Age mansion on a hill. I worked on this book's Alaska chapter while sitting at a desk in the young Pinchot's tower bedroom.

My greatest good fortune in this project was to be able to discuss so many ideas in depth with Diane Krahe, my wife and partner in history. Her dissertation covered the topic of Bob Marshall's roadless-area designations on Indian reservations. We hit upon our mutual fascination with Bob on our second date, while on a hike in Idaho, and we never looked back.

NOTES

INTRODUCTION

1. "News Release: Protest Halts Snowbowl Wastewater Pipeline Construction."
2. Triangle Associates, "Review"; Rob Capriccioso, "Snowy Relations on Sacred Site Development," *Indian Country Today* (Rapid City, South Dakota), April 7, 2010.
3. U.S. Department of Agriculture, Forest Service, *Forest Service Native American Policy*, 2.
4. Skinner, *Vive la difference*, 21. Statistics for Indian forests are rounded from 1996 BIA figures listed in "Summary Statistics," *Evergreen* (June 1998), 50. Statistics for national forests are rounded from figures listed in "Land Areas."
5. *Tribal Relations News* (Summer 2010), http://www.fs.fed.us/spf/tribalrelations/news/tribalrelationsnews_summer2010.html.

CHAPTER 1

1. Otto and Burns, "Traditional Agricultural Practices," 177–83.
2. Krech, *Ecological Indian*, 103–10.
3. Ibid., 113.
4. Cox et al,, *This Well-Wooded Land*, 39.
5. Nash, *Wilderness*, 23–43.
6. Cox et al., *This Well-Wooded Land*, 11–12.
7. Cronon, *Changes in the Land*, 121–22.

8. Cox et al., *This Well-Wooded Land*, 16–17; Cronon, *Changes in the Land*, 109.

9. Williams, *American Indian*, 13–18, 81–83.

10. Miller, *Native America*, 1–8 passim.

11. O'Brien, *American Indian Tribal Governments*, 51; Prucha, *Great Father*, 19–22, 31–34.

12. Prucha, *Great Father*, 21.

13. For a recent excellent account of treaty making with the Dakota in Minnesota, see Westerman and White, *Mni Sota Makoce*, 133–96.

14. The U.S. government negotiated and ratified 389 treaties with Indian tribes. They are compiled in Kappler, *Indian Affairs*.

15. Quoted in Udall, *Quiet Crisis*, 8.

16. Trennert, *Alternative to Extinction*; Sheehan, *Seeds of Extinction*; Tyler, *History of Indian Policy*.

17. For an Indian Service professional's firsthand account of government-to-government negotiations over land-cession agreements in the post-1871 period, see McLaughlin, *My Friend the Indian*, 290–314.

18. O'Brien, *American Indian Tribal Governments*, 55–58.

19. Cox et al., *This Well-Wooded Land*, 111–13.

20. Kinney, *Indian Forest and Range*, 6; McQuillan, "American Indian Timber Management," 74–76.

21. Kinney, *Indian Forest and Range*, 7.

22. Newell, Clow, and Ellis, *Forest in Trust*, 24–30; Kinney, *Indian Forest and Range*, 7.

23. Udall, *Quiet Crisis*, 71–80.

24. Steen, *U.S. Forest Service*, 9–17; Udall, *Quiet Crisis*, 86–96.

25. Steen, *U.S. Forest Service*, 12–25; White, *History of the American West*, 137–54.

26. Hoxie, *Final Promise*, 1–10.

27. U.S. Senate, *Chippewa Allotments* 14, 628–33; Kinney, *Indian Forest and Range*, 11–25; Godfrey, *Forestry History of Ten Wisconsin Indian Reservations*, 27–33.

28. Kinney, "Forestry on Indian Reservations," 473.

29. Hosmer, "Creating Indian Entrepreneurs."

30. Kinney, *Indian Forest and Range*, 11–25.

31. Hosmer, "Creating Indian Entrepreneurs," 4.

32. McQuillan, "American Indian Timber Management," 83.

33. Udall, *Quiet Crisis*, 101.

34. Steen, *U.S. Forest Service*, 26.

35. Ibid, 28.

36. Williams, *USDA Forest Service*, 14–19.

37. Dana and Fairfax, *Forest and Range Policy*, 52–53.

38. Kinney, "Forestry on Indian Reservations," 472–73.
39. Udall, *Quiet Crisis*, 12.

CHAPTER 2

1. Brinkley, *Wilderness Warrior*, 803–5.
2. Pinchot, *Breaking New Ground*, 376–79; Miller, *Gifford Pinchot*, 163–64.
3. Presidential Proclamations 859 through 871, especially, 859, 862–66, and 871, March 2, 1909. The proviso in each of the seven proclamations read as follows:

> Provided, that, nothing herein shall, for the term of twenty-five years from the date hereof, operate to terminate or abridge the rights of the Secretary of the Interior and of the Commissioner of Indian Affairs, under existing laws, to allot to individual Indians any of such of the above described lands as were included in the said . . . Indian Reservation by the said Executive Order modified as aforesaid; to use any of such lands or the timber thereon for Agency, school, or other tribal purposes; to permit the use of any of such lands for grazing purposes; to permit the free use by individual Indians of timber and stone from any of said lands necessary for domestic use upon their allotments; to dispose of the proceeds arising from grazing as provided for by law for other Indian funds; and to dispose of the dead timber standing or fallen upon such lands; Provided further, that said powers and rights of the Secretary of the Interior and Commissioner of Indian Affairs or permittees under or through them or either of them, and of individual Indians, except as to allotments to such Indians, shall be subject to such rules and regulations as the Secretary of Agriculture may from time to time prescribe for the protection of the National Forest; and said powers and rights shall not be construed to apply to any land except such parts of said . . . Indian Reservation as are included in the Forest by this proclamation, and all said powers and rights except the rights of individual Indians and their heirs to hold and enjoy their allotments, shall cease and determine twenty-five years after the date hereof, and thereafter the occupancy and use of the unallotted parts of said lands shall in all respects be subject to the laws governing National Forests.

4. For the relationship between natural resource policy and Indian policy during the Roosevelt presidency, see Hoxie, *Final Promise*.
5. Pinchot, *Breaking New Ground*, 24–25.
6. The quote is attributed to Captain Richard H. Pratt, founder of the Carlisle Indian Industrial School, and comes from a speech he made in Denver in 1892;

"Richard Pratt: 'Kill the Indian, Save the Man,'" http://socrates.bmcc.cuny .edu/bfriedheim/pratt.htm, quoting "Official Report of the Nineteenth Annual Conference of Charities and Correction" (1892), 46–59; reprinted in Richard H. Pratt, "The Advantages of Mingling Indians with Whites," *Americanizing the American Indians: Writings by the "Friends of the Indian" 1880–1900* (Cambridge, MA: Harvard University Press, 1973), 260–71.

7. Prucha, *Great Father*, 269; Hoxie, *Final Promise*, 154–55.

8. McDonnell, *Dispossession*, 88–89.

9. Prucha, *Great Father*, 295.

10. National Forest System lands increased from 75,352,000 acres in 1905 to 172,230,000 acres in 1909. During the whole allotment period, 1887 to 1934, the Indian estate shrank from 138 million acres to 52 million acres. The Indians lost lands in four ways: 38 million acres of surplus land ceded after allotment, 22 million acres of surplus land opened to non-Indian settlement, 23 million acres of fee patented lands lost, and 3 million acres of trust allotments sold. Annual national forest figures are given in USDA, Forest Service, *Land Areas of the National Forest*, 118–19. Figures for Indian land loss are from McDonnell, *Dispossession*, 121.

11. "An Act for the relief and civilization of the Chippewa Indians in the State of Minnesota," January 14, 1889, 25 Stat., 642, in Kappler, *Indian Affairs*, 301–6; Pinchot, *Breaking New Ground*, 203–4, 465.

12. Searle, "Minnesota National Forest," 246.

13. Searle, "Minnesota National Forest," 247–55; Pinchot, *Breaking New Ground*, 205.

14. Searle, "Minnesota National Forest," 255–56; "Indian Assails Morris Bill," *New York Times*, July 6, 1902.

15. "An act amending 'An act for the relief and civilization of the Chippewa Indians in the State of Minnesota,' approved January fourteenth, eighteen hundred and eighty-nine," June 27, 1902, 32 Stat., 400, in Kappler, *Indian Affairs*, 2:756–61; Pinchot, *Breaking New Ground*, 205–7.

16. Pinchot, "Report of the Forester for 1905," *Annual Reports of the Department of Agriculture 1905*, 210.

17. "History," *Leech Lake Band of Ojibwe*.

18. Gifford Pinchot, "Report of the Forester for 1903," 501–2.

19. "An act to authorize the cutting, sawing into lumber, and sale of timber on certain lands reserved for the use of the Menominee Tribe of Indians, in the State of Wisconsin," in Kappler, *Indian Affairs*, 3:259; Hosmer, "Creating Indian Entrepreneurs," 1–7.

20. Howarth quoted in Hosmer, "Creating Indian Entrepreneurs," 9.

21. "An act to authorize the cutting of timber, the manufacture and sale of lumber, and the preservation of the forests on the Menominee Indian Reservation in the State of Wisconsin," March 28, 1908, 35 Stat., 51, in Kappler, *Indian Affairs*, 3:317; Hosmer, "Creating Indian Entrepreneurs," 9–10; Pinchot, "Report by the Forester," 398.

22. Pinchot, "Report by the Forester," 398.

23. U.S. House, Committee on Indian Affairs, *Indians of the United States*, serial no. 6, pp. 4–6; Pinkett, *Gifford Pinchot*, 119.

24. Pinchot, *Breaking New Ground*, 412.

25. Pinkett, *Gifford Pinchot*, 119. The cooperative agreement of January 23, 1908, and Ballinger's letter of July 19, 1909, are reproduced in U.S. House, Committee on Indian Affairs, *Indians of the United States*, serial no. 6, pp. 12–14.

26. Pinkett, *Gifford Pinchot*, 117–24.

27. Pinchot, *Breaking New Ground*, 467.

28. Kinney, *Indian Forest and Range*, 85.

29. Ibid., 84–85.

30. Prucha, *Great Father*, 303; Kinney, *Continent Lost*, 263–64; "Forestry on Indian Reservations," 471–77; McQuillan, "American Indian Timber Management," 86–87.

31. Executive Orders 1475, 1476, 1477, 1478, 1479, 1480, 1481, and 1482, February 17, 1912. There was one more executive order because in the interim one of the seven national forests had been split into two. On Taft's purposes, see U.S. House, Committee on Indian Affairs, *Indians of the United States*, serial no. 14, p. 75.

32. U.S. House, Committee on Indian Affairs, *Indians of the United States*, serial no. 6, p. 3.

33. Ibid., 4–6.

34. Ibid., 7–8.

35. Kinney, *Indian Forest and Range*, 227–28.

36. Ibid., 228; E. A. Sherman, "A Plan for the Disposal of Indian Reservation Timberlands," *Journal of Forestry* 29, no. 4 (April 1921), 360. Snyder had more success when he sponsored the Indian Citizenship Act of 1924, which conferred U.S. citizenship on all U.S. resident Indians who were not already citizens. That measure was also aimed primarily at shrinking the BIA. See Gary C. Stein, "The Indian Citizenship Act of 1924," *New Mexico Historical Review* 47, no. 3 (Summer 1972), 257–74.

37. Kinney, *Indian Forest and Range*, 228–29.

38. Sherman, "Plan for the Disposal of Indian Reservation Timberlands," 354–59.

39. Ibid., 359–60.

40. Kinney, *Indian Forest and Range*, 230.

41. U.S. Senate, Committee on Reforestation, *Reforestation*, 19.

42. Kinney, *Indian Forest and Range*, 231–39. The memo is reproduced in full on pages 233–39. The House Committee on Indian Affairs continued to look for ways to dismantle the BIA during the 1930s, including transfer of the Branch of Forestry to the Forest Service. Commissioner of Indian Affairs John Collier testified before the committee in 1935 that the transfer would not work because of the initiative to develop tribally owned sawmills. See Philp, *John Collier's Crusade*, 175.

43. E.g., part of the Uintah Reservation in Utah was transferred to the Uintah Forest Reserve under a statute enacted in 1905. See Kappler, *Indian Affairs*, 3:146.

CHAPTER 3

1. Kinney, "Forestry on Indian Reservations," 472–73.

2. Newell, "Indian Forest Policy."

3. Philp, *John Collier's*, xiii–xiv.

4. Schwartz, "Red Atlantis Revisited."

5. Collier, Shepard, and Marshall, "Indians and Their Lands," 906.

6. Ibid., 905–6.

7. Ibid., 908.

8. Marshall, "Ecology and the Indians."

9. Technically sustained-yield forestry acquired statutory underpinnings one year before the IRA, when Congress passed the National Industrial Recovery Act (NIRA)and New Dealers wrote sustained-yield principles into the NIRA code for the lumbering industry.

10. Despite the repeal of the General Allotment Act, the Indian estate would go on shrinking for another generation as more allottees or their heirs sold allotments to non-Indians. Eventually, however, tribal repurchase of lands would exceed sale of allotments to non-Indians, allowing the Indian estate to stabilize and actually rebound a bit in the second half of the twentieth century.

11. Prucha, *Great Father*, 321–24.

12. Castile, *Taking Charge*, 9.

13. Ibid., 9–10.

14. Krahe, "Last Refuge," 297.

15. Office of Indian Affairs, "Establishment of Roadless and Wild Areas on Indian Reservations," Order No. 486, October 25, 1937; reproduced in Krahe, "Last Refuge," 280.

16. Krahe, "Sovereign Prescription," 208.

17. Salmond, *Civilian Conservation Corps*, 121; Steen, *U.S. Forest Service*, 214–16.

18. Kinney, "E. C. W. on Indian Reservations," 911.

19. Parman, "Indian and the Civilian Conservation Corps," 40.

20. Naske and Slotnik, *Alaska*, 110–11.

21. Charles H. Flory, Regional Forester, to Chief, Forest Service, August 20, 1936; Chas. G. Burdick, Administrative Assistant, to Regional Forester, August 20, 1936; W. A. Chipperfield, District Ranger, to Regional Forester, August 4, 1936, Records Relating to CCC Work (microfilm), Alaska Historical Library, Juneau.

22. Alaska Native Brotherhood Resolutions, November 14 and 15, 1933; Chas. H. Flory, Regional Forester, to Judson Brown, Alaska Native Brotherhood, December 7, 1933; E. A. Sherman, Acting Forester, to Brown, December 9, 1933; Brown to Flory, January 7, 1934; Flory to Brown, January 12, 1934; Chipperfield to Regional Forester, August 4, 1936; W. A. Silcox, Chief Forester, to Robert Fechner, March 15, 1937; and Chas. G. Burdick to All Divisions, June 25, 1937, Records Relating to CCC Work (microfilm), Alaska Historical Library, Juneau; "CCC Waives Residence Requirement," *Ketchikan Alaska Chronicle*, June 22, 1937; "Morrell Says Indians are CCC Problems," *Daily Alaska Empire* (Juneau), June 25, 1937.

23. Catton, *Inhabited Wilderness*, 48–52.

24. W. A. Chipperfield to Regional Forester, August 4, 1936, Records Relating to CCC Work (microfilm), Alaska Historical Library, Juneau.

25. Parman, "Indian and the Civilian Conservation Corps," 41.

26. "First Aid for Totems," *New York Times*, January 8, 1941.

27. Rakestraw, *United States Forest Service in Alaska*, 98–99; Norris, "Victim of Nature," 8.

28. Rakestraw, *United States Forest Service in Alaska*, 100.

29. Ibid., 101–2.

30. Ibid., 102–3.

31. Ibid., 106.

32. John Autrey interview, October 28, 2010.

33. U.S. Senate, *Western Range*, 473.

34. Steen, *U.S. Forest Service*, 206–7.

35. U.S. Senate, *Western Range*, 473.

36. Ibid., 280–85.

37. Ibid., 472–76.

CHAPTER 4

1. DeMallie, *Sixth Grandfather*, 290.

2. Neihardt, *Black Elk Speaks*, 8.

3. Pauline Esteves quoted in Catton, *To Make a Better Nation*, 25.

4. Harmon, "What Should Foresters Wear?," 192.

5. Clow, "Colorado Game Laws," 24.

6. Fisher, "1932 Handshake Agreement," 188.

7. Ibid., 189–90.

8. Ibid., 190–91.

9. Kappler, *Indian Affairs*, 698–99.

10. Council proceeding quoted in Fisher, "1932 Handshake Agreement," 193.

11. Catton, *National Park, City Playground*, 55–58.

12. Sigler, *Wildlife Law Enforcement*, 162.

13. Other case studies of Forest Service collusion in states' efforts to suppress off-reservation hunting by Indians include Clow, "Colorado Game Laws," and Warren, *Hunter's Game*, chap. 3.

14. Fisher, "1932 Handshake Agreement," 190.

15. Ibid., 196–98.

16. Ibid., 200–3; Catton, *National Park, City Playground*, 55.

17. Fisher, "1932 Handshake Agreement," 203–5.

18. Ibid., 199–200.

19. Ibid., 203–5.

20. Ibid., 204–6.

21. Ibid., 206–9.

22. Ibid., 209–17.

23. Wang, Anderson, and Jakes, "Heritage Management," 365.

24. "Indian Rights and the Forests of Alaska," *Journal of Forestry* 43, no. 6 (June 1945): 391.

25. De Laguna, "Tlingit," 203–5.

26. Naske and Slotnick, *Alaska*, 187.

27. Catton, *Inhabited Wilderness*, 40–49. The discussion in these pages focuses on the National Park Service and the removal of the Huna Tlingit from Glacier Bay National Monument, but events there closely paralleled what occurred on the Tongass. See also John T. Autrey, "Preliminary Investigations into the

Degradation of Traditional Native Subsistence Camps and Smokehouses near the Village of Kasaan, Alaska, During the 1940's and 1950's" (unpublished manuscript, July 5, 2007).

28. Philp, "New Deal and Alaskan Natives," 316–17.

29. U.S. Department of the Interior, *Opinions of the Solicitor*, 1096.

30. Philp, "New Deal and Alaskan Natives," 320.

31. Crichton, "Storm Over Alaska," 75.

32. Philp, "New Deal and Alaskan Natives," 321–26.

33. Catton, *Inhabited Wilderness*, 58, 231; Autrey, "Preliminary Investigations," 5; Haycox, "Economic Development," 29–30.

34. Haycox, "Economic Development," 24.

35. Ibid., 28.

36. Ibid., 27–28, 30.

37. Ibid., 31–34.

38. Ibid., 36–37.

39. Ibid., 37–38.

40. Ibid., 39–43.

41. Catton, *Inhabited Wilderness*, 80; Haycox, "Economic Development," 46.

42. Haycox, "Economic Development," 46.

CHAPTER 5

1. Prucha, *Great Father*, 343; Fixico, *Termination and Relocation*, 33.

2. Parman, *Indians and the American West*, 138–39.

3. "An Act to provide for the termination of Federal supervision over the property of the Klamath Tribe of Indians located in the State of Oregon and the individual members thereof, and for other purposes," August 13, 1954, 68 Stat. 718, in Kappler, *Indian Affairs*, 6:635–41.

4. U.S. Senate, *Amending the Act Terminating Federal Supervision over the Klamath Indian Tribe*, 3; Kephart, "Forestry on the Klamath Indian Reservation," 896–99.

5. U.S. Senate, *Amending the Act Terminating Federal Supervision Over the Klamath Indian Tribe*, 3; Burt, *Tribalism in Crisis*, 98.

6. U.S. Senate, *Amending the Act Terminating Federal Supervision Over the Klamath Indian Tribe*, 7.

7. "Sentiment Grows for Repeal," 25.

8. "To amend the Act terminating Federal supervision over the Klamath Indian Tribe by providing in the alternative for private or Federal acquisition of the part of the tribal forest that must be sold, and for other purposes," August 23,

1958, 72 Stat., 816, in Kappler, *Indian Affairs*, 834–37; *Report of the Chief of the Forest Service, 1958* (Washington: Government Printing Office, 1959), 23.

9. Burt, *Tribalism in Crisis*, 101.

10. *Report of the Chief of the Forest Service, 1961*, 21.

11. Fixico, *Termination and Relocation*, 26.

12. Prucha, *Great Father*, 342.

13. Graybill, "'Strong on the Merits and Powerfully Symbolic,'" 126.

14. Gordon-McCutchan, *Taos Indians*, 3–9.

15. O'Brien, *American Indian Tribal Governments*, 166–68.

16. Graybill, "'Strong on the Merits and Powerfully Symbolic,'" 128.

17. Gordon-McCutchan, *Taos Indians*, 18.

18. Ibid.

19. Ibid., 19.

20. "An Act to Provide for the Protection of the Watershed within the Carson National Forest from which water is obtained for the Taos Pueblo, New Mexico," March 27, 1928, 45 Stat., 372, in Kappler, *Indian Affairs*, 5:37.

21. Gordon-McCutchan, *Taos Indians*, 20–22.

22. "An Act to authorize appropriations to pay in part the liability of the United States to the Indian pueblos herein named, under the terms of the Act of June 7, 1924 … and to amend the Act approved June 7, 1924, in certain respects," May 31, 1933, 48 Stat., 108, in Kappler, *Indian Affairs*, 5:336–38.

23. Gordon-McCutchan, *Taos Indians*, 28–30.

24. Ibid., 31.

25. Ibid., 32–33; Graybill, "'Strong on the Merits and Powerfully Symbolic,'" 129.

26. Graybill, "'Strong on the Merits and Powerfully Symbolic,'" 130–35.

27. Ibid., 135–36.

28. Ibid., 137–38.

29. Ibid., 139–40.

30. Ibid., 140–46.

31. Garment quoted in Graybill, "'Strong on the Merits and Powerfully Symbolic,'" 147; see also Castile, *To Show Heart*, 91–95.

32. Worster, *Under Western Skies*, 113.

CHAPTER 6

1. Clarke and McCool, *Staking out the Terrain*, 45. The percentages come from a study published in 1981. Foresters probably made up an even higher percentage of professional staff in 1970.

2. Hays, *American People and the National Forests*, 55–105; Steen, *U.S. Forest Service*, 278–307.

3. Hays, *American People and the National Forests*, xii–xiii.

4. Ibid., 92–97; Steen, *U.S. Forest Service*, 321–22.

5. Steen, *U.S. Forest Service*, 311; Catton and Mighetto, *Fish and Wildlife*, 142.

6. Freemuth, "Emergence of Ecosystem Management."

7. Kennedy and Quigley, "Evolution of USDA Forest Service."

8. Jack Ward Thomas, interview by Harold K. Steen, 2002, http://www.forest history.org.

9. Silva, "TMO Revisited."

10. Forest History Society, "Gene Bernardi Papers."

11. USDA, Forest Service, Pacific Northwest Region, *Native American Program*, 2–3.

12. Sonia Tamez, personal communication, March 6, 2013.

13. USDA, Forest Service, *Equal Opportunity*, 139–40.

14. Ibid., 2, 103.

15. F. Dale Robertson, interview by Harold K. Steen, August 12–14, 1999, http://www.foresthistory.org.

16. Dan Meza interview, March 8, 2013; "Faces of the Forest Service: Meet Dan Meza," http://www.fs.fed.us/news/2012/faces/meza/indx.shtml.

17. Catton, *Inhabited Wilderness*, 183, 195.

18. Parman, *Indians and the American West*, 153–54.

19. Johnson, *American Indian Occupation of Alcatraz Island*, 53–65.

20. Castile, *To Show Heart*, 112–14.

21. Ibid., 112–14; "Richard Oakes (activist)," https://en.wikipedia.org/wiki/Richard_Oakes_%28activist%29.

22. Smith, *Hippies, Indians, and the Fight for Red Power*, 165.

23. Ibid., 165.

24. Krahe and Catton, *Little Gem of the Cascades*, 226.

25. Smith, *Hippies, Indians, and the Fight for Red Power*, 166.

26. Ibid., 167–68.

27. Sabalow, "Long History."

28. Richard Boyer, "Events Near Four Corners: October 27, 1970," November 6, 1970, Lassen NP Records, Accession 506, Box 43, File 29, W34 Law Enforcement, Indians, 1970–72, Redwoods National Park Archives, Orick, California; Sabalow, "Long History."

29. Parman, *Indians and the American West*, 164–65.

30. Becker, "Fish and Wildlife Management on Tribal Lands," 395.

31. Rankel, "Tribal Fish and Wildlife Management," 408.

32. Durham, "Development of Quality Fishery and Wildlife Management," 399.
33. Ibid., 399.
34. Davis, "Self-Determination and Resources," 24.
35. Castile, *Taking Charge*, 91.
36. Bruggers, "Salish-Kootenai Comeback," 23.
37. "Tribal Forestry," http://www.cskt.org/tr/forestry.htm.
38. Davis, "Self-Determination and Resources," 27.
39. Wilkinson, *Blood Struggle*, 316.
40. Yazzie-Durgio, "Right to Change." 35.
41. Davis, "Self-Determination and Resources," 27.
42. Wilkinson, *Blood Struggle*, 320; Bruggers, "Salish-Kootenai Comeback," 23; Keith Lawrence, interview, August 22, 2012; Diane L. Krahe, "Tribal Natural Resource Employment Needs in the Northwest," survey conducted for the purposes of the advisory committee of Salish Kootenai College's bachelor's program in environmental science, Environmental Studies Department, University of Montana, January 1994, 1–6.
43. Wilkinson, *Blood Struggle*, 310–13.
44. Durham, "Development of Quality Fishery and Wildlife Management," 400.
45. Rankel, "Tribal Fish and Wildlife Management," 410–11; Wilkinson, *Blood Struggle*, 310–11.
46. Rankel, "Tribal Fish and Wildlife Management," 411–13.
47. "History of USET," http://www.usetinc.org/about-uset/history/.
48. Durham, "Development of Quality Fishery and Wildlife Management," 402–3.
49. Morishima, "Indian Forestry," 9.

CHAPTER 7

1. Wang, Anderson, and Jakes, "Legislating the Past," 13; Propper, "The Program," 8; Les McConnell interview, August 24, 2012; Sonia Tamez, e-mail message to author, March 6, 2013.
2. Deloria, *Custer Died for Your Sins*, 78–81.
3. Stapp and Burney, *Tribal Cultural Resource Management*, 11–71.
4. Peerman, "Bare-Bones Imbroglio," 935.
5. Wang et al., "Legislating the Past," 6–7; Rothman, *America's National Monuments*, 6–30; Catton and Hubber, *Commemoration and Preservation*, 19–20. The 1906 edition of the Forest Service's *Use Book* carried the following instructions on national monuments: "All persons are prohibited from appropriating, excavating, injuring, or destroying any historic or prehistoric ruin or monument, or

any object of antiquity situated on lands owned or controlled by the Government of the United States, without the permission of the Secretary who has jurisdiction over the land involved. . . . Forest officers should report to the Forester the location and description of all objects of great scientific or historic interest which they find upon forest reserves, and should prevent all persons from injuring these objects without permission from the Secretary of Agriculture."

6. Wang, Anderson, and Jakes, "Legislating the Past," 7.
7. Stapp and Burney, *Tribal Cultural Resource Management*, 53.
8. DeBloois is quoted at length in a sidebar in Stapp and Burney, *Tribal Cultural Resource Management*, 39.
9. Ibid.
10. Propper, "The Program," 8.
11. U.S. Senate, Subcommittee on Parks, Recreation, and Renewable Resources of the Committee on Energy and Natural Resources, *Archaeological Resources Protection Act of 1979*, 44.
12. Ibid., 44.
13. Watkins, "Antiquities Act," 193; Stapp and Burney, *Tribal Cultural Resources Management*, 50–51.
14. Castillo, "Short Overview."
15. Sonia Tamez, e-mail message to author, March 6, 2013.
16. Platt, *Grave Matters*, 128–30.
17. Dubin, "Preserving California's Indian Heritage," 24.
18. Platt, *Grave Matters*, 143–44.
19. Morris, "Anthropological Culture Shift," 20–22.
20. Stapp and Burney, *Tribal Cultural Resource Management*, 49–50.
21. Sonia Tamez interview, August 31, 2012; Tamez, "Forest Service and Native American Relationships," 40.
22. Bechle, "Shortage of Solitude," 22.
23. Taliman, "Sacred Landscapes," 43.
24. Ervin, "Spirit Dancers," 107.
25. Quotation in Herz, "Legal Protection for Indigenous Cultures, 703.
26. Gulliford, *Sacred Objects*, 67. See also Hughes and Swan, "How Much of the Earth," 247–59.
27. Burton, *Worship and Wilderness*, 105–8.
28. Falk, "*Lyng v. Northwest Indian Cemetery Protective Association*," 516–17; U.S. Senate, Select Committee on Indian Affairs, *Amendments to the American Indian Religious Freedom Act*, 11–13; Merv George Jr. interview, August 27, 2012.
29. Falk, "*Lyng v. Northwest Indian Cemetery Protective Association*," 520–21.

30. King, *Places that Count*, 28.

31. Falk, "*Lyng v. Northwest Indian Cemetery Protective Association*," 521.

32. U.S. Senate, Select Committee on Indian Affairs, *Improvement of the American Indian Religious Freedom Act*, 23–25; Harjo, "American Indian Religious Freedom Act," 131; Ervin, "Spirit Dancers," 107; Burton, *Worship and Wilderness*, 108.

33. U.S. Senate, Select Committee on Indian Affairs, *Improvement of the American Indian Religious Freedom Act*, 23–24.

34. Falk, "*Lyng v. Northwest Indian Cemetery Protective Association*," 522–23.

35. King, *Places that Count*, 29; Sonia Tamez, e-mail message to author, March 6, 2013.

36. Burton, *Worship and Wilderness*, 110; Sonia Tamez, e-mail message to author, March 6, 2013.

37. Harjo, "American Indian Religious Freedom Act," 132–33; Burton, *Worship and Wilderness*, 110.

38. Sonia Tamez, e-mail message to author, March 6, 2013.

39. Yablon, "Property Rights and Sacred Sites," 1623–62.

40. Moore, "National Park Service's Native American Policy," 1–3.

41. Crespi, "Saving Sacred Places," 18.

42. King, *Places that Count*, 33–35.

43. Ibid., 34.

44. Tamez, "Forest Service and Native American Relationships," 40.

45. Adams et al., "Modeling Solutions to Indian Needs," 41–51.

46. Anquoe, "Sacred Sites in Danger"; Baum, "Sacred Places," 34.

47. Sax and Keiter, "Realities of Regional Resource Management," 273; Bruggers, "Forest Service Steps on Blackfeet," 14; Bechle, "Shortage of Solitude," 22.

48. Greiser and Greiser, "Two Views of the World," 9.

49. Bruggers, "Forest Service Steps on Blackfeet," 14; Greiser and Greiser, "Two Views of the World," 10.

50. Greiser and Greiser, "Two Views of the World," 10.

51. Ibid.

52. Adams, "United States Forest Service," 32–35.

53. Stapp and Burney, *Tribal Cultural Resource Management*, 62; Pat Parker, *Keepers of the Treasures: Protecting Historic Properties and Cultural Traditions on Indian Lands* (Washington, DC: U.S. Department of the Interior, National Park Service, Interagency Resources Division), 3–13.

54. Gulliford, *Sacred Objects*, 112.

55. Harjo, "American Indian Religious Freedom Act," 134.

56. Trope and Echo-Hawk, "Native American Graves Protection and Repatriation Act, 136.

57. U.S. House, Committee on Interior and Insular Affairs, *Protection of Native American Graves*, 53–54.

58. Trope and Echo-Hawk, "Native American Graves Protection and Repatriation Act," 136.

59. Peerman, "Bare-Bones Imbroglio," 935.

60. Trope and Echo-Hawk, "Native American Graves Protection and Repatriation Act," 133–34.

61. Dan Meza interview, March 8, 2013; Trope and Echo-Hawk, "Native American Graves Protection and Repatriation Act," 139–40.

62. Trope and Echo-Hawk, "Native American Graves Protection and Repatriation Act," 141–46.

63. Ibid., 151.

64. Morris, "Anthropological Culture Shift," 20–22.

65. Gunsky, "Legacy of Ishi," 4–11.

66. Curry, "Last of the Yahi," 56; Krahe and Catton, *Little Gem of the Cascades*, 318–19.

CHAPTER 8

1. Franklin, "Toward a New Forestry," 37–44.

2. Udall, *Quiet Crisis*, 12.

3. Yaffee, *Wisdom of the Spotted Owl*.

4. Franklin quoted in Davis, "Making of a Revolutionary," 39.

5. Catton and Mighetto, *Fish and Wildlife*, 267; Freeman, "EcoFactory," 635.

6. Hays, *American People and the National Forests*, 106–26.

7. Salka, "Mission Evolution," 221–24.

8. Yaffee, *Wisdom of the Spotted Owl*, 112–13; Freeman, "EcoFactory," 637–39; Salka, "Mission Evolution," 227–28; Catton and Mighetto, *Fish and Wildlife*, 271.

9. White House, Office of the Press Secretary, "Forest Conference"; Tuchmann et al., *Northwest Forest Plan*, 43.

10. Walker and Daniels, "When Talk and Structure Collide," 77–85.

11. Catton and Mighetto, *Fish and Wildlife*, 271–72; Tuchmann, et al., *Northwest Forest Plan*, 2.

12. Thomas quoted in Catton and Mighetto, *Fish and Wildlife*, 263.

13. Pinkham, "Conserving Nature," 21.

14. Morishima, "Indian Forestry," 9.

15. U.S. Senate, Select Committee on Indian Affairs, *Indian Forests and Woodlands*, 66.

16. Gary S. Morishima interview, March 21, 2013.

17. Gary S. Morishima, "A Forest Grows from Tiny Seeds: 30 Years Old and Still Growing: A Retrospective of the Intertribal Timber Council" (undated manuscript), typescript, p. 9.

18. U.S. Senate, Select Committee on Indian Affairs, *Indian Forests and Woodlands*, 210.

19. Morishima, "Indian Forestry," 7; "A Forest Grows from Tiny Seeds: 30 Years Old and Still Growing: A Retrospective of the Intertribal Timber Council" (undated manuscript), typescript, p. 35; U.S. Senate, Select Committee on Indian Affairs, *Indian Forests and Woodlands*, 66.

20. Motanic, "National Indian Forest Resources Management Act," 26–27; Morishima, "Promises to Keep"; Sessions, "Are Indian Forests and Forest Management Improving?," 33.

21. Miller quoted in Petersen, "Forestry in Indian Country," 10.

22. Petersen, "Forestry in Indian Country," 11.

23. Sessions, "Are Indian Forests and Forest Management Improving?" 34–35.

24. USDA (U.S. Department of Agriculture), Forest Service, Office of Tribal Relations, "Tribal Relations Program: History" (undated fact sheet).

25. Catton and Mighetto, *Fish and Wildlife*, 183–85.

26. Hirt, "Biopolitics," 249–50. The controversy continued. The area cleared for the observatory exceeded the area allowed in the exemption by 40 percent. In 2010, the Mount Graham Coalition filed notice of intent to sue the U.S. Department of Agriculture and the U.S. Department of the Interior for failing to reinitiate consultation under the Endangered Species Act; Rambler, "Mount Graham Coalition."

27. DEIS quoted in Rambler, "Mount Graham Coalition."

28. Hirt, "Biopolitics," 249–50; Dougherty, "Star Gate."

29. USDA, Forest Service, *Forest Service Native American Policy*.

30. F. Dale Robertson, interview by Harold K. Steen, August 12–14, 1999, http://foresthistory.org/Research/Robertson%20F.%20Dale%20OHI%20Final.pdf.

31. USDA, Forest Service, *Forest Service Native American Policy*, 2.

32. Ibid., 6.

33. USDA Forest Service, Office of Tribal Relations, "Tribal Relations Program"; Marsha Butterfield interview, December 2, 2010.

34. Les McConnell interview, August 24, 2012.

35. Sonia Tamez, e-mail message to author, March 6, 2013.

36. John Autrey interview, October 28, 2010.

37. Ira Jones interview, October 22, 2012.

38. Susan Johnson interview, October 6, 2012.

39. USDA, Forest Service, State and Private Forestry, *National Resource Book on American Indian and Alaska Native Relations.*

40. Ibid., ix.

CHAPTER 9

1. USDA, Forest Service, *Report of the National Tribal Relations Program*, 10–1; Fred Clark interview, December 1, 2010.

2. USDA, Forest Service, State and Private Forestry, *National Resource Book on American Indian and Alaska Native Relations*, vii.

3. On Forest Service restructuring, see Doug McCleery, "Re-inventing the United States Forest Service: Evolution from Custodial Management, to Production Forestry, to Ecosystem Management," 2008, http://www.fao.org/documents. A sharp reduction in timber sales and receipts resulting from the northern spotted owl crisis and the shift to ecosystem management created strong pressure on the agency to restructure. While the total numbers of Forest Service personnel held steady at about thirty thousand through the turn of the century, Forest Service jobs had to be redistributed to respond to a changing workload. Pressure to relocate personnel and jobs fell hardest on the national forests in the Pacific Northwest in the early to mid-1990s. Pressure to downsize shifted to the higher-grade positions in the Washington office and the research stations in the late 1990s and early 2000s.

4. Mit Parsons interview, October 2, 2012.

5. "Council of Western State Foresters," http://www.wflcweb.org; Parsons interview. The Western Forestry Leadership Coalition was formally established in 2000.

6. Parsons interview.

7. Ibid.

8. Ibid.

9. Minutes, Council of Western State Foresters Annual Meeting, May 25, 1999 (copy provided by Mit Parsons).

10. Parsons interview; Minutes, Council of Western State Foresters.

11. Phil Janik, Janice McDougle, James Hubbard, and Larry Payne, "Forest Service Action Strategy for State and Private Forestry Services," March 27, 1998 (unpublished paper, copy provided by Mit Parsons).

12. Mit Parsons and Tony Martinez, "Issue Paper: Extending Federal State and Private Forestry Programs to American Indian and Alaskan Native People and Tribal Governments"(unpublished paper, n.d., copy provided by Mit Parsons). The ITC prodded the Clinton administration's Domestic Policy Council to do

something about the discriminatory cooperative forestry assistance programs. On April 5, 1999, the Forest Service received a communiqué from the Domestic Policy Council identifying three Forest Service grant programs that provided moneys directly to states but not to tribes. These programs were authorized under the Cooperative Forestry Assistance Act of 1978 as amended by the 1990 farm bill. Under existing legislative authorities, tribes could only access those programs by way of state forestry agencies. The Domestic Policy Council recommended that the Forest Service support legislative changes that would allow tribes direct access to those grant programs.

13. Minutes, Council of Western State Foresters Annual Meeting.

14. Parsons interview; Martinez and Laverty, *Strategic Plan*, 6.

15. Parsons interview.

16. USDA, Forest Service, *Report of the National Tribal Relations Program*, app. A. The names of the task force members were Brad Powell, Sonia Tamez, Marsha Butterfield, Dick Fitzgerald, Carol Jorgensen, Gary Larsen, Joe Mitchell, Gary Morishima, Jacque Myers, Mit Parsons, Lynn Roberts, Cecilia Seesholtz, and Arch Wells.

17. Phil Janik, Chief Operating Officer, to Tribal Chairperson, March 17, 2000, U.S. Forest Service, Office of Tribal Relations, digital files (hereafter OTR digital files).

18. Parsons interview.

19. USDA, Forest Service, *Report of the National Tribal Relations Program*, 3–7.

20. Susan Johnson interview, October 6, 2012.

21. UDSA, Forest Service, *Report of the National Tribal Relations Program*, 1; Parsons interview.

22. "Carol Jorgensen Scholarship for Environmental Stewardship," Society of American Indian Government Employees, http://www.saige.org/member-resources/scholarships/; "Carol Paddock Jorgensen," *Juneau Empire*, September 15, 2009; Robert Schroeder interview, August 8, 2012.

23. Dorothy FireCloud interview, June 10, 2013; Parsons interview; Dale N. Bosworth interview, June 9, 2014.

24. FireCloud interview.

25. Untitled memo beginning "Two Assistant Directors (NFS and S&PF/Research)," n.d., OTR digital files.

26. Joel Holtrop interview, December 3, 2010. Holtrop's four points were as follows. First, it was vitally important that the Forest Service and tribes build relations based on a spirit of collaboration, not conflict. The state and private forestry area was utterly focused on collaboration. The Division of National Forest

Administration worked with partners, too, but not to the same degree that State and Private Forestry did. Second, if the Office of Tribal Relations were put in the Division of National Forest Administration, it would tend to focus the staff on tribal interests and treaty rights wherever those existed on national forest-lands. That narrow focus would in turn tend to make the office more reactive than proactive. Third, the Forest Service needed to be doing more for tribes beyond the National Forest System. It needed to include tribes in cooperative programs that were currently oriented to State and Private Forestry. Holtrop's last point was that the Forest Service needed to devote more attention to traditional ecological knowledge, and he thought the Division of State and Private Forestry, with its more specialized functions, would be better able to nurture that new feature of Forest Service tribal relations.

27. Bosworth interview.
28. Dale N. Bosworth to Regional Foresters, Station Directors, Area Director, IITF Director, and WO Staff, July 17, 2002, copy provided by Susan Johnson.
29. Bosworth interview.
30. "Award Ceremony Recognizes American Indians for Help in Creating Forest Service Office of Tribal Relations," Release No. FS-0503, October 14, 2004, OTR digital files. The other recipients were Butch Blazer, then state forester of New Mexico; Nolan Colegrove, president of the ITC; Keller George, president of the United South and Eastern Tribes; and Susan Masten, former president of the NCAI.
31. FireCloud interview; Gary Harris interview, August 24, 2012; Parsons interview; Dale Kanen interview, October 21, 2010.
32. FireCloud interview.
33. Kanen interview.
34. Ibid.
35. Ibid.
36. Ibid.
37. "History of the Hall of Tribes 2004–2005," July 15, 2005, OTR digital files.
38. Ibid.
39. Ibid.; Office of Tribal Relations, FY 2005 Annual Reports, OTR digital files.
40. USDA Forest Service, State and Private Forestry, "Briefing Paper, Coordination with USDA Concerning a Forest Service Open House in Conjunction with the Opening of the Smithsonian Institution's National Museum for the American Indian," August 11, 2004, OTR digital files.
41. Kanen interview.
42. Ibid.

43. The six items were (1) *Providing forest products for traditional and cultural purposes.* Tribes had special cultural and traditional needs for forest products located on national forestlands, such as logs and planks for cultural structures. The legislation would make exception to the NFMA and allow the Forest Service to provide such products free of charge. (2) *Allowing temporary closure of national forestlands for traditional and cultural purposes.* The legislation would authorize the Forest Service to make temporary closures for the shortest period and minimum area necessary in order to facilitate tribal activities that would otherwise conflict with public access and use. (3) *Encouraging equal access to federal programs by tribal governments.* The legislation would enhance the Forest Service's ability to interact and partner with tribes through grants, agreements, and acquisition programs. (4) *Delivering cooperative forestry assistance to tribes.* By amending the Cooperative Forestry Assistance Act of 1978 and expanding the stewardship program, the Forest Service would be able to ensure that tribal lands were equitably funded under these programs. (5) *Reburying human remains and cultural items.* NAGPRA provided for repatriation of human remains and cultural items to Indian tribes but it did not address their further disposition. Tribes generally wanted to return them to their former resting place, most often on national forestlands. The legislation would give the Forest Service express authority to facilitate such reburials. (6) *Providing confidentiality of cultural information shared during joint Forest Service–tribal research studies and reburials.* The legislation would provide for an exemption from Freedom of Information Act requirements to protect confidentiality of traditional ecological knowledge and reburial location information.

44. Mit Parsons, personal communication, September 19, 2012.

45. Ibid., with attached Word document titled "Draft May 8, 2002 Senate Farm Bill Language on FS and Tribal Governments.doc." The document also contained a "Section X"—apparently eliminated from the final version of the bill but retained with this document for reference purposes—which would have established both the Office of Tribal Relations and the National Tribal Leadership Advisory Council by congressional mandate. USDA's concurrence with the bill is noted in "Tribal Relations Documentation," n.d., copy provided by Mit Parsons.

46. Mit Parsons, personal communication, September 19, 2012.

47. Office of Management and Budget, *Budget of the United States Government, Fiscal Year 2005*:

Also included in the budget is a proposal to improve the ability of the Forest Service and Native American and Alaska Native Tribes to achieve goals of mutual interest. This includes authorities regarding the use of and access to National Forest System lands; forest products for traditional and cultural purposes; repatriation and reburial; and research, development and collaboration with Tribal Governments. These authorities would streamline and clarify several areas of interest between the Forest Service and Native American and Alaska Native Tribes.

48. Teri Cleeland to Dale Kanen et al., e-mail message, March 5, 2004, with draft legislation attached: "Chief and Staff Meeting," March 9, 2004, and "Tribal Relations Documentation," n.d. (copies provided to author by Mit Parsons).

49. Douglas W. Crandall, Director, Legislative Affairs to Deputy Chief for Business Operations et al., June 27, 2008, OTR digital files.

50. U.S. Department of Agriculture, Forest Service, "Briefing Paper, Cultural and Heritage Cooperation Authority in the Farm Bill," July 22, 2009, OTR digital files.

CHAPTER 10

1. Pinchot Institute for Conservation, "Introduction to the National Fire Plan."

2. *10-Year Comprehensive Strategy.*

3. U.S. House, Committee on Resources, *President's Healthy Forests Initiative*, 20.

4. Schoennagel, Veblen, and Romme, "Interaction of Fire," 661–76.

5. Vaughn and Cortner, *George W. Bush's Healthy Forests*, 1–11.

6. Petersen, "New Pioneers," 45; Little, "Un-Common Ground," 45–51. See also *Journal of Forestry* 102, no. 2 (March 2004). The entire issue is devoted to analysis of the Forest Service appeals process. The Government Accountability Office (GAO) is an independent, nonpartisan agency of Congress. In 2004, its name was changed from the General Accounting Office.

7. Kyl quoted in Petersen, "New Pioneers," 45. In FY 2001, fuel reduction projects were accomplished on 2.09 million acres of federal lands. This compared with prescribed burning treatments on 10.1 million acres on national forestlands from 1990 to 2002 (an average of 779,496 acres per year) and 2.8 million acres on other federal lands from 1995 to 2000. See Williams, *Forest Service*, 197–98.

8. "'Stop Fiddling: Save America's Forests': Healthy Forests Act Wins Bipartisan House Approval," *Fort Apache Scout* (Whiteriver, Arizona), May 30, 2003.

9. Lee, "From the Redwood Forests."

10. "Healthy Forests Restoration Act of 2003"; Intertribal Timber Council, *FY 2003 Annual Report.*

11. Andrew H. Fisher, "Working in the Indian Way," 126–28.

12. "White House Initiative Spurs Native American Economic Development"; "Forest Service and Tribal Government Leaders to Meet."

13. "Briefing Paper, Subcommittee on Forests and Forest Health, Committee on Resources, Legislative Hearing on HR 3846 The Tribal Forests Protection Act, Wednesday, April 21, 2004 Room 1334 LHOB, 10:00 a.m.," U.S. Forest Service, Legislative Affairs, Washington.

14. Simon, "Fire Spurs Bush's Long-Stalled 'Healthy Forests' Legislation"; Gary Harris interview, August 24, 2012.

15. Reynolds, "Washington in Brief."

16. Hearing Summary, April 21, 2004, USDA Forest Service, Washington Office, Legislative Affairs; "Tribal Forest Protection Act of 2004," July 22, 2004, 118 Stat. 868; Dale Kanen interview, October 21, 2010.

17. Harris interview.

18. Sonia Tamez, e-mail message to author, March 6, 2013; "Pacific Southwest Region Office of Tribal Relations FY06 Accomplishment Report," n.d., Office of Tribal Relations, digital files (hereafter OTR digital files).

19. Harris interview; Gary S. Morishima interview, March 21, 2013.

20. Fred Clark interview, December 1, 2010.

21. Morishima interview; U.S. House, Committee on Natural Resources, Subcommittee on Public Lands and Environmental Regulation, *State Forest Management*, 113–2; Intertribal Timber Council, "Fulfilling the Promise."

22. Woody Biomass Utilization Database, "Warm Springs Forest Products Industries."

23. Pace, "Biomass Energy Production."

24. "Confederated Tribes of Warm Springs: Oregon Bioenergy, LLC Biomass Project Overview," updated January 3, 2011 (copy provided by Waldo Walker); Oregon Forest Resources Institute, *Woody Biomass Energy*. The tribe developed the plan with help from a $196,735 award by the BIA. U.S. Department of the Interior, "Anderson Announces Funding for Warm Spring Tribes Biomass Demonstration Project Due Diligence Study," October 1, 2004, accessed June 14, 2013 (no longer accessible), http://www.bia.gov/cs/groups/public/documents.

25. Woody Biomass Utilization Database, "Warm Springs Forest Products Industries"; USDA, Forest Service, "Request for Proposal: Woody Biomass Utilization Grants: Hazardous Fuel Reduction on National Forest Lands," February 2005, OTR digital files.

26. "Confederated Tribes of Warm Springs: Oregon Bioenergy, LLC Biomass Project Overview," updated January 3, 2011 (copy provided by Waldo Walker).

27. "Grants: Award Summary, Confederated Tribes of Warm Springs Reservation of Oregon," 1st quarter 2013, accessed June 13, 2013 (no longer accessible), http://www.recovery.gov/transparency/Recovery/Data/pages; "Bullet Points Concerning the Warm Springs Forest Products Biomass to Energy Project," n.d. (copy provided by Waldo Walker).

28. "Warm Springs Biopower Project: A Case Study in Oregon," PowerPoint presentation to Gary Harris by Cal Mukumoto, consulting assistant, Warm Springs Forest Products Industries, n.d. (copy provided by Waldo Walker).

29. Becker et al., "Characterizing Lessons Learned"; "Grants: Award Summary, Confederated Tribes of Warm Springs Reservation of Oregon," 4th quarter 2011, all quarters 2012, and 1st quarter 2013, accessed June 13, 2013 (no longer posted), http://www.recovery.gov/transparency/Recovery/Data/pages.

30. LeVan and Benisch, *2009 Woody Biomass Utilization Status Report*, iv, 1, 35.

31. "Working Together: American Indian/Alaska Natives and the Forest Service," n.d., PowerPoint (presentation provided by Mit Parsons).

32. Intertribal Timber Council, *FY 2004 Annual Report*.

33. "Tribal Relations Program: Making the Vision a Reality," PowerPoint presentation, n.d. (copy provided by Mit Parsons); Mit Parsons, personal communication, September 20, 2012.

34. Mit Parsons and Gary Morishima to Nolan Colegrove, Sr., and Joel Holtrop, August 7, 2003 (copy provided by Mit Parsons).

35. Ibid.

36. "FY06 Significant Accomplishments—Office of Tribal Relations," n.d., and "USDA Forest Service, Office of Tribal Relations Quarterly Report," February 2007, OTR digital files.

37. Petershoare, "Alaska Tribal Leaders Committee."

38. "USDA Forest Service, Office of Tribal Relations Update for ITC," September 2007, OTR digital files.

39. Nolan C. Colegrove Sr. to Jim Hubbard, April 5, 2007, OTR digital files.

40. James E. Hubbard to Nolan C. Colegrove Sr., September 10, 2007, OTR digital files.

41. Ibid.

42. National Association of State Foresters, "Innovations in State & Private Forestry: Redesign Report Card," March 2009, http://www.stateforesters.org/2008_Redesign_Report_Card. The Confederated Salish and Kootenai Tribes contributed

$375,000 to a cooperative forestry project in Montana, the Menominee Nation participated with others in a $304,000 project in Wisconsin, and unnamed tribes were among numerous partners in a $544,000 project in Arizona.

CHAPTER 11

1. Peters, "Postscript," 131.
2. U.S. Forest Service, "Briefing Paper, Sacred Sites Policy Development," July 22, 2009, Office of Tribal Relations, digital files (hereafter OTR digital files); Susan Johnson et al., "Report of the Sacred Sites Policy Development Team," April 2006, copy of draft report provided by Susan Johnson, pp. 7–8.
3. Johnson et al., "Report of the Sacred Sites Policy Development Team"; Susan J. Johnson to Rick D. Cables et al., e-mail message, August 30, 2005 (copy provided by Susan Johnson).
4. Susan Johnson interview, October 6, 2012.
5. Joel Holtrop to Lincoln Bramwell, e-mail message, December 23, 2013 (provided by Lincoln Bramwell).
6. Judith G. Propper to unlisted recipients, e-mail, November 11, 2005, OTR digital files.
7. Glowacka, Washburn, and Richland, "*Nuvutukya'ovi*," 547–48; First Amended Complaint in United States District Court, District of Arizona, *The Navajo Nation et al. v. U.S. Forest Service, et al.*, No. CV 05 1824 PCT PGR, June 2005 (quotation on p. 4); Lawlor, "Snowbowl," 48.
8. Defendants' Response in Opposition to all Plaintiffs' Motions for Summary Judgment in United States District Court, District of Arizona, *The Navajo Nation et al. v. U.S. Forest Service, et al.*, No. CV 05 1824 PCT PGR, n.d.; Nora Rasure interview, August 24, 2012.
9. Glowacka, Washburn, and Richland, "*Nuvatukya'ovi*," 549–50; Zylstra, "Let It Snow," 17–18.
10. National Congress of American Indians, "Resolution #SD-02-018," http://www.ncai.org/attachments/Resolution_nWZuPDaBHvMIoYaRiITHDKwb ATwQcGwFeFxcWYtceJlcRGyjGbF_018.pdf; "Statement of Suzan Shown Harjo, President, the Morning Star Institute, for the Oversight Hearing on Native American Sacred Places Before the Committee on Indian Affairs, United States Senate, Washington, D.C., June 18, 2003," http://www.sacredland .org/PDFs/Harjo_Statement_SIAC.pdf.
11. U.S. Senate, Committee on Indian Affairs, *Religious Freedom Act*, S. Hrg. 108–630, 108th Cong., 2nd sess., 2004, 12, 16.

12. Ibid., 4–5, 29–31.

13. Makley and Makley, *Cave Rock*, 89–92.

14. Ibid., 44; Sonia Tamez interview, August 31, 2012.

15. Tamez interview.

16. Makley and Makley, *Cave Rock*, 92; Tamez interview.

17. Ahtone, "Paying Attention to the Native American Vote."

18. Morning Star Institute, "Protect Native American Sacred Places"; "2011 National Days of Prayer to Protect Native American Sacred Places," June 15, 2011, accessed June 18, 2014 (no longer posted), http://www.culturalsurvival.org.

19. USDA, Office of Tribal Relations, and USDA Forest Service, *Report to the Secretary of Agriculture*, 1.

20. Ibid., 1–2; Fred Clark interview, December 1, 2010.

21. USDA, Office of Tribal Relations, and USDA Forest Service, *Report to the Secretary of Agriculture*, 43.

22. Ibid., 44.

23. "Memorandum of Understanding Among the U.S. Department of Defense, U.S. Department of the Interior, U.S. Department of Agriculture, U.S. Department of Energy, and the Advisory Council on Historic Preservation Regarding Interagency Coordination and Collaboration for the Protection of Indian Sacred Sites," n.d., http://www.fs.fed.us; "Action Plan to Implement the Memorandum of Understanding Regarding Interagency Coordination and Collaboration for the Protection of Indian Sacred Sites," March 5, 2013, http://www.fs.fed.us; "Interagency MOU & Action Plan Guide Protection of Indian Sacred Sites," *Tribal Relations News* (Spring 2013), http://www.fs.fed.us/spf/tribalrelations/documents/news/Spring2013OTRNewsletter.pdf.

24. "Secretary Vilsack Addresses White House Tribal Nations Conference: Unveils Sacred Sites Report," December 6, 2012, http://blogs.usda.gov/page/2/?s=Tribal+Nations+Conference&x=15&y=13&commit=Search.

25. Krehbiel-Burton, "Symposium"; Wahtomy, "President Obama Renews Commitments."

26. National Congress of American Indians, "Comments in Response."

27. Peters, "Postscript," 131–35; Subr-Sytsma, "*In the Light of Reverence*," 60–61.

28. Larry Heady interview, June 12, 2014.

CHAPTER 12

1. Ruth Monihan interview, August 7, 2012.

2. USDA, Forest Service, State and Private Forestry, *National Resource Book on American Indian and Alaska Native Relations*, 42–43.

3. U.S. Department of Agriculture, Forest Service, *The Forest Service in Alaska* (Juneau: U.S. Department of Agriculture, Forest Service, Alaska Region, 1980), 5.

4. ANILCA quoted in USDA, Forest Service, *National Resource Book on American Indian and Alaska Native Relations*, 47–51, (emphasis added); Thornton, "Alaska Native Subsistence," 29–30.

5. Thornton, "Alaska Native Subsistence," 33.

6. Robert Schroeder interview, August 8, 2012.

7. Dale Kanen interview, October 21, 2010; Fred Clark interview, December 1, 2010.

8. USDA, Forest Service, *National Resource Book on American Indian and Alaska Native Relations*, 47.

9. Jorgensen, "Alaska Native View on Subsistence," 10.

10. Thornton, "Alaska Native Subsistence," 33.

11. Kanen interview.

12. Ibid.

13. Ibid.; Lillian Petershoare interview, August 7, 2012.

14. Brelsford, "Meaningful Voice," 72.

15. Armstrong, "Fish and Wildlife," 422–25; Office of Tribal Relations, "Consolidated Accomplishment FY 2005 Annual Reports," n.d., Office of Tribal Relations, digital files (hereafter OTR digital files); USDA Forest Service Natural Resources and Environment Briefing Paper, July 16, 2009, OTR digital files; Beth Pendleton interview, August 8, 2012.

16. Alaska Natives Commission, *Alaska Natives Commission, Final Report* (Anchorage: Alaska Natives Commission, 1994), 1:61–63; Schroeder interview; Ed Thomas and Rob Sanderson interview, August 8, 2012; Wayne Owen interview, August 8, 2012.

17. Owen interview; Petershoare interview; "Feds to Review Subsistence," *Juneau Empire*, October 25, 2009.

18. Alaska Natives Commission, *Final Report*, 1:4.

19. Ibid., 1:71.

20. Ibid., 1:71–73.

21. Clinton, "Remarks," 800–803.

22. Autrey interview.

23. Petershoare interview.

24. Ibid.

25. Ibid.

26. Ibid.

27. Thomas and Sanderson interview.

28. Petershoare interview; Riggs, "Forest Service Presents Ceremonial Staffs"; Walter Soboleff, "My Turn: The Past and Future of the Tongass," *Juneau Empire*, April 8, 2008.

29. Macky McClung, "An Historic Event: The Forest Service Fosters Healing with Southeast Alaska Tribes," *SourDough Notes* (Spring 2008).

30. Petershoare interview.

31. Thomas and Sanderson interview; Jane L. Smith, "A New Smokehouse for Kake Culture Camp," *SourDough Notes* (Summer 2010).

32. Petershoare, "Alaska Tribal Leaders Committee."

33. Pendleton interview.

34. "Youth and Elders: The Perfect Combination," 2011, Douglas Indian Association Diversity Grant, memorandum, Alaska Regional Office files, Juneau, Alaska; Pendleton interview.

35. Pendleton interview; Worl, *Salmon in the Trees*, 73.

36. Mark McCallum interview, August 7, 2012.

37. Lawler, "Tale of Two Skeletons," 171–72.

38. Phil Sammon, "*Kuwóot yas éin*: His Spirit Is Looking Out from the Cave," *SourDough Notes* (Fall 2007).

CHAPTER 13

1. Pinkham, *Sense of Community*.

2. Pinkham, "Conserving Nature," 15; Wilson, "Native Peoples and the Management of Natural Resources," 406; Kawamura, "Symbolic and Political Ecology; U.S. Senate, Subcommittee on Forests and Public Land Management, Committee on Energy and Natural Resources, *Federal Forest Management, Part 1*, 39.

3. Wilkinson, "Indian Tribal Rights," 435–41.

4. Babcock et al., *Forests of the Nez Perce*, chap. 2, pp. 14–17, chap. 8, p. 5.

5. Christine Bradbury interview, August 23, 2012.

6. U.S. Senate, Subcommittee on the Department of the Interior and Related Agencies, Committee on Appropriations, and Subcommittee on Forests and Public Land Management, Committee on Energy and Natural Resources, *Columbia Basin Ecosystem Management Plan*, 47.

7. Babcock et al., *Forests of the Nez Perce*, chap. 2, pp. 15–16, 32–34.

8. Quoted in ibid., chap. 2, p. 23.

9. Ibid., chap. 2, pp. 21–32, Fenn quoted in chap. 2, p. 27.

10. Ibid., chap. 3, pp. 4–17; Kinney, *Indian Forest and Range*, 169.

11. Babcock et al., *Forests of the Nez Perce*, chap. 3, p. 17 to chap. 4, p. 37.

12. Ibid., chap. 6, pp. 9–13.

13. Wilkinson, "Indian Tribal Rights," 449.

14. Babcock et al., *Forests of the Nez Perce*, chap. 7, p. 12 and chap. 8, p. 19; Keith Lawrence interview, August 22, 2012.

15. Quoted in Babcock et al., *Forests of the Nez Perce*, chap. 8, p. 16.

16. Ibid., chap. 8, pp. 12–41; Past and Present, *Forests of the Nez Perce*, 32.

17. Bradbury interview.

18. U.S. Senate, Subcommittee on Forests and Public Land Management, Committee on Energy and Natural Resources, *Federal Forest Management, Part 1*, 39; U.S. Department of Agriculture, Forest Service, *Nez Perce Treaty Rights on National Forest Land: Nez Perce, Clearwater, Payette, Boise, Wallowa-Whitman and Umatilla National Forests* (2011), copy of pamphlet provided in pdf format by Christine Bradbury; Wilkinson, "Indian Tribal Rights," 451.

19. Ira Jones interview, October 22, 2012.

20. Pinkham, "Conserving Nature," 16.

21. Lawrence interview. Pete Hays quoted by Lawrence.

22. Wilson, "Wolves, Politics, and the Nez Perce," 545–47.

23. Ibid., 553.

24. Lawrence interview.

25. Ibid.

26. Wilson, "Wolves, Politics, and the Nez Perce," 554–55; Lawrence interview.

27. Wilson, "Wolves, Politics, and the Nez Perce," 555–57.

28. Montana, "Nez Perce and Grey Wolf"; Lawrence interview.

29. Wilson, "Wolves, Politics, and the Nez Perce," 552, 559.

30. Memorandum of Understanding between the Nez Perce Tribe and the Northern Region, Intermountain Region, and Pacific Northwest Region of the United States Department of Agriculture, Forest Service (1998), copy of original signed document provided in pdf format by Christine Bradbury; Bradbury interview; Wilkinson, "Indian Tribal Rights," 452; Catton and Hubber, *Commemoration and Preservation*, 139–40.

31. Wilkinson, "Indian Tribal Rights," 454–57.

32. Ibid., 454–55. Quotes are from *Winans* by Wilkinson.

33. Ibid., 455. Quote is from *Tulee* by Wilkinson.

34. Memorandum of Understanding between the Nez Perce Tribe and the Northern Region, Intermountain Region, and Pacific Northwest Region of the United States Department of Agriculture, Forest Service (1998), copy of original signed document provided in pdf format by Christine Bradbury.

35. Kevin D. Martin, Steven A. Ellis, Thomas K. Reilly, Jane L Cottrell, and Suzanne Rainville to Rebecca Miles, May 23, 2006, letter provided in pdf format by Christine Bradbury.

36. Southwest regional forester quoted in Wilkinson, "Indian Tribal Rights," 457; Bradbury interview; U.S. Senate, Subcommittee on Forests and Public Land Management, Committee on Energy and Natural Resources, *Federal Forest Management, Part 1*, 39.

37. Barker, "Battle for Bighorns," 34; Lawrence interview; Schommer, "Reestablishment of Big Horn Sheep."

38. Barker, "Battle for Bighorns," 35–37; Lawrence interview.

39. Cheryl Vanderberg interview, October 19, 2012.

40. U.S. Senate, Subcommittee on Forests and Public Land Management, Committee on Energy and Natural Resources, *Federal Forest Management, Part 1*, 40–41.

41. Ibid. 40.

CHAPTER 14

1. Both the tribal resolution and the letter are quoted in Norgaard, "Politics of Invasive Weed Management," 270.

2. Gary Harris interview, August 24, 2012.

3. USDA, Forest Service, State and Private Forestry, *National Resource Book on American Indian and Alaska Native Relations*, 38.

4. USDA, Office of Communications, "Agriculture Secretary Vilsack Signs Regulation."

5. Joel D. Holtrop to Honorable Chief J. Allan, Coeur d'Alene Tribe, December 18, 2009, Office of Tribal Relations, digital files (hereafter OTR digital files).

6. Cheryl Vanderberg interview, October 19, 2012; Fred Clark interview, August 14, 2012.

7. "Tribal Relations Consultation Schedules"; "OTR Director's Corner."

8. Triangle Associates, "Review."

9. Larry Heady interview, June 12, 2014.

10. Harris, *Northwest Forest Plan*, 110–11.

11. Ibid., 3, 13.

12. "Office of Tribal Relations FY 2006 Accomplishment Report Narrative Southern Region," n.d., OTR digital files; Sharmina Manandhar, "Tenth Annual 'To Bridge a Gap' Conference"; Ken Sandri, personal communication, April 18, 2013.

13. "Briefing for FS Chief of Staff," March 2, 2005, OTR digital files.

14. Bill Welton, personal communication, June 12, 2013.

15. F. Dale Robertson, interview by Harold K. Steen, August 12–14, 1999, http://www.foresthistory.org/research/Robertson%20F.%20Dale%20OHI%20Final.pdf.

16. Robertson interview, 80; Sloan, "Haskell Indian Nations University," 48.

17. "Tribal Colleges and Universities."

18. Mike Dockry interview, June 7, 2013.

19. Dockry interview; Hosmer, "Creating Indian Entrepreneurs," 1–5.

20. Dockry interview; College of the Menominee Nation, Sustainable Development Institute, Center for First Americans Forestlands, *Center for First Americans Forestlands: A College of Menominee Nation US Forest Service Partnership.*

21. Dockry interview; "Center for First Americans Forestlands Select Accomplishments 2005–2012," updated 2012, memorandum provided by Mike Dockry.

22. Dockry interview.

23. Dale Kanen interview, October 21, 2010. The Forest Service already employed TEK on many national forests by the year 2000. For an overview of several cases, see Lesko and Thakali, "Traditional Knowledge and Tribal Partnership, 281–301.

24. Kanen interview.

25. Clark interview, August 14, 2012.

26. "Forest Chief Praises Menominee Foresters."

27. Berkes, "Traditional Ecological Knowledge," 1–2.

28. Intertribal Timber Council, *FY 2004 Annual Report.*

29. Heady interview.

30. Clark interview, December 1, 2010.

31. Anderson, *Tending the Wild*, 4–7.

32. Ibid., 3–4.

33. Cunningham and Bagby, *Maidu Stewardship Project*; Little, "Maidu Indians"; Anderson, *Tending the Wild*, 315.

34. "Success Stories, ACT2 and the Maidu Stewardship Project."

35. Cunningham and Bagby, *Maidu Stewardship Project*; "Success Stories, ACT2 and the Maidu Stewardship Project."

36. Baker, "Growing Interest in Special Forest Products."

37. Wang, Anderson, and Jakes, "Heritage Management," 364–65.

38. "Memorandum of Agreement, The Klamath Tribes"; Les McConnell interview, August 24, 2012.

39. McConnell interview.

40. California Indian Basketweavers Association; California Indian Forest and Fire Management Council.

41. Merv George Jr. interview, August 27, 2012.

42. Sonia Tamez, e-mail message to author, March 6, 2013.

43. USDA, Forest Service, *Sierra Nevada Forest Plan Amendment*, 25–26.

44. Office of Tribal Relations, "Special Forest Products," briefing paper, n.d, OTR digital files; Sonia Tamez, e-mail message to author, March 6, 2013.

45. Mike Pool and Bernie Weingardt to Tribal Leaders, July 21, 2006, OTR digital files; Kalt, "Public Lands Traditional Gathering"; George interview.

46. George interview. The letters are contained in two three-ring binders in the OTR.

47. Fawn R. Sharp, President, Quinault Indian Nation to Director, Forest Management Staff, December 18, 2007, and Cory J. Albright, Counsel for the Nisqually Indian Tribe et al., December 20, 2007, OTR binders.

48. John Barnett, General Council Chair, Cowlitz Indian Tribe to Director, Forest Management Staff, January 5, 2008, OTR binders.

49. Connie Reid, Archeologist, North Kaibab Ranger District to wospecialproducts @fs.fed.us (e-mail), December 5, 2007, OTR binders.

50. Monica Marquez, Director of Cultural Preservation, Vincent Randall, Apache Culture, Delores Plunkett, Yavapai Culture, and Chris Coder, Tribal Archaeologist, to Mr. Fitzgerald (e-mail), December 14, 2007, OTR binders.

51. USDA Forest Service, "Briefing Paper, Tribal Aspects of the New Forest Service Regulation on Special Forest Products (SFP)," July 22, 2009, OTR digital files; Marsha Butterfield interview, December 2, 2010.

52. "Tribal Relations Consultation Schedules"; Butterfield interview.

53. Clark interview.

54. Ibid.

55. "New Orleans District Ranger"; Harris, *Northwest Forest Plan*, 111.

BIBLIOGRAPHY

INTERVIEWS

Autrey, John, October 28, 2010

Bradbury, Christine, August 23, 2012

Bosworth, Dale N., June 9, 2014

Butterfield, Marsha, December 2, 2010

Clark, Fred, December 1, 2010, and
    August 14, 2012

Dockry, Mike, June 7, 2013

FireCloud, Dorothy, June 10, 2013

George, Merv, Jr., August 27, 2012

Harris, Gary, August 24, 2012

Heady, Larry, June 12, 2014

Holtrop, Joel, December 3, 2010

Hubbard, Jim, December 3, 2010

Johnson, Susan, October 6, 2012

Jones, Ira, October 22, 2012

Kanen, Dale, October 21, 2010

Lawrence, Keith, August 22, 2012

McCallum, Mark, August 7, 2012

McConnell, Les, August 24, 2012

Meza, Dan, March 8, 2013

Monahan, Ruth, August 7, 2012

Morishima, Gary S., March 21, 2013

Owen, Wayne, August 8, 2012

Parsons, Mit, October 2, 2012

Pendleton, Beth, August 8, 2012

Petershoare, Lillian, August 7, 2012

Rasure, Nora, August 24, 2012

Sanderson, Rob, August 8, 2012

Schroeder, Robert, August 8, 2012

Tamez, Sonia, August 31, 2012

Thomas, Ed, August 8, 2012

Turek, Mike, August 27, 2012

Vanderberg, Cheryl, October 19, 2012

Walker, Waldo, August 24, 2012

REFERENCES

"Action Plan to Implement the Memorandum of Understanding Regarding Interagency Coordination and Collaboration for the Protection of Indian Sacred Sites." Accessed March 5, 2013. http://www.doi.gov/news/upload/SS-MOU-Action-Plan -March-5-2013.pdf.

Adams, E. Charles. "United States Forest Service: Programmatic Issues Concerning Native Americans." In *Tools to Manage the Past: Research Priorities for Cultural Resources Management in the Southwest*, edited by Joseph A. Tainter and R. H. Hamre, 32–35. USDA Forest Service General Technical Report RM-164. Fort Collins, CO: USDA Forest Service, Rocky Mountain Forest and Range Experiment Station, 1988.

Adams, E. Charles, Elizabeth Brandt, Edmund Ladd, Terrance Leonard, Peter J. Pilles Jr., and Sonia Tamez. "Modeling Solutions to Indian Needs Concerning Cultural and Natural Resources on Forest Service and Other Public Lands." In *Tools to Manage the Past: Research Priorities for Cultural Resources Management in the Southwest*, edited by Joseph A. Tainter and R. H. Hamre, 41–51. USDA Forest Service General Technical Report RM-164. Fort Collins, CO: USDA Forest Service, Rocky Mountain Forest and Range Experiment Station, 1988.

Ahtone, Tristan. "Paying Attention to the Native American Vote." *Alaska Natives Commission, Final Report*. Anchorage: Alaska Natives Commission, 1994. Accessed November 4, 2008. http://www.pbs.org/frontlineworld/election2008/2008/11/pay ing-attention-to-the-n.html.

Anderson, M. Kat. *Tending the Wild: Native American Knowledge and the Management of California's Natural Resources*. Berkeley: University of California Press, 2005.

Anquoe, Bunty. "Sacred Sites in Danger." *Indian Country Today*, March 3, 1993.

Armstrong, Fred. "Fish and Wildlife Conservation Agreements in Alaska." In *Transactions of the 64th North American Wildlife and Natural Resources Conference*, edited by Richard E. McCabe and Samantha E. Loos, 420–29. Washington, DC: Wildlife Management Institute, 1999.

Babcock, William A., Timothy F. Light, Manuel A. Machado, Cristina M. Thomsen, Jeffrey A. Weldon, and Gary D. Williams. *The Forests of the Nez Perce: Forest Resource Management on the Nez Perce Reservation 1855–1988*. Report prepared for the Nez Perce Tribe. Missoula: Heritage Research Center, 1991.

Baker, Beth. "Growing Interest in Special Forest Products Yields New Management Challenges." *BioScience* 48, no. 9 (September 1998): 674.

Barker, Rocky. "Battle for Bighorns." *National Wildlife* 49, no. 5 (August/September 2011): 34–35.

Basso, Keith H. *Wisdom Sits in Places: Landscape and Language Among the Western Apache*. Albuquerque: University of New Mexico Press, 1996.

Baum, Dan. "Sacred Places." *Mother Jones* 17 (March/April 1992): 32–38.

Beche, Greg. "A Shortage of Solitude." *Progressive* 54 (April 1990): 22.

Becker, Dale M. "Fish and Wildlife Management on Tribal Lands, Opening Remarks." In *Transactions of the 64th North American Wildlife and Natural Resources Conference*, edited by Richard E. McCabe and Samantha E. Loos, 395–97. Washington, DC: Wildlife Management Institute, 1999.

Becker, Dennis, Dalia Abbas, Kathleen E. Halvorsen, Pamela J. Jakes, Sarah M. McCaffrey, and Casandra Mosely. "Characterizing Lessons Learned from Federal Biomass Removal Projects." *JFSP Research Project Reports*, paper 105. http://digitalcommons.unl.edu/cgi/viewcontent.cgi?article=1104&context=jfspresearch.

Berkes, Fikret. "Traditional Ecological Knowledge in Perspective." In *Traditional Ecological Knowledge: Concepts and Cases*, edited by John T. Inglis, 1–10. Ottawa: IDRC Books, 1993.

Bosworth, Dale. "Fires and Forest Health: Our Future is at Stake." *Fire Management Today* 63, no. 2 (Spring 2003): 4–11.

Brelsford, Taylor. "A Meaningful Voice: Federal Regional Councils and Subsistence Management." *Cultural Survival Quarterly* 22, no. 3 (Fall 1998): 72.

Brinkley, Douglas. *The Wilderness Warrior: Theodore Roosevelt and the Crusade for America*. New York: Harpers Collins, 2009.

Bruggers, James. "Forest Service Steps on Blackfeet." *Progressive* 51 (April 1987): 14.

———. "The Salish-Kootenai Comeback." *Sierra* 72 (July/August 1987): 23–25.

Burt, Larry W. *Tribalism in Crisis: Federal Indian Policy, 1953–1961*. Albuquerque: University of New Mexico Press, 1982.

Burton, Lloyd. *Worship and Wilderness: Culture, Religion and Law in Public Lands Management*. Madison: University of Wisconsin Press, 2002.

California Indian Basketweavers Association. http://www.ciba.org.

California Indian Forest and Fire Management Council (CIFFMC). http://ciffmc.stormloader.com/FrontPage.html.

Capriccioso, Rob. "Snowy Relations on Sacred Site Development." *Indian Country Today*, April 7, 2010.

"Carol Jorgensen Scholarship for Environmental Stewardship." Society of American Indian Government Employees. http://www.saige.org/member-resources/scholarships/.

"Carol Paddock Jorgensen." *Juneau Empire*, September 15, 2009.

Castile, George Pierre. *Taking Charge: Native American Self-Determination and Federal Indian Policy, 1975–1993*. Tucson: University of Arizona Press, 2006.

———. *To Show Heart: Native American Self-Determination and Federal Indian Policy 1960–1975.* Tucson: University of Arizona Press, 1998.

Castillo, Edward D. "Short Overview of California Indian History." California Native American Heritage Commission. 1998. http://www.hazardmitigation.oes. ca.gov/califindian.html.

Catton, Theodore. *Inhabited Wilderness: Indians, Eskimos, and National Parks in Alaska.* Albuquerque: University of New Mexico Press, 1997.

———. *National Park, City Playground: Mount Rainier in the Twentieth Century.* Seattle: University of Washington Press, 2006.

———. *To Make a Better Nation: An Administrative History of the Timbisha Shoshone Homeland Act.* Missoula: University of Montana Printing and Graphic Services, 2009.

Catton, Theodore, and Ann Hubber. *Commemoration and Preservation: An Administrative History of Big Hole National Battlefield.* Missoula, MT: Historical Research Associates, 1999.

Catton, Theodore, and Lisa Mighetto. *The Fish and Wildlife Job on the National Forests: A Century of Game and Fish Conservation, Habitat Protection, and Ecosystem Management.* Washington, DC: USDA Forest Service, 1998.

"CCC Waives Residence Requirement." *Ketchikan Alaska Chronicle,* June 22, 1937.

Clarke, Jeanne Nienaber, and Daniel McCool. *Staking out the Terrain: Power Differentials Among Natural Resource Management Agencies.* Albany: State University of New York Press, 1985.

Clinton, William J. "Remarks to Native American and Native Alaskan Tribal Leaders," April 29, 1994. *William J. Clinton: 1994.* Public Papers of the Presidents of the United States 1994, bk. 1. Washington, DC: Government Printing Office, 1995.

Clow, Richmond L. "Colorado Game Laws and the Dispossession of the Inherent Hunting Right of the White River and Uncompahgre Utes." In *Trusteeship in Change: Toward Tribal Autonomy in Resource Management,* edited by Richmond L. Clow and Imre Sutton, 15–34. Boulder: University Press of Colorado, 2001.

Collier, John, Ward Shepard, and Robert Marshall. "The Indians and Their Lands." *Journal of Forestry* 31 (December 1933): 905–10.

Council of Western State Foresters. http://www.westernstateforesters.org.

Cox, Thomas R., Robert S. Maxwell, Phillip Dennon Thomas, and Joseph J. Malone. *This Well-Wooded Land: Americans and Their Forests from Colonial Times to the Present.* Lincoln: University of Nebraska Press, 1985.

Crespi, Muriel. "Saving Sacred Places." *National Parks* 66 (July/August 1991): 18–19.

Crichton, Kyle. "Storm over Alaska." *Collier's* 115 (March 31, 1945): 75.

Cronon, William. *Changes in the Land: Indians, Colonists, and the Ecology of New England.* New York: Hill and Wang, 1983.

Cunningham, Farrell, and Katie Bagby. "The Maidu Stewardship Project: Blending of Two Knowledge Systems in Forest Management." Taylorsville, CA: Pacific West Community Forestry Center, 2004. Accessed June 20, 2013 (no longer posted). http://www.sierrainstitute.us/archives/MCDG_Final_Report_5_04.pdf.

Curry, Andrew. "The Last of the Yahi." *U.S. News and World Report* 129, no. 7 (August 21, 2000): 56.

Dana, Samuel Trask, and Sally K. Fairfax. *Forest and Range Policy: Its Development in the United States.* 2nd ed. New York: McGraw-Hill, 1980.

Davis, Norah Deakin. "The Making of a Revolutionary." *American Forests* 95 (November/December 1989): 39.

Davis, Shelton H. "Self-Determination and Resources: A Survey of U.S. Indian Forestry." *Cultural Survival Quarterly* 17, no. 1 (Spring 1993): 24–27.

De Laguna, Frederica. "Tlingit." In *Handbook of the North American Indians.* Vol. 7, *Northwest Coast*, edited by Wayne Suttles, 203–28. Washington, DC: Smithsonian Institution, 1990.

Deloria, Vine, Jr. *Custer Died for Your Sins: An Indian Manifesto.* New York: MacMillan, 1969. Reprint, Norman: University of Oklahoma Press, 1988.

DeMallie, Raymond J., ed. *The Sixth Grandfather: Black Elk's Teachings Given to John G. Neihardt.* Lincoln: University of Nebraska Press, 1984.

Dougherty, John. "Star Gate." *Phoenix New Times*, June 16, 1993.

Dubin, Margaret. "Preserving California's Indian Heritage: The Native American Heritage Commission." *News from Native California* 21, no. 3 (Spring 2008): 24.

Duncan, Sally L., and Jonathan R. Thompson. "Forest Plans and Ad Hoc Scientist Groups in the 1990s: Coping with the Forest Service Viability Clause." *Forest Policy and Economics* 9 (2006): 32–41.

Durham, Patrick. "The Development of Quality Fishery and Wildlife Management Programs within Indian Country." In *Transactions of the 64th North American Wildlife and Natural Resources Conference*, edited by Richard E. McCabe and Samantha E. Loos, 398–407. Washington, DC: Wildlife Management Institute, 1999.

Echo-Hawk, Walter. *In the Courts of the Conqueror: The Ten Worst Indian Law Cases Ever Decided.* Golden, CO: Fulcrum, 2010.

Emery, Maria, and Alan Pierce. "Interrupting the Telos: Locating Subsistence in Contemporary U.S. Forests." *Environment and Planning* 37, no. 6 (June 2005): 981–93.

Ervin, Keith. "Spirit Dancers and the Law." *Sierra* 73 (November/December 1988): 107.

Falk, Donald. "*Lyng v. Northwest Indian Cemetery Protective Association*: Bulldozing First Amendment Protection of Indian Sacred Lands." *Ecology Law Quarterly* 16 (1989): 515–70.

Fall, James A. "The Division of Subsistence of the Alaska Department of Fish and Game: An Overview of Its Research Program and Findings, 1980–1990." *Arctic Anthropology* 27, no. 2 (1990): 68–92.

"First Aid for Totems." *New York Times*, January 8, 1941.

Fisher, Andrew H. "The 1932 Handshake Agreement: Yakama Indian Treaty Rights and Forest Service Policy in the Pacific Northwest." *Western Historical Quarterly* 28, no. 2 (Summer 1997): 187–217.

———. "Working in the Indian Way: The Southwest Forest Firefighters Program and Native American Wage Labor." *Journal of Arizona History* 41, no. 2 (Summer 2000): 121–48.

Fixico, Donald L. *The Invasion of Indian Country in the Twentieth Century: American Capitalism and Tribal Natural Resources.* Niwot: University Press of Colorado, 1998.

———. *Termination and Relocation: Federal Indian Policy, 1945–1960.* Albuquerque: University of New Mexico Press, 1986.

"Forest Chief Praises Menominee Foresters." *Tribal College Journal* 16, no. 3 (Spring 2005): 35–36.

Forest History Society. "Inventory of the Gene Bernardi Papers 1971–1991." http://www.foresthistory.org/ead/Bernardi_Gene.html.

"Forest Service and Tribal Government Leaders to Meet." February 3, 2005. http://www.fs.usda.gov/detail/blackhills/news-events/?cid=FSM9_013281.

Franklin, Jerry. "Toward a New Forestry." *American Forests* 95 (November/December 1989): 37–44.

Freeman, Richard. "The EcoFactory: The United States Forest Service and the Political Construction of Ecosystem Management." *Environmental History* 7, no. 4 (October 2002): 632–59.

Freemuth, John. "The Emergence of Ecosystem Management: Reinterpreting the Gospel?" *Society and Natural Resources* 9 (1996): 411–17.

Glowacka, Maria, Dorothy Washburn, and Justin Richland. "*Nuvatukya'ovi*, San Francisco Peaks: Balancing Western Economies with Native American Spiritualities." *Current Anthropology* 50, no. 4 (August 2009): 547–61.

Godfrey, Anthony. *A Forestry History of Ten Wisconsin Indian Reservations under the Great Lakes Agency, Precontact to the Present.* Report prepared for the U.S. Department of the Interior, Bureau of Indian Affairs. Salt Lake City: U.S. West Research, 1996.

Gordon-McCutchan, R. C. *The Taos Indians and the Battle for Blue Lake.* Santa Fe, NM: Red Crane Books, 1995.

"Grants: Award Summary, Confederated Tribes of Warm Springs Reservation of Oregon." 1st quarter 2013. Accessed June 13, 2013 (no longer posted). http://www.recovery.gov/transparency/Recovery/Data/pages.

Graybill, Andrew. "'Strong on the Merits and Powerfully Symbolic': The Return of Blue Lake to Taos Pueblo." *New Mexico Historical Review* 76, no. 2 (April 2001): 126–60.

Greiser, Sally Thompson, and T. Weber Greiser. "Two Views of the World." In *Traditional Cultural Properties: What You Do and How We Think*, edited by Pat Parker. Special issue, *CRM* 16 (1993).

Gulliford, Andrew. *Sacred Objects and Sacred Places: Preserving Tribal Traditions*. Boulder: University Press of Colorado, 2000.

Gunsky, Frederic R. "The Legacy of Ishi." *Living Wilderness* 40 (January 1977): 4–11.

Harjo, Susan Shawn. "American Indian Religious Freedom Act after Twenty-Five Years: An Introduction." *Wicazo Sa Review* 19, no. 2 (August 2004): 129–36.

Harmon, Frank J. "What Should Foresters Wear? The Forest Service's Seventy-Five-Year Search for a Uniform." *Journal of Forest History* 24 (October 1980): 188–99.

Harris, Gary, comp. *Northwest Forest Plan—The First Fifteen Years (1994–2008): Effectiveness of Federal-Tribal Relationship*. Technical Publication R6-RPM-TP-01–2011. Washington, DC: Government Printing Office, 2011.

Haycox, Stephen W. "Economic Development and Indian Land Rights in Modern Alaska: The 1947 Tongass Timber Act." *Western Historical Quarterly* 21, no. 1 (1990): 21–46.

Hays, Samuel P. *The American People and the National Forests: The First Century of the U.S. Forest Service*. Pittsburgh, PA: University of Pittsburgh Press, 2009.

"Healthy Forests Restoration Act of 2003," December 3, 2003, 117 Stat., 1905. http://legcounsel.house.gov/Comps/Healthy%20Forests%20Restoration%20Act%20Of%202003.pdf.

Herz, Richard. "Legal Protection for Indigenous Cultures: Sacred Sites and Communal Rights." *Virginia Law Review* 79, no. 3 (April 1993): 691–716.

Hirt, Paul W. "Biopolitics: A Case Study of Political Influence on Forest Management Decisions, Coronado National Forest, Arizona, 1980s–1990s." In *Forests Under Fire: A Century of Ecosystem Mismanagement in the Southwest*, edited by Christopher J. Huggard and Arthur R. Gómez, 241–86. Tucson: University of Arizona Press, 2001.

———. *A Conspiracy of Optimism: Management of the National Forests since World War Two*. Lincoln: University of Nebraska Press, 1994.

"History." Leech Lake Band of Ojibwe, 2012. http:/www.llojibwe.com.

Hosmer, Brian C. "Creating Indian Entrepreneurs: Menominees, Neopit Mills, and Timber Exploitation, 1890–1915." *American Indian Culture and Research Journal* 15, no. 1 (1991): 1–28.

Hoxie, Frederick E. *A Final Promise: The Campaign to Assimilate the Indians, 1880–1920*. Lincoln: University of Nebraska Press, 1984.

Hughes, J. Donald, and Jim Swan. "How Much of the Earth Is Sacred Space?" *Environmental Review* 4, no. 4 (Winter 1986): 247–59.

"Interagency MOU and Action Plan Guide Protection of Indian Sacred Sites." *Tribal Relations News* (Spring 2013). http://www.fs.fed.us/spf/tribalrelations/documents/news/Spring2013OTRNewsletter.pdf.

Intertribal Timber Council. "Fulfilling the Promise of the Tribal Forest Protection Act of 2004." April 2013. Accessed June 6, 2014 (no longer posted). Update as, "Tribal Forest Protection Act," posted March 29, 2015 (no longer posted). http://www.itc.net.org/issues_projects/issues_2/tfpareports.html.

———. *FY 2003 Annual Report.* http:/www.itcnet.org/support/support_impact.html.

———. *FY 2004 Annual Report.* http://ww.itcnet.org/support/support_impact.html.

Jacoby, Karl. *Crimes Against Nature: Squatters, Poachers, Thieves, and the Hidden History of American Conservation.* Berkeley: University of California Press, 2001.

Jett, Stephen C. "Navajo Sacred Places: Management and Interpretation of Mythic History." *Public Historian* 17, no. 2 (Spring 1995): 39–47.

Johnson, Troy R. *The American Indian Occupation of Alcatraz Island: Red Power and Self-Determination.* Lincoln: University of Nebraska Press, 1996.

Jorgensen, Carol. "An Alaska Native View on Subsistence." In *Alaska Region Overview*, R10-MR-13. Juneau: USDA Forest Service, Alaska Region, 2001.

Kalt, Jennifer. "Public Lands Traditional Gathering Policy Finalized." *News from Native California* 20, no. 4 (Summer 2007): 7–8.

Kappler, Charles J., comp. *Indian Affairs: Laws and Treaties.* 7 vols. Washington, DC: Smithsonian Institution, 1904–71.

Kawamura, Hiroaki. "Symbolic and Political Ecology Among Contemporary Nez Perce Indians in Idaho, USA: Functions and Meanings of Hunting, Fishing, and Gathering Practices." *Agriculture and Human Values* 21, no. 2/3 (2004): 157–69.

Kennedy, James J., and Thomas M. Quigley. "Evolution of USDA Forest Service Organizational Culture and Adaptation Issues in Embracing an Ecosystem Management Paradigm." *Landscape and Urban Planning* 40 (1998): 113–22.

Kephart, George S. "Forestry on the Klamath Indian Reservation." *Journal of Forestry* 39 (November 1941): 896–99.

King, Thomas F. *Places that Count: Traditional Cultural Properties in Cultural Resource Management.* New York: Roman and Littlefield, 2003.

Kinney, J. P. *A Continent Lost—A Civilization Won: Indian Land Tenure in America.* Baltimore: Johns Hopkins Press, 1937.

———. "E.C.W. on Indian Reservations." *Journal of Forestry* 31 (December 1933): 911–14.

———. "Forestry on Indian Reservations." *Forestry Quarterly* 10, no. 3 (September 1912): 471–77.

————. *Indian Forest and Range: A History of the Administration and Conservation of the Redman's Heritage.* Washington, DC: Forestry Enterprises, 1950.

Krahe, Diane L. "Last Refuge: The Uneasy Embrace of Indian Lands by the National Wilderness Movement, 1937–1965." PhD diss., Washington State University, 2005.

————. "A Sovereign Prescription for Preservation: The Mission Mountains Tribal Wilderness." In *Trusteeship in Change: Toward Tribal Autonomy in Resource Management*, edited by Richmond L. Clow and Imre Sutton, 195–221. Boulder: University Press of Colorado, 2001.

Krahe, Diane L., and Theodore Catton. *Little Gem of the Cascades: An Administrative History of Lassen Volcanic National Park.* Report prepared for the National Park Service through the Rocky Mountain Cooperative Ecosystem Studies Unit. Mineral, CA: Lassen Volcanic National Park, 2010.

Krech, Shepard, III. *The Ecological Indian: Myth and History.* New York: Norton, 1999.

Krehbiel-Burton, Lenzy. "Symposium Provides Forum to Discuss Role of Sacred Sites, Preservation." *Native American Times*, October 25, 2013.

Lawler, Andrew. "A Tale of Two Skeletons." *Science* 330 (October 8, 2010): 171–72.

Lawlor, James. "Snowbowl: Can't Use Snow Made from Sewage, Court Says." *Planning* (June 2007): 48–52.

Lee, Tanya. "From the Redwood Forests to the Gulf Stream Waters." *News from Indian Country* (Hayward, Wisconsin), November 1, 2004.

Lesko, Lawrence M., and Renée G. Thakali. "Traditional Knowledge and Tribal Partnership on the Kaibab National Forest with an Emphasis on the Hopi Interagency Management." In *Trusteeship in Change: Toward Tribal Autonomy in Resource Management*, edited by Richmond L. Clow and Imre Sutton, 281–301. Boulder: University Press of Colorado, 2001.

LeVan, Susan, and JoAnn Benisch. *2009 Woody Biomass Utilization Status Report for 2005, 2006, and 2007 Grant Program.* Madison, WI: USDA Forest Service, S&PF, Technology Marketing Unit, 2009.

Lewis, David Rich. "Native Americans and the Environment: A Survey of Twentieth Century Issues." *American Indian Quarterly* 19, no. 3 (Summer 1995): 423–50.

Lipscomb, Brian, and Dale M. Becker. "Tribal Fish and Wildlife Management in the Pacific Northwest." *Transactions of the 64th North American Wildlife and Natural Resources Conference*, edited by Richard E. McCabe and Samantha E. Loos, 458–65. Washington, DC: Wildlife Management Institute, 1999.

Little, Jane Braxton. "Maidu Indians Work to Restore Their Land and Culture." *American News Service*, July 20, 2000. http://www.berkshirepublishing.com/ans/HTMView.asp?parItem=S031000558A.

————. "Un-Common Ground." *American Forests* 109, no. 2 (Summer 2003): 45–51.

MacCleery, Doug. "Re-inventing the United States Forest Service: Evolution from Custodial Management, to Production Forestry, to Ecosystem Management." 2008. http://www.fao.org/docrep/010/ai412e/AI412E06.htm.

Makley, Matthew S., and Michael J. Makley. *Cave Rock: Climbers, Courts, and a Washoe Indian Sacred Place*. Reno: University of Nevada Press, 2010.

Manandhar, Sharmina. "Tenth Annual 'To Bridge a Gap' Conference Planned." 2013. https://www.chickasaw.net/News/Press-Releases/2011-Press-Releases/Tenth -Annual-To-Bridge-a-Gap-Conference-Planned.aspx.

Marshall, Robert. "Ecology and the Indians." *Ecology* 18, no. 1 (January 1937): 159–62.

Martinez, Toby, and Lyle Laverty. *Strategic Plan for Western State and Private Forestry Leadership Coordination, FY 99 Revision*. Denver: Council of Western State Foresters and USDA Forest Service, 1999.

McDonnell, Janet A. *The Dispossession of the American Indian, 1887–1934*. Bloomington: Indiana University Press, 1991.

McLaughlin, James. *My Friend the Indian*. Boston: Houghton, 1910.

McPherson, Robert S. *Sacred Land, Sacred View: Navajo Perceptions of the Four Corners Region*. Provo, UT: Charles Redd Center for Western Studies, Brigham Young University, 1992.

McQuillan, Alan G. "American Indian Timber Management Policy: Its Evolution in the Context of U.S. Forest History." In *Trusteeship in Change: Toward Tribal Autonomy in Resource Management*, edited by Richmond L. Clow and Imre Sutton, 73–102. Boulder: University Press of Colorado, 2001.

"Memorandum of Agreement, The Klamath Tribes and U.S. Forest Service." February 19, 1999 as amended February 17, 2005. http://www.klamathtribes.org/documents/ Special_Use_Permit.pdf.

"Memorandum of Understanding Among the U.S. Department of Defense, U.S. Department of the Interior, U.S. Department of Agriculture, and U.S. Department of Energy, and the Advisory Council on Historic Preservation Regarding Interagency Coordination and Collaboration for the Protection of Indian Sacred Sites." March 5, 2013. http://www.doi.gov/news/upload/SS-MOU-Action-Plan -March-5-2013.pdf.

Miller, Char. *Gifford Pinchot and the Making of Modern Environmentalism*. Washington, DC: Island Press, 2001.

———. "The Once and Future Forest Service: Land-Management Policies and Politics in Contemporary America." *Journal of Policy History* 21, no. 1 (2009): 89–104.

Miller, Robert J. *Native America, Discovered and Conquered: Thomas Jefferson, Lewis and Clark, and Manifest Destiny*. Westport, CT: Praeger, 2006.

Montana, Cate. "Nez Perce and Grey Wolf: Both Banished, They Recover Together." *Indian Country Today*, February 15–22, 1999.

Moore, Jackson W. "The National Park Service's Native American Policy: A Status Report." *CRM Bulletin* 1, no. 3 (September 1978): 1–3.

Morishima, Gary S. "Indian Forestry: From Paternalism to Self-Determination." *Journal of Forestry* 95, no. 11 (November 1997): 4–9.

———. "Promises to Keep: Paradigms and Problems with Coordinated Resource Management in Indian Country." *Evergreen* (June 1998): 22–25.

Morning Star Institute. "Protect Native American Sacred Places." June 15, 2012. http://www.narf.org/nill/resources/Prayer_Sacred_Sites.pdf.

"Morrell Says Indians are CCC Problems." *Daily Alaska Empire* (Juneau), June 25, 1937.

Morris, Virginia. "An Anthropological Culture Shift." *Science* 264 (April 1994): 20–22.

Motanic, Don. "The National Indian Forest Resources Management Act: What Was and What Will Be." *Evergreen* (June 1998): 26–27.

Nagel, Joane. *American Indian Ethnic Renewal: Red Power and the Resurgence of Identity and Culture.* New York: Oxford University Press, 1996.

Nash, Roderick Frazier. *Wilderness and the American Mind.* 4th ed. New Haven, CT: Yale University Press, 2001.

Naske, Claus-M. and Herman E. Slotnik. *Alaska: A History of the 49th State.* 2nd ed. Norman: University of Oklahoma Press, 1987.

National Association of State Foresters. "2009 S and PF Annual Report." March 2009. http://www.stateforesters.org/FY2009-SPF-Annual-Report.

National Congress of American Indians. "Comments in Response to the United States Department of State Draft Supplemental Environmental Impact Statement (DSEIS) for the Keystone XL Project Applicant for Presidential Permit: TransCanada Keystone Pipeline, LP released on March 1, 2013." April 22, 2013. http://www.ncai.org/attachments/Testimonial_UkbhoziSbdrsSGfibMHfjfdK vjlZBHcrVkGDiYgBFhDNBpKeYEJ_KEYSTONE%20COMMENTS%20 APRIL%20222013%20-%20FINAL_1.2.pdf.

Neihardt, John G. *Black Elk Speaks: Being the Life Story of a Holy Man of the Oglala Sioux.* New York: William Morrow, 1932. Reprint, Lincoln: University of Nebraska Press, 1972.

Newell, Alan. "Indian Forest Policy Rooted in Federal Ambivalence." *Evergreen* (June 1998): 19–20.

Newell, Alan, Richmond L. Clow, and Richard N. Ellis. *A Forest in Trust: Three-Quarters of a Century of Indian Forestry, 1910–1986.* Report prepared for U.S. Department of the Interior, Bureau of Indian Affairs, Division of Forestry. Missoula, MT: Historical Research Associates, 1986.

"New Orleans District Ranger." September 11, 2009. http://www.fs.usda.gov/detail/srnf/news-events/?cid=STELPRDB5090751.

"News Release: Protest Halts Snowbowl Wastewater Pipeline Construction; End Destruction and Desecration of Holy San Francisco Peaks." June 20, 2011. http://www.indigenousaction.org/news-release-protest-halts-snowbowl-wastewater-pipeline-construction/.

———. "Indian Assails Morris Bill." July 6, 1902.

Norgaard, Kari Marie. "The Politics of Invasive Weed Management: Gender, Race, and Risk Perception in Rural California." *Rural Sociology* 72, no. 3 (2007): 450–77.

Norris, Frank. *Alaska Subsistence: A National Park Service Management History.* Anchorage: Alaska Support Office, National Park Service, U.S. Department of the Interior, 2002.

———. "A Victim of Nature and Bureaucracy: The Short, Sad History of Old Kasaan National Monument." Paper given at annual meeting of the Alaska Historical Society, Ketchikan, Alaska, October 7, 2000.

O'Brien, Sharon. *American Indian Tribal Governments.* Norman: University of Oklahoma Press, 1989.

Office of Management and Budget. *Budget of the United States Government, Fiscal Year 2005.* https://www.whitehouse.gov/sites/default/files/omb/budget/fy2005/pdf/hist.pdf.

Oregon Forest Resources Institute. *Woody Biomass Energy: A Renewable Resource to Help Meet Oregon's Energy Needs.* Portland: Oregon Forest Resources Institute, 2007.

"OTR Director's Corner." *Tribal Relations News* (Winter 2012): 1. http://www.fs.fed.us/spf/tribalrelations/documents/news/Winter2012OTRNewsletter.pdf.

Otto, John Solomon, and Augustus Marion Burns III. "Traditional Agricultural Practices in the Arkansas Highlands." *Journal of American Folklore* 94, no. 372 (1981): 166–87.

Pace, Felice. "Biomass Energy Production in the Interior West." *High Country News,* May 18, 2011.

Parman, Donald L. "The Indian and the Civilian Conservation Corps." *Pacific Historical Review* 40 (February 1971): 39–56.

———. *Indians and the American West in the Twentieth Century.* Bloomington: Indiana University Press, 1994.

Past and Present. *The Forests of the Nez Perce: A History of Forest Management on the Nez Perce Reservation, 1989–1999.* Report prepared for the Nez Perce Tribe. Missoula, MT: Past and Present, 2001.

Peerman, Dean. "Bare-Bones Imbroglio: Repatriating Indian Remains and Sacred Artifacts." *Christian Century* 107 (October 17, 1990): 935–38.

Peters, Christopher H. "Postscript: Toward a Sacred Lands Policy Initiative." In *Sacred Lands of Indian America*, edited by Jake Page, 1–5. New York: Abrams, 2001.

Petersen, James D. "Forestry in Indian Country: Progress and Promise." *Evergreen* (June 1998): 9–18.

———. "The New Pioneers: Hope Rises from the Ashes in Southwestern Forests." *Evergreen* (Summer 2002): 2–47.

Petershoare, Lillian. "The Alaska Tribal Leaders Committee." *SourDough Notes*. Spring 2010. http://www.fs.usda.gov/Internet/FSE_DOCUMENTS/stelprdb5250792.pdf.

Philp, Kenneth R. *John Collier's Crusade for Indian Reform, 1920–1954*. Tucson: University of Arizona Press, 1977.

———. "The New Deal and Alaskan Natives, 1936–1945." *Pacific Historical Review* 50 (August 1981): 309–27.

Pinchot, Gifford. *Breaking New Ground*. New York: Harcourt Brace, 1947.

———. "Report by the Forester." In *Annual Report of the Department of Agriculture for 1909*. Washington: Government Printing Office, 1910.

———. "Report of the Forester for 1903." In *Annual Reports of the Department of Agriculture 1903*. Washington: Government Printing Office, 1903.

———. "Report of the Forester for 1905." In *Annual Reports of the Department of Agriculture 1905*. Washington: Government Printing Office, 1905.

Pinchot Institute for Conservation. "An Introduction to the National Fire Plan: History, Structure, and Relevance to Communities." March 29, 2002. http://www.pinchot.org/pubs/26.

Pinkett, Harold T. *Gifford Pinchot: Private and Public Forester*. Urbana: University of Illinois Press, 1970.

Pinkham, Jaime A. *A Sense of Community*. Syracuse, NY: New York Center for Forestry Research and Development, 1996. http://www.uvm.edu/rsenr/nr6/Readings/Pinkham.pdf.

Pinkham, James. "Conserving Nature and Sustaining Communities." In *Sustaining Natural Resources in Global Contexts: The 1996 Plum Creek Lectures*, edited by Nick Baker. Missoula: School of Forestry, University of Montana, 1997.

Platt, Tony. *Grave Matters: Excavating California's Buried Past*. Berkeley, CA: Heyday, 2011.

Plaut, Ethan. "Tribal-Agency Confidentiality: A Catch-22 for Sacred Site Management." *Ecology Law Quarterly* 36, no. 1 (2009): 137–66.

Propper, Judith G. "The Program: Managing Cultural Resources in the Southwestern Region." In *Tools to Manage the Past: Research Priorities for Cultural Resources Management in the Southwest: Symposium Proceedings, May 2–6, 1988, Grand Canyon, Arizona*, edited by Joseph A. Tainter and R. H. Hamre. USDA Forest Service

General Technical Report RM-164. Fort Collins, CO: USDA Forest Service, Rocky Mountain Forest and Range Experiment Station, 1988.

Prucha, Francis Paul. *The Great Father: The United States Government and the American Indians*. Abr. ed. Lincoln: University of Nebraska Press, 1986.

Rakestraw, Lawrence. *A History of the United States Forest Service in Alaska*. Anchorage: Alaska Historical Commission, Department of Education, State of Alaska, and the Alaska Region, Forest Service, United States Department of Agriculture, 1981. Reprint, Juneau: USDA Forest Service, 2002.

Rambler, Sandra. "Mount Graham Coalition Included in Notice of Intent to Sue U.S. Forest Service." *Arizona Silver Belt* (Globe, Arizona), January 12, 2011. http://www.silverbelt.com/fe_view_article_window.php?story_id=2264&page_id=77&heading=0.

Rankel, Gary L. "Tribal Fish and Wildlife Management in the United States: Current Status and Trends." *Transactions of the 64th North American Wildlife and Natural Resources Conference*, edited by Richard E. McCabe and Samantha E. Loos, 408–19. Washington, DC: Wildlife Management Institute, 1999.

Reynolds, Jerry. "Washington in Brief." *Indian Country Today* (Oneida, New York), August 4, 2004.

"Richard Oakes (activist)." http://en.wikipedia.org/wiki/Richard_Oakes_%28activist %29.

"Richard Pratt: 'Kill the Indian, Save the Man.'" http://socrates.bmcc.cuny.edu/bfried heim/pratt.htm.

Riggs, Keith. "Forest Service Presents Ceremonial Staffs." *SourDough Notes* (Spring 2008). http://www.fs.usda.gov/Internet/FSE_DOCUMENTS/stelprdb5250792.pdf.

Rogers, Kristine O. "Native American Collaboration in Cultural Resource Protection in the Columbia River Gorge National Scenic Area." *Vermont Law Review* 17 (Spring 1993): 741–800.

Rothman, Hal. *America's National Monuments: The Politics of Preservation*. Lawrence: University Press of Kansas, 1989.

Sabalow, Ryan. "A Long History of Loss for Pit River Tribe." *Redding Record-Searchlight*, September 17, 2011.

Salka, William A. "Mission Evolution: The United States Forest Service's Response to Crisis." *Review of Policy Research* 21, no. 2 (2004): 221–32.

Salmond, John A. *The Civilian Conservation Corps, 1933–1942: A New Deal Case Study*. Durham, NC: Duke University Press, 1967.

Sax, Joseph L., and Robert B. Keiter. "The Realities of Regional Resource Management: Glacier National Park and Its Neighbors Revisited." *Ecology Law Quarterly* 33, no. 2 (2006): 233–312.

Schoennagel, Tania, Thomas T. Veblen, and William H. Romme. "The Interaction of Fire, Fuels, and Climate Across Rocky Mountain Forests." *BioScience* 54, no. 7 (July 2004): 661–76.

Schommer, Tim. "Reestablishment of Big Horn Sheep to Hells Canyon." http://www .fs.usda.gov/detail/wallowa-whitman/landmanagement/resourcemanagement/ ?cid=stelprdb5287260.

Schroeder, Robert F., and Matthew Kookesh. "Subsistence Harvest and Use of Fish and Wildlife Resources and the Effects of Forest Management in Hoonah, Alaska." Technical Paper 142. Juneau: Alaska Department of Fish and Game, Division of Subsistence, 1990.

Schwartz, E. A. "Red Atlantis Revisited: Community and Culture in the Writings of John Collier." *American Indian Quarterly* 18, no. 4 (Fall 1994): 507–30.

Searle, Newell. "Minnesota National Forest: The Politics of Compromise, 1898–1908." *Minnesota History* 42, no. 7 (Fall 1971): 243–57.

"Secretary Vilsack Addresses White House Tribal Nations Conference—Unveils Sacred Sites Report." Farm Service Agency, December 6, 2012. https://fsa.blogs .govdelivery.com/2012/12/06/secretary-vilsack-addresses-white-house-tribal -nations-conference-unveils-sacred-sites-report/.

"Sentiment Grows for Repeal of P. L. 587." *American Forests* 63 (December 1957): 25.

Sessions, John. "Are Indian Forests and Forest Management Improving?" *Evergreen* (Winter 2005–6): 32–37.

Sheehan, Bernard. *Seeds of Extinction: Jeffersonian Philanthropy and the American Indian*. New York: Norton, 1974.

Sherman, E. A. "A Plan for the Disposal of Indian Reservation Timberlands." *Journal of Forestry* 29, no. 4 (April 1921): 354–66.

Sherwood, Morgan. *Big Game in Alaska: A History of Wildlife and People*. New Haven, CT: Yale University Press, 1981.

Sigler, William F. *Wildlife Law Enforcement*. 3rd ed. Dubuque, IA: Brown, 1980.

Silva, Nattie, et al., "TMO Revisited: An Evaluation Report & Building Blocks to Meet 21st Century Challenges." Memorandum, October 1, 1998. http://www .fs.fed.us/cr/correspondence/final_tmo_report.html.

Simon, Richard. "Fire Spurs Bush's Long-Stalled 'Healthy Forests' Legislation." *Los Angeles Times*, November 2, 2003.

Skinner, Dave. "*Vive la difference*: How and Why Tribal Forestlands Are Managed Differently from Federal Forestlands." *Evergreen* (Winter 2005–6): 21–22.

Sloan, Gail. "Haskell Indian Nations University Offers Holistic Education in Natural Resources." *Evergreen* (June 1998): 48–49.

Smith, Jane L. "A New Smokehouse for Kake Culture Camp." *SourDough Notes* (Summer 2010): 41. http://www.fs.usda.gov/Internet/FSE_DOCUMENTS/stel prdb5275314.pdf.

Smith, Sherry L. *Hippies, Indians, and the Fight for Red Power.* New York: Oxford University Press, 2012.

Stapp, Darby C., and Michael S. Burney. *Tribal Cultural Resource Management: The Full Circle of Stewardship.* Walnut Creek, CA: Altamira, 2002.

"Statement of Suzan Shown Harjo, President, the Morning Star Institute, for the Oversight Hearing on Native American Sacred Places before the Committee on Indian Affairs, United States Senate, Washington, D.C., June 18, 2003." http://www.sacredland.org/PDFs/Harjo_Statement_SIAC.pdf.

Steen, Harold K. *An Interview with Jack Ward Thomas.* Durham, NC: Fire History Society, 2002.

———. *The U.S. Forest Service: A History.* Seattle: University of Washington Press, 1976.

Stein, Gary C. "The Indian Citizenship Act of 1924." *New Mexico Historical Review* 47, no. 3 (Summer 1972): 257–74.

"'Stop Fiddling; Save America's Forests'; Healthy Forests Act Wins Bipartisan House Approval." *Fort Apache Scout* (Whiteriver, Arizona), May 30, 2003.

Suagee, Dean B. "The Cultural Heritage of American Indian Tribes and the Preservation of Biological Diversity." *Arizona State Law Journal* 31 (Summer 1999): 485–524.

Subr-Sytsma, Mandy. "*In the Light of Reverence* and the Rhetoric of American Indian Religious Freedom." *Wicazo Sa Review* 28, no. 2 (Fall 2013): 60–86.

"Success Stories, ACT2 and the Maidu Stewardship Project." 2003. http://www.fs.fed.us/plan/par/2003/success/stories/act2.shtml.

Taliman, Valerie. "Sacred Landscapes." *Sierra* 87 (November/December 2002): 38–39.

Tamez, Sonia. "Forest Service and Native American Relationships: Considerations for Research." In *Tools to Manage the Past: Research Priorities for Cultural Resources Management in the Southwest. Symposium Proceedings, May 2–6, 1988, Grand Canyon, Arizona,* edited by Joseph A. Tainter and R. H. Hamre, 40–42. USDA Forest Service General Technical Report RM-164. Fort Collins, CO: USDA Forest Service, Rocky Mountain Forest and Range Experiment Station, 1988.

10-Year Comprehensive Strategy: A Collaborative Approach for Reducing Wildland Fire Risks to Communities and the Environment. August 2001. http://www.forestsand rangelands.gov/resources/plan/documents/7-19-en.pdf.

Thornton, Thomas E. "Alaska Native Subsistence: A Matter of Cultural Survival." *Cultural Survival Quarterly* 22, no. 3 (Fall 1998): 29–33.

Trennert, Robert A. *Alternative to Extinction: Federal Indian Policy and the Beginnings of the Reservation System, 1846–51.* Philadelphia: Temple University Press, 1975.

Triangle Associates. "Review of USDA and Forest Service Policies and Procedures for the Protection of Indian Sacred Sites: National Listening Session Final Themes Summary." November 29, 2010 and February 14, 2011. http://www.fs.fed .us/spf/tribalrelations/documents/sacredsites/20110214NationalSacredSitesSummary_Final.pdf.

"Tribal Colleges and Universities." 2013. Accessed June 12, 2013 (no longer posted). http://www.aihec.org/colleges/index.

"Tribal Relations Consultation Schedules." May 24, 2013. http://www.fs.fed.us/spf/ tribalrelations/documents/consultation/USFSTribalRelationsConsultation Schedule.pdf.

Trope, Jack F., and Walter R. Echo-Hawk. "The Native American Graves Protection and Repatriation Act Background and Legislative History." In *Repatriation Reader: Who Owns American Indian Remains?* Lincoln: University of Nebraska Press, 2000.

Tuchmann, E. Thomas, Kent P. Connaughton, Lisa E. Freedman, and Clarence B. Moriwaki, eds. *The Northwest Forest Plan: A Report to the President and Congress.* Portland, OR: U.S. Department of Agriculture, Forest Service, Office of Forestry and Economic Assistance, 1996.

"2011 National Days of Prayer to Protect Native American Sacred Places." June 15, 2011. http://www.culturalsurvival.org/current-projects/native-language-revitalization -campaign/2011-national-days-prayer-protect-native--o.

Tyler, S. Lyman. *A History of Indian Policy.* Washington, DC: U.S. Department of the Interior, Bureau of Indian Affairs, 1973.

Udall, Stewart. *The Quiet Crisis.* New York: Holt, Rinehart and Winston, 1963.

USDA (U.S. Department of Agriculture), Forest Service. *Alaska Region Overview.* R10-MR-13. Juneau: USDA Forest Service, Alaska Region, 2001.

———. *Equal Opportunity Is for Everyone: 1988 Civil Rights Report.* Washington, DC: Government Printing Office, 1988.

———. *The Forest Service in Alaska.* Juneau: U.S. Department of Agriculture, Forest Service, Alaska Region, 1980.

———. *Forest Service Native American Policy: Friends and Partners.* FS-446. Washington, DC: USDA Forest Service, 1990.

———. *Land Areas of the National Forest System as of September 1997.* FS-383. Washington, DC: USDA Forest Service, 1998.

———. *Report of the Chief of the Forest Service.* (Annual reports, titles vary, 1900s–1960s.)

———. *Report of the National Tribal Relations Program Implementation Team.* Washington, DC: USDA Forest Service, 2003.

————. *Report of the National Tribal Relations Program Task Force.* Washington, DC: USDA Forest Service, 2000.

————. *Sierra Nevada Forest Plan Amendment: Final Supplemental Environmental Impact Statement.* Vallejo, CA: USDA Forest Service, Pacific Southwest Region, 2004.

USDA (U.S. Department of Agriculture), Forest Service, Alaska Region. *Land and Resource Management Plan, Tongass National Forest.* Juneau: USDA Forest Service, Alaska Region, 1997.

————. *Tongass Land Management Plan Revision: Final Environmental Impact Statement.* Juneau: USDA Forest Service, Alaska Region, 1997.

USDA (U.S. Department of Agriculture), Forest Service, Pacific Northwest Region. *The Native American Program.* Washington, DC: Government Printing Office, 1979.

USDA (U.S. Department of Agriculture), Forest Service, State and Private Forestry. *Forest Service National Resource Book on American Indian and Alaska Native Relations.* Washington, DC: USDA Forest Service, 1997.

USDA (U.S. Department of Agriculture), Office of Communications. "Agriculture Secretary Vilsack Signs Regulation Confirming 'Government to Government' Consultation with Tribes." January 31, 2013. http://www.usda.gov/wps/portal/usda/usdahome?contentid=otr_001_13.xml.

USDA (U.S. Department of Agriculture), Office of Tribal Relations, and USDA Forest Service. *Report to the Secretary of Agriculture: USDA Policy and Procedures Review and Recommendations: Indian Sacred Sites.* Washington, DC: U.S. Department of Agriculture, 2012.

U.S. Department of the Interior. *Opinions of the Solicitor of the Department of the Interior Relating to Indian Affairs, 1917–1974.* Vol. 1. Washington, DC: U.S. Department of the Interior, 1979.

U.S. House, Committee on Indian Affairs. *Indians of the United States: The Condition of Various Tribes of Indians.* 66th Cong., 1st sess., September 29, 1919, serial no. 6. Washington, DC: U.S. Government Printing Office, 1919.

U.S. House, Committee on Indian Affairs. *Indians of the United States: The Condition of Various Tribes of Indians.* 66th Cong., 1st sess., October 17, 1919, serial no. 14. Washington, DC: U.S. Government Printing Office, 1919.

U.S. House, Committee on Interior and Insular Affairs. *Protection of Native American Graves and the Repatriation of Human Remains and Sacred Objects: Hearing Before the Committee on Interior and Insular Affairs.* 101st Cong., 2nd sess., July 17, 1990, serial no. 101–62. Washington, DC: U.S. Government Printing Office, 1991.

U.S. House, Committee on Natural Resources, Subcommittee on Public Lands and Environmental Regulation. *State Forest Management: A Model for Promoting*

Healthy Forests, Rural Schools and Jobs. 113th Cong., 1st sess., February 26, 2013, serial no. 113–2. Washington, DC: U.S. Government Printing Office, 2013.

U.S. House, Committee on Resources. *The President's Healthy Forests Initiative and H.R. 5214, H.R. 5309 and H.R. 5319.* 107th Cong., 2nd sess., September 5, 2002, serial no. 107–150. Washington, DC: U.S. Government Printing Office, 2003.

U.S. House, Subcommittee of the Committee on Appropriations. *Department of the Interior and Related Agencies Appropriations for 1996: Hearings Before a Subcommittee of the Committee on Appropriations, Part 5, Testimony of Public Witnesses for Indian Programs.* 104th Cong., 1st sess., March 13, 1995. Washington, DC: U.S. Government Printing Office, 1995.

U.S. Senate. *Amending the Act Terminating Federal Supervision over the Klamath Indian Tribe by Providing in the Alternative for Private or Federal Acquisition of the Part of the Tribal Forest That Must Be Sold.* 85th Cong., 2nd sess., S. rept. no. 1518, 1958. Washington, DC: U.S. Government Printing Office, 1958.

———. *Chippewa Allotments of Lands and Timber Contracts.* 50th Cong., 2nd sess., S. rept. no. 2710, 1889. Washington, DC: U.S. Government Printing Office, 1889.

———. *The Western Range.* 74th Cong., 2nd sess., S. doc. no. 199, 1936. Washington, DC: U.S. Government Printing Office, 1936.

U.S. Senate, Committee on Indian Affairs. *Indian Forest Resources Management Act: Hearing Before the Committee on Indian Affairs.* 104th Cong., 1st sess., September 20, 1995, S. hrg. 104–350. Washington, DC: U.S. Government Printing Office, 1996.

———. *Inter-tribal Council's Indian Forest Management Assessment Team Report: Hearing Before the Committee on Indian Affairs.* 108th Cong., 2nd sess., March 30, 2004, S. hrg. 108–483. Washington, DC: U.S. Government Printing Office, 2004.

———. *Native American Free Exercise of Religious Freedom Act: Hearing Before the Committee on Indian Affairs.* 103rd Cong., 2nd sess., March 23, 1993, S. hrg. 103–639. Washington, DC: U.S. Government Printing Office, 1994.

———. *Native American Grave and Burial Protection Act (Repatriation); Native American Repatriation of Cultural Patrimony Act; and Heard Museum Report: Hearing Before the Select Committee on Indian Affairs.* 101st Cong., 2nd sess., May 14, 1990, S. hrg. 101–952. Washington, DC: U.S. Government Printing Office, 1990.

———. *Religious Freedom Act.* 108th Cong., 2nd sess., July 14, 2004, S. hrg. 108–630. Washington, DC: U.S. Government Printing Office, 2004.

U.S. Senate, Committee on Reforestation. *Reforestation.* 67th Cong., 4th sess., 1923. Washington, DC: U.S. Government Printing Office, 1923.

U.S. Senate, Select Committee on Indian Affairs. *Amendments to the American Indian Religious Freedom Act: Hearing Before the Select Committee on Indian Affairs.* 102nd

Cong., 2nd sess., November 12, 1992, S. hrg. 102–950. Washington, DC: U.S. Government Printing Office, 1992.

———. *Improvement of the American Indian Religious Freedom Act: Hearing Before the Select Committee on Indian Affairs.* 100th Cong., 2nd sess., May 18, 1988, S. hrg. 100–879. Washington, DC: U.S. Government Printing Office, 1988.

———. *Indian Forests and Woodlands; and the Indian Environmental Regulatory Enhancement Acts,* 101st Cong., 2nd sess., 1990. Washington, DC: U.S. Government Printing Office, 1990.

U.S. Senate, Subcommittee on the Department of the Interior and Related Agencies, Committee on Appropriations, and the Subcommittee on Forests and Public Lands Management, Committee on Energy and Natural Resources. *Columbia Basin Ecosystem Management Plan: Joint Hearing Before the Subcommittee.* 105th Cong., 2nd sess., 1999, S. hrg. 105–906. Washington, DC: U.S. Government Printing Office, 1999.

U.S. Senate, Subcommittee on Forests and Public Land Management, Committee on Energy and Natural Resources. *Federal Forest Management, Part 1: Hearing Before the Subcommittee on Forests and Public Land Management of the Committee on Energy and Natural Resources.* 104th Cong., 1st sess., March 8, 1995. Washington, DC: U.S. Government Printing Office, 1995.

U.S. Senate, Subcommittee on Parks, Recreation, and Renewable Resources of the Committee on Energy and Natural Resources. *The Archaeological Resources Protection Act of 1979; and the Frederick Law Olmsted National Historic Site: Hearing Before the Subcommittee on Parks, Recreation, and Renewable Resources of the Committee on Energy and Natural Resources.* 96th Cong., 1st sess., May 1, 1979, pub. no. 96–26. Washington, DC: U.S. Government Printing Office, 1979.

Vaughn, Jacqueline, and Hanna J. Cortner. *George W. Bush's Healthy Forests: Reframing the Environmental Debate.* Boulder: University Press of Colorado, 2005.

Wahtomy, Roselynn. "President Obama Renews Commitments to Indian Country." *Sho-Ban News* (Fort Hall, Idaho), November 21, 2013.

Walker, G. B., and S. E. Daniels. "The Clinton Administration, the Northwest Forest Conference, and Conflict Management: When Talk and Structure Collide." *Society and Natural Resources* 9, no. 1 (1996): 77–85.

Wang, Grace A., Dorothy H. Anderson, and Pamela J. Jakes. "Heritage Management in the U.S. Forest Service: A Mount Hood National Forest Case Study." *Society and Natural Resources* 15 (2002): 359–69.

———. "Legislating the Past: Cultural Resource Management in the U.S. Forest Service," *Society and Natural Resources* 9, no. 1 (1996): 3–18.

Ward, Robert C. "The Spirits Will Leave: Preventing the Desecration and Destruction of Native American Sacred Sites on Federal Land." *Ecology Law Quarterly* 19 (1992): 795–816.

Warren, Louis S. *The Hunter's Game: Poachers and Conservationists in Twentieth-Century America*. New Haven, CT: Yale University Press, 1997.

Watkins, Joe E. "The Antiquities Act at One Hundred Years: A Native American Perspective." In *The Antiquities Act: A Century of American Archaeology, Historic Preservation, and Nature Conservation*, edited by David Harmon, Francis P. McManamon, and Dwight T. Pitcaithley, 187–98. Tucson: University of Arizona Press, 2006.

Watkins, T. H. "The Perils of Expedience." *Wilderness* 54, no. 191 (Winter 1990): 23–71.

Welch, John R. and Ramon Riley. "Reclaiming Land and Spirit in the Western Apache Homeland." *American Indian Quarterly* 25, no. 1 (2001): 5–12.

Westerman, Gwen, and Bruce White. *Mni Sota Makoce: The Land of the Dakota*. St. Paul: Minnesota Historical Society Press, 2012.

White, Richard. *"It's Your Misfortune and None of My Own": A History of the American West*. Norman: University of Oklahoma Press, 1991.

"White House Initiative Spurs Native American Economic Development; President's Healthy Forests Initiative to Help Native American Tribal Areas." December 1, 2004. http://www.prnewswire.com/news-releases/white-house-initiative-spurs-native -american-economic-development-75619082.html?sGiRef.

White House, Office of the Press Secretary. "The Forest Conference." March 30, 1993. http://clinton6nara.gov/1993/03/1993-03-30-forest-conference-participants.html.

Wilkinson, Charles. *Blood Struggle: The Rise of Modern Indian Nations*. New York: Norton, 2005.

———. "Indian Tribal Rights and the National Forests: The Case of the Aboriginal Lands of the Nez Perce Tribe." *Indian Law Review* 34 (1997/1998): 435–63.

Wilkinson, Todd. "Skis Carve a Path of Controversy in Arizona." *Christian Science Monitor*, March 30, 2005.

Williams, Gerald W. *The Forest Service: Fighting for Public Lands*. Westport, CT: Greenwood, 2007.

———. *The USDA Forest Service: The First Century*. Washington, DC: USDA Forest Service, 2000.

Williams, Robert A., Jr. *The American Indian in Western Legal Thought*. New York: Oxford University Press, 1990.

Wilson, Patrick Impero. "Native Peoples and the Management of Natural Resources in the Pacific Northwest: A Comparative Assessment." *American Review of Canadian Studies* 32, no. 3 (Autumn 2002): 397–414.

————. "Wolves, Politics, and the Nez Perce Wolf Reintroduction in Central Idaho and the Role of Native Tribes." *Natural Resources Journal* 39 (Summer 1999): 543–64.

Wood, Mary Christina. "Fulfilling the Executive's Trust Responsibility Toward the Native Nations on Environmental Issues: A Partial Critique of the Clinton Administration's Promises and Performance." *Environmental Law* 25 (1995): 733–800.

Woody Biomass Utilization Database. "Warm Springs Forest Products Industries." N.d. Accessed June 14, 2013 (no longer posted). http://www.nationalbiomassutilization.org/program/331.

Worl, Rosita. *Salmon in the Trees: Life in Alaska's Tongass Rain Forest.* Seattle: Mountaineers Books, 2010.

Worster, Donald. *Under Western Skies: Nature and History in the American West.* New York: Oxford University Press, 1982.

Yablon, Marcia. "Property Rights and Sacred Sites: Federal Regulatory Responses to American Indian Religious Claims on Public Land." *Yale Law Review* 113, no. 7 (2004): 1623–62.

Yaffee, Steven Lewis. *The Wisdom of the Spotted Owl: Policy Lessons for a New Century.* Washington, DC: Island Press, 1994.

Yazzie-Durgio, Victoria. "The Right to Change Tribal Forest Management." *Journal of Forestry* 96, no. 11 (November 1998): 33–35.

Zellmer, Sandi B. "Conserving Ecosystems Through the Secretarial Order on Tribal Rights." *Natural Resources and Environment* 14, no. 3 (Winter 2000): 162–65, 211–14.

Zylstra, Sarah Eckhoff. "Let It Snow." *Christianity Today* (August 2009): 17–18.

INDEX

ABOUT THE AUTHOR

Theodore Catton is coproprietor of Environmental History Workshop and associate research professor in the History Department at the University of Montana. He is the author of numerous books, articles, and reports on the national parks and national forests, including *Inhabited Wilderness: Indians, Eskimos, and National Parks in Alaska* and *National Park, City Playground: Mount Rainier in the Twentieth Century.* In 2012 he received a Fulbright Senior Scholar award to make a comparative study of U.S. and New Zealand national parks. Catton resides in Missoula, Montana, with his wife and writing partner, Diane Krahe. His other interests include backpacking in the Northern Rockies and walking vacations in the British Isles.